York St John
Library and Information Services

Please return this item on or before the due date stamped below (if using the self issue option users may write in the date themselves), **If recalled the loan is reduced to 10 days.**

RETURNED 1 5 JAN 2008		
1 3 JAN 2012		

Fines are payable for late return

PSYCHOLOGICAL SUBJECTS

Psychological Subjects

Identity, Culture, and Health in Twentieth-Century Britain

MATHEW THOMSON

OXFORD
UNIVERSITY PRESS

OXFORD
UNIVERSITY PRESS

Great Clarendon Street, Oxford OX2 6DP

Oxford University Press is a department of the University of Oxford.
It furthers the University's objective of excellence in research, scholarship,
and education by publishing worldwide in

Oxford New York

Auckland Cape Town Dar es Salaam Hong Kong Karachi
Kuala Lumpur Madrid Melbourne Mexico City Nairobi
New Delhi Shanghai Taipei Toronto

With offices in

Argentina Austria Brazil Chile Czech Republic France Greece
Guatemala Hungary Italy Japan Poland Portugal Singapore
South Korea Switzerland Thailand Turkey Ukraine Vietnam

Oxford is a registered trade mark of Oxford University Press
in the UK and in certain other countries

Published in the United States
by Oxford University Press Inc., New York

© Mathew Thomson, 2006

British Library Cataloguing in Publication Data

Data available

Library of Congress Cataloging in Publication Data

Data available

Typeset by Newgen Imaging Systems (P) Ltd., Chennai, India
Printed in Great Britain
on acid-free paper by
Biddles Ltd., King's Lynn, Norfolk

ISBN 0-19-928780-5 978-0-19-928780-2

1 3 5 7 9 10 8 6 4 2

Acknowledgements

This book began its life in research on mental hygiene in the first half of the twentieth century, looking, in retrospect rather too ambitiously, to adopt an international comparative approach. For a brief period this research was funded by a British Academy Postdoctoral Fellowship, based at the Wellcome Unit for the History of Medicine at the University of Oxford, under the guidance in particular of my former supervisor Paul Weindling and with the benefit of further advice from its then Director, Richard Smith. During this period, I received a scholarship from the Rockefeller Foundation to visit their superb archive, resulting in a body of research that if not directly evident in this book does profoundly shape several of its underlying assumptions. The Fellowship was cut short by my appointment as a Wellcome Lecturer in the History of Medicine at the University of Sheffield, where I spent five happy years in the Department of History. Here I must thank John Woodward for his constant support. I also benefited immensely from being in a department led with such energy by Ian Kershaw. I was lucky to find such a good friend in the department as Stephen Salter, who always helped me to keep things academic in proper perspective. Bob Shoemaker, David Martin, Robert Cook, Peter Gurney, and Graham Smith were all good companions in the Clarkehouse Road building. And Erica Sheen in English was always ready to talk ideas and dogs. During this time at Sheffield, the focus of my research became more narrowly British, but it took wings in other ways, and I thank the department for providing an environment to make this possible. In 1998, I moved to the Department of History at the University of Warwick, which has been quietly long-suffering about the slow pace of progress on the promised book. The University, the Arts and Humanities Research Council, and the Wellcome Trust have all helped me towards completion. At Warwick, I have found myself once again in a hugely stimulating environment, not just in terms of the staff, but also the undergraduate and postgraduate students who have been such a pleasure to teach. Postgraduates past and present, Vicky Long, Sheryl Root, and Brooke Whitelaw are all now in a position to teach me about aspects of this study. Trips up and down the M40 have been made so much better through being able to share talk with Maxine Berg, Margot Finn, and Colin Jones, who have all been hugely supportive. I have also been fortunate to have Hilary Marland as a colleague, and to have benefited from the collegiate environment of seminars, workshops, and research projects that she has fostered in the Centre for the History of Medicine. Outside of Warwick, Rhodri Hayward has accompanied me in this path of research, and I have learnt much from him in discussion, as I have from Peter Barham, Ben Shephard, Deborah Thom, Graham Richards, and Jonathan Toms. For help and encouragement over the years, I owe thanks to Roy Porter, Michael

Neve, Roger Cooter, Jose Harris, Peter Mandler, and Carolyn Steedman. I have also benefited from invitations to hear about the Dutch experience in conferences organised first by Marijke Gisjwijt-Hofstra and now Frank Huissman and Harry Oosterhuis, with their wonderful hospitality. At Oxford University Press, I would like to thank Anne Gelling, Kay Rogers, and Katie Ryde. I also owe a debt of gratitude to Peter Mandler and the other reader on the initial manuscript for supporting it and offering such useful advice on revision. Finally, life would have been far duller, though quieter, if it had not been for the wonderful presence of my children Grace and Joseph, and impossible without the support of Michelle.

M.T.
Wolvercote, 2005.

Contents

List of Abbreviations

BJEP	*British Journal of Educational Psychology*
BLPES	British Library of Political and Economic Science
BMA	British Medical Association
BMJ	*British Medical Journal*
CAPA	Campaign against Psychiatric Activities
CMAC	Contemporary Medical Archives Centre
HMSO	Her Majesty's Stationery Office
JNIIP	*Journal of the National Institute for Industrial Psychology*
NAMH	National Association for Mental Health
NIIP	National Institute for Industrial Psychology
PRO	Public Record Office
UNESCO	United Nations Educational, Scientific, and Cultural Organization
WEA	Workers' Educational Association
WFMH	World Federation for Mental Health

Introduction

This is a book about how twentieth-century Britons viewed both themselves and their world in psychological terms.[1] It examines the extent to which psychological thought and practice could mediate, not just understanding of the self, but also a wide range of social and economic, political, and ethical issues that rested on assumptions about human nature. Despite some fine studies of the institutional development of psychology as an academic discipline and profession and of the diffusion of psychoanalytic thought to an educated public, this broader historical subject remains strikingly undeveloped.

Psychological Subjects argues that if we want to pursue this line of inquiry we need to be wary of projecting back our own view of what constituted psychological modernity and confining the scope of analysis accordingly. It sets out to broaden our appreciation of the types of psychological thinking that were available, and examines some of the hitherto largely unappreciated practices, movements, and debates that this inspired. On this basis, it develops a picture of the appeal, style, and ramifications of psychology within this culture that is more variegated and therefore vigorous, and of a rather different overall character, than is often assumed. In order to achieve this, the range of the book has been necessarily broad. It brings together high and low psychological cultures, and something in between the two: the professional and academic, the popular and here the 'practical', and the intellectual. It addresses not just psychology's relation to thinking about the individual, but also about the social. It focuses not just on health, but also on education, economic life, and politics. It also reaches from the start of the century right up to the 1970s. Such scope has benefits as well as drawbacks. It enables the book to arrive at a number of theses about the correspondence between expert and popular thought and about the nature of change over time. It also, however, means that coverage has necessarily been selective and that the

---

[1] It does not attempt to analyse the past in psychological terms, though its findings may help to develop more nuanced work in this area. On the psycho-historical approach: P. Gay, *Freud for Historians* (New York and Oxford, 1985), P. Loewenberg, *Decoding the Past: The Psychoanalytic Approach* (New York, 1983). For an example of application to the history of modern Britain: G. Dawson, *Soldier Heroes: British Adventure, Empire and the Imagining of Masculinities* (London, 1994). Nor is it directly a contribution to a history of emotion, whose focus is more specific, and which is more interested in charting patterns of behaviour in the past. See for instance, Carol and Peter N. Stearns (eds.), *Emotion and Social Change: Toward a New Psychohistory* (New York and London, 1988); W. Reddy, *The Navigation of Feeling: A Framework for the History of Emotions* (Cambridge, 2001). Nevertheless, its findings about the shifting position of emotionality in psychological thought, particularly the ongoing reservations and modes of accommodation, should be of interest for such work.

picture that emerges is incomplete. The hope is that it will help to open up a territory and a series of questions for further investigation. It already owes a huge
amount to those who have provided us with more focused studies of particular
episodes and currents of thought. The fact that its emphases and conclusions have
often pointed in a rather different direction is not because it rejects the value of
this earlier work; rather, it is that in looking elsewhere one begins to see some of
these existing stories in new light.

To date, study of the impact of psychological thought within the Britain of this
period has concentrated on the reception of Freud and psychoanalysis. There is still
nothing to compare with the impressive histories of the place of psychoanalysis
within twentieth-century culture as a whole in the United States.[2] However,
several historians have now looked in some detail at the arrival of psychoanalysis
in the Britain of the first decades of the century, to a degree revising the view that
Britain was so notably reticent and resistant in this respect.[3] Whether this will
wholly dislodge a contrast that has some firm roots in economics, social structure,
and culture when it comes to demand, and in professional organisation when it
comes to supply, is another matter. Although this book will have something to say
on such limitations, it does not offer itself as another story of the impact of Freud;
indeed, one of its main points is that this is too narrow a way to frame a history of
the modern psychological subject when it comes to Britain.[4]

The development of psychological ways of thinking is a subject that should be
of interest well beyond the traditional audience of the history of psychology.
A central aim of the book is to make this apparent, and this accounts for two principles behind its design and focus. Firstly, it concentrates on uncovering a more
varied and widespread culture of psychological thinking than has been hitherto
recognised. It does not claim that psychological ideas normally, centrally, or
independently guided the lives and broader intellectual outlook of twentieth-
century Britons, even if it does establish that this was the case for a more socially
diverse section of the population than has been thus far appreciated. It is keen to
highlight issues of resistance, and in doing so to differentiate between the relative
acceptability or appeal of a variety of psychological models and practices. Even

[2] In particular: N. Hale Jr., *Freud and the Americans: The Beginnings of Psychoanalysis in the United
States, 1876–1917* (New York, 1971); N. Hale Jr., *The Rise and Crisis of Psychoanalysis in the United
States: Freud and the Americans, 1917–1985* (Oxford, 1985); J. Burnham, *Paths into American
Culture* (Philadelphia, 1988).

[3] S. Ellesley, 'Psychoanalysis in Early Twentieth Century England: A Study in the Popularisation
of Ideas', Ph.D. thesis (University of Essex, 1995); D. Rapp, 'The Early Discovery of Freud by the
British General Educated Reading Public, 1912–1919', *Social History of Medicine*, 3 (1990), 217–45;
D. Rapp, 'The Reception of Freud by the British Press: General Interest and Literary Magazines,
1920–1925', *Journal of the History of the Behavioural Sciences*, 24 (1988), 191–201; G. Richards,
'Britain on the Couch: The Popularization of Psychoanalysis in Britain, 1918–1940', *Science in
Context*, 13 (2000), 183–230.

[4] This is also a conclusion that emerges in work on the impact of Freud: J. Forrester, ' "A Whole
Climate of Opinion": Rewriting the History of Psychoanalysis', in M. Micale and R. Porter (eds.),
Discovering the History of Psychiatry (1994), 174–90; D. Pick, 'The Id Comes to Bloomsbury',
Guardian (16 August, 2003).

when it comes to the enthusiasts, it emphasises limitations and in particular accommodation within traditional moral frameworks. However, reframed as this more complex process of negotiation and dialogue, the story emerges as one that has a broader resonance than does the narrower narrative of rejection or acceptance of a particular Freudian model: it suggests a messier but also a richer history of the path to psychological modernity. Secondly, this is a history of psychological thinking that, rather than looking inwards to theoretical debates and professional struggles, subjects already attracting the attention of the historians of psychology, instead turns outwards to highlight the ways in which such psychological thought impinged on issues not normally associated with this field of history. Thus, the book concludes with consideration of the women's movement of the late 1960s and 1970s, and earlier touches on subjects such as workers' education, and thinking about religion, war, and economic life. Again, the point is to open up exploration of psychology mattering in unexpected areas well beyond its own province, an integral part of the broader intellectual, but also increasingly humanistic spiritual, and even shifting political landscape.

It is important to emphasise, here at the start, not only that popular psychological thinking is not the exclusive focus of what follows, but also that only with careful qualification would the popular be a wholly appropriate frame for the substantial proportion of the book that does attend to the theme of thinking outside the academy or profession. Coverage of the latter has indeed been more cursory than it could well have been. This is partly because the development of the discipline itself—the influence of its key thinkers, its institutional politics, and the role of its applications such as the mental test—has already benefited from some excellent scholarship, providing an opportunity to build outwards from such foundations.[5] More crucially, it is because of a desire to write a history that situates psychology within its broader culture and therefore necessarily pushes beyond such disciplinary boundaries. Nevertheless, the presence here of the professional and academic alongside the popular is still crucial. This is a history, in part, of that encounter and relationship, of the tensions, the contrasts, but also the similarities, the dialogue, and at times the problem of drawing sharp boundaries between the two.[6] Even in the one chapter (Chapter 1) that focuses most directly on the popular, the relationship to the professional is still crucial in making sense of development. Subsequent chapters focus on the operation of psychological thought within intellectual elites, within other disciplines, and within other professional groups—all examples of the popular only if one radically stretches the concept and in doing so willingly obscures the importance of countervailing professional or elitist and anti-popular attitudes.

[5] L. Hearnshaw, *A Short History of British Psychology, 1840–1940* (London, 1964); G. Bunn, G. Richards, and S. Lovie (eds.), *Psychology in Britain: Historical Essays and Personal Reflections* (Leicester, 2001).

[6] M. Thomson, 'The Popular, the Practical and the Professional: Psychological Identities in Britain, 1901–1950', in Bunn et al. (eds.), *Psychology in Britain*, 115–32.

It also needs to be emphasised that this is not a book that centres on the attitudes of the majority. If it were, it would need to say even more about resistance towards and sometimes ridicule of psychological enthusiasm on the one hand, and about sheer ignorance and lack of interest, pragmatism, and anti-intellectualism on the other. It seems sensible to assume that throughout the century, just as now, those who had little developed or active everyday interest in psychological ideas were a silent majority. Without actively seeking it, however, they met the language and assumptions of psychology on a regular basis. This complicates interpreting such silence. The historian of this subject will need to analyse far more systematically than has been possible here the traces of psychological thought within the mass media of the popular press, novels, film, radio, and eventually television: each a vast project. *Psychological Subjects* does indicate potential orientations for attitudes towards psychology among this majority but leaves such research for others to take up. The problem here is not just one of scope; it is also that evidence in such sources tends to be top-down in nature, scattered, and relatively superficial, making it very difficult to arrive at conclusions about the particular character and logic of popular psychological thought. In search of the latter one turns to sources that more directly engaged with the subject of psychology, and this is the purpose of this book.

Although it avoids making any definite claim about the majority, what this book indicates about the character of thinking among and the scale of a more committed section of the population will nevertheless have implications for our assumptions about the position of psychology within the culture as a whole. It will support an emerging body of work on the popularisation of Freud as well as the psychological dimension within such phenomena as spiritualist thought, mysticism, psychical research, and the occult to conclude that there has been a tendency to underestimate interest and enthusiasm for new psychological ideas in the early twentieth century.[7] However, it will extend and modify this line of argument in three ways. First, it will push such analysis of popular psychological thinking much further into the century. Secondly, it will set practical, active engagement alongside the passive encounter of the reader. Thirdly, it will decentre the psychology that was such an easy target of the critics—a psychoanalytic psychology of the bohemian elite, obsessed with sex, open about emotion, and introspective. Not only did the latter not necessarily reflect a more populist psychology, but it also existed alongside rather different currents even within the bohemian culture itself. Instead, the book will highlight currents of psychological thought and practice that reveal the appeal of psychology that was often far more pragmatic, ethically conventional, and less individualist or introspective. The story of resistance,

---

[7] On mystical, spiritualist, psychical research, and occult movements and the interest in the psychological: A. Owen, *The Place of Enchantment: British Occultism and the Culture of the Modern* (Chicago and London, 2004); J. Dixon, *Divine Feminine: Theosophy and Feminism in England* (Baltimore, 2001); A. Gauld, *The Founders of Psychical Research* (London, 1968); R. Hayward, 'Popular Mysticism and the Origins of the New Psychology, 1880–1910', Ph.D. thesis (University of Lancaster, 1995); J. Hazelgrove, *Spiritualism and British Society between the Wars* (Manchester, 2000).

ridicule, and rejection ignores this other strand of popular psychological culture. One of the aims of the book is that this will be harder in the future.

PSYCHOLOGICAL SUBJECTS

If analysis of psychological thinking is the main line of investigation of this book, what it addresses are the psychological subjects of the title. This term demands some discussion. It refers both to people and to ideas. In both cases, it is important to emphasise that the title announces a field for exploration, rather than a conclusion. The first reason for this is that the book's emphasis on the culturally embedded nature of psychology, its existence in close relation to broader values, makes it difficult to accept without serious qualification the idea that the period saw either a new pre-eminence of the psychological over other influences in thinking about the self or a fundamental disjuncture. The second reason is methodological. The book concentrates on uncovering ideas and practices, and on making a series of judgements as to the extent, character, and cultural resonance of such phenomena. When it comes to influence and meaning for the individual—their psychological subjectivity—there are additional, and extremely challenging, questions for the historian. Such a subject demands far more focus on particular individuals, more rigorous analysis of sources such as memoirs, autobiographies, oral history, and clinical records than is possible here, even an engagement with psychohistory. This book may offer a new steer to such work, by indicating a broader range of ideas on offer, but it ventures only tentatively down that line. Indeed, it actually raises new difficulties. Certainly, in highlighting the variety, complexity, and at times unexpected nature of contemporary psychological thought and practice, it challenges work that considers psychological subjectivity through the tool of a rather universal psychoanalytic model. At the very least, it makes more pressing the question of whether we also need to think more rigorously and open-mindedly about how these people thought about themselves in psychological terms.

When it comes to Britain, the most important existing work on the modern psychological subject centres on processes of measurement, normalisation, and adjustment made possible by the spreading gaze and technologies of psychology. Here, psychological subjectivity is either imposed on the individual through the discipline's increasing influence as a tool of governance within the modern welfare complex, or is internalised in the individual through the growing influence of experts and their advice within private life. The relative weakness of a narrative of Freudian liberation in the British context has perhaps contributed to the strength of this disciplinary narrative in its place. Particularly influential has been the work of two British sociologists in the 1980s, both heavily influenced by the ideas of Michel Foucault. The first of these was David Armstrong, with his study of the expanding 'gaze' of twentieth-century medicine, *The Political Anatomy of the Body*, which included analysis of the extension of medico-psychological interest to the borderland territory of the neuroses. The second was Nikolas Rose, with two interrelated books on the role of psychology in the governance of modern subjectivity in twentieth-century Britain, *The Psychological Complex* and *Governing the Soul*.[8] Initially, interest was largely among those working on closely related fields, such as the histories of crime, psychiatry, and medicine. However, Rose's *Governing the Soul* is now emerging as a reference point for locating the position of psychological thought in studies of aspects of cultural and social history in twentieth-century Britain.[9]

What this work very properly attempted to demonstrate was a history of psychology that lay outside that of professional formation and theoretical advance, which had become the whiggish staple of a discipline anxious to defend its own rather tenuous claims to scientific authority and firm disciplinary boundaries. Its first strategy, particularly that of Rose in his *Psychological Complex*, was to highlight the importance of psychology as an applied discipline—an area neglected as relatively unimportant in the discipline's own theory-centred histories.[10] In doing so, it argued that the discipline emerged as a science of individual difference because of what it could provide for a state increasingly concerned about managing its population. This found support in historical studies of national efficiency and eugenics. Anxiety about eugenic fitness, in particular, is presented as providing the opportunity to define and mark out mental, and in truth social, abnormality, but also thereby to highlight normality itself as a problem, through a new psychological scale. In sites like the new universal education system, and in the mobilisation of men for the war of 1914–18, the population was suddenly visible in an unprecedented way. Anxiety about national efficiency would subsequently provide opportunities in the advance of industrial psychology and in campaigns to establish mental hygiene as equally important in preventive medicine as its physical counterpart. The second strategy has been to set this story of regulation, measurement, and normalisation from the outside alongside one of psychological governance, passed down by the expert, but so internalised that it appeared to come from within. Because of the tensions between the more authoritarian approach and the dominant liberal culture of the era, the second strategy of internalisation would be both increasingly ascendant and ultimately far more pervasive and influential, binding us 'to a subjection that is more profound because it appears to emanate from our autonomous quest for ourselves, it appears as a matter of freedom'.[11]

The case for such processes has been in many respects a compelling one. Partly because it has already been presented so influentially, this book will contribute

[8] D. Armstrong, *The Political Anatomy of the Body* (Cambridge, 1983); N. Rose, *The Psychological Complex: Psychology, Politics and Society in England, 1869–1939* (London, 1985); N. Rose, *Governing the Soul: The Shaping of the Private Self* (London, 1989).

[9] For instance, P. Joyce, *Democratic Subjects: The Self and the Social in Nineteenth-Century England* (Cambridge, 1994), 18–19.   [10] Rose, *Psychological Complex*, 2–3.

[11] Rose, *Governing the Soul*, 254, 256. See also N. Rose, *Inventing Ourselves: Psychology, Power and Personhood* (Cambridge, 1996), 17.

instead, first through pointing to some of the limitations of this approach, and secondly and more fundamentally by pointing to two rather different ways of addressing the history of the psychological subject. In terms of limitations, one of the problems is that facing all more schematic accounts: the difficulty of reconciling the complexities that tend to emerge in detailed historical research. There is a focus on the aims, ideas, and even the practical tools of the professionals, but sometimes a tendency to assume their influence, without attending in sufficient detail to the way these failed or changed because of messy politics, competing interests, and economic realities. With little attempt to gauge the scale of influence, there is a danger of producing an impression that the story of intention, or of regulation in rather select sites, stands for the whole. There is also a limitation of focus, with the emphasis on professional literature meaning that it can be hard to break free altogether from the conventional narrative within the history of psychology. Thus, the story changes to one of control, regulation, and the constitution of psychological subjectivity 'around the pole of abnormality', a mirror image to that of scientific progress and liberation that it seeks to replace, but one still working within the parameters of the approach it criticises.[12] Such a perspective holds back recognition of a psychology that lay beyond the profession itself, and of psychologies that rejected the constitution of psychological subjectivity around a pole of abnormality for routes of transcendence instead. It also holds back consideration of the interplay with other systems of thought—scientific, religious, political, and cultural—and in general of the importance of a shifting historical context. It offers us, in sum, a story which takes as its context a rather undifferentiated modernity and which offers little sense of the way that psychology has been embedded in the more particular circumstances of its own times. It provides us with an important argument about the relationship between internalisation of psychological thinking and liberal modes of governance, but it thereby closes down the space for exploring the full nature of excitement about psychology and for its modification in relation to a broader set of interests and values. One of the aims of this book is to open up such cultural space. In doing so, it shares the belief that there is an important relationship between psychological and social democratic subjectivity, but rather than looking at this in terms of the internal ideology of psychological modes of governance turns to specific historical examples of a more direct engagement between the two.

The book also opens up thinking about subjects of knowledge as psychological subjects in the period. First, by addressing the interrelationship between popular and professional or academic psychology, and between the latter and the broader culture, it offers some contribution towards our understanding of how psychology struggled to constitute itself as a subject.[13] Secondly, it points to the ways in which excitement about psychology offering an important new understanding of human

[12] Rose, *Psychological Complex*, 5.

[13] G. Bunn, 'Introduction', in Bunn et al. (eds.), *Psychology in Britain*, 1-29; G. Richards, 'Of what is History of Psychology a History?', *British Journal for the History of Science*, 20 (1987), 2–11;

nature had the potential to influence, or draw influence from, other fields: most obviously those, such as sociology, economics, politics, and anthropology, so dependent upon a model of human nature. In this respect, as in others, the book is more concerned with looking outwards from psychology than in analysing the constitution of knowledge within the discipline itself. In fact, it sets the drive towards specialisation of knowledge in tension with a continuing dream of synthesis. Psychology for much of this period was located on either side of the divide: for some a science whose ambitions had to be contained if it was to justify such a status; for others a key to making sense of everything, a source of values for the new age, even a new way of reconciling science with religion.[14]

The second way this book looks beyond the narrative of governance is to examine what the psychological populists were actually writing, what intellectuals and radicals were hoping to do with psychology, and what ordinary people were reading. Here we find suspicion of the expert and resistance to a supposedly dominant psychology and its regimes of regulation, and instead a vision of the psychological subject that centred on the individual taking control yet at the same time offered meaning beyond mere individualism. From the start of the century, there was a radical expansion in the popular appeal of explicitly psychological systems of thought. The point in the first chapters of this book, but also one resonating throughout, is that this drew influence from a psychology that came from above, but also to some extent emerged out of processes and movements that already existed independently, below. If there was one psychological idea that acted as a trigger to accelerate this process, it was the idea that a vast area of human consciousness and associated potential lay hidden in the normal waking mind, both in the force of instinct and in the unconscious. The idea was not new, but circumstances both broadened its diffusion and made it more urgent but also potentially transformative in the new century: no longer something simply to suppress, if not yet something without due modification to fully embrace.[15] This too was partly why popular practice was initially so important, with a range of tools like autosuggestion emerging as ways to access, mobilise, and channel this hidden power and thereby attain full self-realisation. Much of the story of the next half century would centre on the challenge of responding to and accommodating this most fundamental and radical proposition of the new psychological thought. Throughout this period, psychology provided a language and topography of self to access these hidden levels and harness them towards ethical, social, and sometimes spiritual ends. It is this psychological subject—one that was to be

R. Smith, 'Does the History of Psychology have a Subject?', *History of the Human Sciences*, 1 (1988), 147–77; see also Ch. 2.

[14] On the latter: P. Bowler, *Reconciling Science and Religion: The Debate in Early Twentieth-Century Britain* (Chicago, 2001); and R. Smith, 'Biology and Human Values: C. S. Sherrington, Julian Huxley and the Vision of Progress', *Past and Present*, 178 (2003), 210–42.

[15] H. Ellenberger, *The Discovery of the Unconscious: The History and Evolution of Dynamic Psychiatry* (New York, 1970).

present at its own making (hence again the importance of the practical, as well as the popular)—rather than that imagined in the apparent determinism of behaviourism on the one hand, or of instinct-driven Freudianism on the other, that dominates much of the story that follows.

IDENTITY, HEALTH, AND CULTURE

Of the three sub-themes of this book, identity is important but more elusive than might appear likely. In highlighting the existence of a rich and multi-faceted psychological culture and therefore the need to recognise that many people understood themselves through the filter of such language, knowledge, and practices, this book does aim to contribute to what is a well-developed interest in the subject. On the other hand, for the reasons already outlined, it stops well short of the leap of faith that is necessary to claim that we thereby can understand or know identity. It does however challenge certain conventional thinking on the subject. In particular, in charting a narrative of the psychological subject over the century as a whole, the book suggests that a fixation on personal identity—some would say narcissism—that is so central in our own view of the impact of psychology has been encouraged by some relatively recent developments. In fact, in terms of both perceptions but also actual thought and practice, it stands in contrast to much of what went before. In that sense, the book offers a case for shifting us beyond a focus on psychological identity in its currently dominant individualist and emotionalist form. Instead, we are encouraged to think more about how psychology in different circumstances could foster the imagining of social dimensions of the self, and even offered practices to help realise such identity. More specifically, what follows will offer some new insights for those interested in the identities associated with gender, class, and nation.[16]

When it comes to the sub-theme of health, it is worth pointing out that this project originated in a study of the expansion of medical and psychiatric concern in Britain during the first half of the century from mental illness to mental health. Partly because this way of framing the impact of psychology has already attracted consideration, partly because the sources revealed an excitement about psychology spilling outside this frame, this has turned into a study in which the field of medicine is now just one example of the subject's influence. However, the issue of health is not as easily contained as the others to a single chapter and remains a concern throughout. This is still, then, a study that speaks to the historian of medicine and psychiatry; albeit one that attempts to move beyond what has become a rather stale paradigm of 'the asylum and after'. It points to the psychological as an area that

[16] Race, the other key category of identity, attracts less attention here. For thoughts on its relation to psychological thinking in the first part of the period: M. Thomson, ' "Savage Civilisation": Race, Culture and Mind in Britain, 1889–1939', in W. Ernst and B. Harris (eds.), *Race, Science and Medicine, 1700–1960* (London, 1999), 235–58.

epitomised some of the difficulties of twentieth-century medicine in satisfying its clients and in alleviating disease. It highlights the tensions that resulted when it came to defining the boundaries of health and illness. And it suggests that we might locate this story, not as some inevitable outcome of modernity for the self, but perhaps as something of a more unique interlude of peculiarly psychological subjectivity, situated between two eras of greater biological and genetic determinism, encouraged as much by social and political circumstances as new medical and psychological ideas.[17] Finally, it is worth pointing out that this book avoids attempting any reconstruction of patterns of psychological health and illness, though the sources that it has uncovered do offer views on this as well as rich, untapped data for anyone willing to address the methodological and epistemological challenge.

There are several reasons for labelling this as a history of culture. First, there is the simple one that the alternatives of the social and economic, the political, the intellectual, or the medical were all too narrow on their own. The cultural better encompasses the aim of demonstrating that a story of psychological subjects infiltrated and inflected so many aspects of British life and thought in the period. It also reflects the fact this is far more a history of beliefs than of policy. The reasons are also, however, more specific. The book examines how psychological theory, both elite and popular, has imagined the relationship between the individual and culture; in particular, how culture has at times come to be seen as embedded within the self, at times to be in conflict with it. It also explores the role of culture in shaping the psychologies of the age. It traces this, in particular, in relation to what many have seen as the key cultural shift of the age, from a Victorian culture of character, to the permissiveness of our age. Along the way, it has something to say about national culture and the emergence of a self-consciously British way in psychology.[18] At the same time, in its engagement with anthropology, in its location in an era of increasing interest about Eastern systems of thought, and in the universalistic ambitions of its visions of self-realisation, it also highlights some of the ways in which the project of the psychological subject had the potential to collapse such national cultural boundaries. There is also a question of the influence of, and comparison with, developments in America. In what follows, there will be some clear instances of such influence, though also of modification, even explicit identification against an American way. The book does not directly address the comparative issue. This is partly because to do so would demand

[17] Also relevant, though not explored here, is the increasing interest in computational models of consciousness in the second half of the century. This area has recently begun to receive serious attention in the work of Rhodri Hayward, for instance ' "Our Friends Electric": Mechanical Models of Mind in Postwar Britain', in Bunn et al. (eds.), *Psychology in Britain*, 290–308; and 'The Tortoise and the Love-Machine: Grey Walter and the Politics of Electro-Encephalography', *Science in Context*, 14 (2001), 615–41.

[18] See Ch. 7 in particular, in relation to thinking about German culture and its psychology in both wars, but also the allusions to an American style in Chs. 1, 8, and Conclusion. Throughout, the book has attempted to maintain a focus on literature that was of British provenance, or if not that which was notably influential in Britain perhaps in modified form. The aim here is to capture the particular national character of this culture.

analysis of the American situation, and properly independent study of it, that lies beyond the scope of the present study. The second reason for resisting what has been a dominant frame of comparison with the United States is that this has tended to hold back considering the British case in its own right, or has at least framed the story in a rather limiting way as one of backwardness, resistance, or failure, and hence of little unique interest. This is a perspective that perhaps needs to be circumvented before new and more interesting comparative questions can arise. The final significance of culture in what follows is as a way to mark out communities of shared ideas and enthusiasm for the psychological. To date, attention has focused on the relatively exclusive, culturally authoritative, intellectual elite of Bloomsbury and its environs. This book offers a different view of psychological currents within this type of setting.[19] More importantly, it suggests that such cultures, in which psychology played a key role, existed well beyond this geographical and intellectual space. In doing so, it acknowledges the importance of the type of cultural boundaries so evident in both the elitism and the group identity of Bloomsbury, attending also to the role of the psychological within this, but it explores their formation and function well beyond this arena as well as the relationships that existed across such borders.

STRUCTURE

The book has three main parts. The first focuses on the excitement about a change in human character that opened the century. Here, the year 1900 is of course something of an artificial starting date.[20] Indeed, part of the point of these chapters is to set a sense of the new alongside a story of cultural continuities.[21] The three chapters of this opening section each concentrate on a different level of psychological culture. The first is devoted to a type of popular psychological culture that other historians have either overlooked or largely ignored, partly because of the way it jars with assumptions about the relationship between psychology and modernity. The third moves to the arena of the intellectual that has attracted attention, though recasts the story in several significant respects. In between, the second reframes the interest of academic and professional psychologists by setting it alongside the two others. Though the chapters take the opening of the century

19 See Ch. 3 for the interwar era and then Ch. 8 for the 1970s.
20 This is explored further in M. Thomson, 'Psychology and the Consciousness of Modernity', in B. Rieger and M. Daunton (eds.), *Meanings of Modernity: Britain from the Late-Victorian Era to World War II* (Oxford, 2001), 97–115.
21 There is an obvious lineage, for instance, with areas uncovered in: J. Oppenheim, *Shattered Nerves: Doctors, Patients and Depression in Victorian England* (New York, 1991); A. Winter, *Mesmerized: Powers of Mind in Victorian Britain* (Chicago, 1998); R. Cooter, *The Cultural Meaning of Popular Science: Phrenology and the Organization of Consent in Nineteenth-Century Britain* (Cambridge, 1984); and C. Steedman, *Strange Dislocations: Childhood and the Idea of Human Interiority, 1780–1930* (London, 1995).

and the excitement surrounding the 'new age' as their starting point, they each look beyond it. The third of the chapters develops the context of the problem of industrial civilisation as a way to link it with the section that follows. Together, they introduce a central theme within the book: the existence of different but interrelating levels of psychological culture. The parallels identified indicate the importance of a common context and the interrelation with existing cultural formations, and as such do something to downplay the significance of the psychological discipline and its theories.

The three chapters of Part II focus on psychology in relation to industrial civilisation. They each attend to a particular psychological problem and its associated institutional structures and sites, but also foreground the excitement and the prospects thereby unleashed. The first chapter focuses on education. It argues that this was the site of greatest potential influence for psychological thought, but one in which the excitement about changing human character was just as significant as the development of mental testing. A second chapter on industry, the worker, and economic life provides the opportunity to develop the context of the problem of industrial civilisation and to bring to the fore the theme of class. The third chapter focuses on health and the medical profession. In each of these chapters, the aim has been to indicate the difficulties faced by a psychology that aimed to control and regulate, and to emphasise instead the narrative of prospects. In selecting these three areas for analysis, others have been omitted, notably that of the military, which has already benefited from several important studies in relation to shellshock and its successor conditions, but also that of psychology within the legal and penal system.[22]

The two chapters of Part III focus on particular historical moments as possible ends to this story: first the mid-century international crisis, secondly the emergence of a permissive society. Here, the book locates its subject in relation to what have been the two central narratives for making sense of the history of the period as a whole. In doing so, it presents the Second World War as the point of greatest opportunity for realising some of the ambitions that had developed in the first half of the century. It was also an important event in shifting the balance between a psychology that looked backwards, tied closely to the nineteenth century in terms of its moral and spiritual stance, and a psychoanalytic strain that centred on the problem of the emotions. However, such a transition was complex and still faced major obstacles. The second chapter takes this story into the era of the permissive society of the 1960s and 1970s, providing an epilogue that both rethinks developments in

---

[22] On the military, see Ch. 6. Particularly important is B. Shephard, *A War of Nerves: Soldiers and Psychiatrists, 1914–1994* (London, 2000). There is no comparable view of its role in the penal sphere. Useful here is D. Garland, *Punishment and Welfare* (Aldershot, 1985). There is also a rapidly developing literature on homosexuality, for instance: I. Crozier, 'Taking Prisoners: Havelock Ellis, Sigmund Freud and the Construction of Homosexuality, 1897–1951', *Social History of Medicine*, 13 (2000), 447–66; C. Waters, 'Havelock Ellis, Sigmund Freud and the State: Discourses of Homosexual Desire in Interwar Britain', in L. Doan and L. Bland (eds.), *Cultural Sexology: Labelling Bodies and Desires, 1890–1940* (London, 1998), 165–79.

this period in light of what went on before and begins to connect the story of the first half of the century with the psychological culture of our own times.

Overall, the book tends to align itself with the view that Britain was a country that saw some strong cultural continuities, particularly in the realm of values, from the late nineteenth century into at least the 1950s.[23] Throughout this period, psychological thinking was not yet common sense, but there was a strong reason to argue that it should be. Because of this, it mattered perhaps even more intensely to those people who were seduced by its promise, and it was a subject of considerable excitement and curiosity for many others. In what can be seen as the protracted afterlife of Victorianism within British life, psychology provided a bridge between tradition and modernity, a source for the re-articulation and full realisation, rather than the end, of a subjectivity realised in service, character and values, and in the self's relation to the social and the spiritual. It had vocal supporters—and detractors—because it seemed new (even, if in many respects, it may not have been); because it attempted to change and operated at the margins of common sense, and at times well outside it; and because it functioned, consequently, often as a source of inspiration and a guide for transformation. *Psychological Subjects* tells the story of the emergence and spread of this excitement, but also attends to resistance and the frequent distance between utopian ambition and practical realisation. In doing so, it calls for a fresh appraisal of the psychological culture that our own has emerged out of, not only suggesting that the degree of interest was stronger earlier in the century than generally appreciated, but also that the character of the earlier culture was often markedly different to our own. In charting a story of psychological modernisation, the temptation of existing scholarship has usually been to emphasise those developments—most obviously, the impact of Freud, or the development of psychology as a tool of governance—that most obviously point to the present. *Psychological Subjects* does not set out to deny the importance of these histories, but it does aim to decentre and thereby recast them alongside a more neglected, less obviously modern, psychological modernity. It tells a story of what fell away: of largely forgotten alternative subjectivities and visions of society fostered by often hugely inflated expectations of psychology. At the same time, it also thereby indicates elements of continuity: on the one hand, the traces of utopianism, longing for values, and even mysticism hidden within our psychological common sense; on the other, the possibility that this psychology may still operate at some distance from a more pragmatic psychological subjectivity of the majority. In doing so, it should help to reveal our own 'common sense' psychological thought, and its valuing in particular of the expression of individual emotion, as one that emerges, not out of the discovery of some natural truths about our needs, but as a product of its own particular cultural context.

---

[23] J. Harris, *Private Lives. Public Spirit: A Social History of Britain, 1870–1914* (Oxford, 1993), 252–3.

PART I

PSYCHOLOGIES OF THE NEW AGE

1

Practical Psychology

Until relatively recently it tended to be assumed that, apart perhaps from a bohemian minority, the British at the start of the last century had been sceptical and resistant to a new psychology particularly associated with the ideas of Sigmund Freud and the practice of psychoanalysis. This was subject to little searching scrutiny, certainly nothing to compare with the impressive studies of the popularisation of Freud and the embrace of the psychotherapeutic in the United States, which by way of contrast made the British absence even more striking.[1] It gained acceptance because it fitted a more general view that the British were reluctant modernists, culturally conservative, anti-intellectual and resistant to the sway of theory just as they were to ideology. Recently, however, historians have begun to test, not just the broad assumption about Britain, but also the more specific view about psychology and a new view of the self within this context. Unsurprisingly, this work has concentrated on the popularisation of Freud—the touchstone for a psychological modernity. Some of it homes in on what is already the one relatively familiar territory of Bloomsbury, albeit to offer us a far more nuanced picture. Others, however, have begun to reveal through analysis of press and periodical literature that there was a considerably broader interest and enthusiasm than hitherto recognised, even if in doing so they also confirm to some extent the existence of causes for suspicion and caution.[2] What this work also suggests, but leaves largely unexplored, is a hinterland of popular, but more unorthodox, psychology beyond.

Recognition of the widespread existence of what we might call a low culture of popular psychology is not altogether new. In his still unsurpassed history of British psychology of 1964, Leslie Hearnshaw noted the popularity of what he called practical psychology, though given his conventional disciplinary focus paid

---

[1] On the reception of Freud in the United States: Hale, *Freud and the Americans; Hale, The Rise and Crisis of Psychoanalysis in the United States*; Burham, *Paths into American Culture*, 96–110; T. J. Jackson Lears, 'From Salvation to Self-Realization', in R.W. Fox and T. J. Jackson Lears (eds.), *The Culture of Consumption: Critical Essays in American History, 1880–1980* (New York, 1983), 3–38; J. Pfister and N. Schnog (eds.), *Inventing the Psychological: Toward a Cultural History of Emotional Life in America* (New Haven and London, 1997).

[2] Rapp, 'The Early Discovery of Freud by the British General Educated Reading Public, 1912–1919'; Rapp, 'The Reception of Freud by the British Press'; Ellesley, 'Psychoanalysis in Early Twentieth Century England'; Richards, 'Britain on the Couch'.

it little attention.[3] When it comes to Victorian Britain, there has been some very important research on the influence and popularity of popular psychological thought and practice, in particular in relation to thinking about shattered nerves, phrenology, spiritualism, and most recently mesmerism.[4] However, this has tended to leave unanswered the question of what happened to such energies afterwards. The assumption has tended to be that they made way for the modernity of Freudianism, even if this jars with the idea of resistance.[5] Historical studies of the continuing appeal of spiritualism and the occult in the Britain of the first decades of the twentieth century are now beginning to indicate that such a transition was less abrupt, offering us detailed insight into the mystical territory that so often ran alongside, shared goals with, and often interconnected with interest in the psychological.[6] This chapter builds on this developing picture, putting flesh on the bones of that 'practical psychology' noted but left unexplored by Hearnshaw.[7] In doing so, the point is not to discount the significance of those areas—the psychoanalytic, on the one hand, the occult and spiritual, on the other—that have already received attention. What follows should help us to interconnect these different areas, exposing a middle ground in which they met, explored their differences, and to some extent found a common language. However, it will also introduce something new, highlighting an attraction to psychological thought and practice that went far beyond Freud and psychoanalysis. This will modify the overall picture of the psychological culture of the period that is beginning to emerge, not just in terms of its character, but also its scope.

Practical psychology was a term used by many of the writers and organisations in the analysis that follows. Others may not have used the same term, or may have used it inconsistently, but had enough in common, in thought, practice, and institutional identity, with the first group to justify inclusion. The term serves here as the most effective way to describe a type of psychological thought and practice very largely overlooked to date. It existed in a space between the two main areas of popularisation that have already attracted attention: the popularisation of Freud, on the one hand, and occultism and spiritualism, on the other. Here, it acted as a channel for interconnection and dialogue; it also, however, attracted people who rejected the path on either side and in certain respects looked in significantly different directions. Its defining characteristic was an emphasis on the practical.

---

[3] Hearnshaw, *Short History*, 292–7.

[4] Oppenheim, *Shattered Nerves*; Cooter, *The Cultural Meaning of Popular Science: Phrenology and the Organisation of Consent in Nineteenth-Century Britain*; J. Oppenheim, *The Other World: Spiritualism and Psychic Research in England, 1850–1914* (Cambridge, 1985); Hayward, 'Popular Mysticism and the Origins of the New Psychology, 1880–1910'; A. Owen, *The Darkened Room: Women, Power and Spiritualism in Late Victorian England* (London, 1989); L. Barrow, *Independent Spirits: Spiritualism and English Plebians, 1850–1910* (London, 1986); Winter, *Mesmerized*.

[5] Oppenheim, *Shattered Nerves*, 304–11.

[6] Hazelgrove, *Spiritualism and British Society between the Wars*; Owen, *The Place of Enchantment: British Occultism and the Culture of the Modern*. Although Owen's book concentrates on the period 1880–1914, she argues that this occultism evolved into the new psychology of the post-war generation of occultists: ibid. 235.   [7] Hearnshaw, *Short History*, 292–7.

At its most extreme, this could mean outright hostility to a professional monopoly on psychology knowledge and practice: a factor that was strongest at the start of the period. More commonly, it meant enthusiasm for psychology as a practical tool within regimes of self-improvement.

Other than the fact of its general neglect to date, there are several reasons why a focus on practical psychology can add something to our existing understanding. First, it can help us to think critically about what we might mean by a popular psychology. In this regard, existing work has exhibited several limitations. There has been a tendency to focus on an elite Bloomsbury or an 'educated reading public', leaving relatively little insight into more middlebrow, let alone working-class, attitudes. There is the problem that a focus on the downward diffusion of ideas from the great psychologists—Freud in particular—tends to leave out of the picture a more eclectic range of intellectual influences, let alone the possibility that ideas and practices might emerge from below. Finally, where it focuses on the fact of publication as a sign of diffusion, or on the existence of debate in still relatively elite periodicals as evidence of popular interest, its picture of popularisation has been a largely passive one. It has paid relatively little attention, either to processes of resistance and translation, or to the nature of the audience itself. This has also meant that there has been little study of practice, as opposed to probable thought, or of the relationship between the two. Analysis of practical psychology will both help to expose these limitations and point towards a more active and independent strand of popular psychological culture.

The second benefit is that one emerges from consideration of this practical psychology with a markedly different appreciation of what type of psychology often appealed to the public. In this instance, Freud was important and of great interest, but, particularly at first, not central. He was far more likely to appear in a bastardised form, usually only once translated into a more acceptable idiom. Qualities often associated with the embrace of the psychotherapeutic—introspection, emotional expression, an interest in sex and relationships, and the use of some kind of talking cure—were all, in fact, notable far more for their absence than regular presence. Rather than being a threat to values, psychology offered a route to higher values in a cultivation of personality that drew on existing discourses of character and spiritual growth. The unconscious was embraced, but as a path to untold new powers, rather than as a danger, that either needed to be managed, or in the case of the libertine let loose. Mind, memory, and instinctive energies were to be harnessed, put together, and enhanced, not taken apart in self-critical analysis. Such qualities, so different to those conventionally associated with the appeal of psychoanalysis, were fundamental in making this psychology both popular and practically appealing.

The final reason for paying attention to practical psychology is that it offers something new in terms of sources and scope of evidence. First, the existence of practical psychology clubs and journals, with histories stretching across the first half of the century, offers a dynamic picture to set beside the more static one

gained from existing work on coverage in the press or via publication in the first
two decades of the century. Secondly, the dialogic and multi-vocal nature of much
of the material from within this culture, including the social activities of the clubs,
publication of letters, advice literature, correspondence teaching, and question-
naires, offers insight into a relationship between thought and practice that has
been largely absent in work that has rested on analysis of the downward diffusion
of knowledge.

FREUD AND THE PUBLIC

It is important to recognise that the recent revisionism about the popularity of
Freud in the British context is one that rightly points to a growing awareness and
interest but does generally stop well short of suggesting any widespread embrace.
It modifies previous assumptions about resistance, but it leaves in place a caution
based on the existence of some major cultural hurdles.[8] Even when it comes to the
highbrow culture of Bloomsbury, a centre for the interest in psychoanalysis, the
picture remains a very mixed one: enthusiasm amidst suspicion, scepticism, and
ignorance.[9]

The first hurdle stemmed from attitudes surrounding sex. Here, for all the
attempts to exhume the active sexuality of the Victorians, the vast majority of the
evidence continues to support the idea that public prudishness and ignorance prevailed. On the other hand, as popular demand for sex advice literature indicates, a
substantial section of this public was keen to know more.[10] As such, the idea that
the British dismissed or avoided Freud, simply because he broached the subject, is
of course something of a myth. However, there were serious misgivings, both
about the way psychoanalytic ideas challenged sexual orthodoxy, and about the
fact that they seemed to concentrate on nothing but sex. It was all too easy for

[8] Richards does go considerably further, suggesting an embrace comparable to that in the United
States and an exaggeration of cultural barriers. However, this is partly because, as in the case of this
chapter, he pushes the boundaries of what was significant in terms of psychological thought: 'Britain
on the Couch'.

[9] Caine, 'The Stracheys and Psychoanalysis', 144–69. Suggesting that the understanding in
Bloomsbury was 'not deep': M. Pines, 'The Development of the Psychodynamic Movement', in
G. Berrios and H. Freeman (eds.), *150 Years of British Psychiatry, 1841–1991*, 1 (London, 1991),
226–9. A sign of this is that although Virginia Woolf was treated by a series of doctors for her depression, not one was a clear Freudian: S. Trombley, *'All that Summer She was Mad': Virginia Woolf and her
Doctors* (London, 1981). Her view of Freud was ambivalent: H. Lee, *Virginia Woolf* (London, 1996),
722–6. Emphasising a high level of bohemian interest in a more eclectic range of new psychological
ideas, see Ch. 3.

[10] H. Cook, 'Sex and the Doctors: The Medicalization of Sexuality as a Two-Way Process in Early
to Mid-Twentieth-Century Britain', in W. de Blécourt and C. Usborne (eds.), *Cultural Approaches to
the History of Medicine* (Basingstoke, 2004), 195; H. Cook, *The Long Sexual Revolution: English Women,
Sex, and Contraception, 1800–1975* (Oxford, 2004), 167–73. For the reassertion of Victorian sexuality
in private life: M. Mason, *The Making of Victorian Sexuality* (Oxford, 1994); P. Gay, *The Bourgeois
Experience: Victoria to Freud: The Tender Passion* (Oxford, 1986).

critics to caricature Freud's work and that of his followers as little more than pornography.[11] The second main problem was that he suggested a model of the self in which the individual will—such a central theme in Victorian ideology—was no longer in command.[12] Presenting an acute conflict between human instinct and the conventions of civilisation, Freudiauism raised the dangerous prospect of blame shifting to the Victorian moral code itself. Psychoanalytic therapy was also a problem in this regard, seen by critics as a form of confession that would actually indulge and even encourage underlying problems. The same concern about the will lay behind criticism of hypnosis, so closely associated with psychoanalysis at first, which seemed to be placing the patient in a pathological state of loss of control, and giving dangerous power to potentially unscrupulous quackery.[13] Other reasons for caution or resistance at the popular level were less central. There was the objection that Freud's proposals had their basis in hypothesis rather than concrete evidence, particularly in criticism from the medical profession. There could also be an undercurrent of anti-Semitism and national xenophobia, though this was probably only a serious factor during the First World War.[14]

Through a careful survey of the periodicals of the educated reading public, Dean Rapp has helped to revise, to some degree, this idea that the British lacked enthusiasm for or were ignorant of Freud.[15] Rapp casts light, in particular, on the views of the literary and journalistic community who produced these articles, and thereby demonstrates diffusion of awareness (rather than understanding), to the middle-class audience. This interest peaked in the early 1920s, when there was much talk of a 'craze', and declined thereafter. However, a serious appreciation of Freud had emerged as early as 1912 (before the First World War, so often seen as the harbinger of his ideas, though still slightly later and less favourably than in Germany and the United States). Freud's own writing only established a very small audience, but accounts by interested British academics and psychologists summarising his ideas were more wide reaching. The botanist A. G. Tansley probably attracted the greatest number of readers with his book *The New Psychology*, first published in 1920 and already in its fifth impression by 1922. It sold five times more copies than the more orthodox account by the British Freudian,

[11] Oppenheim, *Shattered Nerves*, 306.

[12] On this problem in nineteenth-century British psychiatry: M. Clark, 'The Rejection of Psychological Approaches to Mental Disorder in Late Nineteenth-Century British Psychiatry', in A. Scull (ed.), *Madhouses, Mad-Doctors, and Madmen: The Social History of Psychiatry in the Victorian Era* (London, 1981), 271–312.

[13] D. Pick, *Svengali's Web: The Alien Enchanter in Modern Culture* (New Haven and London, 2000).

[14] Oppenheim, *Shattered Nerves*, 304–11; Rapp, 'Early Reception'. On racism: Ellesley, 'Psychoanalysis', 159–61; Rapp, 'Early Discovery', 231. See also Pines, 'Development of the Psychodynamic Movement', 206–31; and R. D. Hinshelwood, 'Psychodynamic Psychiatry before World War I', in Berrios and Freeman (eds.), *150 Years of British Psychiatry*, vol. 1, 197–205. For a more detailed examination of attitudes in the medical profession, see Ch. 6.

[15] Rapp summarises the findings in his two articles: 'Reception of Freud' and 'Early Discovery'.

Barbara Low. Even so, only 19,000 copies were printed.[16] What was more important in terms of public awareness was that these ideas and publications did spark off a reaction in the general press. In total, the 43 periodicals Rapp surveys had published over 170 items of some kind about Freud, Jung, and their more eclectic British followers by 1920. These pieces were generally favourable to the idea of the dynamic unconscious (as long as it was not pushed to a deterministic extreme). They were less favourable, indeed invariably critical, of his emphasis on the sexual instinct, and often showed a preference for Jung and Adler for this reason. There was also much concern about the abuse of psychoanalysis in practice by unqualified practitioners. Rapp suggests that the media's selectively favourable view was important in the British public's receptivity to the eclectic form of psychoanalysis that was to emerge in Britain over the next decades.[17]

Sandra Ellesley largely confirms such conclusions in her study of the popularization of psychoanalysis in England.[18] Based again on analysis of general readership periodicals—26, covering the period 1900 to 1926—she points to a similar level of interest, with 68 articles, 46 reviews, and 29 letters. She also highlights coverage in both the national and provincial press and regards this as the main channel for popularisation.[19] She offers a nuanced reading of this material, recognising the limitations of a purely quantitative gauge. In general, despite her evidence on the rising profile of psychoanalysis, she tends to acknowledge the strength of a contemporary view that the interest in Freud was something of a fashionable, faddish, and thus superficial craze—the 'game of psychoanalysis' as G. K. Chesterton called it—with dedicated followers a minority cult.[20] In this respect, she also highlights its proximity to a range of occult, religious, and variously unorthodox ideas. On the other hand, she does note that such a dismissal also had class and gender connotations: a female and mass audience was seen as particularly suggestible and led by desire rather than rationality.[21]

These histories tell us a great deal about the responses of a literary elite and the construction of an elite-led, public opinion, and we can assume consequently a broader growing awareness of figures like Freud via the pages of the press. However, they reveal much less when it comes to practice. Neither is there much if any ground level evidence to substantiate the claims about popularisation or to cast light on what this actually meant in terms of thought. In passing, they do reveal that the interest in Freud was invariably tied up with a much broader set of ideas and movements: with other psychologists such as Jung and Adler, and with occultism, psychic research, Theosophy, spiritualism, Christian Science, faith healing, and quackery (indeed until the 1920s, psychoanalysis was rarely

[16] Rapp, 'Reception of Freud', 197. For more on writers like Tansley and Low and a popularisation from above, see Ch. 2.   [17] Rapp, 'Early Discovery'; Rapp, 'Reception of Freud', 191–201.
[18] Ellesley, 'Psychoanalysis'.   [19] Ibid. 200.
[20] G. K. Chesterton, 'The Game of Psychoanalysis', *Century Magazine*, 106 (1923), 34–43. This was accepted in the influential early social history of the period, first published in 1940: R. Graves and A. Hodge, *The Long Weekend: A Social History of Great Britain, 1918–1939* (London, 1971), 98–100.   [21] Ellesley, 'Psychoanalysis', 176–87.

discussed in its own right). However, these histories remain bound by the paradigm of a 'Freudian Revolution'. Thus, they tend to see resistance as a sign of lack of interest in psychology, rather than interest in another sort of psychology. Similarly, they tend to see complexity as a reflection of the confusion, weak purchase, or eclecticism of the new psychology in Britain, rather than as an indication that psychological popularisation was a much broader and pervasive phenomenon, and that much of it was of a rather different hue.[22] What follows is an attempt to take seriously this other psychology, one that was in truth perhaps the truly popular psychology of the era. In terms of our own Freudian perspective, it is a less obviously modern and in some ways more intellectually mundane story, hence its neglect to date; however, in terms of helping us to understand how many normal people actively engaged with psychology before gradually moving on towards a more Freudian psychology, it adds a crucial element to our existing picture.

PELMANISM

The traditional story of psychological modernity would have it that the encounter with shellshock in the First World War was crucial in changing attitudes, in a turn in particular towards Freud and psychotherapy. In fact, the extent to which shellshock transformed public minds, not just the minds of a select group of doctors, remains subject to debate.[23] If one is looking for a great public enthusiasm for psychology in the War, one might in fact turn in an altogether different direction: to the explosion of interest in the practical psychology of Pelmanism.[24]

Founded in 1899 by William Joseph Ennever, this system of mental training through correspondence course was already popular by the start of the war. Based initially on an ability to improve memory as a route to success, it claimed to have enrolled some 200,000 by 1915.[25] Conditions of war fuelled interest into a frenzy.[26] In 1918 alone, there were 100,000 reported new enrolments, making 400,000 since foundation.[27] The idea that Pelman training could substantially add to the nation's mental efficiency—help the 'British brain' regain 'its position of predominance'—won influential backers in circumstances of war, and effective self-promotion made the most of this.[28] By accepting regular advertising, *The*

---

[22] Ibid. 170.   [23] See pp. 182–6, 211–13.
[24] E. Anton, 'The Psychological Factor', *The Times* (10 Nov. 1917). Coverage in *Truth* in 1916 was important in bringing it to the fore of public attention.
[25] '£2,000 a Year: The Road to a Big Income', *The Times* (11 May 1915). Courses were advertised as early as 1903: 'Memory Means Money', *The Times* (21 Feb. 1903).
[26] E. Anton, 'The Biography of an Idea—Pelmanism', *The Times* (28 Jan. 1918).
[27] 'Pelmanism Sweeps the Country', *The Times* (4 Feb. 1919); 'Pelmanism and the Press', *The Times* (6 Feb. 1919).
[28] E. Anton, 'The Biography of an Idea—Pelmanism', *The Times* (28 Jan. 1918).

Times gave establishment approval.[29] A series of luminaries also offered public support. Member of Parliament, Sir James Yoxall, spoke in favour of Pelmanism as a tool in education, and proposals emerged by 1919 for every schoolchild to pass the course, even for a 'Ministry of Pelmanism'.[30] More crucially, the war effort itself provided in the view of Major-General Sir F. Maurice a pressing case for Pelmanism as a kind of 'mind drill', and he was far from being alone in highlighting this potential.[31]

Whether such feelings can account for the surge in membership is another matter. In the case of the motor manufacturer, Herbert Austin, the death of his son on the Western Front was a precipitating factor; the focus of Pelmanism in this instance perhaps attractive as a distraction from loss, holding emotion in check, but also for its supposed ability to end moods at will.[32] There was particular emphasis on its appeal for men in the forces:[33] Pelmanism sold itself as something that could be practiced anywhere, and this meant even in the trenches. Soldiers may well have seen it as a useful way to kill time, a distraction, through focused attention, from everyday stress and fear, but also from the boredom and resulting 'intellectual hunger' experienced behind the front lines or in hospital.[34] Marketing, however, continued to place most emphasis on the promise of success, much as in peace, albeit here with the added dimension of the soldier's insecurity about return. The particular appeal to officers—supposedly, 18,000 by 1918— may also reflect its attraction as a source of efficiency to those somewhat desperate for answers and without much training cast into such difficult circumstances.[35] War, then, probably did broaden appeal. Though, even in 1917, enrolment was mainly middle class: accountants and bankers (8.3 per cent); businessmen (7.4 per cent); clerks and salesmen (12.5 per cent); businesswomen (10.3 per cent); doctors (2.6 per cent); clergymen and teachers (8.5 per cent); engineers (8.1 per cent); solicitors and barristers (2.5 per cent); government and other officials (5.8 per cent); authors, editors, and journalists (1 per cent); as well as army and navy (12.3 per cent); and an unclassified group (20.7 per cent).[36]

Pelmanism, as was typical of practical psychology, combined common sense with a little basic psychological theory, and hard work through practice with a missionary zeal and at times a millennial ambition. For the *Daily News*, the

---

[29] 'Pelmanism in 1917: Remarkable Response from Readers of the Times', *The Times* (5 Sept. 1917).

[30] Sir James Yoxall, 'Pelmanism as an Educational Factor', *The Times* (26 July, 1918); 'Pelmanism Sweeps the Country', *The Times* (4 Feb. 1919).

[31] Maj.-Gen. Sir F. Maurice, 'The Military Value of Pelmanism', *The Times* (10 Aug. 1918).

[32] Information on Austin from the *Dictionary of National Biography*. E. Anton, 'Pelmanism and Moods', *The Times* (8 May 1918).

[33] 'Army and Navy "Solid" for Pelmanism', *The Times* (17 Sept. 1917).

[34] There is a widespread misapprehension that these soldiers were simply playing a version of the memory-based card game that later came to be known by the name of Pelmanism (as well as several others). On appeal: G. Henry, 'A Pelmanist Regrets', *The Times* (10 Oct. 1918).

[35] E. Anton, 'The Biography of an Idea—Pelmanism', *The Times* (28 Jan. 1918).

[36] 'Rapid Spread of Pelmanism', *The Times* (25 June 1917).

Pelmanists were the 'apostles of common sense'.[37] As a 'gospel of action' it offered, not just principles for practical living, but impelling, vivifying spirit.[38] Ennever always maintained that there was no great secret or personal insight behind the method.[39] It was just modern psychology distilled for mass consumption and use: 'all the best that has been written of psychology is in Pelmanism in tabloid form', as he put it, rather appropriately, in an interview in the *Daily Mail*.[40] Rather than depending on experts, Ennever had enlisted as teachers the help of any man or woman with a 'psychological mind'.[41] Expert ideas, too, were useful rather than essential. As he put it, 'The science of mind-training is over-ridden by theories. Almost every psychologist has his own theory, and most are exceedingly plausible. But our work is essentially practical.'[42]

Although best known for its techniques of training memory, Pelmanism found itself in an environment in which the potential of psychology was coming to be recognised as far broader and now attempted to present itself as something that could help with 'moods', 'character', 'self-realisation' and 'self-expression'.[43] After a brief flirtation with continuing to emphasise its national value, now in terms of reconstruction for peace, the New Pelman Course of 1920 indicated a post-war reorientation towards the concerns of 'everyday life'.[44] Evidence suggests that those who enrolled did indeed look for something much broader than mere memory technique. Like many other adherents, Miss Lillah McCarthy welcomed the lessons of its now twelve 'Little Grey Books' as something, perhaps as religion once had, that provided rhythm and security to life: 'Pelmanism is now my Sunday recreation. I take a dose of this new mental tonic, and at once feel braced up, ready for my week's work.'[45] General Lionel Dunsterville, friend of Rudyard Kipling and model for his character Stalky, likewise found Pelmanism attractive as something that could give order and direction to life after the Great War. Taking it up in 1921, at the age of fifty-six, he reported the transformative effect in his diary. 'I think Pelmanism is waking me from my mental lethargy', he recorded on initial encounter.[46] Two weeks later, he was even more convinced: 'It gives me the

[37] 'Pelmanism and the Press', *The Times* (6 Feb. 1919).
[38] 'Pelmanism: The Gospel of Action', *The Times* (2 Jan. 1919).
[39] The original idea may have been that of Christopher Lewis Pelman who published several books on the subject in the first decade of the century with the Pelman School of Memory Training.
[40] From an interview in the *Daily Mail* in October 1921, extracted in 'Pelmanism in 1922: Personal Statement from the Founder of the Pelman Institute', *The Times* (2 Jan. 1922).
[41] E. Anton, 'The Biography of an Idea—Pelmanism', *The Times* (28 Jan. 1918).
[42] Ibid.
[43] E. Anton, 'Pelmanism and Moods', *The Times* (8 May 1918); M. Pemberton, 'The Romance of Pelmanism', *The Times* (17 July 1918); *Pelmanism: The First Principles. Lesson No 1* (London, n.d., c.1916), 5.
[44] Corporal A. F. Thorn, 'Pelmanism and Peace', *The Times* (11 Oct. 1918); 'Peace, Pelmanism and Prosperity', *The Times* (27 Nov. 1918). The shift to a concern about everyday life is developed later in this chapter.
[45] 'The New Pelman Course—The Psychology of Everyday Life', *The Times* (9 Feb. 1921).
[46] Diaries of General Lionel Dunsterville: http://www.gwpda.org/Dunsterville/Dunsterville_1921.html: entry for 11 Aug. 1921.

power to *exert* my will, the will was always there, but no driving force behind it. It takes the slackness out of your mind.'[47] What is particularly notable is the emphasis on control, perhaps something that the veteran missed in civil society. Partly this was an issue of Pelmanism giving structure to the day: a session of reading and then physical exercises in the morning, with further exercises before bed.[48] Partly, it was here an issue of fending off over-indulgence and the temptations of alcohol and tobacco: 'It all leads to *control* which is what all of us lack—*control yourself* and you at once stand out from your fellowmen, the *uncontrolled*.'[49] Whether this was a long-term solution to readjustment seems doubtful: just three months into the course of study, Dunsterville was reporting that 'Pelmanism is not prospering and my mental state is rather chaotic'.[50]

In the early 1920s, Ennever's Pelman Institute also found itself struggling with mounting debt.[51] Perhaps the wartime boom had led to inflated ambitions and overextension, or perhaps it was a case of such a psychology now facing more competitors, or not adequately addressing new psychological demands. Survival now depended as much on projecting the memory techniques into books on teaching foreign languages.[52] Pelmanism remained a persistent reminder, through its advertisements, of the continuing appeal of a psychology centred on success, but with Ennever slipping from the helm through ill health and financial difficulties, it never fully regained the level of appeal and national profile that it temporarily had during the War.[53]

THE PSYCHO-THERAPEUTIC SOCIETY

Pelmanism provides one end of the spectrum of popular thought and practice in this chapter: practical psychology at its most pragmatic. Located at the more mystical and bohemian extreme was the London Psycho-Therapeutic Society. What they had in common was a belief, both that psychology was of central value as a guide to life, and that the key was to put theory and practice into the hands of the individual. If Pelmanism highlights a lineage back to Victorian self-improvement, the Psycho-Therapeutic Society helps us to understand a lineage to occult, spiritualist, and mesmerist thought and practice.

---

[47] Diaries of General Lionel Dunsterville. 30 Aug. 1921.   [48] Ibid. 17 Sept. 1921.
[49] Ibid. 12 Sept. 1921.
[50] Ibid. 25 Sept. 1921. On the psychological problems of re-adjustment and its relation to masculinity and new psychological ideas: M. Roper, 'Between Manliness and Masculinity: The "War Generation" and the Psychology of Fear in Britain, 1914–1950', *Journal of British Studies*, 44 (2005), 343–62.   [51] 'Winding up the Pelman Institute, Ltd', *The Times* (26 Oct. 1921).
[52] For instance, 'How to Speak French like a Frenchman', *The Times* (2 Oct. 1923).
[53] 'Pelmanism in 1922: Personal Statement from the Founder of the Pelman Institute', *The Times* (2 Jan. 1922). Ennever filed for bankruptcy in 1941: *The Times* (24 April 1941). Under the aegis of the Ennever Foundation, Ennever would publish two further books: *Brain Building for Success* (London, 1938); *Your Mind and How to Use It* (London, 1942). He would die in 1947.

Founded in 1901, the Society's driving force, Arthur Hallam, was Secretary of the London Association for the Prevention of Premature Burial, which worked to reform burial practice in light of claims that conditions of trance and suspended animation were often mistaken for death.[54] His call for a new society to investigate magnetic healing sprang from the same aim of bringing the concerns of spiritualism to bear on issues of practical reform. An initial meeting was held in the rooms of Dr George Wyld, one of the 'oldest mesmerists in England', with tensions immediately emerging over whether the new society would be independent or part of the broader spiritualist movement.[55] In the end, it aimed to serve as a broad church, which could demonstrate the relationship between the growing number of groups currently interested in psychic phenomena, including the Spiritualist, Theosophical, Mental Science, Christian Science, and Divine Science movements.[56] It would reject the struggle for pre-eminence that put so many people off these groups; instead, it would highlight a unifying theory that placed man at the very centre of psychic and mental force.[57] In its earliest days it constructed a lineage back to early nineteenth-century Mesmerism, and positioned itself against a medical profession which had attacked pioneers, such as Dr John Elliotson, and now stood against any revival.[58] As well as Wyld, the input of Dr Forbes Winslow and phrenologist Dr Bernard Hollander tied the Society to a radical and alternative strain within Victorian medical psychology, which had persisted despite the increased regulation of the profession.[59] The Society also looked to recent continental (especially French) research both in psychiatry, and in physical science.[60] It saw its function as spreading an understanding of these new scientific ideas against

[54] Such concerns can be traced in the journal *Burial Reformer* (1905–8).

[55] A. Hallam, 'The Psycho-Therapeutic Society—Its Origins and Principles', *Health Record*, 13, 149 (1914), 83–4. Wyld had practised mesmerism since 1839 and was interested in hypnotism and Christo-Theosophy: *Psycho-Therapeutic Journal*, 3 (1904), 11. He was also a phrenologist, theosophist, spiritualist, and homeopath: Oppenheim, *The Other World*, 231–2. The subject of spiritual healing is the subject of Sheryl Root's Ph.D thesis (University of Warwick, 2006) 'Healing, Touch, and Medicine, *c*.1890–1950'.

[56] Oppenheim estimates that the number of active spiritualists by this time was in the (wide) range 10,000 to 100,000, with some 200 local spiritualist lyceums on the eve of World War I: *The Other World*, 50, 103.   [57] *The Psycho-Therapeutic Journal*, 1, (1901), 1–3.

[58] The medical profession was intensely concerned about clamping down on quackery at this time. In this atmosphere, the Psycho-Therapeutic Society struggled to gain legal recognition from the Board of Trade, who eventually accepted its incorporation in 1910: *Health Record*, 9 (1910), 17.

[59] For instance: Forbes Winslow, 'Hypnotism', *Psycho-Therapeutic Journal*, 1 (1902), 43; Forbes Winslow, 'Political Madness', *Psycho-Therapeutic Journal*, 5 (1906), 6–7; G. Wyld, 'Mesmerism and Hypnotism: Their Affinities and their Differentiations', *Psycho-Therapeutic Journal*, 1 (1902), 38–9; B. Hollander, 'The Psycho-Therapeutics of Insanity: Can Insanity be Treated by Suggestion?', *Health Record*, 7 (1908), 83–4. Hollander continued to find an audience for his ideas on phrenology: British Phrenological Society, *In Commemoration of Bernard Hollander* (London, 1965); B. Hollander, *Scientific Phrenology: Being a Practical Mental Science and Guide to Human Character* (London, 1902).

[60] See, for instance, the report on the hypnotic movement in Paris: *Psycho-Therapeutic Journal*, 1 (1902), 49. For report on autosuggestion in Paris see ibid. Review of Dr H. Baraduc's *The Human Vibrations* and French reports of the discovery of N-Rays emanating from the human body: *Psycho-Therapeutic Journal*, 3 (1904), 3–5.

both the prejudice of British doctors, and the anti-materialism and claims for exclusive authority of movements like Christian Science.[61]

The antagonism of the medical profession was inflamed as the Society established a 'psycho-therapeutic clinic'. Here, it used the force of mind over body and the transmission of energy by 'operators', free of charge, to cure or at least ameliorate an extraordinary range of conditions: pains of all descriptions, sleeplessness, functional paralysis, anaemia, irregularities of menstruation, loss of appetite and all nervous digestive disturbances, constipation and diarrhoea, gastric and intestinal dyspepsia, psychical impotence, pollutions, 'onanisms' and perverted sexual appetites, alcoholism and drug habits, chronic muscular and arthritic rheumatism, lumbago, neurasthenic disturbances, neuritis, stammering and nervous disturbances of vision, sickness and sea sickness, vomiting in pregnancy and troubles of childbirth, nocturnal weaknesses, hysterical attacks of all kinds, phobias, bad habits, epilepsy, haemorrhages, general debility, mental depression, obsessions, stage fright, and want of confidence.[62] Though it recognised the need to suppress mere quackery and criticised the use of hypnotism in séances and drawing-room entertainment as degrading, the Society viewed the medical profession's growing criticism of psychotherapeutics as little more than selfish and ignorant protectionism, and its drug-based therapies as seriously restricting the efficacy and scope of medical care.[63]

The psychotherapeutic clinic developed rapidly. In 1904, 'operators' already saw 141 patients and provided 1,324 free treatments and diagnoses, nearly half performed by the medical clairvoyant George Spriggs.[64] By 1907, the three leading operators were all women, with total treatments now 3,868.[65] This peaked in 1910, with over 4,262 cases that year.[66] However, growth stopped here. There was a feeling that the National Insurance Act of 1911 was a factor, obliging the poorer classes to pay for outdoor medical attendance and leaving them unable to afford the additional expense of fares to the Society's rooms.[67] Nevertheless, by the outbreak of war, the clinic had dealt with 4,051 patients and provided 35,741 free treatments.[68] Similar work was also undertaken privately and by allied groups.[69]

---

[61] A. Lovell, 'Psycho-Therapeutics and Science', *Psycho-Therapeutic Journal*, 1 (1902), 2–5; A. Hallam, *Health Record*, 10 (1910), 66. On Christian Science: C. F. Gartrell-Mills, 'Christian Science: An American Religion in Britain, 1895–1940', D.Phil. thesis (University of Oxford, 1991).

[62] A. Hallam, 'Psycho-Therapeutics—A Rational Cure for a Variety of Complaints', *Health Record*, 12 (1913), 74–5.

[63] *Psycho-Therapeutic Journal*, 1 (1902), 25–31; 'Out-Patients', *Psycho-Therapeutic Journal*, 2 (1903), 29.

[64] 3rd Annual Report, *Psycho-Therapeutic Journal*, 3 (1904), 50. Spriggs had been interested in medical clairvoyance since the 1870s. He spent the 1880s and 1890s in Australia. Since his return, he had been a central figure in the Society and also a councillor in North Sheen: 'Obituary', *Health Record*, 11 (1912), 26–7.

[65] 6th Annual Report, *Health Record*, 6 (1907).

[66] 9th Annual Report, *Health Record*, 9 (1910), 76.

[67] 12th Annual Report, *Health Record*, 12 (July 1913), 58.

[68] *Psycho-Therapeutic Society 13th Annual Report* (London, 1914), 6.

[69] For instance, Dr Francis Gilbert Scott and Dr Edwin Ash ran the London Nerve Clinic and School of Psychotherapy: *Health Record*, 12 (1913), 98. For more on Ash, see pp, 179–80. An editorial

The primary aim of the Society was to demystify and propagate psycho-therapeutic practice. Anyone could be a therapist. However, practice and experience helped, particularly when it came to diagnosis and the Society started training classes in a range of therapeutic techniques.[70] Hallam also published detailed practical instructions in hypnotic and magnetic 'passing' techniques.[71] The idea that health depended on an inner, vital energy and that a trained operator could encourage the return of a positive flow in the patient, partly through sensitivity and partly through ability to project energy, meant that therapy was at first firmly within an established tradition of mesmerism and animal magnetism. However, the integration of new theories and practices of mind was rapid. This included hypnosis and suggestion, but also new theories about the existence of hidden forms of energy such as X-rays and the possibility of human N-rays. The older terms came to seem too restrictive, and the 'psycho-therapeutic', or occasionally the 'mental therapeutics' label, emerged instead.[72] What this psychotherapy did not entail, at least not explicitly, was any kind of talking cure; rather, it was psychological in the sense that it regarded physical (and mental) illness, like health and even power, as dependent on levels of psychic energy and attitudes of mind.[73] Mind and body were part of the same system, both key to a state of harmony and vitality.[74] For this reason, psychotherapeutics allied itself closely with and utilised a host of other health regimes: among them were vegetarianism, fruitarianism, clothes reform, chromotherapy, electrotherapy, hydrotherapy, deep breathing, and physical culture.[75] The unifying idea was that health and happiness depended on maintaining the body's vital energies: restrictive clothes were rejected and those absorbing energy and projecting colours worn instead, the putrefaction and toxins of meat-eating and alcohol were to be avoided, and poise was to be gained through harmonious movement.[76] In each instance, medicine's narrow emphasis on cure

---

on 'Advancement' highlighted a 'rapid increase of schools, teachers, and practitioners of psychic and mental healing': *Health Record*, 12 (1913), 115. Hallam, himself, ran a private practice in Maida Vale, offering free consultations, treatments, and lessons: *Health Record*, 12 (1913), 105, 107. There were also adverts for numerous recuperative homes and magnetic healers. For instance, Mr and Mrs M. W. Wragg, magnetic healers, specialising in rheumatic and nervous diseases, and their Harvard Institute of Vibration and Psycho-Therapeutics, in Isleworth, Middlesex: *Health Record*, 10 (1911), v.

[70] *Psycho-Therapeutic Journal*, 3 (1904), 22.

[71] A. Hallam, 'Practical Instruction in Psycho-Therapeutics', *Psycho-Therapeutic Journal*, 3 (1904), 33–5; A. Hallam, *The Key to Perfect Health (And the Successful Application of Psycho-Therapeutics: A Practical Guide to both Operator and Patient)* (London, 1912).

[72] 'Wanted—A Term', *Psycho-Therapeutic Journal*, 1 (1902), 13.

[73] A. Hallam, 'Mental Therapeutics', *Health Record*, 10 (1911), 49–54.

[74] A. Hallam, 'Psycho-Therapeutics: A Course of Instruction in Curative Human Radiations, Medical Hypnotism, and Suggestive Therapeutics', *Psycho-Therapeutic Journal*, 4 (1905), 98; A. Hallam, 'A Course of Instruction (cont.)', *Psycho-Therapeutic Journal*, 5 (1906), 16.

[75] For the eclecticism of treatment: 'Some Recent Cases Successfully Treated by the Psycho-Therapeutic Society', *Psycho-Therapeutic Journal*, 4 (1905), 51–2. On chromotherapy: D. D'A. Wright, 'The Effects of Light Energy on Man', *Health Record*, 8 (1909), 134–7.

[76] On chromotherapy: Wright, 'Effects of Light Energy', 134–7. On the rejection of a 'biceps culture' in favour of a synthesis between mind and body action in exercise: W. St Clair Phillips, 'Health, Strength, and Symmetry: A System and an Argument', *Health Record*, 8 (1909), 63–5. On

was criticised, and a life of prevention and elevation of mind and body power was set in its place. Psychotherapy brought these movements together and stood above them, just as it aimed to bring together Spiritualism, Christian Science, Theosophy, and New Thought, because it provided both a unifying theory of the role of vital energy and the power of thought and of mind over body, and a series of practical techniques for cure and management.[77] Although Psychotherapy allied itself with the esoteric adherents of a 'cosmic consciousness', it was always important that this theory rested on science, or 'natural law', rather than mysticism; vital energy was variously traced to the physical attraction between blood cells or to forms of energy and matter still hidden from modern science but no less real than those already discovered.[78]

Ultimately, psychotherapy was designed, not simply as something which could be proffered in a curative role to others, but as a theoretical basis for and practical guide towards a more balanced, happy, and powerful self. The path to control over one's own vital energies, and to the health and power this offered, was one of gaining absolute self-control over body and mind.[79] This re-educative role was just as important as the magnetic healing in the regular treatment sessions.[80] Thus, Hallam's book on the subject was to act as a guide for patients, as well as operators.[81] And an emphasis on some form of hypnosis or suggestion made way for teaching people how to exercise suggestion on themselves.[82]

This reorientation also saw a secular emphasis on health superseding a mystical, occult, and spiritual one, symbolised in the renaming of the Society's monthly periodical as the *Health Record* in 1907. Perhaps this was also a reflection of the need to attract a broader range of advertising, catering to a market for health food and retreats. Despite this, financial problems were so serious that Hallam had to step in to save the journal in 1912.[83] One of the problems was that membership of the Society (and thus subscription to the journal) had struggled to expand. In 1904, it had stood at 64, with 39 associate members; by 1906, this had risen to 157 and 46 respectively, but here it had levelled off. Despite its schemes of free treatment and placing free copies of the journal in public libraries, it had clearly struggled to reach beyond its original rather bohemian, metropolitan audience.[84] The significance of

---

diet: S. H. Beard (President of the Order of the Golden Age), 'Diet in Relation to Health', *Health Record*, 6 (1907), 134–6. On breathing correctly: A. Hallam, 'Psycho-Therapeutics', *Health Record*, 6 (1907), 9.

[77] On the primacy of psychotherapy over (still valuable) physical health regimes: A. Hallam, 'Perfect Health: How to Acquire it', *Health Record*, 9 (1910), 62–3.

[78] For instance, H. V. Knaggs (LRCP, MRCS, LSA), 'Methods of Mind Control', *Health Record*, 12 (1912), 38–9; H. V. Knaggs, 'The Psychical Element in Blood', *Health Record*, 11 (1911), 14–16.

[79] A. Hallam, 'Course of Instruction (cont.)', *Psycho-Therapeutic Journal*, 5 (1906), 69–70.

[80] A. Hallam, 'Hypnotism—Its Educational and Reformatory Value', *Psycho-Therapeutic Journal*, 1 (1902), 30–1.   [81] A. Hallam, *The Key to Perfect Health* (London, 1912).

[82] The phrenologist Dr Bernard Hollander was an influential advocate: 'The Power of Suggestion', *Health Record*, 11 (1912), 50–3.

[83] 11th Annual Report, *Health Record*, 11 (1912), 74–6.

[84] Around eighty such copies were donated in 1908, a few overseas, but most to public libraries, hotels, health homes, corresponding societies, reading rooms, spas and sanatoria. Copies even

the Society lies therefore, not in its scale or longevity, but in it as a symbol of transition and as a meeting point highlighting the commonalities between what at first sight might appear an extraordinary range of groups and interests.[85] Yet in forging a unified, non-sectarian path, the Society ultimately struggled to reconcile the tensions between supporters of the primacy of mind, body, and spirit. Perhaps because he was conscious of the challenge of movements that did now place even more emphasis on primacy of mind, Hallam appears to have stepped back from exaggerating the claims of mental therapeutics.[86] Instead, what was on offer from the Society was a more pragmatic message about management of nerves in everyday life and as an adjunct to physical care in the maintenance of health.[87] Because of this moderation, bridges were left open to those within the medical profession who were at last becoming interested in the relationship between mind and body and the use of hypnotism, Freudian psychoanalysis, and persuasion.[88] At first, the outbreak of war appeared to offer Psycho-Therapy great opportunities.[89] Shortages, however, hit small publications, forcing the *Health Record* to shift to a quarterly in 1915.[90] Later that year, publication ceased while Hallam served in the war. In 1921, it made a brief reappearance, though now with a far less distinctive identity and epistemology, descending into the more banal fare of recipes, ideas about headache cures, general household tips, and advice on healthy places to visit such as Bognor Regis and Southwold.[91] Acknowledgement that the medical profession was now waking up to the value of psychotherapy—evident for instance in the pronouncements of figures like Professor Robertson in Edinburgh or Dr Helen Boyle in Brighton—is a further indication of how a role was being lost.[92] After just three issues, the journal disappeared.

reached unlikely venues such as the Cwmavon Tinworks Reading Room and Institute: *The Psycho-Therapeutic Society: 10th Annual Report* (London, 1911), 33–5. There was some limited institutional expansion beyond London, with a Psycho-Therapy Society opened in Brighton, a healing class opened after a lecture in Newcastle-on-Tyne, and a clinic opened in Liverpool: *Health Record*, 6 (1907), 132; *Psycho-Therapeutic Journal*, 1 (1902), 34; *Health Record*, 11 (1912), 55.

[85] This is very apparent in its library holdings published in annual reports. In 1908, there were well over two-hundred entries, ranging across subjects from animal magnetism, animal rights, the aura, auto-suggestion, bathing, beauty, the brain, breathing, burial reform, cancer, Christo-Theosophy, Christian Science, Clairvoyance, the conquest of death, diet, diptheria, education, electricity, flesh-eating, gymnastics, healing, herbs, human radiations, hydropathy, hypnotism, massage, mesmerism, motherhood, N-rays, the occult, pasteurism, phrenology, physiognomy, psychic phenomena, the new psychology, reincarnation, seeing the invisible, somnambulism, soul culture, spiritualism, self synthesis, telepathy, theosophy, uncontrollable drunkenness, vaccination, vegetarianism, vivisection, wholemeal flour, women of the era, worry, yoga, and perpetual youth (to give only a selection): *The Psycho-Therapeutic Society: 7th Annual Report* (London, 1908), 28–35.

[86] A. Hallam, 'Mental Therapeutics', *Health Record*, 10 (1911), 52–3.

[87] For instance, A. P. Call, 'Nerves and Common Sense', *Health Record*, 12 (1913), 14–16.

[88] M. Rittenburg, 'Mind Surgery', *Health Record*, 12 (1912), 26. The Society republished an article from the *British Journal of Inebriacy* by H. C. Miller (future Director of the Tavistock Clinic: 'Psychotherapy and the Inebriate', *Health Record*, 12 (1912), 47–8. For more on Miller, see Chs. 2 and 6.

[89] Editorial: 'The War and Mental Depression', *Health Record*, 13 (1914), 99.

[90] Editorial: 'The Brightest Stage of the War', *Health Record*, 13 (1915), 111.

[91] *Health Record*, 14 (1921), 9.   [92] Ibid. 41.

PRACTICAL PSYCHOLOGY AFTER
THE FIRST WORLD WAR

Between the poles of Pelmanism and the Psycho-Therapeutic Society lay the practical psychology that came to the fore after the First World War. What follows is an outline of its landscape and scope, before further sections on its initial epistemology and its evolution in the 1930s. The club was a central feature of practical psychology. It provided a site for regular lectures and meetings, libraries of psychological literature, courses of self-improvement, and perhaps even therapeutic attention; though the latter was usually far less central than it had been within the Psycho-Therapeutic Society. Some of these clubs formed into federations; others were the offspring of a central figurehead. These are the easiest to trace through journals and other publications, but smaller clubs may have existed without leaving such obvious records.

In the 1920s, the term practical psychology was increasingly that chosen to describe the clubs and publications that were springing up across the country. This development took place most vigorously in London, the north east, and the north west of England, but clubs could also be found in the Midlands, the south, and in Scotland. In 1925, the *Practical Psychologist* began publication. Although this journal centred on the Practical Psychology club of London and its activities and ideas, it had links to clubs around the country: for instance, in Bristol, Leeds, Liverpool, Manchester, Nottingham, and Sheffield. These clubs united under the umbrella of the Federation of Practical Psychology Clubs of Great Britain, which was founded in 1922 when Miss Anna Maud Hallam, said to be the foremost lecturer and teacher of the subject, came to Britain from the United States aiming to set up an educational centre to teach practical psychology.[93] No relation, despite the coincidence of name, with the leader of the London Psycho-Therapeutic Society, Arthur Hallam, she had supposedly cured herself of near blindness and nervous collapse through harnessing the power of the subconscious mind, and her story had already acted as the inspiration for a network of Anna Maud Hallam Practical Psychology Clubs in the United States. She claimed to have brought the term 'practical psychology' to Britain, and became Life President of the British Federation.[94] Her evangelism took her even further afield, lecturing and conducting classes in South Africa (where she formed five further clubs) and studying and

---

[93] *Practical Psychologist*, 1/1 (1925), 6–8; *Practical Psychologist*, 2/4 (1926), 170: Hallam formed 'Psychological Educators Ltd' to take over the magazine when she returned abroad. The Federation's first convention was in 1923: *Practical Psychologist*, 1/2 (1925), 11. Hallam's ideas also spread through her course of instructions, *Practical Psychology* (London and Philadelphia, 1922).

[94] A. Howland, 'Anna Maud Hallam and Her Followers at Toronto', *Psychology*, 1/4 (1923), 24–5, 42. Thanks to Ben Harris for information about Hallam in America and for correcting my earlier suggestion of a possible line of descent from Arthur Hallam: M. Thomson, 'The Popular, the Practical and the Professional: Psychological Identities in Britain, 1901–1950', in Bunn et al. (eds.), *Psychology in Britain*, 131.

researching in India. When she toured Britain, she attracted reportedly huge and enthusiastic audiences. Such activity helped the continued expansion of the movement, with further clubs setting up in Bradford, Derby, Leicester, Northumberland, and Scotland.[95]

Despite this growth, the *Practical Psychologist* struggled to keep afloat and ceased publication after just two years.[96] It would be tempting to see such a rapid collapse as a sign that the movement was something of an ephemeral craze, the transplantation of an American psychological idiom that lacked real roots in the indigenous culture and faded away without the presence of its inspirational figurehead. However, the affiliated groups continued to thrive and other periodicals emerged. One of these was the *Emblem*, published for the Federation of British Practical Psychologists in Sheffield—a shift of the centre of gravity that reflected the growing importance of the provincial movement relative to the metropolitan.[97] By 1932, this journal alone claimed to be printing 1,500 copies of each edition and almost selling out.[98] Meanwhile, in Harrogate, Albert Osbert Eaves turned his *New Thought Journal* in a practical psychological direction, renaming it as *Applied Psychology* in 1924.[99] Such a transition was taking place across the country.[100] There was another particularly active centre in the north west, with the journal *Practical Psychology*, dedicated to 'Health, Success, and Happiness', published in Blackpool between 1924 and 1925. Like Eaves, the editor, Mr A. Myddleton, also ran classes and published books.[101] He aimed to establish

[95] *Practical Psychologist*, 1/1 (1925), 44; 'Club News', *Practical Psychologist*, 1/4 (1925), 34; 'Club News', *Practical Psychologist*, 1/5 (1925), 35; 'Club News', *Practical Psychologist*, 2/1 (1926), 45–6.

[96] 'Club News', *Practical Psychologist*, 2/1 (1926), 45.

[97] Its founder was Alexander Anderson Naylor, manager of a bookshop near the University. He was formerly a worker at Patrick Geddes' Outlook Tower in Edinburgh and continued his magnetic healing in Sheffield at the Clinic of the Human Service League and in the homes of the sick: Obituary, *The Emblem*, 2 (1929), 21–2.

[98] Editorial, *The Emblem*, 10 (1931/1932), 204.

[99] Eaves' publications included: *The Colour Cure: A Popular Exposition of the Use of Colour in the Treatment of Disease* (London, 1901); *The Art of Luck* (Harrogate, 1904); *Eaves' Home Course of Lessons in Mental Science. Series 1* (Harrogate, 1904); *Modern Vampirism* (Harrogate, 1904); *Situations: How Obtained, How Retained (Heart to Heart New Thought Talk, 3)* (Harrogate, 1908); *Thought, the Builder* (Harrogate, 1908); *Your Position: How Improved* (Harrogate, 1908); *The Cult and Path of Beauty, or Beauty Imperative: How Obtained* (Harrogate, 1917); *Your Powers and How to Use Them* (Harrogate, 1918). On termination: *Applied Psychology*, 28 (1930), 109.

[100] *International New Thought Alliance (INTA) Record*, 1/4 (1928), 6–12. On the importance of New Thought in the emergence of a therapeutic culture in the United States during this period: E. Moskowitz, 'The Therapeutic Gospel: Religious Medicine and the Birth of Pop Psychology, 1850–1910', *Prospects: An Annual of American Cultural Studies*, 20 (Cambridge, 1995), 57–86. On the important role of women in American New Thought: B. Satter, *Each Mind a Kingdom: American Women, Sexual Purity, and the New Thought Movement, 1875–1920* (Berkeley and Los Angeles, 1999). There is no history of the movement in Britain. Moskowitz claims that its self-help manuals reached best-seller levels (100,000+) in the United States and that one of its leading periodicals reached 45,000 subscribers and sold some 150,000 copies in total.

[101] See for instance the advertisement for '16 Lessons in Practical Psychology', *Practical Psychology*, 1/1 (1924), 32. Titles selling at 1s. each, included: *Practical Psychology. Suggestion that Wins; Life Building; How to Analyse Yourself; Psychology of Health and Healing; Psychology in Business*.

a 'Psychology Institute' in every town, with facilities for teaching, healing, discussion, and practical help.[102] By 1925, there were reports of activity in Barnsley, Bradford, Halifax, Harrogate, Huddersfield, Hull, Leeds, Sheffield, and Wakefield, many of these towns benefiting from their own teachers.[103] Myddleton was clearly excited about the prospects for the future. He noted how psychology was suddenly appearing everywhere: on the lips of public speakers, in sermons, and in magazines as well as the daily press.[104]

Ironically, this attention may have turned out to be a problem for the practical psychology journals, facing them with more competition and perhaps with changes in taste. Nearly all of them struggled to survive or collapsed in the late 1920s and early 1930s. However, this was partly the result of the general economic downturn, which hit all small publications. The networks of clubs around the country not only survived, but also expanded, in the 1930s. This is traceable through the journal *Practical Psychology*, which began publication in 1936 as the official organ of the British Union of Practical Psychologists.[105] By this time, there were thirty-four local clubs in addition to that in London, suggesting that there had been no dimming of enthusiasm in the intervening years. Moreover, expansion continued through the second half of the decade, with the formation of four regional amalgamations to coordinate the growing number of local clubs: a Northern Federation, a Yorkshire Association, a Lancashire Group, and the British Federation centred on London, mirroring the still uneven distribution of activity across the country. By 1939, the total number of local clubs stood at fifty-three.[106]

Such activity reflects a dedicated enthusiasm within many British cities and towns. The membership of such clubs would have been small, but their local influence would have extended further through lectures, classes, and also the provision of some kind of healing service. In Leicester, a children's class was set up in the 1930s, in the hope of establishing contacts with other groups, with members as young as four years of age encouraged to think positively and rewarded with psychology badges.[107] Sheffield also had an active club, meeting twice weekly for study and concentration classes and had a well-stocked library. With annual fees set at two pounds, it advertised itself as a non-sectarian and non-political club, representing the best intellectual elements of the city, and

[102] *Practical Psychology* 1/11 (1925), 29–30.   [103] Ibid. 2/14 (1925), 26.
[104] Editorial, *Practical Psychology*, 1/12 (1925), 2.
[105] The British Union was established in Southport in 1933: *You*, 3 (1939), 374–8.
[106] Some of these were within the established heartlands of activity, but others pushed the movement into new territories such as Bath, Birmingham, Blackpool, Bournemouth, Bradford, Brighton, Bristol, Broadstairs, Darlington, Derby, Dundee, Edinburgh, Glasgow, Halifax, Hanley, Harrogate, Kirkcaldy, Leicester, Liverpool, London, London North, Long Eaton, Maidstone, Manchester, Nelson, Newcastle-on-Tyne, Nottingham, Perth, Portsmouth, Preston, Reading, Rochdale, Sheffield, Stockport, Southport, Torquay, Wakefield, Wallasey, Wolverhampton, Worthing, and even an outpost in Perth, Australia: *You*, 3 (1938), 58–9; *You*, 4, 7 (1939).
[107] *The Emblem*, 15 (1933), 314.

welcoming all people who were sincerely concerned in achieving 'individual and corporate efficiency'.[108] Invited speakers presented ideas on subjects like 'Psychology and Sight', 'The Subconscious and its Functions', and 'Psychological Healing'.[109] The club members even met to sing practical psychology ballads and published these in a collection.[110] A psychology club was still active in the city as late as 1946.[111]

The reach and influence of practical psychology was far greater, however, through the diffusion of published literature. In particular, there appears to have been a thriving trade in self-help guides, mail-order courses, and advice books. Virtually all the main practical psychology teachers and groups provided such services; indeed, they were probably vital in maintaining the financial basis of the movement. A common strategy was to provide a course in a series of instalments. The British Institute of Practical Psychology sold a series of eight separate lessons, with accompanying practical exercises and tests to be sent back for examination and comment. In the first, it taught relaxation, recognition of conscious and sub-conscious thought, and control of the latter via concentration. A second instalment focused on autosuggestion and control of instincts. The third covered knowing yourself (are you an extrovert or introvert?). The fourth looked at the influence of infancy on personality development, and how to remedy problems by suggestion (with a word association test, which was to be returned to the Institution for analysis and comment). The fifth covered conflict between conscious desires and sub-conscious impulses. The sixth dealt with complexes and their sublimation. A seventh focused on willpower and its reinforcement. The final instalment was devoted to channelling impulses towards goals.[112] Such courses offered self-education, but also the opportunity for self-improvement, self-realisation, and even therapy. Through correspondence, they offered access to apparent expertise for the isolated, but also a sense of individual analysis, and privacy in tackling potentially sensitive issues. Their serial design also helped to create an appetite for more.[113]

Alongside the clubs, the journals, and correspondence courses, there was also a boom in the publication of psychological advice books. There are traces of such a literature in the second half of the nineteenth century.[114] However, the first decade of the century was the real take off point for the practical psychology

---

[108] *Practical Psychology,* 1/1 (1925), ix.

[109] Advertisement, *Practical Psychologist*, 1/3 (1925), xii.

[110] *Practical Psychology*, 2/4 (1926), 212.

[111] Letter advertising the club's activities, *Sheffield Telegraph*, 25 June 1946, 2.

[112] British Institute of Practical Psychology, *Complete Course on Psychology*, (London, 1933).

[113] For another example: British Institute of Practical Psychology, *Personal Adjustment and Vocational Guidance through Personalysis* (London, 1934).

[114] Nineteenth-century precursors included J. Ashman, *Psychopathology or the True Healing Art* (London, 1874). Ashman was Principal of the Psychopathic Institution in London and offered cure through magnetism. See also G. Richards, 'Edward Cox, the Psychological Society of Great Britain (1875–1879) and the Meanings of an Institutional Failure', in G. Bunn et al. (eds.), *Psychology in Britain*, 35–53.

advice book that covered everything in a single volume or series.[115] By the mid-1930s, the volume increased further, as it became more common to concentrate on particular psychological problems or qualities, a specialisation that reflected a growing sophistication within popular psychology.[116] Such literature reached well beyond the more dedicated followers in the clubs. The maxims of practical psychology spilled over into such unexpected areas as books on how to improve one's golf with techniques of concentration, directing of imagination, and mastery of the subconscious.[117] The novelist Arnold Bennett was deeply interested in psychology and published articles and manuals on mental efficiency through self-control and a well-oiled mind, for instance *Mental Efficiency* (1912); *How to Live on 24 Hours a Day* (1907); *The Human Machine* (1908); and *Self and Self Management* (1918). Such books promised 'Big, strong vital thinking... thoughts that make a man reach up to his highest self'.[118] General advice books and health

[115] In addition to titles already mentioned, other post-1900 popular psychological guides included: R. Harte, *The New Psychology, or the Secret of Happiness, Being Practical Instructions as to How to Develop and Employ Thought Power* (3rd edn., London, 1903); S. D. Kirkham, *The Philosophy of Self-Help: An Application of Practical Psychology to Daily Life* (London, 1909); H. Fox, *Dreamland Speeches on Homeland Problems: The Practical Psychology of Life* (London, 1914); F. C. Haddock, *Practical Psychology: An Advance Manual in the Science of Mental Development in Eleven Lessons* (London, 1915); H. Maxim, *Practical Psychology of Cooperative Conduct* (London, 1920); R. Elsdon, *Notes on Class Lectures on Practical Psychology* (Colne, 1925); P. Fennelly, *Practical Psychology* (Hull, 1929); C. A. Dunlop, *Practical Psychology: Embodying the New Principle for the New Age in the Art of the Science of Living* (London, 1930); D. E. Cameron, *Auto-Psychology* (London, 1934); P. Fennelly, *Charts for Reading Physiological and Psychological Data* (Sheffield, 1935); P. Fennelly, *Practical Analysis* (Southport, 1935); M. Dainlow, *Personal Psychology: A Practical Guide to Self-Knowledge, Self-Development, and Self-Expression* (2nd edn., London, 1936); D. Simmons, *Private Lessons in Practical Psychology (The Realization System)* (Manchester, 1936); T. Inch, *Self Analysis: A Book of Practical Psychology* (London, 1947).

[116] For instance, the *Psychologist* magazine published a successful series of Practical Psychology Handbooks which continued through the Second World War into the early 1950s, including: J. M. Graham, *Neurasthenia: Its Nature, Origin and Cure* (London, 1936); W. J. Macbride, *The Conquest of Fear through Psychology* (London, 1936); W. J. Macbride, *The Inferiority Complex: Its Meaning and Treatment* (London, 1936); W. Northfield, *Curing Nervous Tension* (London, 1936); H. Littleton Philp, *Memory: How to Make the Most of It* (London, 1936); Psychologist, *Nervousness: Its Cause Prevention and Cure* (London, 1936); J. Kennedy, *Worry: Its Cause and Cure* (London, 1937); W. Northfield, *Sound Sleep: Proved Methods of Attaining it* (London, 1937); J. M. Graham, *Personality: How it Can be Developed* (London, 1938); J. Kennedy, *Will Power: Ways to Develop it* (London, 1938); M. Cardwell, *How to Keep Well: A Simple Outline of the Proved Laws of Health* (London, 1938); M. Chadwick, *Chapters about Childhood: The Psychology of Children from 5–10 Years* (London, 1939); P. Fletcher, *How to Practise Auto-Suggestion* (London, 1939); R. Ladell, *The First Five Years from Birth to School: How to Help your Child Develop its Personality* (London, 1939); C. H. Teear, *The Art of Making Friends* (London, 1939); W. Northfield, *Frayed Nerves: Simple Ways of Restoring their Tone* (London, 1940); A. Kornhauser, *How to Study*, 2nd edn. (London, 1941); R. Ladell, *The Parents' Problem: Or How to Tell Children about Sex* (London, 1941); C. H. Teear, *Mastering Shyness* (London, 1941); R. W. Wilde, *Psychology: How it Can Help You* (London, 1942); R. Ladell, *Blushing: Its Analysis, Causes and Cures* (London, 1949); R. Ladell, *A Dictionary of Psychological Terms with Definitions and Explanations* (London, 1951).

[117] L. Schon, *The Psychology of Golf* (London, 1922), which was also serialised in the *Daily Mail* reaching a mass audience; C. W. Baily, *The Brain and Golf: Some Hints for Golfers from Modern Mental Science* (London, 1923).

[118] G. Lafourcade, *Arnold Bennett: A Study* (London, 1939), 222.

manuals increasingly saw psychology as an important dimension, and in doing so were more likely to integrate the language and essentially self-improving message of practical psychology than they were to project an undiluted Freudianism. Take, for instance, what readers found in the New Health Society's popular, educational text on the 'hygiene of life'. First, there was a no-nonsense directive about practice: 'The mind must be exercised and its activity stimulated by selected interests, if mental health is to be preserved; the attention must be engaged, the memory employed, the senses cultivated, the instincts controlled, the reason used, and the will directed so that the desires are moderated.'[119] Alongside this, there was the promise of health and success by harnessing the full potential of will, with Benito Mussolini a model.[120] When it came to emotion, rather any discussion of the problem of repression, we find another peon to will and mental energy:

We must refrain from indiscriminate and impulsive responses to our emotions for such bad habits are wearing to mind and body. Rather we should strengthen our will and give it a purpose by controlling and directing our emotions; such controlled emotions will in turn give more power to the will. Especially should we endeavour to cultivate *joyful* emotions, for these can be used to fortify the *will to health*.[121]

Ultimately, there was that familiar practical psychological optimism about being on the threshold of some new era: 'To-day, telepathy is an accepted fact. So it will be with mind-healing.'[122]

In the popularisation of the ideas of Emile Coué, and of his technique of autosuggestion, with its positive-thinking mantra of 'every day, in every way, I am getting better and better', there is a further example of the broad reach of the practical psychology ethos. Coué was in fact confirming an approach that was already well-established within practical psychology, and as such was already known and welcomed in these circles, though not regarded as having a unique message. Nevertheless, his two visits to England in 1922, when he lectured at the Wigmore Hall and at Eton as well as holding private séances, did help to create an atmosphere of intense fascination with his personality as well as his practice, even if he tried to downplay the idea that he was some kind of miracle worker.[123] The episode helped to present the practical psychology of positive thinking, not as a new religion, but as part of common sense.[124] Its grip on the popular imagination was such that a *Daily Express* report on suicide could expect its readers to understand that this was a case of 'Couéism Reversed'.[125] A series of popular

[119] Sir R. Armstrong-Jones, 'Mind and Body', in Sir W. Arbuthnot Lane (ed.), *Safer Motherhood and the Hygiene of Life* (London, 1934), 449.
[120] G. Somerville, 'Healing through the Mind', in Lane (ed.), *Safer Motherhood and Hygiene of Life*, 465.   [121] Ibid. 467.
[122] Ibid. 468.
[123] 'M. Coué's Cures', *The Times* (29 Mar. 1922); 'M. Coué's Sixty Patients', *The Times* (30 Mar. 1922); 'M. Coué Explains: No Miracle Worker', *The Times* (9 June 1922); 'M. Coué's Return', *The Times* (15 Nov. 1922).
[124] H. Macnaghten, *Emile Coué: The Man and his Work* (London, 1922), 38.
[125] 'Couéism Reversed', *Daily Express*, 2 May 1922.

translations of his work, by the fellow Nancy School supporter of autosuggestion Charles Badouin, and also the writing of British proponent Harry Brooks, helped to maintain interest well beyond the initial craze.[126]

Advertising also indicates the broad appeal of the practical psychology message. 'Rest your Mind' was the sales pitch for the Willie Holt Billiards Table: 'If every business man could be plainly shown the power of his MIND, he would be struck with wonder. MIND Rest helps you to uncover that power, because you see clearer ahead. Mind Rest comes through change of thought.'[127] The high volume of advertising for tonics such as Wincarnis, Sanatogen, Phospherine, Halls Wines, and Dr Cassell's Tablets, with extraordinary claims to solving problems of mind as well as body, suggests that a considerable section of the population remained at least open-minded on this issue.[128] Celrox, for instance, a tonic wine made with celery—the 'most perfect nerve food'—claimed to cure neuralgia and sleeplessness, even depression and mental breakdown.[129] The focus on women in such advertising reflects continuing assumptions about female fragility, but perhaps more crucially the importance of a female market. Other therapies emphasised the mental over the physical. Thus, 'Neu-Vita' offered a mental route to the cure of poor sight, an approach taken most famously by Dr Bates, leading to its adoption by the American Army in the First World War, as well as by Aldous Huxley.[130] Despite the objections from the medical profession to such inflated claims, the press appears to have been more interested in the value of selling advertising space and therefore remained largely silent on the issue.[131] More generally, it also recognised the appeal of catering to the popular interest in psychology, offering an invitation to an eclectic, optimistic, and morally uncontroversial psychology that was still more likely to be pursued further in the practical psychology literature than by delving into psychoanalysis.[132]

---

[126] See for instance: E. Coué, *Self Mastery through Conscious Autosuggestion* (London, 1922); E. Coué and J. L. Orton, *Conscious Auto-Suggestion* (London, 1924); C. H. Brooks, *The Practice of Autosuggestion by the Method of Emile Coué* (London, 1922). Attention was first raised by Eden and Cedar Paul's translation of Charles Badouin, *Suggestion and Autosuggestion: A Psychological and Pedagogical Study Based Upon the Investigations made by the Nancy School* (London, 1920). By 1954, Brooks' *The Practice of Autosuggestion* was in its 16th impression; and Coué's *Self Mastery through Conscious Autosuggestion* went into its 16th impression in 1956; E. Coué and C. H. Brooks, *Better and Better Every Day: Two Classic Texts in the Healing Power of Mind* (London, 1960). Coué was born in 1857 and after practising as a chemist for thirty years had opened a free clinic at Nancy in 1910.

[127] Advertisement, *Efficiency Magazine*, 1/1 (1915), 22.

[128] For further discussion of psychology and advertising, see pp. 155–7. For examples of adverts for Wincarnis and Sanatogen: *Evening News*, 9 Sept. 1915. The continuity in popular understanding and demand is indicated by the fact that tonics like Sanatogen were being advertised in very similar terms after the Second World War: *Picture Post* (7 Dec. 1946).

[129] *Manchester Daily Dispatch* (8 May 1909), 7. This issue also contained adverts for Wincarnis and Phospherine.

[130] W. H. Bates, *The Cure of Imperfect Sight by Treatment without Glasses* (New York, 1920); A. Huxley, *The Art of Seeing* (London, 1943).

[131] A. Bingham, *Gender, Modernity, and the Popular Press in Inter-War Britain* (Oxford, 2004), 93.

[132] Bingham, *Popular Press*, 102–3. See for instance the questionnaire 'Are you Ruled by your Head or your Heart?', *Daily Mirror* (2 Feb. 1937).

The practical ethos meant that this psychology had little truck with the idea, associated in different ways with both the psychoanalysts and the occultists, that self-realisation rested on some secret or expert knowledge to be exercised carefully only by an elite. Eaves spoke of his ambition to reach 'men and women who are not scholars' and who 'have not been fortunate, have not gained all they would desire, have not been blessed with either healthy bodies or purses'.[133] His primary appeal, like that of the broader movement, was to those with ambitions of personal improvement and upward social mobility. Pelmanism made a similar pitch: 'Unless you were born with a silver spoon in your mouth, your brain is the only weapon with which you can hope to fight the battles of life . . . It is the open sesame to the best society; it is the key to every kind of success.'[134] More frequently than any other group, the aspiring salesman was singled out for special attention, and these lower-middle class men clearly formed a key element within the movement, particularly in the first decades of the century.[135] Practical psychology could be unsympathetic, by contrast, towards the poor and unemployed, seeing their circumstances as nobody's fault or responsibility but their own: 'The poorhouse does not come to us. We go to the poorhouse and we are taken there because we wanted to go.' The solution lay in harnessing mental power, rather than an over-protective state. On the other hand, in the case of the mind that broadcast its discord, the use of some sort of segregation might be justified.[136] The emphasis on practice, self-improvement, and education, even the harsh attitude towards indigence, albeit here reframed in terms of mind, was not unattractive to a large section of the working class. Men who had risen up from such a background were in fact prominent within the leadership of the practical psychology clubs by the 1930s.[137] The preponderance at this time of articles on subjects such as the driving of motor cars, travel, leisure, and culture suggests a solidly middle-class audience.[138] Perhaps unsurprisingly then, psychology now validated the inherent healthiness both of class division, and more particularly of being middle class: aspiration for social betterment was a sign of mental health.[139]

---

[133] *New Thought Journal*, 2/20 (1904), 293.

[134] *The First Principles of Pelmanism: Lesson Number 1*, 3–4.

[135] L. D. Fort, 'Salesmanship', *Practical Psychology*, 1/3 (1924), 27–9; 'Sweetening Sour Customers', *Practical Psychology*, 1/4 (1925), 7; H. E. Hunt, 'Psychology and Business', *Practical Psychology*, 2nd ser., 2 (1937), 9–11.

[136] P. Fennelly, 'Hard Times', *The Emblem*, No. 4 (1931), 163–5. Similarly: *Applied Psychology*, 28 (1930), 97. On the popular support for segregation of 'mental defectives': M. Thomson, *The Problem of Mental Deficiency: Eugenics, Democracy and Social Policy in Britain*, 1870–1959 (Oxford, 1998).

[137] See the list of Presidents of the British Union of Practical Psychologists: *You*, 3 (1939), 374–8.

[138] For instance, on the problems of increased leisure time: E. Salter Davies, 'Leisure', *Practical Psychology*, 1/5 (1936), 39–40; P. H. Prideaux, 'Boredom and its Lure', *Practical Psychology*, 2nd ser., 2 (1937), 263–5.

[139] W. J. Pinnard, 'Personal Psychology—Class Consciousness', *You*, 3 (1938), 165, 159–65; G. Warwick, 'Am I Middle Class?', *You*, 3 (1938), 202–4.

THE EPISTEMOLOGY OF PRACTICAL PSYCHOLOGY

Thus far, this chapter has presented the case for the existence of a culture of practical psychology in the first decades of the century. It will now probe further what this meant in terms of belief, first in relation to academic and professional psychology, and then to body, mind, and spirit. Practical psychologists did not reject the value of academic psychology; indeed, they demonstrated a considerable appetite for it, albeit translated into a more accessible idiom. What they did believe, however, was that it had far less to offer when it came to practical results. They also objected to anyone claiming exclusive authority in the area.[140] It was simply untrue, they argued, that psychology was inaccessible for the ordinary individual. Any attempt by academics to restrict such knowledge or to disparage its popularisation was condemned.[141] The practical psychologists could also point out that for all the recent academic advances, many fundamental questions about mind remained unanswered. Academic psychology might have made great strides in beginning to map the structure of the mind, but in revealing formerly hidden unconscious depths it also opened the door to speculation about further levels and powers, possibilities that practical psychology, with less inhibitions, was so keen to embrace. The situation was similar when it came to the nature of the psychic force behind mind, with no consensus within academic psychology and lingering support within this community for the possibility of 'psychic' phenomena such as telepathy.[142]

Practical psychology also viewed with considerable suspicion the prospect of the State and its experts using psychological knowledge to control and regulate citizens. Mental testing in school and factory, for instance, appeared a very crude and reductive way to judge the individual when set against the holistic perspective of practical psychology.[143] At the more religious end of the spectrum, the main object of attack was different, with followers called on to 'know more of their own selves' and to reject the 'Old Thought' religion which made them into 'grovelling worms, only fit to be crushed by the heel of a man-made deity'.[144] Here again, the idea that modern science was coming to accept a metaphysical dimension of knowledge provided room for accommodation.[145]

Although it is most significant in representing a reorientation of popular self-help culture towards mind, the success of practical psychology also depended on doing this in a way that incorporated existing emphases about the importance of both body and spirit. The assumption of a close interplay between mind and body

[140] 'Society News' (Halifax), *Practical Psychology*, 2/14 (Nov. 1925), 27; A. M. Hallam, 'The Threshold of Practical Psychology', *Practical Psychologist*, 1/1 (1925), 2; E. M. Fraser, 'An Outline of Academic Psychology. Part I: The Growth of Mental Life', *Practical Psychologist*, 2/1 (1926), 8–13.

[141] Editorial, *Practical Psychology*, 2nd ser., 2 (1937), 290.

[142] *Applied Psychology*, 28 (1930), 109. On academic psychology, see Ch. 2.

[143] W. Myddleton, 'Mental Stature' and Editor's remarks, *Practical Psychology*, 1/3 (1924), 18–21.

[144] *New Thought Journal*, 2/20 (1904), 293.   [145] *INTA Record*, 1/11 (1928), 9.

appealed to a population comfortable with the idea that mental suffering often had somatic origins and consequences, but still concerned that a wholly psychological perspective was dangerously close to denying the reality of illness or blaming it on the individual.[146] It was then a traditional, more than a radical, position. The New Thought wing of the movement did downplay the physical, in favour of the psycho-spiritual, though rarely went as far as Christian Science in discounting it altogether.[147] Elsewhere, there was a regular interest in bodily health, breathing technique, nutrition, mastication, and exercise as crucial adjuncts to the health of mind. A figure like Eustace Miles, for instance, contributed articles in most of the practical psychology periodicals, offering self-health advice on the psychological body, at the same time as advertising his own services, which included a restaurant as well as a clinic.[148] Sometimes the tensions between the two positions came to the surface.[149] In the view of novelist Winifred Holtby, the cult of the body, in which products became essential for personal salvation, fuelled by the mass suggestion of the advertisers, was now taking the place of religious revivalism.[150] More common, however, was an attempt at synthesis; and certainly a belief in the spiritual as fundamental in health did not preclude an often obsessive concern about life-management on the physical plane. Even a leading advocate of 'cosmic consciousness' like Anna Maud Hallam would spend time detailing the rights and wrongs of body management and diet.[151] Thus, exercise was an act of training the mind, as much as the body. Abstinence from flesh-eating was a way to avoid autotoxaemia disrupting brain and body, but also helped to advance mind and spirit to a loftier plane through the rejection of such degrading behaviour, and trained the mind and body in self-control. Similarly, breathing exercises improved the flow of blood to mind and massaged the internal organs, but also trained the subconscious mind in the art of bodily control, and educated the spirit through mental awareness of life force and the rhythms of the natural world.[152] By the mid-1930s, the growing understanding of hormones and vitamins gave new justification to belief in the close interplay between body and

[146] As argued more generally in E. Shorter, *From Paralysis to Fatigue: A History of Psychosomatic Illness in the Modern Era* (New York, 1992).

[147] 'Conference of Medical Men and Others to Discuss Mental Therapeutics', *New Thought*, 2/22 (1929), 6–11.

[148] E. Miles, 'The Power of Body over Mind', *Practical Psychologist*, 1/1 (1925), 23–5. On walking, posture, clothing and their importance for body and brain: C. Jeffrey, 'The Psychology of Walking', *Practical Psychologist*, 1/5 (1925), 18–21.

[149] See Miles's dig at New Thought students: 'The Mental Attitude Towards Exercise', *Practical Psychologist*, 1/2 (1925), 28.

[150] W. Holtby, 'The Psychology of Revivalism', *The Realist*, 1/1 (1929), 54–63.

[151] A. M. Hallam, 'A Lesson on Health', *Practical Psychologist*, 1/5 (1925), 1–6.

[152] E. Miles, 'The Mental Attitude Towards Exercise', 25–9; H. B. Smith, 'Practical Psychology Postulates Perfect Poise', *Practical Psychologist*, 1/6 (1925), 33–5; C. Forward, 'The Psychology of the Slaughterhouse', *Practical Psychologist*, 1/3 (1925), 26–30; C. Forward, 'Psychology and Diet', *Practical Psychologist*, 1/6 (1925), 17–20; Q. Woodbridge, 'Rhythmic Breathing', *Practical Psychologist*, 1/2 (1925), 39–42.

mind.[153] It did not follow, however, that such discoveries necessarily led to a primacy of the physical over the mental. Mental health might have depended on the quality of food, but it also depended on ability to digest this food properly: on human action that was ultimately psychological, depending on mental engagement, an absence of stress, and personality.[154] Thus, a concern about the physical persisted, but in no way did it threaten to swamp the psychological.

As with attitudes towards the body, positions on the spiritual did vary, with tension between extremists at either end of the spectrum. More characteristic, however, was an accommodation and integration of the spiritual into a holistic model of the self. At the New Thought end of the spectrum, the theology and language of Christianity, albeit radically transmuted, was still central. Since Christ had taught that the Kingdom of God lay within and that man was one with the Father, man's body could be envisaged as a kind of Holy Temple, each function, organ, member, and cell controlled by Divine Intelligence, with an inexhaustible, divine supply of energy within. The path to love, truth, peace, health, and elevation of the self to the spiritual plane was a process of realising 'oneness' with this greater whole.[155] In practice, this meant that thought became the supreme fact of life, with New Thought fascinated by the potential of a subconscious as well as a conscious mind in healing the physical body and integrating it with the Universal Spirit.[156]

Practical psychology groups tended to distance themselves from the explicitly religious stance of New Thought. First, and foremost, they believed that their philosophy rested on science. On the other hand, they were invariably sympathetic towards religion, especially Christianity (though also Eastern religions), regarding its key tenets as compatible with practical psychology and good common sense; and many practical psychologists were actively religious.[157] For Myddleton, practical psychology stood for 'a safe and sane exposition of psychology from the definitely Christian standpoint as the basis upon which the whole structure of human character must rest.'[158] Nevertheless, it was not 'a new religion, nor did it aim at supplanting any form of religion. It was a science dealing with life, and it made for the enrichment of the religious life of the individual.' Thus, it was important to avoid any title that associated practical psychology with any particular creed.[159]

The spiritual dimension of practical psychology could also lie in its vision of the individual mind connecting with a universal consciousness, which opened up

---

[153] For instance, E. S. Chesser, 'Glands, Temperament and Personality', *Practical Psychology*, 2nd ser., 1 (1936), 61–2; E. S. Chesser, 'Minerals that Make Us', *Practical Psychology*, 2nd ser., 1 (1936), 41–2.

[154] E. S. Chesser, 'Food and Personality', *Practical Psychology*, 2nd ser., 1 (1936), 21–2; R. F. English, 'Digestion and Mental Function', *Practical Psychology*, 2nd ser., 2 (1937), 298–9.

[155] See, for instance, the 'Declaration of Principles' regularly printed in the New Thought literature: *New Thought*, 2/22 (1929), 2.

[156] For instance, 'Super-Vision', *New Thought*, 2/22 (1929), 3–5.

[157] For an example of the influence of Eastern religion and thought see the profile of Quetta Woodbridge, 'England's foremost exponent of Eastern Philosphy' and her Eastern Temple of Healing in Mayfair: *Practical Psychologist*, 2/1 (1926), 2–4.   [158] *Practical Psychology*, 1/1 (1924), 3.

[159] Ibid. 1/11 (1925), 29.

both a transcendental level of self-development for the individual, and the prospect of a higher plane of evolution for humanity.[160] Here, science was not ignored, but 'reenchanted', given a spiritual dimension as the ultimate truth—the 'Natural Law'.[161] The role of a mystical deity, if not rejected, was downplayed and instead life itself was invested with spirituality, the transcendental life replacing the promise of heavenly salvation. With science now suggesting that all forms of energy including thought might be interchangeable, the universe became a vibrating, vital whole, connecting all, and disrupting any notion of the atomised individual. Individual consciousness was therefore located in a sea of energy. The majority were unaware of this, because it was hidden in the vast realm of the subconscious. Practical psychology offered a path into this interior and through this to a spiritual understanding—as some put it, a 'cosmic consciousness'—of man's true position in the universe.[162]

By the mid-1930s, an overtly spiritual dimension was becoming less prominent within popular psychology. By 1936, for instance, the Aims and Objects of the British Union of Practical Psychologists made no mention of spirituality.[163] Nevertheless, religious contributors to the literature were still able to find spiritual values and insights in psychology.[164] Links were also emerging with a more orthodox Christianity that was interested in using psychology and psychological healing in modernising its pastoral role.[165] The *Daily Mirror* reported one London vicar who had opened a spiritual clinic arguing that 'ideally a parish should be governed by a priest, a doctor, and a psychotherapist.'[166] However, the most powerful manifestation of this ongoing spiritual dimension, albeit now in a largely secular form, was its influence on an ethics of self, captured as often as not in a discourse of personality.[167] This built on existing ideas about character, and it paralleled the hold in this period of a culture and ethics of citizenship that drew on

---

[160] For examples of the way man's potential for creative evolution was invested with a kind of spirituality: Rev. A. Porter, 'Resist or Die', *Practical Psychology*, 2nd ser., 1 (1936), 24–2; W. J. Pinard, 'Personal Psychology', *Practical Psychology*, 2nd ser., 2 (1937), 3–4.

[161] A. M. Hallam, 'The Threshold of Practical Psychology', *Practical Psychologist*, 1/1 (1925), 1–6; W. Attwood, 'The Reign of Natural Law', *Practical Psychologist*, 1/2 (1925), 1–9. This paralleled a process in the high culture of science and religion: Bowler, *Reconciling Science and Religion*. On the accommodation between the rational and irrational, and science and the mystical in the occult: Owen, *Place of Enchantment*.

[162] A. M. Hallam, 'Evolution, or the Growth of Human Personality', *Practical Psychologist*, 1/6 (1925), 1–8; L. Bosman, 'The Psychology of Religious Belief: A Personal God', *Practical Psychologist*, 1, 6 (1925), 36–44; L. Bosman, 'The Purpose of Individuality in Evolution', *Practical Psychologist*, 2/4 (1926), 219. [163] *Practical Psychology*, 2nd ser., 1 (1936), 15.

[164] C. A. Hope, 'A Lesson on Attainment', *Practical Psychology*, 2nd ser., 1 (1936), 173–5; C. A. Hope, 'Mind and Health: The Wider View', *Practical Psychology*, 2nd ser., 1 (1936), 203–4.

[165] See the positive review of Miss A. Graham Ikin's *The Background of Spiritual Healing: Psychological and Spiritual*, in *Practical Psychology*, 2nd ser., 2 (1937), 213. Also: Rev. G. Needham, 'The Future of Practical Psychology', *You*, 3 (1938), 313–14. The relationship between the Church and psychology is further explored on pp. 72–4, 187.

[166] *Daily Mirror*, 10 Nov. 1937, reported in *Practical Psychology*, 2nd ser., 2 (1938), 387.

[167] For instance, M. Cardwell, 'Have you Personality?', *Practical Psychology*, 2nd ser., 1 (1936), 235–7.

idealist philosophy.[168] Where the emphasis had changed was that Victorian character had centred on control of self, moral conduct, and fulfilment of duties, and as such was primarily an issue of public conduct rather than psychological management.[169] Thus, in Samuel Smiles' best-selling *Character*, first published in 1871, the ideal had been 'truthfulness, chasteness, mercifulness; and with these integrity, courage, virtue, and goodness in all its phases'.[170] The exception was the stress on the control of will over primitive instincts, though even here the conceptualisation of a path to self-control struggled to move beyond the terms of public conduct. Practical psychology reasserted the powers of the will and self-control, but through an interpretative shift that allied them with their former enemy, the subconscious, that was now an essential element if any individual was to develop true personality.[171] Deriving from the Latin term *persona*—the mask worn by actors and literally meaning to sound through—a language of personality developed within the psychology of this period, though particularly within a strain of academic psychology, to suggest a self that was more mutable, relational, and quantifiable in its parts than before.[172] Yet, its use within practical psychology invariably reaffirmed the idea of some essential true, whole, even higher self. Thus, in contrast to the 'change of human character' famously evoked by Virginia Woolf and associated with modernism, this more popular shift saw a reconfiguration, rather than a rejection, of existing dominant tropes for conceptualising self-development.[173] Practical psychology could have descended into a merely selfish, individualist drive for personal advancement. Instead, not just personality but

[168] For instance in relation to its impact on social policy: J. Harris, 'Political Thought and the Welfare State, 1870–1940: An Intellectual Framework for British Social Policy', *Past and Present*, 135 (1992), 116–41.

[169] S. Collini, *Public Moralists: Political Thought and Intellectual Life in Britain, 1850–1930* (Oxford, 1991), 94.

[170] S. Smiles, *Character* (London, 1908), vi.

[171] For instance, L. Bosman, 'What is an Individual?', *Practical Psychologist*, 1/4 (1925), 36–42; W. J. Vanstone, 'Personality and Personification', *Practical Psychologist*, 1/2 (1925), 19–21; W. J. Pinard, 'Personal Psychology—Will', *Practical Psychology*, 2nd ser., 2 (1937), 187–90; T. E. Drabble, 'Personality', *Practical Psychologist*, 1/2 (1925), 8–12. On the use of 'personality' in the United States: W. Susman, 'Personality and the Making of Twentieth-Century Culture', in J. Higham and P. Conkin (eds.), *New Directions in American Intellectual History* (Baltimore, 1979), 212–26; S. Smith, 'Personalities in the Crowd: The Idea of the "Masses" in American Popular Culture', *Prospects*, 19 (Cambridge, 1994), 273–83.

[172] N. Rose, 'Assembling the Modern Self', in R. Porter (ed.), *Rewriting the Self: Histories from the Renaissance to the Present* (London, 1997), 224–48. The growing sway of this psychological construction is suggested by the *Oxford English Dictionary* dating for the usage of: 'personality-type' (1919); 'personality-traits' (1921); 'personality-defect' (1927); 'personality tests' (1927); 'personality factors' (1932); 'personality disorder' (1938); 'personality structure' (1939); 'personality pattern' (1949); and 'personality system' (1951).

[173] Woolf used the phrase in her talk on 'Character in Modern Fiction' in May 1924, subsequently published as the essay 'Mr Bennett and Mrs Brown'. Though her focus was a shift in representation of character from an older generation of novelists like Arnold Bennett to that of D. H. Lawrence and Lytton Strachey, the moment of December 1910 as a turning point reflected contemporary shock at the Post-Impressionist exhibition held at the Grafton Galleries. Striking in relation to the focus of this chapter is Bennett's association with practical psychology, in contrast to that of Lawrence and Strachey with Freud. What this chapter suggests is that the old guard were involved in a psychological reframing of

also 'service' provided it with higher goals. Fostering the spirit of service and brotherhood among members, and spreading this principle and knowledge of the psychological path to attaining it beyond, were enshrined as core aims of one leading practical psychology group.[174] This was the case, even when it came to business efficiency and salesmanship. Indeed, this constituency was particularly concerned about the distinction, attempting to suggest that a new conception of business, resting on mutual service, could be 'an integral part of the wave of spiritual reconstruction'.[175] With mental development seen as providing the ultimate meaning in life, it was the duty of all practical psychologists to develop, not only their own full potential, but also that of others. This meant that the individual had to develop beyond the traditional boundaries of an atomised, conscious self. Reaching into the subconscious, the individual would become sensitive, both to the memories of generations in the past, and to the thoughts and feelings of fellow 'citizens'. The individual would thus discover a 'greater self': a self that was inherently social, as well as more truly individual.[176] In sum, in looking beyond the individualist self, in offering higher meaning to life, and in tying ideal self-development to ethical goals, the popular psychology of this era inherited what we might see as a kind of secular, human-centred spirituality.

Despite the importance of the physical and the spiritual dimensions, the mental was at the very heart of the practical psychology cosmology, and crucial in linking the other two into a holistic system. It was the excitement that man was on the threshold of discovering a greater psychological self that was crucial in animating the movement. Certainly, the findings of academic psychology played their part in this. The interwar practical psychologists were alert, for instance, to the work of Sigmund Freud, Carl Jung, and Alfred Adler, and summarised their findings in accessible form for their readers. Just as important, though, was the influence of an eclectic mix of less orthodox or celebrated thinkers. The now rather obscure William McDougall was the most likely British academic psychologist to gain a mention.[177] Just as influential, however, were figures well outside the psychological mainstream, such as Henri Bergson with his concept of 'vital force'. The crucial point is that no single figure was of fundamental importance or exclusive authority. Their ideas, instead, were set within a framework of general revelation.

their own that deserves serious consideration. For more on intellectuals and psychology, see Ch. 3. On Woolf and the 'change': P. Stansky, *On or About December 1910: Early Bloomsbury and its Intimate World* (Cambridge, Mass., 1996); P. Brooker, *Bohemia in London: The Social Scene of Early Modernism* (Basingstoke, 2004), 171–7; Lee, *Virginia Woolf*, 287–91; C. Harrison, *English Art and Modernism, 1900–1939* (London, 1981), 291.

[174] Aims and objects of the British Union of Psychologists: *Practical Psychology*, 2nd ser., 1 (1936), 15.
[175] H. Ernest Hunt, 'Buying and Selling', *You*, 3 (1938), 227–9; 'The Joy of Service', *Practical Psychology*, 1/3 (Dec. 1924), 16–17; Mr Taylor, 'Society News', *Practical Psychology* (Dec. 1925), 28; Q. Woodbridge, 'Business Psychology', *Practical Psychologist*, 2/1 (1926), 41–4.
[176] L. Bosman, 'What is an Individual?', *Practical Psychologist*, 1/4 (1925).
[177] For further discussion, see Ch. 2.

If any single psychological idea was central, it was the concept of a multi-level mind, with the greater part lying in the subconscious. The suggestion that the majority of the population simply ignored nine tenths of the self, its powers wasted, had an extremely powerful attraction.[178] Practical psychology directed its efforts towards uncovering this hidden potential, and equipping followers with the tools to harness it. Health, happiness, and success would naturally follow.

Practical psychology was also often home to the idea that thought was simply another form of energy. This had implications, as already noted, for thinking about the relationship between mind and body. Sometimes it could lead to the idea that mental energy had the potential to move between individuals, and that mental training might promote ability in both projection and reception.[179] By the late 1930s, such a model of mind was on the wane, though it had not disappeared altogether.

For practical psychology, technique was just as important as theory. Here, magnetism, hypnotism, and suggestion, which had been so important for the Psycho-Therapeutic Society in the first decade of the century, made way for autosuggestion, mind concentration, and visualisation: tools that shifted power to the individual. Autosuggestion, as already noted, was popularised through trans-lations of the work of Emile Coué, the French popular psychologist. Coué's tech-nique aimed to harness the power of the imagination (recognised as more influential than conscious will) in order to control the subconscious mind. Practical psychology continued this quest well into the interwar period, autosug-gestion transcending in importance the narrower phenomenon of Couéism.[180]

A psychology that acted as an apostle for positive thinking and the liberation of latent energies had only a limited appetite for the gloomier Freudian view of a sexual, aggressive, and destructive unconscious. In the mid-1920s, practical psy-chologists tended to be in the position of defending Freud and psychoanalysis against some strong criticism in the national press, supporting in particular his emphasis on the importance of the unconscious. At the same time, they had seri-ous misgivings of their own.[181] In part, this was because they often shared the broader feeling that his ideas placed too much emphasis on sex. They also objected to the way medical men used Freudianism to claim an exclusive ability to practise psychotherapeutics (noting also the practical limitations of the highly time-consuming psychoanalysis), and looked instead to make the individual into his or her own psychoanalyst.[182] More generally, they regarded psychotherapy as overly

[178] For instance, A. M. Hallam, 'The Threshold of Practical Psychology', *Practical Psychologist*, 1/1 (1925), 3.

[179] Pilgrim, 'Broadcasting', *The Emblem*, No. 1 (1929), 4; 'The Significance of Broadcasting', *Practical Psychologist*, 1/1 (1924), 30–4.

[180] For instance, C. Ashwell Hope, 'A Lesson in Autosuggestion', *Practical Psychology*, 2nd ser., 1 (1936), 43–5.

[181] R. C. Owen, 'Is Psycho-Analysis Trustworthy?', *Practical Psychology*, 1/1 (1924), 6–9.

[182] 'Stray Thoughts', *New Thought*, 26, 122 (1926); H. Reinheimer, 'Psycho-Analysis', *Practical Psychologist*, 2/4 (1926), 205–9.

obsessed with abnormality, and as such with little to offer the normal person, and potentially a danger to real individuality.[183] Adler, with his far more positive and 'practical' call for personal readjustment of false perspectives in achieving happiness, would be considered more favourably, and even forged some direct links with the movement in the 1930s.[184]

Ultimately, it would be impossible to explain the emergence and development of the practical psychology movement in terms of the ideas of Freud alone, or indeed of any other canonical figure from the annals of psychology. The very idea of dutifully following in such footsteps was an anathema to the practical philosophy. Although there was an undoubted interest in such figures, their relative absence is far more striking. When they did appear, it was often after a process of dilution, translation, even transformation. This was not a culture to worship the expert. The book reviews and library lists in the practical psychology periodicals suggest that the work of academic psychologists was rarely what the average follower or the interested member of the public was likely to read. Instead, psychology was diffused by non-professionals, who probably did read some of this work, but took from it what they wanted or understood, and added it to an eclectic mix. Some of these figures appear to have based whole careers on this popularising role, living off the proceeds of their books and associated practices.

FEMINISATION AND THE DECLINE
OF UNORTHODOXY

By the mid-1930s, medical psychology, which had advanced considerably from an initially insecure position over the last three decades, was becoming increasingly prominent within the discourse of practical psychology. It was now more common to find the language of 'instincts' and 'complexes', for instance, and to find contributions from qualified doctors and psychologists.[185] There was no great difficulty in integrating such ideas and language into the existing cosmology. Practical psychologists were well versed in the art of synthesis. The aim of reinforcing subconscious mental powers continued to distinguish practical psychology, and advertisements for courses indicate still strong demand.[186] However, a change was taking place. The promise, both of spiritual transcendence, and of success

[183] Paonne, 'Are you Normal? The Tyranny of Words', *Practical Psychologist*, 1/6 (1925), 12–15; E. Hopewell-Ash, 'Psychology and the Essential Self III', *Practical Psychology*, 2nd ser., 3 (1936), 45–7.

[184] Editorial, *Practical Psychology*, 2nd ser., 1 (1936), 2; 'Notes on Modern Psychological Theory' and an advertisement for Adler's British lecture tour, *Practical Psychology*, 2nd ser., 1 (1936), 70–1; Editorial, *Practical Psychology*, 2nd ser., 1 (1936), 86; A. Adler, 'Prevention of Neuroses and Delinquency', *Practical Psychology*, 2nd ser., 1 (1936), 122–5. For more on Adler, see Ch. 3.

[185] For instance, E. Severn, 'Don't be Afraid of Your Instincts', *Practical Psychology*, 2nd ser., 1 (1936), 148–9.

[186] For instance, the Theiron Method and School of Life (offering renewed personality and achievement): *Practical Psychology*, 2nd ser., 1 (1936), 77; 'The Power that Autopsychology Gives',

based on developing, if not supernatural, then supernormal psychological power, was fading. It now stood alongside a more temperate survey of how an understanding of psychology could help in everyday life.[187]

This shift was not simply the result of ideas filtering down from above; it also reflected the increasing importance of a female market and the gradual feminisation of the literature. This in turn reflected the growing prominence of women as consumers and shapers of a modernity that centred on home and family.[188] An increasing volume of articles now marked out a specifically female audience and addressed their particular personal concerns. Often, though, this was less explicit. One article on the general problem of treating a person with depression revealingly assumed that the answer was to persuade 'her' to take up an occupation.[189] General articles were now also more likely to address issues that might traditionally have been of largely female concern, such as the psychology of skin problems, extremes in weight, and self-consciousness. Most importantly, the subjects of child psychology and sex, largely ignored until this time, began to receive serious coverage.[190] In coming to recognise that women might have distinctive psychological concerns, the character of the movement as a whole was also to some extent feminised.[191] It also became both less distinctive, and less aggressively practical and independent, as its interests merged with those of doctors and psychologists who were now becoming more active in promoting a top-down form of popular psychology often in the form of 'mental hygiene'.[192] Thus, a figure like Dr Elizabeth Sloan Chesser published on the

Practical Psychology, 2nd ser., 1 (1936), 187; 'Don't Let Nerves Run Your Life!', *Practical Psychology*, 2nd ser., 2 (1937), 285; 'Man Can Now Create at Will!', *Practical Psychology*, 2nd ser., 2 (1937), 288; or that for Noel Jacquin: *Practical Psychology*, 2nd ser., 1 (1936), 131.

[187] A new series covered 'Mental Hygiene in the Home': *Practical Psychology*, 2nd ser., 1 (1936), 239–40. See also J. G. Mackenzie, 'The Art of Living', *You*, 4 (1939), 20–7.

[188] A. Light, *Forever England: Femininity, Literature, and Conservatism between the Wars* (London, 1991); J. Giles, *Women, Identity, and Private Life in Britain, 1900–1950* (London, 1995); C. Pursell, 'Domesticating Modernity: The Electrical Association for Women, 1924–1986', *British Journal for the History of Science*, 32 (1999), 47–67. The parallels between the role of women in this area and that of psychology are suggested by the contribution of the Director of the Electrical Association for Women, Caroline Hazlett, 'Psychology and the Home: The Value of Electricity', *Practical Psychology*, 2nd ser., 2 (1937), 314–15. The shift was also reflected in the content of the tabloid press: Bingham, *Popular Press*.

[189] L. A. E. Porter, 'Some Suggestions for Treating Depression', *Practical Psychology*, 2nd ser., 2 (1937), 278–9.

[190] E. Severn, 'On Child Training', *Practical Psychology*, 2nd ser., 1 (1936), 24; M. Cardwell, 'Misfits—Some Causes of Maladaptation in Families', *Practical Psychology*, 2nd ser., 2 (1937), 191–4; R. Fay (S.R.N.), 'Child Psychology: The Early Months', *Practical Psychology*, 2nd ser., 2 (1937), 195–6; M. Cardwell, 'Some Simple Causes for Mental Ill Health', *Practical Psychology*, 2nd ser., 2 (1937), 269–71.

[191] See for instance, K. Porter, 'Men and Women . . . the Difference', *You*, 3 (1938), 7–10; and the Editorial, *You*, 3 (1938), 322–3.

[192] Advert for *New Health* and its psychological advice service: *Practical Psychology*, 2nd ser., 2 (1937), 213; W. J. Pinard, 'Personal Psychology—Mental Hygiene', *Practical Psychology*, 2nd ser., 2 (1938), 403–5. On top-down popularisation, see Chs. 4–6; on mental hygiene, see Ch. 6.

psychology of sex, not just in the practical psychology journals, but also in the *Daily Express*, the *Sunday Express*, the *Glasgow Herald*, *Good Housekeeping*, and *Women's Pictorial*, as well as her own popular books such as the *The Woman who Knows Herself* of 1926.[193]

Such a transition was symbolised in 1938, when the journal *Practical Psychology* transformed its identity in an attempt to appeal to a broader market. First, it shifted to a more personal, but also fashionable and accessible pocket-size format. Secondly, its title was changed to *You*, with 'practical psychology' dropped to the subtitle, a relegation that reflected, perhaps, the sense that the drawing power of such a concept and movement had served its time. The new title heralded a reorientation away from abstract and often hugely ambitious speculation about the potential powers of the self towards a focus on personal, everyday life and its problems. The new journal was 'to make psychology incidental to life, rather than life incidental to psychology.'[194] This could sometimes mean a rather more trivial line of inquiry: articles on pets, travel, and clothes, replacing complex topographies of the self, theoretical debate, and self-education.[195] The new remit was one of amusing readers, showing them that psychology was no complicated or 'gloomy science'. Gone was the strident, evangelistic tone about being on the threshold of fundamental knowledge about human nature. Instead, psychology had become something that needed masking or lacing with sweeteners if it was to be fit for popular consumption:

You is not dull, even though psychology does enter its columns. Not that psychology is a dull subject. Indeed, it is exciting when used in relation to all human experience. To import principles of psychology by suggestion through normal reading is our aim. Even though the word 'psychology' may not be used once in the course of the article, it is implied and suggested.[196]

The new editor, Raymond Henniker-Heaton, a Fellow of the Society of Arts, looked now to the mental hygiene of culture (what films should we watch, what music should we listen to if we want to be mentally healthy), rather than to psychological development itself as the path to some higher type of culture. More often than not, it was simply a way to enliven the subject, with articles on the

---

[193] Along with contributions on child rearing and sex from fellow doctor Mary Cardwell, and those from nurse Ruby Fay, Elizabeth Sloan Chesser's articles demonstrate the entry of the expert into this popular psychological literature. Chesser's articles included: 'Glands, Temperament and Personality', *Practical Psychology*, 2nd ser., 1 (1936), 41–2; 'The Psychology of Sex', *Practical Psychology*, 2nd ser., 2 (1937), 46–7. *The Woman who Knows Herself* was in its third impression by 1934. Chesser is not one of the 104 writers (18 per cent female) surveyed by Hera Cook as writers of sex advice literature in Britain in this period: *Long Sexual Revolution*, 341–54. She has, however, attracted attention through her interest in eugenics: G. Jones, 'Women and Eugenics in Britain: The Case of Mary Scharlieb, Elizabeth Sloan Chesser, and Stella Browne', *Annals of Science*, 52 (1985), 481–502.   [194] Editorial, *You*, 3 (1938), 67–8.

[195] For instance, G. Warwick, 'Do You Hate Cats?', *You*, 3 (1938), 106–7; H. E. Hunt, 'Road Sense', *You*, 3 (1938), 143–5; N. Brookes, 'Does your Dress Dress You?', *You*, 3 (1938), 26–8.

[196] Editorial, *You*, 3 (1938), 4.

psychology of art, music, writing, and the cinema over the next few years.[197] Confidence that an ethic of psychological development on its own could inspire readers, let alone create an active following in clubs up and down the country, was in retreat.

It would be wrong, however, to see this period in terms of a decline in the ambition of popular psychology. In particular, the emerging willingness to tackle personal relations is striking in its contrast to earlier practical psychology. Here, the concerns of a female readership often seem to have been to the fore.[198] It was within this context that the advice column emerged, with Susan Grant, for instance, offering readers of *You* 'Practical Advice on Everyday Life'. Such a reorientation was also evident in the women's pages of the popular press, with coverage of 'relations', that had stood at an average of just 3 per cent for much of the interwar period, leaping by 1939 to 27 per cent in the *Daily Mirror*, 12 per cent in the *Daily Express*, and 11 per cent in the *Daily Mail*.[199] Given that the provision of practical advice had been such a central feature of practical psychology since the start of the century, this might appear hardly a novel departure. In fact, there may have been a strong tradition of publishing testimonials as to the success of psychological cures, but open discussion of personal problems and the handing down of advice had never previously been a feature. It was partly that the boundaries of privacy were beginning, albeit slowly, to shift, with new psychological tastes better seen as facilitating such reorientation, rather than dictating it. It also reflected a decline in the earlier practical ethos, in particular a breakdown in the suspicion towards authority, both in accepting advice from above, and in focusing on specific problems rather than general principles.[200] Thus, the increasing prominence of the advice page represented, in one respect a reinvigoration of the 'practical' tradition, yet in another a move towards placing authority in the hands of the experts.[201] The latter echoed the broader shift within the literature, already alluded to, which saw the coming together of 'high' and 'low' psychological cultures. Significantly, such periodicals now began to include lists of professional psychological clinics. Earlier suspicion and open hostility towards the advance of psychological regulation also disappeared, with calls for instance for psychologists to inspect car drivers before the granting of a licence, and to be placed within every department of government.[202] Even the dangers of popularisation in the hands of

[197] This interest in art was also, in part, a concern about the mental hygiene of culture: R. Henniker-Heaton, 'The Psychology of Art', *You*, 3 (1938), 32–4; H. E. Hunt, 'At the Cinema', *You*, 3 (1938), 534–6; 'Psychology of Music', *You*, 3 (1938), 355–7.

[198] N. Brookes, 'Are Women Mean?', *You*, 3 (1938), 99–101; I. Campbell, 'The Egotist Husband', *You*, 3 (1938), 103–5; I. Campbell, 'Jealousy kills Love', *You*, 3 (1938), 135–6; T. Browne, 'Sex', *You*, 3 (1938), 146–8; G. Warwick, 'The Dissatisfied Woman', *You*, 3 (1938), 157–8.

[199] Bingham, *Popular Press*, 251 (Figure A6).

[200] The subject matter ranged from advising readers on what books to read to answering questions on child abuse: *You*, 3 (1938), 50–2; *You*, 4 (1939), 393–6.

[201] For the advice column in the press, see also p. 210.

[202] *You*, 4 (1939), 171; Editorial, *You*, 4 (1939), 347.

the non-expert, and the errors of over-enthusiasm in the past, began to be acknowledged.[203]

CONCLUSION

The analysis of the phenomenon of practical psychology in this chapter has concentrated on mapping the shifting contours of a largely uncharted territory. It has suggested a more diverse culture of psychological thought and practice in the first decades of the century than has been hitherto appreciated, and one that integrated the new psychology with existing attitudes and movements associated with the interrelationship of mind, body, and spirit. It has also pointed towards a process of transition and a decline in independence and unorthodoxy over the interwar period, partly because of the growing importance of the psychological concerns of a female constituency. It has said less about context. This conclusion will suggest that we might usefully pursue four lines of inquiry in this respect. The first involves consideration of the extent to which this practical psychology was shaped by a consciousness of living in a 'new age' normally associated with a more exclusive modernist elite: one of exciting new prospects, as well as a series of stresses and strains which contemporaries associated with the experience of modernity. Here, both do appear to have encouraged, not only a re-conceptualisation of the self and its psychology, but also a sense of the modernity of this self.[204] This was encouraged further by reactions to the human devastation of 1914–18 and the social disruption that followed, though not as far as sometimes assumed, and it was certainly not created by this experience.[205] Whether we see a radical re-conceptualisation of self, where contemporaries did, is another matter. In the tendency towards fragmentation and complexity of the self, we might. In that this practical psychology moved in an often very different direction to Freud (still the dominant touchstone of modernism in the field), in that it so often looked to integrate a spiritual dimension, and in that it evolved relatively seamlessly out of an existing discourse of character, we might well not. Indeed, it shared, to a considerable extent, that desire for unity and connectedness in thought and identity that Jonathan Rose suggested was so characteristic of an 'Edwardian temperament', and in its rich associational culture extended this well into the interwar period.[206]

A second context was the impact of new intellectual ideas. However, this chapter has attributed less significance to this factor than has often been the case. The impact of canonical figures has been de-emphasised, notably that of Freud. At the popular level, there was a deep suspicion of the expert. Here, the cult of the

---

[203] T. Gilbert Oakley, 'The Real Psychology that Works', *You*, 4 (1939), 304–7.

[204] For instance, R. Whitwell, 'The New Age', *The Emblem*, 14 (1932/3) 291–3; Thomson, 'Consciousness of Modernity'.

[205] *Applied Psychology*, 21/118 (1925). The impact of war will be discussed further in Ch. 7.

[206] *The Edwardian Temperament, 1895–1919* (London, 1986).

practical was in considerable tension with that popularisation from above that has attracted most attention to date. New psychological ideas were important, but only through a process of translation, and through merger with existing values and systems of ideas. Psychology, moreover, was simply one element in a broader and longer-term revision of the scientific worldview that helped reconfigure views of the self at the popular level.

A third potential context was the disappearance, or more likely the weakening and reformation, of established discourses and practices for locating the individual in a social and spiritual world. Of particular significance was the process of secularisation. This could lead to the loss of a higher order of meaning in life and a felt need for re-enchantment. Alternatively, it could lead to a splintering of orthodox religion into a range of man-centred sects. Both encouraged an interest in psychology. The period also saw the destabilisation of a series of social identities. In this respect, the attraction of practical psychology to the upwardly mobile and to women is noteworthy. Practical psychology was able, not only to reinvest the world with a spiritual dimension, but also to provide the individual with new social moorings. It accomplished the latter, first through involvement in the practical activities of the movement, secondly through the idea of a self within a sea of consciousness, and finally through providing a practical resource and guide for the individual whose identity was in flux. Building on, rather than wholly rejecting, the dominant Christian and democratic/idealist world views of the era, development of self was now increasingly likely to be imagined, not simply as an issue of conduct, good citizenship, Christianity, and character development, but as a psychological, interiorised journey towards integration of 'personality'. The fact that such an identity was still rooted in the older discourses, and was still far less comfortable with talking about emotions and relationships, made it more social, far less individualistic or narcissistic than would be characteristic of the psychological self-help culture that emerged towards the end of the century.[207]

The final main context was the existence of a burgeoning commodity culture, which reshaped and made possible a heightened individual pursuit of physical, mental, and even spiritual health. Mass marketing and the emergence of new opportunities for leisure were crucial in facilitating the spread of a culture that offered commodity solutions to the discovery of identity, the construction of health as well as cure of illness, and the redesign and psychological management of ever more aspects of lifestyle.[208] However, in the struggle of so many of the practical psychology journals in the economic climate of the 1920s and 1930s we have an indication, both of the fragility of such markets, and of practical psychology's limitations in this regard. In truth, the vehicle of the club, rooted in a still vibrant

---

[207] This is explored further in Ch. 8.
[208] T. Richards, *The Commodity Culture of Victorian England: Advertising and Spectacle, 1851–1914* (Stanford, Calif., 1990); J. Benson, *The Rise of Consumer Culture in Britain, 1880–1980* (London, 1994); G. Cross, *Time and Money: The Making of a Consumer Culture* (London, 1993).

associational culture, was in this period at least as significant, and this was probably crucial in maintaining its distinctive practical orientation. The reorientation
of the 1930s, the loss of independence, and the merger with more mainstream
psychological concerns about relationships, reflected, not just the growing influence of popularisation from above, but also the feminisation of the market and the
resulting demands from below.

2

Reframing the Discipline

As the opening chapter of this book will have made clear, this is not a history of psychology as traditionally written, framed by the institutional perspective and interest of the psychological discipline itself. The proposition is that a history of psychology's significance in twentieth-century Britain extends far beyond such narrow disciplinary horizons.[1] There is a second point that follows from this and which has implications for the more traditional history: the history of the psychological discipline itself—its institutional boundaries, theoretical moorings, and practical applications—may look different when set within the broader framework. This chapter begins such an exploration, setting the disciplinary development alongside the more popular rethinking of human character explored in the previous chapter. In doing so, it questions the very idea of an absolute division between the popular and the academic, or between the amateur, practical, and mystical, on the one hand, and the scientific and the professional, on the other.[2] In particular, it argues that the discipline had to establish itself through accommodation to many of the same broader cultural circumstances that shaped the popular psychologies of the era, and it attempts to explain why this was the case. As in the case of the popular movements, there was intense excitement about psychology's new potential at the start of the century, and similar inflated ambition in some quarters. This encouraged the idea that psychology had profound implications for any study that involved calculations about human actions: anthropology, economics, history, politics, and sociology among them. Yet, this psychology also had to adapt itself to be acceptable in relation to still powerful existing languages of self, such as those centred on character and religion. This dual cultural inheritance, both hugely ambitious in its modernity, yet shaped by traditional values, reflected the particular circumstances at the start of the century, the key formative period for the British discipline. Hence its position at this point of the book. Though there was an obvious tension, this largely resolved itself

[1] For broader exploration of this problem: Smith, 'Does the History of Psychology have a Subject?'; G. Richards, 'Of What is History of Psychology a History?', *British Journal for the History of Science*, 20 (1987), 201–11.

[2] Elaborated in Thomson, 'The Popular, the Practical and the Professional', 115–32. See also: G. Richards, 'Edward Cox, the Psychological Society of Great Britain (1875–1879) and the Meanings of Institutional Failure', in Bunn et al. (eds.), *Psychology in Britain*, 54–71.

through a common interest in values. The result was that the British psychology of the first half of the century developed as a profoundly moral subject.[3]

THE STRANGE CASE OF WILLIAM McDOUGALL

William McDougall was the most celebrated British psychologist of the first half of the century. Since then he has virtually disappeared from view. What made him significant at the time no longer seems important, or in some respects acceptable. This contrast makes him very relevant for a study aiming to highlight the relationship between psychology and its own culture. Not only was McDougall's contemporary reputation within the discipline a very considerable one, but his appeal crossed the divide from an academic arena, to a semi-popular realm of teaching and training, to a popular sphere of practical and even spiritual psychology. More famously, the imported ideas of Freud, Jung, and Adler also transcended this divide. However, McDougall is especially valuable for this account, not just because of the decision to concentrate on British sources where possible, leaving him as the most influential and widely known British psychologist of his day, but because he was in some respects viewed as even more foundational. The others, particularly Freud, addressed the psychology of pathology; McDougall provided a framework for the whole.

The reasons for forgetting or at least marginalising McDougall have been numerous. He was the figurehead for a psychology based on instinct that would lose out in the disciplinary struggle for supremacy with another centred on behaviour. The philosophical bent of much of his writing, his efforts in the realm of psychical research, and his exploration of the 'riddle of life' and solution of 'animism' would all come to be seen as out of touch with the path of progress in the period; though such disciplinary perceptions do change and there are recent signs of renewed attention.[4] Interest in a 'group mind' would likewise come to be regarded as a misguided departure from science to metaphysics. He was recognised as by far the most important British psychologist of his day in Hearnshaw's history of British psychology of 1964, the only one to have a whole chapter devoted to his work. Nevertheless, the overriding impression in Hearnshaw's account is of frustration at a man so well prepared in terms of training turning out to be so poor as a scientist and contributing in the long term so little to the discipline.[5] Despite its revisionist agenda, the most significant contribution to the history of twentieth-century British psychology since Hearnshaw saw McDougall

---

[3] For a similar conclusion about American psychology: G. Richards, ' "To Know our Fellow Men to do them Good": American Psychology's Continuing Moral Project', *History of the Human Sciences*, 8 (1995), 1–24. On Britain and biology more generally: R. Smith, 'Biology and Values', 210–42.

[4] For instance, M. Boden, 'Purpose, Personality, Creativity: A Computational Adventure', in Bunn et al. (eds.), *Psychology in Britain*, 354–6. Boden recalls her interest in McDougall in the 1960s as akin to the raising of the dead: ibid. 355.   [5] Hearnshaw, *Short History*, 185–95.

falling even further into the background.[6] The most important contribution in recent decades in fact came from a historian operating well outside the history of psychology itself, and in highlighting McDougall's elitist attitudes hardly acted as a boost to his reputation.[7]

To some extent, this falling out with his own discipline was already a feature in his own life. Relocating to the United States and a Chair at Harvard in 1920, where he would remain until 1928, and thereafter taking a position at Duke University until his death in 1938, he would find his instinct psychology under attack from the rise of behaviourism.[8] However, this was to a considerable extent a reflection of American attitudes, with the British discipline of his era remaining much closer to his instinct model than to behaviourism. The impression that he was a reactionary intellectual dinosaur, ill-equipped to be taking up such a prestigious appointment in the country that was at the cutting edge of psychological development, was not helped by the fact that he chose this moment to publish a populist account highlighting the eugenic danger of the race problem in the United States.[9] On the other hand, psychology and eugenics were not strangers to one another in this period, and, in certain respects, McDougall's instinct theory would point to commonalities as well as differences across human history and civilisations.[10] His idea of the 'group mind' would also come under attack from contemporaries, with sociologists to the fore; though again, one needs to recognise both that there was an issue of professional interest at stake here, and that McDougall's use of the term was more metaphorical and less negative than some of his critics acknowledged.[11] It was not simply what McDougall said, therefore, but how he said it, that lost him friends within the discipline. He was not an easy man. He was conscious of this, but too arrogant to do anything about it; indeed, he revelled in courting controversy.[12]

A related problem was that he so often communicated through semi-popular channels. Even the book that brought him to prominence, his *Introduction to Social Psychology* of 1908, was in a popular series, reaching 62,000 copies of the

    [6] Bunn et al. (eds.), *Psychology in Britain*.

    [7] R. Soffer, 'The New Elitism: Social Psychology in Prewar England', *Journal of British Studies*, 8 (1989), 111–40; R. Soffer, *Ethics and Society in England: The Revolution in the Social Sciences 1870–1914* (Berkeley and Los Angeles, 1978), 217–51.

    [8] J. B. Watson and W. McDougall, *The Battle of Behaviourism: An Exposition and an Exposure* (London, 1928).

    [9] W. McDougall, in C. Murchison (ed.), *A History of Psychology in Autobiography*, 1 (New York, 1961; 1st edn., 1930), 212–13.

    [10] The book, really an essay on eugenics, with minor adaptations, went under different titles on the two sides of the Atlantic: *National Welfare and National Decay* (London, 1921); *Is America Safe for Democracy?* (New York, 1921). McDougall would claim that his raising of the racial question lay behind much of the criticism that subsequently haunted him in America: *History of Psychology in Autobiography*, 213. For a recasting of McDougall's racism: Thomson, ' "Savage Civilisation": Race, Culture and Mind in Britain', 235–58.

    [11] W. McDougall, *The Group Mind* (Cambridge, 1920).

    [12] McDougall, *A History of Psychology in Autobiography*, 192, 203; W. McDougall, *Religion and the Sciences of Life* (London, 1934), x.

English edition by 1936.[13] It was not his only such success. *Psychology, the Study of Behaviour*, published by the Home University Library of Modern Knowledge in 1912, was in its nineteenth edition by 1937. In 1927, he went further still in translating his ideas into a popular and practical idiom, with *Character and the Conduct of Life: Practical Psychology for Everyman*. Other ventures in this direction included a series of talks broadcast on the BBC in 1931.[14] The fading of McDougall's views from fashion subsequently, but also during his lifetime to some degree, particularly in the American academic context so influential in the longer term perspective of the discipline, have obscured the huge reputation that he had in his lifetime. Even if his ideas fell out of favour within an academic discipline that was moving in other directions, tastes changed more slowly amongst teachers, and to a lesser extent within other groups such as social workers, who were among the key actors in bringing psychology into applied settings. For such groups, McDougall remained a foundational authority. The regularity with which he was cited as a key authority at an even more popular level is equally noteworthy, and should alert us to the danger of assuming that the public shared the later view of him as an elitist.

For Hearnshaw, McDougall, rather than being insignificant, is symbolic in his contemporary importance of what was wrong about British psychology in the first half of the century, and of the 'wide divergence' from the path of progress as represented by developments in the United States.[15] In 1870, Britain had been 'in the van of psychological progress', an international leader in the field, with a long tradition of psychologically-orientated philosophy going back to John Locke, and now a new generation of figures like Francis Galton, Herbert Spencer, and Charles Darwin at the cutting edge of the discipline and with international reputations.[16] Thereafter, things went downhill. Having been a leader in turning towards a physiological and evolutionary approach, British psychology suddenly found itself handicapped by the importation of a German idealism which swamped a native tradition of associational psychology that had lent itself more to a marriage with physiology, and instead encouraged purely mental, philosophical, and even semi-mystical ideas of mind. The path of progress, followed in Germany and the United States, lay in science. Britain struggled to move in this direction. Such a psychology was too closely associated with a philosophical tradition that was anti-religious in tone. A psychology in line with idealist thought was more conducive to the dominant evangelical conscience. By 1900, Britain was well behind in a discipline whose progress could now be measured in terms of laboratories, university positions, and of course the long-term, scientific significance of research; by 1940, it had begun

[13] McDougall, *A History of Psychology in Autobiography*, 208; McDougall, *Introduction to Social Psychology* (London, 1967), xxi. The references that follow refer to this edition.
[14] The latter were published as *Love and Hate: A Study of the Energies of Men and Nations* (London, 1931). For full details of McDougall's extensive publications: A. L. Robinson, *William McDougall: A Bibliography* (Durham, NC, 1943). [15] Hearnshaw, *Short History*, 215.
[16] Ibid. 120.

moving, but in relative terms was as backward as ever. Hearnshaw does his best to account for such a falling away of British psychology in terms of internal disciplinary development, but it is notable how often he falls back on allusions to the broader cultural mood. In accounting for his contemporary reputation, he tells us, for instance, that McDougall's 'views fitted in with the mood of the time', that in its elevation of the irrational and saving of the 'soul', his theory 'provided just what was required', and that his system was 'both solid and reassuring'.[17] The aim of the analysis that follows is to develop this line of inquiry. In doing so, it is less concerned about failure, and regards this anyway as a rather whiggish perspective that tells us as much about the situation of the discipline from which Hearnshaw was constructing such a narrative. Instead, what follows is an analysis that regards the cultural circumstances for divergence as a worthy subject in its own right.

A NEW PSYCHOLOGY

In 1901, McDougall gathered together with ten like-minded individuals in London to form the Psychological Society, the forerunner of the British Psychological Society, which would emerge as the institutional face of the discipline in twentieth-century Britain.[18] Of course, a British psychological tradition existed well before this moment. Looking for a starting point, Hearnshaw takes us back to 1840 and Alexander Bain, despite acknowledging that Hobbes was writing about human nature and mind in a way that could be recognised as not only characteristically psychological, but also characteristically British, a full two centuries earlier.[19] The choice of Bain as a starting point was also that of the earliest history of British psychology, written in 1933 by J. C. Flugel, a psychoanalyst and a former pupil of McDougall. It is a choice, then, that probably tells us something significant about how the discipline wanted to understand itself in this period.[20] Hearnshaw recognised that Bain did build on others who had preceded him, but saw his more scientific approach as a powerful reason for starting here a history that in his view centred on scientific progress. On the other hand, he noted that it was not until mid-century that use of the term 'psychology' caught on; though even then it retained an 'exotic' flavour.[21] Recent work on developments in the 1870s not only confirms the need to look before 1901 (even if this is described at one point as a 'prehistory'),[22] but also indicates that this psychology was contested

[17] Hearnshaw, *Short History*. 185–95.

[18] Though the group was brought together by James Sully, it has been suggested that McDougall was the initial driving force and this is what he himself claimed: S. Lovie, 'Three Steps to Heaven: How the British Psychological Society Attained its Place in the Sun', in Bunn et al. (eds.), *Psychology in Britain*, 98. [19] Hearnshaw, *Short History*, 1–2.

[20] J. C. Flugel, *A Hundred Years of Psychology, 1833–1933* (London, 1933).

[21] Hearnshaw, *Short History*, 1–14.

[22] G. Bunn, 'Introduction', in Bunn et al. (eds.), *Psychology in Britain*, 15.

and intellectually insecure territory, overshadowed by the presence of philosophy on the one hand and a rising physiology on the other.[23]

Neither was psychology new as an academic subject at the start of the century (an issue linked to the first, but not the same, since many of the leading nineteenth-century authorities on the subject were amateurs in this sense). However, it often went on under the umbrella of philosophy—'mental philosophy'—and had the most fragile of footholds. Only at Liverpool did psychology emerge under the alternative umbrella of physiology, though even here such development depended on the leadership of C. S. Sherrington from 1899 and fell away after his departure to Oxford before the First World War.[24] The path to academic credibility has generally been presented as one of putting psychology on a scientific and experimental basis, following the influential German example, and in this respect progress was slow, with the first, small, research laboratories at University College London and Cambridge not properly established until 1897.[25] McDougall, who took up the Wilde Readership in Mental Philosophy at Oxford in 1904, was forbidden by the terms of the post from conducting laboratory work (even if he did manage to flout this on a small scale), and found himself dismissed by the scientists as a metaphysician.[26] His departure to the United States was clearly a sign of Britain's own backwardness. Though he would note signs of progress after the war, he would publicly voice his concern about the neglect of the subject in his own country.[27] It was not until 1919 that Britain had its first full-time professor of psychology (until then chairs had been in departments of philosophy or physiology), and as late as 1939 there were still only six university chairs, with three of these in London, and about thirty lectureships in total.[28] The Scottish system was a little more propitious, but this was because its Batchelor in Education degree entailed a significant psychological element after the First World War.[29] From Hearnshaw's perspective, the general situation was one of academic 'starvation and emaciation', with the university sector remaining unreceptive to the subject until after the Second World War.[30] The only caveat here is that this does probably underplay the significance of new development within what was a generally conservative academic system.

As a profession with its own institutions, there is a stronger case for regarding the start of the twentieth century as a point of origin. In particular, 1901 saw the

[23] On developments in the 1870s: Richards, 'Edward Cox, the Psychological Society of Great Britain'; F. Neary, 'A Question of "Peculiar Importance": George Croom Robertson, *Mind* and the Changing Relationship between British Psychology and Philosophy', in Bunn et al. (eds.), *Psychology in Britain*, 54–71.   [24] Hearnshaw, *Short History*, 180.

[25] For details: Bunn, 'Introduction', in Bunn et al. (eds.), *Psychology in Britain*, 2–5.

[26] McDougall, *A History of Psychology in Autobiography*, 207; A. Costall, 'Pear and his Peers', in Bunn et al. (eds.), *Psychology in Britain*, 188.

[27] W. McDougall, 'Our Neglect of Psychology', *Edinburgh Review*, 245 (1927), 299–312.

[28] Bunn, 'Introduction', in Bunn et al. (eds.), *Psychology in Britain*, 21; Costall, 'Pear and his Peers', 188; Hearnshaw, *Short History*, 168–81.   [29] Hearnshaw, *Short History*, 179.

[30] Ibid. 181, 215.

foundation, as already noted, of the British Psychological Society, and 1904 saw the first edition of the *British Psychological Journal*. However, the challenge of popular psychological organisations meant that the claim to a distinctive professional identity was not initially secure. Development of careers in educational, industrial, and clinical psychology would only begin to take off, and then more falteringly so than often claimed, in the interwar period—the subject for later chapters—and such specialisation also had its negative side in that it threatened to fracture a single identity. Not until 1921 would psychology have its own section in meetings of the British Association, before then going under the heading of physiology.[31] Membership of the British Psychological Society was very low in its first two decades, with even fewer attending meetings. By 1918, it had reached just 98. Membership became easier after rule changes in 1919, though this to some extent resulted in a retreat from strict professionalism, much of the increase accounted for by doctors interested in shellshock in the immediate aftermath of the war. It was not until the 1940s that membership again took off, rising from around 800 to 2,000, setting the slow pace and small scale of professional development until that point in perspective.[32]

In sum, whichever way we look at it—as a subject of intellectual inquiry, as an academic discipline, or even perhaps as a profession—it makes little obvious sense to regard psychology as new in 1900: in most respects it had older origins, while much of the most important development was yet to come. What was new, however, was a belief in the existence of a 'new psychology', and a belief that the subject, and thereby the discipline and nascent profession, were of key importance to society as a whole. It was this sense that psychology could help herald a new age that the discipline, or at least an important section within it, had in common with the popular psychological movements of the day. In both cases, the idea of newness served an obvious purpose of accentuating the significance of ideas and practices but also reflected broader belief that this was an age of transition. As such, the break with the past was often exaggerated, but it is the belief and the importance of this belief to subsequent development that is of as much concern in the analysis that follows.

McDougall's *Introduction to Social Psychology* of 1908 was a key text in the marking out of a transition to a new era of psychology, even if in content it shared much with the systematising psychologies of his immediate predecessors like James Sully, G. F. Stout, and James Ward.[33] McDougall would emphasise the novelty of his own system by setting it against a psychology that had continued influence within the social sciences but had largely already been superseded in his own discipline. '[P]sychologists must cease to be content with the sterile and narrow conception of their science as the science of consciousness', he argued, drawing a line between the introspective approach of the past and the science of

[31] Hearnshaw, *Short History*, 183–4

[32] Lovie, 'Three Steps to Heaven', 98–106. See also: H. Steinberg (ed.), *The British Psychological Society 1901–1941: Supplement to the Bulletin of the British Psychological Society* (London, 1961).

[33] Hearnshaw, *Short History*, 132–43.

conduct and behaviour of the future.[34] This was ironic, considering his later falling out with a more determined behaviourism. The contrast was also in actuality far less sharp, with introspection an unavoidable element of a new psychology that could not escape conclusions arising from the psychological subject's own experience. It was a necessary contrast, nevertheless, if psychology was to set itself free from philosophy. McDougall looked not simply to science, but to a 'positive science'.[35] For at the heart of this new psychology was the view that mind was no blank slate, passively receiving impressions from the outside world, rather it was the origin for the most crucial of purposive forces for all life: the instincts—*horme*, as he would later call it.[36] Accepting this meant accepting that the earlier focus on consciousness had been much too narrow, with the unconscious mind now emerging as a crucial terrain for exploration. It also exploded the idea of a purely rational, utilitarian, psychological subject, acting according to a calculus of pleasure and pain, as a hedonistic fiction. The instinct-driven, purposive mind—a mind with a mind of its own—demanded a more dynamic psychology to comprehend it. The analytical, descriptive psychology of the past had to make way for one that recognised its subjects as changing rather than fixed, biological heritage in constant dialogue with environment. With the psychological subject so reconfigured, the door was open for psychology, not simply to record human nature, but to turn to the study of how to change it.

McDougall's topography of instincts, emotions, and sentiments was so broad in its reach that it appeared to provide a model for all kinds of human behaviour. This model and others like it would be able to accommodate, not only Freud, but also his offspring and rivals Adler and Jung. Instinct theory provided a platform that helped to make these theories seem less incompatible, more members of a single family, and in the process less threatening. Despite his subsequent falling out with the behaviourists, McDougall's was also a model that went some way to bringing together the behaviourist and psychoanalytic approaches. This may help to account for his appeal at the popular level, where there was a tendency to overlook difference and to regard the multitude of theory as reinforcing an essential underlying message. Equally important, the emphasis on instinctive drives— present in all forms of life in parallel systems of hierarchical organisation—gave McDougall's work a biological appearance, and thus a crucial scientific and evolutionary authority, even if it rested on little actual biological research.[37]

By the time botanist A. G. Tansley published his account of *The New Psychology and its Relation to Life* in 1920, the idea of a new psychology and an old was widely accepted, even if the 'old psychologists' might have grumbled that the new was less

---

[34] *Social Psychology*, 13.   [35] Ibid.

[36] He would borrow this phrase from British educationalist Percy Nunn and would regret not having such an expression at the time to mark himself out as representing a particular school of thought: McDougall, 'Preface to the Twenty-Second Edition', *Social Psychology*, xix–xx.

[37] His most sustained piece of experimental research only came in the last stages of his career in a ten-year exploration of Lamarckian inheritance using rats.

novel than its proponents thought it was.[38] In the intervening years since McDougall's *Social Psychology*, greater awareness of the ideas of Freud and his followers regarding psychopathology, as well as the controversy provoked in some quarters, and then the encouragement given by the shell-shock phenomenon of the First World War, all further encouraged the sense of a division. A keen Freudian, Tansley took full advantage, setting the findings of the psychopathologists alongside the foundations laid by figures like McDougall. From now on, the new psychology would come to be more closely associated with the findings of psychopathology.[39]

Tansley was a respected scientist with a serious interest in psychoanalysis.[40] His book appealed to experts and public alike, reprinted eleven times in just four years. However, he was not a psychologist himself, and as such was perhaps freer than McDougall to write a book that was a little more touched by the broader excitement of its day. He was also more enthusiastic about diffusing psychological understanding to encourage a change in human character than the conservative McDougall. For Tansley, the old psychology 'seemed to be divorced from life as it is actually lived': it was too abstract, not practical enough.[41] The new psychology would help individuals to understand themselves and to live and prosper in a new way.[42] Such a vision is even more apparent in another of the key texts of British new psychology, J. A. Hadfield's *Psychology and Morals* of 1923, with its central message of self-realisation and its three key principles of psychological health: 'know thyself; accept thyself; be thyself'.[43]

In his criticism of a psychology based on introspection and in his desire to draw on evidence from life, including his own experience of other cultures as part of the Cambridge anthropological expedition to the Torres Straits Islands and then Borneo in 1898–9, McDougall too had contrasted the old and the new in terms of the latter's readiness to engage with real life: to study individuals within their social settings. Absent, however, is any indication that McDougall saw the way to a new age as lying through the path of self-realisation so prevalent within the practical psychology culture. Indeed, he could express violent opposition to the diffusion and confusion of the new psychology taking place at the popular level. Psychology might now have become 'the most popular of sciences', but he found no encouragement in this. In many ways, it was 'a disturbing and distorting influence'. The public was turning to the 'extreme, ill-balanced, fantastic, and bizarre'. By contrast, a psychology based on science was:

too difficult, too laborious, too lacking in sensational claims, in promises of immediate solutions of practical problems, too humdrum, too tame, too full of unverified hypotheses

[38] A. G. Tansley, *The New Psychology and its Relation to Life* (London, 1922), 13.

[39] Ibid. 19–25.

[40] L. Cameron, 'Histories of Disturbance', *Radical History*, 74 (1999), 5–13; J. Forrester and L. Cameron, ' "A Nice Type of the English Scientist": Tansley and Freud', *History Workshop Journal*, 48 (1999), 64–100.   [41] *New Psychology*, 19.

[42] Ibid. 296–7.

[43] J. A. Hadfield, *Psychology and Morals: An Analysis of Character* (London, 1923).

and confessions of ignorance. What the public likes is to be told straight-forwardly and dogmatically that it has an Unconscious, source of all mysteries and solutions; or a terrible Oedipus Complex, source of all disorders; or an Inferiority Complex, source of all achievement; or a few Conditioned Reflexes that explain all human activity; or a miracle-working power of Auto-Suggestion; or an Etheric body; or an imperishable Soul. And whatever the dogma, it must be one that promises immediate profits in health, or pocketbook, or domestic harmony and relief from personal responsibility.[44]

The hostility and distaste for the popular is resounding. In this, he was certainly not alone.[45] Here, there is a striking contrast to the way that popularisation would be embraced in the second half of the century by a figure such as Hans Eysenck.[46]

PSYCHOLOGY AND NEW SUBJECTS OF KNOWLEDGE

What animated McDougall, what makes him not only a new psychologist but a psychologist of a new age, was not any vision of reaching out directly to the public, rather it was his belief that this new understanding had profound implications for all subjects of knowledge.[47] His *Introduction to Social Psychology* was a manifesto for a psychology whose significance transcended the discipline itself: for psychology as a key tool in any subject which made assumptions about human nature, ultimately a key tool of statecraft.[48] In 1920, his study of the *Group Mind* would act as a sequel, amplifying his claim for psychology's importance for any understanding of social action. Such a grandiose vision undoubtedly had a personal dimension, reflecting McDougall's ambition, arrogance, and elitist inclination.[49] But so many others shared at least some of this excitement and ambition that explanation based on personal qualities alone becomes difficult to sustain.[50] The vision also stemmed from the nature of psychological ideas at the time and the set of circumstances in which they came to the fore.

McDougall's complaint was not simply that other disciplines had ignored psychology, when it should have been central, but that when they had paid it lip service the psychology had been grossly inadequate. He particularly had in mind the influence of a hedonistic psychology, which explained behaviour through the attraction of pleasure and the avoidance of pain. This had come to the fore in the work of the Utilitarians in the first half of the nineteenth century, but it remained influential in some circles, while its inadequacies had turned others away from an engagement with psychology altogether. The problem with the focus on pleasure

[44] McDougall, *A History of Psychology in Autobiography*, 222.
[45] Thomson, 'The Popular, the Practical and the Professional'; and in relation to medicine see Ch. 6.
[46] See Ch. 8.   [47] *Social Psychology*, p. 1.
[48] This is particularly evident in the opening salvo. See also: W. McDougall, *Anthropology and History* (Oxford, 1920).   [49] Soffer, 'New Elitism'.
[50] For instance, W. Brown (ed.), *Psychology and the Sciences* (London, 1924); J. A. Hadfield (ed.), *Psychology and Modern Problems* (London, 1935); and C. S. Myers, *In the Realm of the Mind* (Cambridge, 1937).

was that it described an emotional response rather than actually explaining anything: the question should have been, why was pleasure experienced, and was behaviour determined by such pleasure? The vehemence of what was a more general attack on hedonism also reflected moral discomfort about such a self-interested and hedonistic psychological subject.[51]

Whether consciously, or not, it was impossible to avoid making psychological assumptions in the study of any subject involving predictions about human action. Indeed, it had a part to play in all subjects of knowledge, for if man was not an object of study, as he was in the human and social sciences, then he was still present in even the hardest of sciences in his psychological role of observation and interpretation.[52] The new psychology made this more important than ever. It had placed behaviour at the very heart of psychology. It also offered new tools for understanding the modification of behaviour in its social setting. Gregariousness, tenderness, and protectiveness were all among McDougall's core instincts. In various manifestations, such social instincts would appear as a regular feature of the new psychology, most memorably as Wilfred Trotter's 'herd instinct', but also in the focus on love which came to the fore in the interwar period in a moralisation of the Freudian emphasis on the sex instinct.[53] The new psychology would also make much of the power of suggestion. Finally, in the idea of the modification of instinct through culture, psychology drew on the findings of history and anthropology and recast them in psycho-biological guise as keys to understanding the society of its own day.

When McDougall brought these tools of analysis together in his study of the *Group Mind*, he was criticised by those who felt that he was pushing the line of argument too far by implying some sort of consciousness outside the individual mind. He would always deny this, arguing that he was simply pointing to the way in which individuals behaved differently in groups. However, he was arguing that, particularly when these groups contained individuals with similar types of mental constitution (as in the nation), this behaviour did take on mind-like qualities: the interplay between individuals mirroring the interplay between purposive forces in an individual mind. This did imply that there was the possibility of a functional similarity between individual and group mind. It is easy to understand the concern of the critics towards a theory that, pushed to its extreme, challenged the very idea of individual autonomy. However, many key aspects of this social psychology, such as the role of instinct in modifying behaviour, did have broad currency. Indeed, the idea that all psychology was social psychology, and thus that the isolated individual of past psychology was a fiction, reverberated throughout the British psychological literature of the era.

[51] For instance, Hadfield, *Psychology and Morals*, 89–90.

[52] On this implication for scientific knowledge: W. McDougall, *The Frontiers of Psychology* (London, 1934), ix.

[53] W. Trotter, *Instincts of the Herd in Peace and War* (London, 1919); I. Suttie, *The Origins of Love and Hate* (London, 1935).

Circumstances were also important in encouraging psychology to stake a claim to a central position in relation to other subjects. The still primitive state of disciplinary boundaries made exchange both easier and more pressing. At the same time as he was playing a formative role in establishing the Psychological Society, McDougall was active in, among others, the Society for Psychical Research, the new Sociological Society, the Royal Anthropological Society, the Medico-Psychological Association, the Royal Society of Medicine, the Mind Association, and the Aristotelian Association.[54] Psychology also remained at an uneasy border between and in dialogue with physiology and philosophy, even if this was a key period for the emergence of a more independent identity.

The proximity and permeability between disciplines at this time is apparent in psychology's relationship to anthropology. Leading figures of the new psychology, McDougall, W. H. R. Rivers, and C. S. Myers were all members of the Cambridge Anthropological Expedition to the Torres Strait of 1898.[55] The experience would shape their subsequent approach to psychology.[56] This is apparent in examples scattered throughout McDougall's *Social Psychology*. Rather than emphasising racial otherness, as one might have expected with a figure of McDougall's reputation, the encounter with the primitive highlighted the parallels across the history of civilisation and the roles of instinct, the irrational, and the interplay between culture and mind. It was true, argued McDougall, that the natives 'are very unlike the typical civilised man of some of the older philosophers, whose every action proceeded from a nice and logical calculation of the algebraic sum of pleasures and pains to be derived from alternative lines of conduct; but we ourselves are equally unlike that purely mythical personage.'[57] For Rivers, anthropology had pointed towards the value of understanding present society through knowledge of its past—he would call his study of Melanesian Society a 'History'—and this, accordingly, would be the necessary way forward in constructing a science of social psychology.[58] The idea of a 'savage within', at the heart of the civilised psychological subject, was reinforced by increasing awareness of the parallels between the customs, rituals, and magic encountered in the new anthropological field and those uncovered closer to home in the study of ancient myth and folklore as well as the emerging psychology of dreams. The persistence of such cultural traits, evident for instance in the folklore revival, seemed to offer further confirmation that such impulses remained active in the subconscious mind.[59]

[54] McDougall, *A History of Psychology in Autobiography*, 206–7.

[55] R. Slobodin, *W. H. R. Rivers* (New York, 1978). See also: I. Langham, *The Building of British Social Anthropology: W. H. R. Rivers and his Cambridge Disciples in the Development of Kinship Studies, 1898–1931* (London, 1981); A. Herle and S. Rouse (eds.), *Cambridge and the Torres Strait: Centenary Essays on the 1898 Anthropological Expedition* (Cambridge, 1998).

[56] H. Kuklick, *The Savage Within: The Social History of British Anthropology, 1885–1945* (Cambridge, 1991).

[57] C. and W. McDougall, *The Pagan Tribes of Borneo*, 2 (London, 1912), 211. Though published after his *Introduction to Psychology* (London, 1908), the research preceded it.

[58] W. H. R. Rivers, *The History of Melanesian Society*, 2 (Cambridge, 1914), 596.

[59] W. H. R. Rivers, 'Dreams and Primitive Culture', *Bulletin of the John Rylands Library*, 4 (1917–18), 387–410; W. H. R. Rivers, 'Sociology and Psychology', *Sociological Review*, 9 (1916),

If the anthropological encounter helped to change the psychological subject, it also suggested that psychology on its own would not be able to explain social phenomena. As such, McDougall's ambitions for the discipline exceeded those of his peers. Recognising that when McDougall spoke of a 'social psychology', he was assuming that individual psychology could explain social phenomena, Rivers felt the need to add a note of criticism. He wanted a close alliance between psychology and sociology or anthropology, not a merger. Granted, all psychology was social psychology, but on its own psychology could not explain the culture that modified individual psychology.[60] The same point would be made after the war by Bronislaw Malinowski, Professor of Social Anthropology at the London School of Economics, who was attracted by Freudian theory but recognised the fallacy of the universalism of something like the Oedipus Complex.[61] In sum, the encounter between psychology and anthropology stopped short of accepting psychology as a tool for explaining how cultures developed, but it did help to introduce a social dimension to British psychology. The latter was one of the things that helped distinguish a British way in psychology throughout the first half of the century.[62]

The same kind of outcome emerged in the encounter with sociology. Again, circumstances of primitive and loose disciplinary boundaries at the start of the century encouraged dialogue. If the founding of the *British Journal of Psychology* marked a coming of age of psychology as a conscious subject, then that of the *Sociological Review*, four years later in 1908, did something similar for a discipline whose roots were perhaps even more tenuous. This sociology looked to psychology in its first years as an answer to the problem of being scientific. Again, the relationship that eventually emerged out of this dialogue was to be a disappointment for someone of McDougall's ambition. In 1908, sociologist Graham Wallas had suggested that psychology might be the key to going beyond an arid rational model of human nature in sociology; by 1914, he was more cautious and even highlighted it as something that threatened to engulf the discipline in irrationalism.[63] In the interwar period, sociologist Morris Ginsberg would reiterate the call for a rejection of irrationalism. Like Wallas, however, he did still recognise that psychology might be useful in explaining why humans responded in the way that they did to the primary determinant of social or political circumstances.[64] Thus,

1–13, reprinted in W. H. R. Rivers, *Psychology and Ethnology* (London, 1926), 17; R. Marett, 'A Sociological View of Comparative Religion', *Sociological Review*, 1 (1908), 48–60; R. Marett, *Psychology and Folk-Lore* (London, 1920), 1–26.

[60] Rivers, 'Sociology and Psychology'.

[61] Malinowski, letter to the Editor, *Nature*, 3 Nov. 1923, 650–1.

[62] For the ongoing interaction: Sir F. Bartlett, M. Ginsberg, E. J. Lindgren and R. H. Thouless (eds.), *The Study of Society: Methods and Problems* (London, 1939).

[63] G. Wallas, *Human Nature in Politics* (London, 1908); G. Wallas, *The Great Society: A Psychological Analysis* (London, 1914). On Wallas: M. Wiener, *Between Two Worlds: The Political Thought of Graham Wallas* (Oxford, 1971).

[64] M. Ginsberg, *The Psychology of Society* (London, 1921).

he would criticise McDougall's idea of an inherent national character, but accept the value of psychology in the study of the pressing issue of nationalism.[65] Even if this dialogue was cautious, it is still significant bearing in mind the peculiarly empirical and anti-theoretical reputation of British sociology in this period.[66]

Within the discipline, there is a belief that social psychology did not arrive in Britain until after the Second World War. 'Social psychology was an American invention', asserts the leading British figure in the field of the last decades of the twentieth century, Michael Argyle: 'there had been almost nothing in Britain until the 1950s, and I had never met a social psychologist.' This, however, is a view based on the idea that the only lineage deserving of the name is that which runs without too much deviation from the past to the present. It also reflects the view-point of the 1950s and a British psychology that was rejecting its more independent character of the interwar era.[67] A social psychology of sorts certainly did exist in the first half of the century. It was a trajectory that had opened up in the first decade of the century, and that would gain new momentum through the pressing nature of social problems and concerns about international relations in the 1930s.[68] Indeed, for all the talk of psychology emerging because of its applications as a discipline of defining individual difference, it needs to be recognised that in theoretical terms the psychological subject of the era was accepted as having a necessarily social dimension.[69]

The interdisciplinary encounter must also be set within the context of a deep cultural objection in Britain to the mechanisation of human nature that could easily have resulted from psychology. McDougall was not alone in situating psychology at a rather unique frontier, speaking to the arts as well as science, and as a key force for humanising the latter.[70] Charles Myers was one of the few who could challenge McDougall as the most important British psychologist of the interwar period, playing a key role in institutional development and in his role as pioneer and figurehead for industrial psychology.[71] However, he also continued to write about psychology in a much more general and philosophical way, emphasising its value for all subjects of knowledge, well into the interwar period.[72] Indeed, it was particularly important for an area like industrial psychology to demonstrate that

[65] M. Ginsberg, 'National Character and National Sentiment', in J. A. Hadfield (ed.), *Psychology and Modern Problems* (London, 1935), 29–50.

[66] M. Bulmer, 'The Development of Sociology and Empirical Social Research in Britain', in Bulmer (ed.), *Essays on the History of British Sociological Research* (Cambridge, 1985), 3–36.

[67] M. Argyle, 'The Development of Social Psychology in Oxford', in Bunn et al. (eds.), *Psychology in Britain*, 333.

[68] M. Roiser, 'Social Psychology and Social Concern in 1930s Britain', in Bunn et al. (eds.), *Psychology in Britain*, 169–87. These concerns are discussed further in the chapters that follow, especially Ch. 7.

[69] For the emphasis on defining individual difference: Rose, *Psychological Complex*.

[70] W. McDougall, *The Frontiers of Psychology* (London, 1934).

[71] On his role in the British Psychological Society: Lovie, 'Three Steps to Heaven'. On industrial psychology, see Ch. 5.   [72] C. S. Myers, *In the Realm of the Mind* (Cambridge, 1937).

psychology did not look to a mechanisation of humanity.[73] Alongside sections of
the British Psychological Society devoted to education and medicine, both with
their own journals, another set up in 1922 and active until 1937 was devoted to
aesthetics.[74] Many of the leading British psychologists were active in this field.
Myers, for instance, had a long-running interest in the relation between psychology and music.[75] Cyril Burt conducted significant research on the psychology of
aesthetics. In one experiment, he questioned readers of the *Listener* about their
artistic judgements, with the results broadcast on the BBC.[76] The linguistic
theory of I. A. Richards drew on engagement with psychology.[77] There was also a
dialogue between British psychology and theoretical writing on modern art.[78] In
sum, although interwar British psychology is best known for its diversion of
energy toward establishing itself on an applied basis in schools, clinics, and
factories, this sat alongside a more theoretical, philosophical, humanistic, and
outward-looking project. A narrative that focuses only on the longer-term
development of the field is in danger of neglecting this ambitious dimension of
the subject in the first decades of the century.[79]

BODY AND MIND

When it came to psychology's position in relation to more general intellectual
concern and thus its social purpose, the problem with nineteenth-century
psychology was that it had not been interested in the right things. Attention to
classification of mental states and a focus on perception and intellectual processes
had only been of very indirect broader relevance. Biology and Darwinism opened
up human nature to scientific investigation and explanation, yet in doing so
deterred speculative thinking. Its scientific status much enhanced by the end of the
century, it was important for physiology to avoid the leap of faith in projecting
what could now be said about nerves, if not yet brain, onto mind. Evolution,

[73] C. S. Myers, 'The Human Side of Industry', *Journal of the National Institute for Industrial Psychology* (JNIIP), 1/8 (1923), 309.
[74] Steinberg, *British Psychological Society*, 12, 19.
[75] See the chapter on music in C. S. Myers, *In the Realm of the Mind* (Cambridge, 1933).
[76] L. Hearnshaw, *Cyril Burt, Psychologist* (London, 1979), 215–21; C. Burt (ed.), *How the Mind Works* (1932), 267–310.
[77] F. G. Crookshank, 'The Importance of a Theory of Signs and a Critique of Language in the Study of Medicine', in C. K. Ogden and I. A Richards, *The Meaning of Meaning*, 2nd edn. (London, 1927), 337–55. For more on Crookshank, see pp. 86, 196.
[78] E. Miller, 'The Artist in Modern Civilisation', in Hadfield, *Psychology and Modern Problems*, 159–86. See also W. H. Auden, 'Psychology and Art', in G. Grigson (ed.), *The Arts To-day* (London, 1935), 1–24. The critic Herbert Read was particularly interested, as were surrealist artists like Roland Penrose, and figures like Arthur Segal explored the role of art in therapy: S. Hogan, *Healing Arts: The History of Art Therapy* (London, 2001).
[79] Perhaps this is why the older members of the British Psychological Society would become criti-
cal of a new lack of breadth and triviality: Steinberg, *British Psychological Society*, 12.

meanwhile, provided a scientific framework for conceptualising organisation of mind, but in doing so similarly held back questions about how mind itself operated.

One of the significant things about psychology at the start of the century was that it had the confidence to break away, not just from philosophy, but also from physiology and its constraints. The mind–body problem remained, but now rather than responding to this by jettisoning one or the other, psychology fudged the question. It claimed the mental as a valid territory for science, as it had to do if it was to advance itself, yet it had no convincing answer to the question of how one could talk of science when there was no clear physiological basis for the subject of this science, mind.[80] Such a leap of faith—there was little to differentiate the concepts of mind and soul—was crucial in the type of mentalist psychological subject that came to the fore. The unanswered questions about mind's relation to body meant that this remained a realm for considerable speculation, within the discipline as well as without. Such circumstances helped to bring psychoanalysis to the fore as a putative science of mind, but it also left the existence of mental energy outside of the body, even beyond bodily death, within the realm of possibility in the first decades of the century.[81] The fact that the physical science of the interwar period appeared to make the world a more rather than a less mysterious place than before, provided further reason for such open-mindedness.[82]

Thus, psychology took on a philosophical and at times a mystical dimension, albeit under the guise of science. Even Cyril Burt, a figure now renowned for his contributions to statistics and the psychology of individual difference, was in fact just as concerned with the philosophy of mind.[83] Like others in Britain, he resisted the behaviourist rejection of mind as something unknowable. Following McDougall, his tutor at Oxford, he also objected to the closing down of a space for human freedom inherent in the behaviourist model.[84] McDougall's solution was to regard mind as the recorded imprint of a purposive force that was the basic function of life at all levels from the amoeba up to the instincts of man, its function being to guide future striving in the light of experience.[85] Such a model had the essential scientific and biological veneer. It also postulated a crucial freedom at the heart of the psychological subject, its Lamarckian model of psychological evolution offered as an alternative to Darwinian fatalism on the one hand and behaviourism on the other.[86] McDougall's solution may have been just one of

[80] On the absence of physiology from the mainstream of British psychology in the period: R. Smith, 'Brain and Mind in the Age of C. S. Sherrington', in Bunn et al. (eds.), *Psychology in Britain*, 226.

[81] For instance, F. Aveling, *Directing Mental Energy* (London, 1927).

[82] W. McDougall, *The Riddle of Life* (London, 1938), 53–6.

[83] Hearnshaw, *Burt*, 292–306.   [84] Ibid. 305.   [85] McDougall, *Riddle of Life*, 263–5.

[86] On the appeal of Lamarckian model: P. Bowler, *The Eclipse of Darwinism: Anti-Darwinian Evolution in the Decades around 1900* (London, 1992). One implication of this was an interest in the possibility that memory like instinct might be inherited. This also led to an interest in Jung: L. Otis, *Organic Memory: History and the Body in the Late Nineteenth and Early Twentieth Centuries* (London, 1994).

many to this fundamental problem, but it does indicate at the very least the way in which this could open up a space for ethical as much as scientific speculation.

ACCOMMODATION

For all the talk of a new psychology, one of the reasons for success was that along-side the attraction of the new came a series of messages that acted as a salve to existing values and concerns rather than fundamentally challenging them. Yet, to place the biology of instincts, let alone the unconscious, at the very centre of a model of human nature was potentially radical and destabilising for existing morality and for an existing confidence in the rational individual. What follows is an attempt to explain how the new psychology overcame this problem.

Man may have shared a basic set of instincts with animals but was still unique in the way these instincts manifested themselves. A dynamic model of development explained how instinct modified in the history of civilisation, just as in the history of the individual life in the passage from childhood to maturity.[87] The self-regarding instinct was fundamental in this respect: behaviour modified by an idea and ideal of self.[88] Even in its Freudian form, the new psychology maintained this essential moral restraint, now in the guise of the ego ideal.[89] Rather than something that placed control beyond the individual, instinct was a vehicle for purpose, agency, and ultimately humanity, thus avoiding the alternative mechanistic scenario against which British psychology mobilised throughout the period. Social instincts also came into play, directing individual behaviour towards the interests and approval of others, thus also avoiding the potential determinism of an empha-sis on base instinct that was sometimes a criticism of Freud. In this regard, McDougall's gregarious instinct and Trotter's herd instinct were far more than reflections of elite anxiety about the irrationality of the masses.[90] In McDougall's hands, social instincts could play a vital role in curbing and giving social and moral direction to potentially destructive human drives. And if Trotter's instinct of the herd could have negative results in the aggression and blind adherence to authority that he imagined among the German population, it was also key to a cooperative effort in Britain that might defeat aggression and ensure a civilised and tolerant society thereafter.[91]

The second way in which the new psychology accommodated itself to the existing moral climate was through its position on psychological integration. Just as the new psychology argued that one could no longer think in terms of an

---

[87] McDougall, *Social Psychology*, ch. 8 'The Advance to the Higher Plane of Social Conduct', 180–96.   [88] Hadfield, *Psychology and Morals*, 82–8.

[89] McDougall, *Social Psychology*, 150–79; J. C. Flugel, *Man, Morals and Society: A Psycho-Analytic Study* (London, 1945), 50–64. Emphasising this lineage, Flugel had been another of McDougall's Oxford pupils.   [90] Soffer, 'New Elitism'.

[91] Trotter, *Instincts of the Herd*.

individual who was not a social individual, it came to be regarded as equally artificial and dehumanising to imagine individual psychological capacities in isolation. The individual, unlike the machine, was more than the sum of parts.[92] Character, recast but essentially revivified in psychological terms as 'personality', was the sum of sentimental and instinctual arrangements characteristic of the individual, each linked one to the other, and each therefore both constitutive and reflective of a unique individuality. In the project of harmonising and integrating the system of instincts and sentiments into a coherent whole, personality inherited something akin to that moral dimension so integral to the Victorian concept of character.[93] Thus, this was a vision, which for all the talk of the importance of the unconscious and of the need to recognise rather than simply repress drives and urges, was in the end primarily and reassuringly one of conscious self-determination and the channelling of mental energies towards higher ends.[94] In its valuing of authenticity, in its integration of instinct with higher ideals, and in its emphasis on purposive self-responsibility, it had considerable appeal in a culture that still largely expected and looked for a moral framework for the self.[95]

Connected to the new psychology's accommodation with a culture of character was its position on heredity. In its role in mental testing, its assumptions about the inheritance of intelligence and susceptibility to mental illness, and its class-based sympathies with broader anxieties about national fitness, the psychology of the early twentieth century was in some respects a natural ally of eugenics.[96] Reframed in terms of the ideological situation of psychology, the situation emerges as more complex. Going too far down the deterministic hereditarian track would have been to undermine the accommodation with character; not to have done so at all would have been flying in the face of the evolutionary framework that was a virtual necessity for any science of life. Again, there was a process of accommodation. One possibility was to forsake evolutionary moorings altogether, taking the behaviourist path where psychology could simply ignore biology. For a set of reasons already discussed, the British were loath to follow this route. Instead, a system like McDougall's presented itself as biology and set itself very firmly within an evolutionary context, yet in its translation of these themes into the language of mind operated at the same time as a psychology of character. In a less overt way, this slippage and accommodation

---

[92] Take, for instance, Cyril Burt's *Young Delinquent* (London, 1925), where the range of capacities, environmental as well as hereditary, taken into account, reveal a surprisingly holistic vision given his reputation.

[93] The centrality of character in Victorian Britain is discussed on pp. 42–5 See also Collini, 'The Idea of Character', 91–118. This influential account makes only a brief allusion to development in the twentieth-century. Here, he suggests that behaviourist psychology as well as sociology created a less hospitable environment for character, yet he remains cautious about accepting how far such change actually did take place: ibid. 117. The current chapter, like the first, supports such caution.

[94] For instance, F. Aveling, *Personality and Will* (London, 1931), 214; W. Brown, *Mind and Personality: An Essay in Psychology and Philosophy* (London, 1926), 2–14; W. Brown, *Science and Personality* (London, 1929), 236–8.

[95] For instance, Hadfield's *Psychology and Morals*, which was in its fifteenth edition by 1949.

[96] For instance, Rose, *Psychological Complex*.

between biology and character was also a feature of the psychodynamic psychology of the interwar years. Such models helped to present psychology as science. They also catered to a popular appetite for evolutionary and hereditarian models often overlooked in a literature that accounts for the advance of eugenics in this period simply in terms of its attractions to the elite as a tool of social engineering. In the work of a figure like McDougall, heredity became an issue, not simply of levels of ability, but also of culture and national character.[97] Elsewhere, this embedding of the history of culture in the individual self could be less nationalist, attractive instead to those looking to liberate but master instinct by acknowledging the savage within.[98] Such psychological models of inheritance spoke to the contemporary desire for affirmation of an identity that went beyond an atomised, isolated individualism. They looked to a self that was only fully realised if it came to understand and experience its relation to a hidden history within as well as its social position within a network of affective relations. As such, it reconfigured the path to character, rather than rejected it; indeed, it pointed to the way in which character, or now more commonly 'personality', could reach a higher level.

This psychology also left doors open to religion.[99] It has been suggested that psychology was one of the more difficult hurdles in a more general reconciliation between science and religion during the period.[100] In particular, it potentially undermined the position of the individual as a freely self-determining agent that was at the heart of Christianity. Behaviourism rejected the very idea of mind and replaced free will with the mechanism of the reflex. Psychoanalysis, pushed to its extreme, likewise fundamentally challenged the idea of a rational self, and it recast religion itself in psychodynamic terms. However, in the British context, behaviourism was largely rejected because of its mechanistic implications, while psychoanalysis was rarely pushed to its extreme or at least popularly understood in this way. New psychologists like Hugh Crichton Miller, first Director of the Tavistock Clinic, were comfortable in reconciling psychoanalysis and religion.[101] J. A. Hadfield, who had initially undergone theological training before turning to psychotherapy, wrote *Psychology and Morals* to counter the idea that the new psychology and morality inherently opposed one another. Another of the great semi-popular success stories of the new psychology, it received a particularly enthusiastic reception from a religious audience.[102] The relationship would become more contentious in the 1930s, but it was still reconcilable. There were those who chose to make a fight out of potential incompatibilities. One of the

[97] On the latter, see in particular his *Group Mind*.			[98] Thomson, ' "Savage Civilisation" '.
[99] On the nineteenth-century origins of this meeting: Hayward, 'Popular Mysticism and the Origins of the New Psychology', 197.
[100] Bowler, *Reconciling Science and Religion*.
[101] H. C. Miller, *The New Psychology and the Preacher* (London, 1924); H. C. Miller., 'The Priest and the Doctor in the Treatment of Nervous and Mental Disorder', *Mental Hygiene*, 2 (1936), 23–9. Also see the report on the debate following the paper, the thrust of which, like the paper, pointed to scope for collaboration in the field of mental health between medicine and religion: ibid. 30–9.
[102] See the preface to the sixteenth edition: Hadfield, *Psychology and Morals* (London, 1964), vii.

most prominent was the Revd J. C. M. Conn, who had spent five years as a research student in experimental psychology, but who now attacked the new psychology as a 'menace'. Conn was particularly hostile towards the idea that religion could be explained in psychological terms, especially when this meant its dismissal as a kind of narcotic or some unhealthy source of repression: God no more than a 'Freudian Frankenstein'.[103] However, a far more prevalent feature of the period was the readiness of psychoanalysts to be open-minded or supportive of religion, and for religious progressives to experiment with psychology as an adjunct to a pastoral role and a vital tool for modernising religion in the light of science.[104] This indeed was part of the context for Conn's attack.[105] In the Britain of the 1930s, William James's work on religion being integral to the human self was far more likely to be regarded as important and worthwhile than a psychoanalytic dismissal of religious behaviour in terms of psychopathology.[106] The new psychology and its psychotherapeutics might narrow the opportunities for calling on religion as a guide on issues of morality; the case was severely weakened, for instance, for treating as sinful perversions and obsessions that were now recognised as emerging from the unconscious. However, this could be to the advantage of religion, providing it with a legitimate case for ceding disputed moral territory and thus adapting to social change. Psychology could also offer religion a vital role as the type of ideal necessary as a unifying force for the self. In general, the case certainly remained stronger for seeing religion as a positive rather than negative factor in individual mental health.[107] In fact, there was real optimism about 'psychological experts exercising their art of mental therapy inspired by the Christian gospel'.[108] The reverse of this process was also taking place, as across denominations psychology became attractive as a modernising adjunct to ministry.[109] This interest was already developing, but it gained added impetus through the experience of chaplains with shell-shocked soldiers in the First World War. It was also a way to counter the challenge of spiritualist healing that became a pressing issue in the interwar period.[110] Psychological ministers, like the Methodists Leslie Weatherhead and Eric Waterhouse, and the Anglican L. W. Grensted, spread this new psycho-spiritual message through their preaching (the reach of which was now dramatically extended through the advancing

[103] Revd J. C. M. Conn, *The Menace of the New Psychology* (London, 1939), 59.

[104] Hearnshaw, *Short History*, 293–5; G. Richards, 'Psychology and the Churches in Britain, 1919–1939: Symptoms of Conversion', *History of the Human Sciences*, 13 (2000), 57–84. For further discussion, see pp. 187–8.   [105] Conn, *Menace of the New Psychology*, 24.

[106] W. James, *Varieties of Religious Experience* (London, 1902); R. H. Thouless, *Introduction to the Psychology of Religion* (Cambridge, 1923); Hearnshaw, *Short History*, 293.

[107] For instance, Revd A. E. J. Rawlinson, 'Psychology and Theology', in Brown (ed.), *Psychology and the Sciences*, 107.

[108] Revd Dean Inge of St Paul's, 'Psychology and the Future of Religion', in J. A. Hadfield (ed.), *Psychology and Modern Problems* (London, 1935), 233.

[109] Hearnshaw, *Short History*, 293–5.

[110] S. Mews, 'The Revival of Spiritual Healing in the Church of England, 1920–26', in W. J. Shiels (ed.), *The Church and Healing* (Oxford, 1982), 299–331.

medium of the radio), publication of popular advice books, and an influence on how religion was taught (with Jesus—the 'greatest of psychologists'—leading the way).[111] The process showed no sign of dying away in the 1930s, with 1936 seeing the foundation of the Jungian-influenced Guild of Pastoral Psychology.[112] As late as the 1950s, Weatherhead's latest book sold its first print run of 10,000 books within three months, with three further editions within the decade.[113]

These were practical reasons for accommodation. However, in psychology's venture to comprehend mind, this period also saw a more philosophical and at times mystical case put forward, albeit in the guise of science. Here psychology offered the prospect of finding in mind something that was both of and yet beyond the material, of and yet beyond the individual, and so fundamental to life itself that it was akin to the object of religion. Even an atheist like McDougall saw soul-like qualities in mind.[114] The idea that some kind of purposive and thus psychological force was at the core of all life and was key to evolutionary progress reassured those who recognised the need for an accommodation between religion and evolution but objected to the mechanistic implications of Darwinism.[115] Psychology could also offer a sort of religion of humanity to those who struggled any longer to accept traditional Christian teaching but found themselves disenchanted by materialism. It provided purpose to life, ideal direction, and a vision of the self that transcended mere individualism and looked ultimately to at-oneness with the universe.[116] For William Brown, Wilde Reader in Mental Philosophy at Oxford, this was a psychological vision that advanced man 'inevitably from a religion of humanity to a religion of God'.[117] Within the scientific humanism that emerged during this period, the language remained secular, but the emphasis on purposive personality being at the heart of psychosocial evolution played a comparable role to religion in giving a meaning and value to life.[118]

CONCLUSION

This chapter has attempted to reframe the history of the British psychological discipline in the first decades of the twentieth century. In terms of institutional expansion and a certain sort of science centred on laboratory, it has accepted the

[111] Hearnshaw, *Short History*, 293–5; J. C. Travell, 'Psychology and Ministry with Special Reference to the Life, Work and Influence of Leslie Dixon Weatherhead', Ph.D. thesis (University of Sheffield, 1990). For a taste of their approach: L. Weatherhead, *Psychology and Life* (London, 1934); E. S. Waterhouse, *An ABC of Psychology: For Sunday School Teachers and Bible Students*, 4th edn. (London, 1933), 114; E. S. Waterhouse, *Psychology and Religion: A Series of Broadcast Talks* (London, 1930).

[112] W. H. Kyle (ed.), *The History of the Guild of Personal Psychology, 1936–1970* (London, 1970).

[113] Travell, 'Psychology and Ministry', 197.

[114] McDougall, *Religion and the Sciences of Life*, viii; Bowler, *Reconciling Science and Religion*, 43.

[115] Bowler, *Reconciling Science and Religion*, 181–4, 308–14.

[116] Brown, *Mind and Personality*, 318.

[117] Ibid. P. T. de Chardin, *The Phenomenon of Man* (London, 1959), 285.

[118] J. Huxley, *The Humanist Frame* (London, 1961).

view that this was a period of backwardness. What it has suggested, however, is that one result of this weak position is that British psychology was more inclined to look beyond itself, both to engage with other disciplines and to be influenced by cultural constraints. Because of this, it was a psychology that mirrored some of the key features of the more popular change in human character considered in the last chapter. These included an attempt to reconcile psychological science with religion, and a consequent search for purpose in life; an emphasis on wholeness, whether of self, or of the relationship between the self and the world; and the forging of a renewed morality through a revivified mission of character-development in the new guise of personality. From the perspective of the discipline, the period may seem like something of an aberration; from the perspective of the historian of culture, one can recognise the cultivation of a psychological subjectivity that addressed more successfully many of the key concerns of its age. This was a psychological subjectivity, moreover, of a very different hue to the regulated, normalised, quantified, individualised subject that we have come to know in accounts of psychology's emergence as an applied discipline in this period. Whether this means the picture in relation to these areas of application needs similar modification is a subject for later chapters.

3

After the New Age

The opening chapter of this book uncoverd a popular and practical psychological culture that came to the fore in the first decades of the century. The second set this alongside the simultaneous emergence of a professional and academic discipline of psychology. This chapter turns to an intellectual culture between the two. Again, one of the aims is to explore the politics of knowledge, and this means highlighting differences, mutual suspicions and even antipathies across both divides, but also the striking similarities when it came to the content, ambition, and style of psychological thought and practice. Existing views about the popularisation of psychology often rest on this type of intellectual culture, rather than the low culture that was the subject of the first chapter. In that sense, the book has already made its case for altering our view of the popular. This chapter will put the intellectual culture itself under scrutiny.

In terms of charting a spectrum of opinion from the popular to the professional, it might have made sense if this chapter had come in between the two others. Instead, it follows them, because it provides an opportunity to move from the first historical context for this book to the second: from the new age, to the problems of industrial civilisation. Not only has the latter been a central frame in the writing of modern British history as a whole, but it has also been particularly important when it comes to the interwar period that is the focus of this chapter. However, the recent reorientation away from labour, social, and economic history towards cultural history has tended to shift our attention to new subjects, such as identity, sex, domesticity, leisure, and consumption, rather than encouraging a reappraisal of industrial civilisation itself. The same has been the case with work touching on psychological thought and practice. This chapter and the three that follow will begin to explore the extent to which such narratives did connect.

The Chapter title also alludes to the specific point of origin for the story that follows. The chapter makes its argument by tracing the subsequent pathways of a group of intellectuals associated with the modernist journal *New Age* who had met to explore the opportunities presented by the new psychology in the aftermath of the First World War. In doing so, the aim is to point to the ongoing centrality of a concern and excitement surrounding the psychological, but at the same time to highlight the variety of forms that this would take in the decades that followed.[1] By tracing lines of descent and illuminating a web of connections, it suggests that a concern about the psychological had a more pervasive and multi-form presence than is generally recognised. In doing so, it sets out to reposition the areas of intellectual interest that have dominated attention to date: in particular, Freud, psychoanalysis, introspection, and even sex are decentred, while our attention is drawn to mysticism, the will, attention, and a preoccupation with putting the self together but also transcending the confines of individualism. We need to be open, in sum, to looking beyond what is sometimes a rather whiggish, Freudian-centred model of psychological modernity. What follows suggests a more complex and intellectually messy situation, one more constrained and shaped by contemporary problems.

The final purpose of the Chapter title is to signal an engagement with a grand narrative for the psychological subject over the century as a whole. In part, the point here is to highlight some parallels between the situation at the end and at the start of the century: in short, the way in which our 'new age' succeeds another; the way in which ours is neither the first moment of excitement about mixing ideas of East and West, nor the first psychotherapeutic culture.[2] However, in pointing out the parallel and even the existence of some direct links in terms of people and practices from one to the other, it also notes differences between the two, differences to which the final chapter of the book will return. In particular, it will point to the social, spiritual, and ethical emphases of the visions of the psychological subject in the earlier period, framed in the context of an acute awareness of the problems of industrial civilisation, which contrast with what has tended to be described as a more individualist, introspective, some might say narcissistic, vision later on.[3]

This chapter also contributes to the book's exploration of how ideas and practices of psychological subjectivity circulated. The first chapter opened up the channel of a burgeoning market of popular publications, on the one hand, and the role of the club, on the other. The second chapter looked to the challenge of spreading ideas from an academic base that was intellectually fluid, to its advantage, but professionally insecure, to its disadvantage. This chapter opens up the role of the guru and the disciple. In doing so, it also highlights, on the one hand, the existence of a global intellectual market, with the guru a point of contact for

---

[1] There were also close connections and parallels with the interwar occult and spiritualist movements: A. Owen, 'Occultism and the "Modern Self" in *Fin-de-Siècle* Britain', in Rieger and Daunton (eds.), *Meanings of Modernity*, 71–96; Dixon, *Divine Feminine*; Hazelgrove, *Spiritualism and British Society between the Wars*.

[2] Though the late-twentieth-century new age movement tended to claim ancient roots, the most important study of the phenomenon emphasises its relationship to modernity and highlights fin de siècle origins: P. Heelas, *The New Age Movement: The Celebration of the Self and the Sacralization of Modernity* (Oxford, 1996), 41–9. Also relevant: A. Falby, 'Gerald Heard (1884–1971) and British Intellectual Culture between the Wars', D.Phil. thesis (Oxford, 2000).

[3] Dixon, too, notes that despite a shift towards a more individualist self-actualization, interwar Theosophy continued to engage with the social and political in a way that is at odds with Heelas's less differentiated picture of a vaguely liberal philosophy of everyone finding their own truth: *Divine Feminine*, 232–3.

the exchange of ideas and people between East and West, and on the other hand, the importance of local physical and intellectual spaces in creating networks of individuals.

The figure of the guru, who would also be known to contemporaries as the 'prophet', 'sage' and 'seer', had a prominence in the period, and in particular within its psychological cultures, that calls out for historical investigation.[4] It also needs emphasising that this phenomenon of the charismatic leader was to be found, not only in the kind of elite and at times mystical circles that provide the subject for this chapter, but also within practical psychology, and there was even of course an element of the guru–disciple relationship within the psychoanalytic movement.[5] The neglect by historians of this important feature of intellectual life in the first part of the century reflects a tendency to dismiss from serious consider-ation what has come to appear as, at best eclectic but amateur synthesis, at worst intellectually confused, wrongheaded, and indulgently fanciful mysticism.[6] The prominence of the guru had something to do with the factors that made a popular culture so vibrant and the profession so insecure: the guru benefited from the mar-ket, even though this was sometimes less important because of a tendency towards elitism; and it was important that a space had been opened up by the limits of professional authority. Outside of orthodoxy and professional or academic con-straints, the guru was able to take advantage of a climate that was advantageous for the drawing together of an idea of Eastern thought with the new of the West. In its emphasis on the development of personality and higher levels of consciousness as routes to individual influence over others, the psychological theory of this era

[4] The *OED* reveals that the term 'guru' came to Britain from India in the nineteenth century. The interwar period, however, seems to have seen its popularisation. By 1940, H. G. Wells was using the expression in popular dialogue: 'I ask you, Stella, as your teacher, as your Guru, so to speak, not to say a word more about it' (*Babes in Darkling Wood*, 205). By 1966, it had descended to an item of fashion, with *Vogue* advertising the 'Guru Jacket'—buttoned up high, Chinese style. For contemporary views: R. B. Kerr, *Our Prophets* (Croydon, 1932); R. Landau, *God is my Adventure: A Book on Modern Mystics, Masters and Teachers* (London, 1935). Novelist John Buchan drew on the guru P. D. Ouspensky for his 'Professor Moe' in *The Gap in the Curtain* (London, 1932). Despite its subtitle, there is disappointingly little light shed on the origins of the phenomenon as a whole in Peter Washington's *Madame Blavatsky's Baboon: Theosophy and the Emergence of the Western Guru* (London, 1993). The term implied a drawing of knowledge from the East, but often so too did the terms 'seer', 'sage', and 'prophet' used for figures like Patrick Geddes, Edward Carpenter, and Havelock Ellis.

[5] On practical psychology, see Ch. 1. At times, such figures did self-consciously take on some of the characteristics of the seer. For instance, William Margrie, styled himself 'Sage of Camberwell' and leader of the 'South London Immortals Club': W. Margrie, *Brainy Britons and Brainless Britons* (Peckham, 1947). For the link with psychoanalysis: D. Pick, *Svengali's Web: The Alien Enchanter in Modern Culture* (New Haven and London, 2000). On the related figure of the 'sorcerer' within the more secret realm of the occult: A. Owen, 'The Sorceror and his Apprentice: Aleister Crowley and the Magical Exploration of Victorian Subjectivity', *Journal of British Studies*, 36 (1997), 99–133.

[6] For thoughts along the same lines in relation to Gerald Heard: Falby, 'Gerald Heard and British Intellectual Culture between the Wars'. For the neglect of the intelligentsia in Britain: T. Heyck, 'Myths and Meanings of Intellectuals in Twentieth-Century British National Identity', *Journal of British Studies*, 37 (1998), 192–221. For an important reinterpretation of interwar science that does emphasise the interplay with religion and what might be deemed mysticism: Bowler, *Reconciling Science and Religion*.

itself played a key role in fostering a culture for the guru. However, in this regard, there was a tension at the heart of many of the psychological movements of the era. On the one hand, followers were often drawn in because a powerful, charismatic leader seemed to represent all that might be gained from a psychological programme, and sometimes this programme was a secret mystery to be divulged only to select, loyal disciples. On the other hand, these movements positioned themselves as believers in self-improvement and self-realisation, and practice rather than mere theory, and invariably on these grounds set themselves in opposition to elitist—expert–dependent—therapeutic traditions, such as within orthodox medicine (even as represented by psychoanalysis). This tension between the cult of the leader and the democratic impulses of the age clearly touches on a central theme of the period. Later chapters will develop this in relation to the mid-century ideological crisis and professional psychology.

Finally, a note about sources is appropriate at this stage. Much of what follows in this chapter rests on the rich memoir material left by disciples. As such, it needs careful interpretation. Clearly, some disciples exaggerated the achievements of their psychological leaders. But this was not universal. Many wrote from a position of some distance and even hostility, having rejected their earlier beliefs. Once any such bias is recognised, these memoirs can still provide an important source. Even the biases are revealing when it comes to understanding the shifting relationship of the guru and his disciples. It would certainly be foolish to dismiss their value on this basis. In the more popular realm explored in the opening chapter of the book, the sources are very unrevealing on questions of personal motivation. This is the great value of the rich memoir material of the intellectual classes. We gain real insight into not just what people may have believed, but why. We gain a sense of how one intellectual position led to another. We also find the type of personal detail unavailable elsewhere to recreate a picture of the intense intellectual and social interconnection that surrounded the excitement about psychology: here definitely a social phenomenon. Indeed, this may help to explain why psychology—as the subject that explained and offered command over personal relations—could be such an important part, not just of intellectual life, but also of the social life of the intellectual.

THE *NEW AGE* AND PSYCHOLOGY

In the aftermath of the First World War, a small circle of people affiliated with the weekly *New Age* met to discuss their excitement about new psychological ideas. Alongside A. R. Orage, the influential editor of the magazine, there were four doctors: David Eder, regarded as one of Freud's most important early followers in Britain, and also important for his involvement in socialism and Zionism; Maurice Nicoll, who has come to be regarded as one of the leading British Jungians of the following decades; James Carruthers Young, based in lucrative

Harley Street and a representative of the Adlerian camp; and J. A. M. Alcock, the main contributor on psychoanalysis in the pages of the *New Age*, an advocate of 'psychosynthesis' rather than any of the main psychological theorists of the day. There were two who were or had been influential editors of the left: former Editor of the *Daily Herald*, Rowland Kenney; and Editor of the *New Statesman*, Clifford Sharp. There were also two men who are perhaps best described as seers in the range and mystical colouring of their interests: Havelock Ellis (difficult to categorise as a doctor, despite training, or even as a psychologist, despite being author of the multi-volume *Psychology of Sex*); and the Eastern European émigré, Dmitri Mitrinovic.[7] The chapter will not trace all these figures in detail, and some are less central anyway.[8] It will focus on Orage, the four doctors, and Mitrinovic, saying also something about other characters outside of this original circle whose stories intersect in important ways with those of the main protagonists. The naming of names and the tracing of links that follows has several purposes. The first is to point to an era in which ideas crossed, relatively freely, the boundaries between the arts, medicine, and politics—something that became harder in the second half of the century. The permeability of such boundaries was fundamentally important in making possible and in shaping the vision of psychological subjectivity that emerged in the period. The second is to contribute to a case about significance; though this also rests on the argument that there was an engagement with the social problems of the period, and that the names helped to mobilise a broader constituency looking for a new type of progressive politics.

Set up in 1907 with financial support from George Bernard Shaw but also a theosophist banker, the *New* Age, under the editorship of Orage, emerged as the liveliest literary forum of its day in Britain, unique in the British context for its combination of modernism and political radicalism. The journal's brief post-war flirtation with psychoanalysis gains passing attention in all the standard accounts, and is seen as a sign of its broader path-breaking unconventionality but in the end a factor in its subsequent decline. Such histories agree that from being in the vanguard of a radical encounter between socialism and modernism, Orage led the *New Age* in two wrong-headed trajectories. The first mistake was to support Major Douglas and his theory of Social Credit as a solution to Britain's economic problems. The second was the brief flirtation with psychoanalysis and subsequent descent into mysticism. The latter, in particular, has been both confusing and

---

[7] These names are repeated in most accounts of the *New Age* with usually a brief coverage of Orage's flirtation with psychoanalysis, for instance the most recent of these: G. Taylor, *Orage and the New Age* (Sheffield, 2000), 126–9. It is very possible that others were also involved. Though Ellis is generally mentioned as part of the circle, he does not figure in any of the accounts of the subsequent interest in Ouspensky and Gurdjieff. Though still an important influence, he can also be regarded as representing an older generation.

[8] The literary figure J. D. Beresford is also reported as having attended these first meetings. By the 1930s he was the presiding figure in the *Aryan Path*, a Theosophical magazine, and he was involved in the Theosophical wing of the Peace Pledge Union: J. Webb, *The Harmonious Circle: The Lives and Works of I. D. Gurdjieff and P. D. Ouspensky and their Followers* (London, 1980), 395, 441.

embarrassing for Orage's admirers. The net result, so the argument goes, was disastrous. Readership fell, from around 4,500 in 1913, to 2,000 by 1920, and Orage left on his chase for spiritual enlightenment, with the journal never to return to its former glory. The relationship between the simultaneous turn to Social Credit and mysticism remains unclear. Implicit in most accounts is the belief that there is no need to draw any rational relationship. What tied the two, after all, was a common thread of foolishness: Orage's fatal attraction towards mysticism, gurus, and their simple panaceas. Such accounts tend to dismiss out of hand the value of engaging with these beliefs in their own right. The suggestion that the mysticism compensated for the materialism of his economics is the best, albeit undeveloped, overture in this direction.[9] This chapter will attempt to cast a little more light not just on the mysticism but on the strange coupling with economic theory, positioning it as part of the broader interwar engagement between psychological subjectivity and the problem of industrial civilisation.

In light of our new appreciation of interest in psychoanalysis in the pages of the educated press of this period, the mere fact that an avant-garde forum like the *New Age* covered the issue comes as no surprise. Written before this awareness of a broader interest, accounts of the *New Age* generally assumed that this owed much to the contributions of the pioneering psychoanalyst, Dr David Eder, regarded by Freud himself as 'the first, and for a time the only doctor to practice the new therapy in England': in other words, a rather top-down view.[10] This chapter will suggest a rather different picture. In due course, it will situate Eder as an integral figure in the literary as much as the psychoanalytic world. First it will argue that his contribution sat alongside that of others, who may not have been explicitly psychological let alone psychoanalytical in their language, but who in their analysis of art, literature, and politics were still centrally concerned with a new view of psychological subjectivity. The *New Age* was in fact decidedly wary about what psychologists themselves were up to; anything else would have jarred with its anti-authoritarian attitudes. Even Eder attacked medicine and its crude use of psychology as a tool of diagnosis in the area of mental deficiency.[11] What was wanted was a psychology that put man together with his world and in doing so transformed both: a psychology of personal as well as political revolution. This type of position was exemplified by the man who, rather than Eder, was the most frequent writer on the subject after the War: J. A. M. Alcock, a young doctor, born in India and with a taste for Eastern philosophy, 'who had never been able to take *materia medica* seriously'.[12] Alcock attacked academic psychologists like W. H. R. Rivers

[9] A. Rigby, *Initiation and Initiative: An Exploration of the Life and Ideas of Dimitrije Mitrinovic* (Boulder, Colo./New York, 1984), 65.

[10] J. B. Hobman (ed.), *David Eder: Memoirs of a Modern Pioneer* (London, 1945); M. Thomson, 'Mind in Socialism: Montague David Eder, Socialist, Psycho-Analyst, and Zionist' (unpublished paper). Ernest Jones was not pleased to see his position as Freud's leading British acolyte usurped: V. Brome, *Ernest Jones: Freud's Alter Ego* (London, 1982), 210–11.   [11] Hobman, *Eder*, 81–2.

[12] R. Kenney, *Westering: An Autobiography* (London, 1939), 324.

and William McDougall as materialists: 'they profess psychology and practise physics . . . one of them will one day doubtless locate the unconscious in, say, the cerebellum, and then there will be nothing more to it.' They might have supported psychoanalysis in word, but this was not the psychoanalysis of 'ever-becoming' deed that inspired Alcock, and others like him.[13] He condemned psychotherapy for treating symptoms not causes.[14] He dismissed the value of all writing on shellshock (apart from that of Ernest Jones and Maurice Nicoll).[15] And he portrayed the founder of the industrial psychology movement in interwar Britain, C. S. Myers, as a mechanist with no real interest in psychology, failing to appreciate that the real problem was the inferiority complex that lay behind class-consciousness and that because of this it was only natural that workers would resist any attempted efficiency gains.[16]

ORAGE AND THE PSYCHO-MYSTICAL PATH

Orage's own interest in psychological subjectivity originated well before he had ever heard about Freud. It had its roots in an engagement with mysticism, but also with socialism. The *New Age* emerged in the context of dissatisfaction with the increasing state collectivism of the Fabians and a desire for a socialism that might integrate the vision of self-realisation that someone like Orage had already found in Nietzsche and Theosophy.[17] Its initial great enthusiasm was Guild Socialism, which was attractive not just in socialist but in psychological terms: it viewed the worker as a dynamic human individual, yet it avoided mere individualism in its vision of integration in a greater psychological whole.[18] However, as future head-master of the progressive Summerhill school, A. S. Neill, pointed out, if Guild Socialism and its system of self-government within industry was going to work it had to change the human material it was dealing with. He knew this all too well through his dispiriting personal experience as an elementary school teacher. One had to rid the worker of fear, and this would mean going right back to the schoolroom, rather than thinking that economic freedom would suffice on its own. The poor were constantly reminded of their inferiority, and the class war emerged as compensation: consciously it may have been presented as economic

[13] J. A. M. Alcock, 'Psycho-Analysis', *New Age* (1 Jan. 1920), 138.

[14] J. A. M. Alcock, 'Psychotherapy', *New Age*, (5 Feb. 1920), 222–3.

[15] J. A. M. Alcock, 'War-Shock', *New Age* (1 April 1920), 353–5.

[16] J. A. M. Alcock, *New Age*, (20 May 1920), 42–3. However, G. D. H. Cole, a key figure in the pre-war Guild Socialism debate, was supportive of the setting-up of Myers' National Institute for Industrial Psychology, seeing it as leading to an analysis of labour that went beyond mere economics to flesh and blood individuals: *New Age* (12 June 1919), 115–16.

[17] On Orage's earlier interests: Taylor, *Orage and the New Age*. On the relation to Fabians: N. and J. MacKenzie, *The First Fabians* (London, 1977), 344–5. For the broader appeal of a new type of politics: C. Nottingham, *The Pursuit of Serenity: Havelock Ellis and the New Politics* (Amsterdam, 1999), 231–3.   [18] Martin, *The New Age under Orage*, 209–11.

war; unconsciously, and more fundamentally, it was psychological and emotional. Following this logic, psychological change was the real solution to the problem of the classes; class warfare was a symptom, rather than a solution.[19]

Orage's creation of a circle to discuss psychoanalysis was continuous with these earlier concerns.[20] This is why psychoanalysis itself could not provide the answers. The encounter with psychoanalysis appears merely to have brought to the fore a mental crisis that heightened his attraction for a psychology that, like mysticism before it, could put the self together rather than simply expose its problems.[21] Psychoanalysis was undoubtedly a powerful stimulus in opening up the unconscious, but it did little to satisfy hunger for a new morality and guide to life.[22] Orage's engagement with such issues was intense, and by the summer of 1921 he had virtually stopped contributing to the *New Age*.[23] Instead, alongside Kenney and Alcock, he struggled to marry the strengths of psychoanalysis and mysticism in the alternative of psychosynthesis.[24]

By the start of October, Orage had found a figurehead for such a movement in the Russian mystic P. D. Ouspensky, who had recently arrived in the country from Constantinople, supported by Lady Rothermere.[25] The core of the psychoanalytic circle followed him: Orage, Nicoll, Alcock, Eder, Young, Kenney, and Mitrinovic.[26] For those who regarded Orage with some reverence, it was a shock to see him rapidly accepting the role of pupil.[27] Ouspensky's talks, at first in Lady Rothermere's study in St John's Wood, and then at Warwick Gardens, attracted a crowd that also included T. S. Eliot, Herbert Read, Aldous Huxley, and Gerald Heard.[28] For a while, followers attempted to integrate his exercises of self-observation in their everyday lives, whether by undertaking counting exercises on the London Underground or the abjuring of favourite foods. However, this fashion for attacking mechanism while continuing one's everyday life was rather superficial.[29] The seriously committed would abandon all commitments. In Orage's case, this meant selling his stake in the *New Age* to make the journey to immerse himself in the 'Work' at the 'Institute for Harmonious Development', at the Château du Prieuré, in Fontainebleau outside Paris. Here, another Eastern guru, Gurdjieff, had settled after failing to get permission to stay with his

[19] A. S. Neill, 'Psycho-Analysis in Industry', *New Age* (4 Dec. 1919), 69.

[20] Webb, *Harmonious Circle*, 200–31.

[21] P. Mairet, *Autobiographical and Other Papers* (Manchester, 1981), 180.

[22] Rigby, *Initiation and Initiative*, 85.   [23] Mairet, *Autobiographical Papers*, 184.

[24] Kenney, *Westering*, 325–6.

[25] Mairet, *Autobiographical Papers*, 185. The post-war exodus of such figures from Eastern Europe appears to have left a significant impact on the culture of the West and would deserve some of the attention now devoted to the impact of émigrés from Nazism. On the attraction of Theosophy in Russia before forcible eviction in the 1920s: M. Carlson, *'No Religion Higher than Truth': A History of the Theosophical Movement in Russia, 1875–1922* (Princeton, 1993). J. Moore, *Gurdjieff: A Biography* (Shaftesbury, 1991), 359–60.   [26] Mairet, *Autobiographical Papers*, 186.

[27] Kenney, *Westering*, 329; Webb, *Harmonious Circle*, 199.

[28] L. Welch, *Orage with Gurdjieff in America* (London, 1982), 23.

[29] J. C. Young, 'An Experiment at Fontainebleau—A Personal Reminiscence', *The New Adelphi*, 1 (1927), 32.

followers in England, but having spent enough time there to impress someone like Orage that he not Ouspensky was the real master.[30] After several years at the Prieuré, Orage would travel with Gurdjieff to the United States and remained there as his representative, based in New York for much of the rest of the decade.

What Philip Mairet called the 'Orage Mystery' was his subsequent return to England and his former interests.[31] Here, he took on a key editorial role in the *New English Weekly* that was trying to fill the modernist gap left by the *New Age*, which had become a much less dynamic entity after Orage's departure. He also resumed an active role in the campaign for Social Credit, which had found new legs in response to the crisis of international finance that had devastated the world economy at the start of the decade.[32] It has been easy to conclude that Orage's Gurdjieffian episode was a misjudgement, the result perhaps of some kind of mental breakdown, and something that he both retreated from and probably rejected. This misreads the situation.[33] Orage held many of these ideas well before the encounter with Gurdjieff, even before his interest in psychoanalysis; and there is no evidence of any recantation when he returned to England.[34] What is more, his ideas of this period, when scrutinised in their own right, emerge as very different to the mysticism that one might have expected. Indeed, when the *Nation* reviewed his book of *Psychological Exercises*, there was disappointment in finding that mysterious higher truths came down to such rather mundane practical operations: 'no more remarkable than cross-word puzzles, anagrams and other parlour games'.[35] In fact, there has been little attention to this work since its influence was mainly confined to the United States, where Orage was highly influential at the time and for some time after (Herbert Croly, Editor of the *New Republic*, and other important literary and publishing figures were among his followers).[36] Orage would reiterate, though translate into a common-sense language accessible for the American audience, the Gurdjieffian 'Work's' emphasis on the importance of attention: the need to be aware of one's behaviour at its time of occurrence. Undoubtedly, part of the attraction was in the exotic trappings, including the use of dance. However, Orage's writing was highly accessible, with little if any occult obfuscation. Essays on 'how to learn to think', 'the control of temper', 'how not to be bored', 'life as gymnastics', paralleled the language and focus on everyday practice to be found in many of the popular psychological manuals of the era. The

---

[30] He had visited briefly and Orage had been deeply impressed and resigned from the *New Age*. The Home Office did eventually grant permission for Gurdjieff to settle but not his colony of followers. His brief stay in England did not attract him to the prospect anyway. For details of the debate in the Home Office: Moore, *Gurdjieff*, 154–71. [31] Mairet, *Autobiographical Papers*, 193.
[32] The immediate context for the return was partly the arrival of Gurdjieff in the United States and his disappointment at what Orage had put in place: Webb, *Harmonious Circle*, 365. For some details on the *New Age* involvement in Social Credit in the rest of the 1920s: J. W. Hughes, *Major Douglas: The Policy of a Philosophy* (Glasgow, 2002), 62–6.
[33] Mairet also suggests this: *Autobiographical Papers*, 193.
[34] On his ongoing interest: Webb, *Harmonious Circle*, 376.
[35] Ibid. 365. Asked whether Orage was a mystic, David Eder is reported as responding: 'Only in the sense that we are all mystics': Ibid. 378. [36] Welch, *Orage with Gurdjieff in America*.

emphasis on self-observation, rather than introspection, and on practical technique over theory, likewise echoes such a culture. Indeed, he published his essays in popular psychology magazines in the US, and had the reputation as a 'lecturer in psychology'.[37] Orage framed this psychology as one of rescuing the individual from the mechanical impetus of the age, awaking him or her to full consciousness. This was the psychological counterpoint to his fascination with first Guild Socialism and then the Economics of Social Credit. They formed a joint and interrelated response to the psychological problem of the individual within industrial civilisation.

YOUNG AND THE ADLERIAN PATH

One of the lesser-known figures in the *New Age* psychological circle was Dr James Carruthers Young, a successful Harley Street doctor, who had already worked under Jung in Zurich.[38] Young also followed Gurdjieff to Paris. In this case, disenchantment rapidly followed. Despite a rather bitter subsequent attack, Young was also keen to set out both his reasons for attraction in the first place and what he continued to regard as the merits of Gurdjieff's ideas.[39] Once again, and making more understandable the venture of the Harley Street doctor in the first place, we see what he called 'the experiment at Fontainebleau' as having to contemporaries at least and even a later apostate, a serious and potentially valuable psychological message. Some might have been attracted because of the occult trappings, but it was the actual practices and the way that they centred on the exercise of the will that were crucial. Here, the central aim of self-development through deepening or expanding the limits of self-consciousness was at the very heart of what was so exciting about modern psychology more generally. Previously, Young had felt somewhat dissatisfied by his experience of analytical therapy, which might reveal the cause of neurosis in an inability to address reality, but did not tend to be so successful when it came to providing the solutions. 'To put it in a nutshell', he wrote, 'analytical knowledge is not necessarily effective knowledge.'[40] In his experience, a problem of will was at the heart of the neurotic cases that he and other doctors in this period were so preoccupied with, and the ideas, but most importantly the practical techniques, of Ouspensky and Gurdjieff bore real promise in this respect. This would lead other doctors into an important engagement with the ideas of Alfred Adler. Indeed, Young himself would later be one of the founding members of the Medical

[37] A. R. Orage, *The Active Mind* (London, 1954), 121.
[38] Mairet, *Autobiographical Papers*, 191.
[39] Initially an address to the Medical Section of the British Psychological Society, this was subsequently published in the first edition of the literary journal, *The New Adelphi*, edited by John Middleton Murry, whose wife, the short story writer Katherine Mansfield, was at the time under the influence of Gurdjieff and would die at the Prieuré: J. Carswell, *Lives and Letters: A. R. Orage, Beatrice Hastings, Katherine Mansfield, John Middleton Murry, S. S. Koteliansky, 1906–1957* (London, 1978), 174–93. [40] Young, 'An Experiment at Fontainebleau', 27.

Section of the London arm of Adler's International Society for Individual Psychology, one of the era's most important pressure groups for the integration of a psychological dimension in all medical work.[41]

The key influence among these early medical Adlerians was the brilliantly clever, but unstable, Francis Crookshank, himself something of a guru within the circle. As such, after he took his own life in 1933, the dynamism of the movement fell away.[42] Crookshank would look to Nietzsche, as much as Adler, for inspiration (indeed, he would not submit to the indignity of personal psychoanalytic training).[43] Both were attractive as guides away from a philosophy of 'I think therefore I am', to one of 'I think therefore I will'.[44] Crookshank launched a fundamental critique on the materialism of modern medicine and offered in its place a new, liberating holism. Individual psychology would rescue the minds and spirits of the masses from the alienating effects of an industrial civilisation; the advance of state medicine only threatened to compound the situation.[45] Writing in the literary journal, the *Adelphi*, in 1932, Young however argued that in an age in which there had been a vast increase in psychological problems, caused in part by social and economic conditions, it was no longer adequate for the psychologist to regard this as simply an issue of personal maladjustment. Society itself needed readjustment, with psychologists therefore having a key role to play in the future political process.[46]

In sum, Young is representative of a line of descent that drew medicine, via a combination of the encounter with the mystics, Adler, and the foregrounding of the will, into psychology and in some cases on to politics. It even had friends close to the heart of the medical establishment.[47] However, the Adlerian approach was also viewed with much suspicion. No doubt the close alliance with political causes

---

[41] See also pp. 195–6.

[42] Perhaps best known and notorious for his degenerationist vision: *The Mongol in Our Midst: A Study of Man and his Three Faces* (London, 1924). Born in 1873, Crookshank had medical credibility through membership of the Royal College of Surgeons and the Royal College of Physicians. For a sketch of the movement: W. Langdon-Brown et al., *The History of the Medical Society of Individual Psychology of London*, Individual Psychology Pamphlet 23 (London, 1943), 11–16. See also the account by the wife of one of Adler's closest British friends: P. Bottome, *Alfred Adler: Apostle of Freedom* (London, 1939), 290–1.   [43] Bottome, *Adler*, 290–1.

[44] F. G. Crookshank, *Individual Psychology and Nietzsche*, Individual Psychology Pamphlet 10 (London, 1933), 9. On the interest in Nietzsche in interwar Britain: D. Stone, *Breeding Superman: Nietzsche, Race and Eugenics in Edwardian and Interwar Britain* (Liverpool, 2002).

[45] F. G. Crookshank, *The New Psychology and the Health of the People*, Individual Psychology Pamphlet (London, July–Sept. 1932), 6–7.

[46] J. C. Young, 'Implications of Adlerism', *Adelphi*, 4 (1932), 517–24, 581–9. See also also M. Robb in W. Langdon-Brown et al., *Individual Psychology and Psychosomatic Disorders (I)*, Individual Psychology Pamphlet 4 (London, 1932). Robb also contributed an appendix on the psychosexual roots of neurosis related to unemployment in D. Beales and M. Lambert (eds.), *Unemployed Man* (London, 1934). This is discussed further in Ch. 5.

[47] Here the emphasis on the whole person was attractive to elite practitioners threatened by biomedicine: C. Lawrence, 'Still Incommunicable: Clinical Holists and Medical Knowledge in Interwar Britain', in C. Lawrence and G. Weisz (eds.), *Greater than their Parts: Holism in Biomedicine, 1920–1950* (Oxford, 1998), 94–111. Figures like Langdon Brown, Horder, and Brackenbury support Lawrence's model better than others like Crookshank—his Nietzschean elitism being of a

contributed to this. So too did resistance to the idea of lay therapists, with the gradual rise to prominence within the profession of medical Freudians making the situation worse.[48] Several Adlerian clinics were established, but they remained rare.[49] Significantly, when Adler visited England in 1934, he was able to count on the help of influential lay supporters like Lady Astor, who provided him with access to Society soirées and even to a meeting with Ministers at the House of Commons, but he was treated rudely by the medical profession itself.[50]

MITRINOVIC AND THE PSYCHO-POLITICAL PATH

Born in 1887, Dimitri Mitrinovic was a native of Serbia in the Austro-Hungarian Empire, arriving in Britain at the start of the First Word War. He had been editor of an avant-garde journal in Belgrade and a leader of one of the movements for a greater Serbia. Losing out to those in favour of violent methods, he left the country before the murder by his political opponents of the Archduke, which acted as a catalyst for War throughout Europe.[51] His missionary pan-humanism and support of a united Europe in the post-war era would spring in part from his sense of a deep personal involvement in the devastation of 1914–18.[52] Coming to England via Munich, where he exchanged ideas with artists Paul Klee and Wassily Kandinsky and the pioneering Dutch psychotherapist Frederick Van Eeden,[53] he was employed by the Serbian Ambassador to promote a British understanding of his nation which was currently epitomised by 'To hell with Serbia' headlines. He soon came to impress as he took tours around the Victoria and Albert Museum exhibition on Serbia, displaying his vast knowledge about human history as these excursions soon spilled over into other areas of the V&A and beyond to the British Museum. This was where writer Philip Mairet, soon to be one of Mitrinovic's closest followers and among the most admiring of many memoirists, first encountered him. Like others, he was soon investing Mitrinovic with the qualities of the sage, a leap of faith that drew on his exotic foreignness, as well as his learnedness, but was also very physical and sensual: his 'beauty of voice and intonation' often remarked upon.[54] Even Paul Selver, who was ill-disposed to the mystical, reported something hypnotic and deeply impressive about his mere presence: 'Hardly had I shaken hands with him than I found myself so affected by his mere presence that

different brand—or Young, who seems to haven been drawn to a more radical engagement with social and economic problems and was also keen to engage with modernist thought.

[48] Bottome, *Adler*, 295–6.

[49] Dr Franz Plewa, Dr Hamburger, and Dr James Moore worked out of the Victoria Club, Kennington; Mrs Nagelschmidt, a Geman lay psychotherapist had a clinic for backward and defective children in Manchester; Dr Stallybrass provided Adlerian therapy in Liverpool; and in London an Adlerian approach was also present at the Child Clinic at Friends House and in the work of Dr H. C. Squires of the Torrington Square Group: Bottome, *Adler*, 300–1.

[50] Ibid. 296, 308–12.   [51] Mairet, *Autobiographical Papers*, 116.   [52] Ibid. 137–8.

[53] Ibid. 128.   [54] Ibid. 85.

I lost consciousness.'[55] Mitrinovic's talk of a journey beyond individual consciousness was undoubtedly even more powerful because of the feeling that he literally embodied such a vision. Mitrinovic would deliberately cultivate such an impression, shaving his head to leave striking black wing-like eyebrows that marked out his eyes as tools of enchantment.[56]

Mairet's detailed accounts are particularly interesting for what they reveal about the relationship between the leader and the led. He recalled finding it liberating to adopt the identity of 'a believer, a neophyte', as he puts it, and felt that he became more rather than less conscious in letting go of himself.[57] Swept off his feet, Mairet resigned from his wartime posting with the Red Cross to follow Mitrinovic. He spent the second half of the war with his wife, Ethel Mary, the weaver, in Ditchling, Sussex, where the printer and calligrapher Douglas Pepler had set up a craft-based community that aimed at retrieving pre-industrial values and reviving living traditions of work and religion.[58] Here, the loss of self in the close attention and physical exertion of work had parallels to Gurdjieff, though it was also firmly located in the British tradition of Ruskin and Morris. This was not the only community of its type. Inspired by the arts and crafts movement and guild socialism, documentary filmmaker Humphrey Jennings's parents, for instance, founded the Walberswick Peasant Pottery Company and were readers of the *New Age*, and his mother would go on to be a follower of Gurdjieff after the War.[59] Helen Sodden, another of the small group of Mitrinovic's acolytes, also moved to Ditchling, and the group as a whole would meet in her Woodbine Cottage. Mairet would end the war in Wormwood Scrubs, as the authorities caught up with him as a Conscientious Objector.[60] Mitrinovic would resign from the Serbian Legation as his pan-humanism emerged as incompatible with the post-war nationalist vision.[61] After the war, while Mairet took his exploration of persona onto the stage before becoming literary editor of the *New Age*,[62] Mitrinovic would begin to cultivate new connections via the groups who met at Valerie Cooper's flat in Fitzroy Street and Lilian Slade's

---

[55] Mairet, *Autobiographical Papers*, 86. There are parallels with John Buchan's description of conversion under Professor Moe in his novel *The Gap in the Curtain* (London, 1932). Of course, conversion—as in the practical psychology culture—could take place through the inspiration of reading rather than the power of the individual. See for instance the account of composer Cyril Scott: *My Years of Indiscretion* (London, 1924), 110.

[56] It appears that his shaved head emerged some time after the arrival in London. This description comes from Alan Watts' recollections of meeting him in the late 1920s: A. Watts, *In My Own Way: An Autobiography, 1915–1965* (London, 1973), 108–9. The striking qualities are confirmed by photographic portraits from the period. On the role of the eyes in enchantment: Pick, *Svengali's Web*.

[57] Mairet, *Autobiographical Papers*, 108.

[58] On Ethel Mairet: M. Catts, *A Weaver's Life: Ethel Mairet, 1872–1952* (Bath, 1983). The origins of the community went back to sculptor Eric Gill's arrival in 1907. Gill and Pepler would found the Catholic Guild of St Joseph and St Dominic in 1921. Descendants of the original community remain in this area of Sussex to this day and a museum at Ditchling displays work by original members: http://www.ditchling-museum.com/arts_crafts-intro.html, consulted June 2005.

[59] M. Jennings and C. Madge (eds.), *Pandaemonium, 1660–1886: The Coming of the Machine as Seen by Contemporary Observers* (London, 1995), ix.

[60] Mairet, *Autobiographical Papers*, 127.   [61] Ibid. 129

[62] Ibid. 130–1. Mairet was in the Shakespeare Company at the Old Vic for four years.

house at Golders Green. Such locations, scattered throughout the memoirs that surround the figures in this chapter, remind us of the important function, in the spread of ideas and practices, of networks of people and opportunities for face-to-face contact and thus the sway of personality, primarily in the intense environment of the city, but also spilling over into the countryside retreat.[63]

It was during this period that Mitrinovic began to cultivate Orage at the *New Age*. Mairet argues that most accounts of Orage underestimate this influence.[64] The closeness and importance of the relationship is indicated by the decision to offer Mitrinovic a column on 'World Affairs' and to co-write this under the pseudonym of M. M. Cosmoi, in an attempt—unsuccessful—to tone down Mitrinovic's style of 'towering abstractions, metaphysical allusions and extraordinary neologisms'.[65] This column appears to have upset readers, and to have supported it, even after Orage himself found it impossible to modify the column, suggests a deep fascination, even if this stopped short of complete conviction.[66] Mitrinovic came to develop a distinct and in some ways contrasting vision of the psychological subject to that of both the psychoanalysts and the mystics (which, in turn, had a surprising amount in common).[67] What made his writing psychological was not simply its content, but its style. It was so difficult to follow, so packed with mythological allusions, because it appealed to the subconscious, not simply the rational mind. In addressing the whole of human history and myth, Mitrinovic was also addressing the deeper levels of the individual mind: the imprint of the former embedded subconsciously in evolutionary layers within the latter. There was nothing novel about this notion: it was at the heart of other influential visions of mind at the turn of the century—notably in the founder of Theosophy, Madame Blavatsky's *Secret Doctrine*, and in the vision of British socialist and seer Edward Carpenter. Such a model meant that the individual could find within himself the whole of humanity. There was a universal psychic thread, a unity and continuity of mind. Mapped on to this, however, was a model of difference. Each nation, each race, had a different location in this history of mental and cultural evolution. In particular, there had been a continuous process of evolutionary change in human consciousness, from the primacy of instinct of the East, to the self-consciousness and rationalism of the West. The West was now at some kind of crisis point: having lost a collective unconscious, and having emphasised in its place individual self-consciousness, individuals might have become free agents but they were also isolated and this was the basis for conflict. It was vital in Mitrinovic's view, as in that of so many others during this period, to bring this Western mind back towards the East: to cultivate a merger between the two.[68]

[63] On the city and modernism: Brooker, *Bohemia in London*.
[64] Mairet, *Autobiographical Papers*, 184.   [65] Ibid. 181.   [66] Ibid. 181–2.
[67] For an exploration of common themes in the occult and psychoanalysis of the period: Owen, 'Occultism and the "Modern" Self in *Fin-de-Siecle* Britain', 71–96; Owen, *The Place of Enchantment*.
[68] For elaboration of Mitrinovic's complex system of thought: Rigby, *Initiation and Initiative*, 67–83.

Soon after the arrival of Ouspensky and Gurdjieff on the scene, Mitrinovic stopped writing his *New Age* column. Mairet suggests that he could not compete with the new challenge.[69] Instead, he turned his energies to launching a series of more broadly based movements that claimed an interest in changing the world, rather than simply changing the individual.[70] He argued that there was a limit to how long it was healthy for the master–pupil relationship to continue; and indeed a time came when serious moral problems emerged, when rather than being an initiation into life, study became an escape from life altogether. Now was the time to turn to more 'objective work under public auspices'.[71] Again, this points to a trajectory from the new age cultivation of self towards public engagement with the problems of industrial civilisation.

The first of these ventures was his key role in cultivating the Adlerian movement. Meeting Adler in Britain in 1926, he helped to found an English branch of the Adlerian International Society for Individual Psychology in 1927.[72] Mitrinovic was attracted because this estranged disciple of Freud was less concerned with mining the depths of the unconscious than either Freud or Jung and was more interested in what the individual could consciously do to change himself and thereby the world. To someone with such a broad-ranging synthetic mind, its emphasis on the whole individual was also attractive.[73] The Adler Society was very active in London until 1932, meeting most nights at its premises at 55 Gower Street, and with sections on education, sociology, philosophy, arts and crafts, music, eurythmics, and medicine, and also a man's group and woman's group: a range of activities indicative of its outward-looking inclinations. Although all the work on popularisation to date has concentrated on Freud, it has been said that there was as much 'head knowledge' of Adler's ideas in Bloomsbury as in half of Vienna.[74] The turning of an interest into a movement owed much to Mitrinovic's own force of personality.

Tensions would arise over the politicisation of what some saw as a medical issue. The movement had close links and overlapping membership with the Chandos Group, set up in response to the General Strike and publishing reports on social and economic issues of the day. Their *Coal: A Challenge to the National Conscience* of 1927 was an attempt to grapple with one of the central industrial and social issues of the day, merging economic argument and psychology in its Adlerian emphasis on the need for a will to power and for individual responsibility. Despite the Medical Section's own concern with broader issues, such obvious political association, let alone the challenge to medical control over psychological therapy implicit in the broad remit of the Society, led to separation in 1930. Adler, too, was increasingly concerned and saw dissociation from such currents as a necessity if he was to protect his followers elsewhere in Europe from charges of political association.[75] Nevertheless, the dialogue between Adlerian psychology

---

[69] Mairet, *Autobiographical Papers*, 187–9.   [70] Ibid. 190, 133–4.   [71] Ibid. 131–2.
[72] Bottome, *Adler*, 287–8.   [73] Rigby, *Initiation and Initiative*, 87.
[74] Bottome, *Adler*, 289.   [75] Ibid. 94–8.

and the sense of crisis in the social, economic, and political situation would continue through the 1930s, with Mitrinovic taking an active role. The journal *Purpose*, founded in 1929, acted as a forum for exploring this relationship. In its first year, it would carry regular contributions from Mitrinovic, but also Chandos Group members and Adlerians Alan Porter, W. T. Symons, and Philip Mairet.[76] Rescuing the individual through psychology was the counterpart to rescuing the economy through Social Credit. An economics based on Marx was criticised as no longer sufficient: it did not foresee the new economy of abundance; and it had not had the opportunity to integrate the insights of the new psychology. Major Douglas, the central theoretician of Social Credit, provided an economic parallel to Adler's individual psychology in that the drive for power over others—in this case, the financiers' control over credit—came to be recognised as a central and neurotic feature of the economic situation. The solution lay, not in redistributing wealth under the current system, but in transforming the financial system altogether and nationalising credit. Again, this found support from an Adlerian perspective, for simply to attack wealth was to evade personal responsibility and did nothing to challenge the more fundamental underlying problem of the inferiority complex of the working class; this indeed was the persistent strategic mistake of the Labour movement. Individual Psychology and Social Credit both looked to end a neurotic struggle for egoistical safety by supplying social safety, but in so doing they saw a place within socialism for an 'aristocracy' of true individual self-fulfilment. The real issue was to bring the situation into consciousness and to cancel it: Adler did this through individual psychology; Douglas promised this through his campaign for Social Credit; and both in this sense offered a psychological solution.[77]

In the 1930s, Mitrinovic would launch a further series of linked, phoenix-like movements to bring together his vision of personal development and a new world order, now presenting the transformation of the individual as an alternative to the current struggle between fascism and communism.[78] In 1931, he founded the Eleventh Hour Flying Club movement, which supported European federation and the establishment of clubs around the country. The same year also saw the founding of the Women's Guild for Human Order. The most successful was the New Britain movement, emerging out of these existing organisations but officially launched on Empire Day, 24th May 1933. His adoption of the nationalist banner reflected recognition of its populist appeal but also went back to his vision of

---

[76] Porter, described as a poet and psychologist in Hughes' account of Social Credit, left Britain for the United States after the publication of the Group's *Coal* study. Symons had also acted as Treasurer of the *New Age* between 1923 and 1934. Other Social Credit intellectuals such as Maurice Reckitt would look to Anglo-Catholicism for a vision of the human and spiritual to set alongside their economics: Hughes, *Major Douglas*, 60–70.

[77] W. T. Symons, 'Marx's Succession in Economics and Psychology', *Purpose*, 1/ 3 (1929), 117–23.

[78] Attracting little attention from historians, its significance has however been highlighted in L. Passerini, *Europe in Love, Love in Europe: Imagination and Politics in Britain between the Wars* (London, 1999), 131.

bringing East and West together and his view that the British Empire was thereby
of fundamental importance. This is a vision that, rather, strikingly, does not
conform to the conventional picture of a comfortable, introverted, and backwards-
looking national identity in the period.[79] It was a vision of the new nation, a nation
that would find itself by looking beyond, not only to Empire, but also to its position within Europe. With financial aid from the wealthy daughter of a millionaire
manufacturer behind it, the movement launched a glossy weekly, boldly illustrated,
with futurist design sitting happily alongside photographic imagery of an Ancient
and Eastern past that was now being excavated as part of the subconscious mind
of the present. Claimed sales rapidly reached 32,000 (far surpassing publications
like the *New Age* of course); and lest the readership doubted this, Mitrinovic publi-
cised that such figures had official certification behind them.[80] Within two
months, there were already 57 groups around the country, and by November 1933,
groups existed in 47 towns with a further 30 across London.[81] The newly founded
group in Rugby, to take just one example, had its own office, with members taking
a 100 copies of the *New Britain*, selling a further 250, and hoping in future to hand
out free copies to the unemployed.[82] Bearing in mind the scale of the movement,
and its relevance for a longstanding historiography on interwar, fringe political
movements and a more recent interest in Englishness and Britishness, the absence of
the New Britain phenomenon in these existing scholarships is surprising. Perhaps
part of the problem is that its ideas appear so odd set against the conventional political landscape of left and right, and more fundamentally that it fits the conventional remit of neither the political nor the cultural movement.[83] Indeed, there was
a fundamental tension about whether the priority was political or personal and
spiritual development. Rapid success meant that some wanted to turn this into an
organised mass movement. However, Mitrinovic opposed such a development and
returned to his cultivation of a smaller elite until these activities were disrupted by
the outbreak of war.[84]

Perhaps historians have also neglected the movement because they have not been
interested in the frame of psychological subjectivity that can help make sense

---

[79] M. Wiener, *English Culture and the Decline of the Industrial Spirit, 1850–1950* (Cambridge,
1981); R. Colls and P. Dodd (eds.), *Englishness: Politics and Culture, 1880–1920* (London, 1986).
There has been a recent move to pay more attention to the relationship with Empire and wider world
in the imagining of the nation, indicated for instance in the new account by one of the editors of these
books: R. Colls, *Identity of England* (Oxford, 2002). The European dimension is mainly a focus of
studies on post-war Britain, where the post-imperial context is also prominent; though as often as not
these are seen as cosmopolitan threats resisted by a still predominantly inward-looking nation:
C. Waters, ' "Dark Strangers" in Our Midst: Discourses of Race and Nation in Britain, 1947–1963',
Journal of British Studies, 36 (1997), 207–38.   [80] *New Britain*, (21 June 1933), 287.
[81] Rigby, *Initiation and Initiative*, 116–22.
[82] 'News of the groups', *New Britain* (21 June 1933), 160.
[83] For a study that breaks away from such parameters and notes the significance of an engagement
with psychology, though includes only a passing mention of the New Britain movement:
P. Coupland, 'Voices from Nowhere: Utopianism in British Political Culture 1929–1945', Ph.D.
thesis (University of Warwick, 2000), 65–8.   [84] Rigby, *Initiation and Initiative*, 125.

of it.[85] Recollections suggest that this was a central issue among followers. Drawn into the New Britain movement in the early 1930s, socialist and former miner D. R. Davies recalled it not only as containing many 'psychoanalysts' both professional and amateur, but as being an environment in which one 'lived psychoanalysis'.[86] No doubt, he was using the term very loosely, as was common at the time. Adler continued to be an important influence. Freud and Jung were also part of the landscape, albeit with their individualist limitation emphasised. Lesser known figures stood alongside them, like the American Trigant Burrow, author of *The Social Basis of Consciousness*, and Georg Groddeck, author of *The Book of the It*.[87] The idea of personality being under threat in the age of mass man was at the very heart of the movement. Personal Alliance, centring on a kind of group therapy system aiming at a 'socialized consciousness', was to be at the core of members' day-to-day life.[88] Groups of six or seven would sit together in three to four hour sessions, 'truth speaking' about themselves, criticising one another, destroying and then putting back together each others' personalities, sometimes subjected to public analysis and humiliation by Mitrinovic. Looking back on his own youthful involvement, Alan Watts, new age guru of the second half of the century, would recognise it as a precursor to the later vogue for encounter groups.[89] Davies's memoir is far less sympathetic. Coming to see Personal Alliance, like psychoanalysis, as imprisoning people in self-obsession, he would reject it for Marxism.[90] However, he acknowledged that Mitrinovic's ambitions had been broader. The problem was that the vision of a socialised consciousness was ultimately impossible, and in practice it struggled to get beyond the painful psychodrama of 'group work'.[91]

It is harder to establish whether the centrality of psychology in the London-based circle around Mitrinovic extended to the movement across the country. Some indication comes in the New Britain journal, variously going under the titles from 1932 to 1934 of *The New Atlantis, New Albion*, and *New Britain*. Initially, it was published as a quarterly, but from June 1933 it came out weekly at just 2 *d.*, and this low price must have facilitated the expansion of readership. If one is looking for the dissemination of orthodox psychology, then one would have to conclude that the journals reveal some interest, but still a rather marginal one. If, however, it is recognised that the problem of psychological subjectivity was addressed through the language of personality and human-ness, then it emerges as a far more central preoccupation. National identity provided an opportunity to extend the appeal of a politics centred on personality far beyond Mitrinovic's own circle. The West, Europe in particular, was the 'Civilisation of Personality', though one in crisis. The 'New Albion' in the

[85] This is, however, part of what has drawn Passerini to the subject: *Europe in Love*. Rigby's main interest is in relation to questions of international relations: *Initiation and Initiative*.

[86] D. R. Davies, *In Search of Myself: The Autobiography of D. R. Davies* (London, 1961), 130.

[87] Rigby, *Initiation and Initiative*, 159. Adler Society lectures were also advertised, for instance *New Britain: Quarterly Organ of the XIth Hour Group*, 1/1 (Oct. 1932), inside back cover.

[88] Davies, *In Search of Myself*, 130–4, 139–40; Watts, *In My Own Way*, 111.

[89] Watts, *In my Own Way*, 111.   [90] Davies, *In Search of Myself*, 139–145.

[91] Ibid. 140–1.

form of the giant Britain of Empire was the key to rebirth, the 'giant nation of indi-
viduation and self-presence'.[92] Psychology was important, not just because of a new
understanding since the start of the century, but because consciousness had changed
under new conditions.[93] In the context of unemployment and economic stagnation
alongside prosperity and the expansion of leisure, the problem of industrial civilisation was being reframed as one of adjusting to a world in which work would be less
central.[94] There were huge opportunities to channel human energies in other
directions—towards culture in particular (the movement continuing that bringing
together of a political, individual, and artistic project begun in the *New Age* itself).
Indeed, the psychological problem of achieving a reorientation of will from work to
culture lay at the very heart of what was seen by so many as a crisis for industrial civilisation. Indicative of the way that an issue such as this could be used to reach out to a
broader constituency, links were forged with the 'Society of Good Companions', an
organisation of clubs for the unemployed, aiming to help themselves with
Mitrinovic-like inner circles which promoted the study of human nature and codes
of conduct on the 'Road of Life'.[95] The falling birth rate led to a similar reorientation
when it came to the politics of reproduction, with a case emerging for seeing the will
to sex, and thus culture and erotics, rather than mere biology, as the crucial eugenic
issue of the day.[96] We also see some intriguing contributions in Mitrinovic's journals
from a new generation of political and cultural figures. There was a contribution
from filmmaker John Grierson. There was an advertisement for a lecture by psychoanalyst (and sister-in-law to Eder), Barbara Low, on 'Psychological Resistance to
Leisure and Plenty', suggesting parallels to the *New Britain* psychological exploration of the problems of industrial civilisation.[97] There was a contribution from
G. Scott Williamson, inspiration behind the modernist Peckham Health Centre.[98]
Even a young Harold Macmillan made an appearance.[99]

NICOLL AND THE PSYCHO-SPIRITUAL PATH

Like Eder and Young, Maurice Nicoll trained in medicine but maintained
broader literary and intellectual ambitions that brought him into the *New Age*
orbit. Unlike his fellow doctors, whose trajectory after the *New Age* was one of

[92] 'The Sacred Duty and Right of Albion', *New Albion*, 1 (April 1934), 1.

[93] 'Psychology in Politics', *New Britain* (16 Aug. 1933), 389.

[94] For instance, Philip Mairet, 'The Cultural Integrity of the State', *New Britain*, 1/2 (Jan.–March 1932), 36–7.

[95] There were 32 of these clubs reported in 1933: T. Ernest Jackson, 'How the Unemployed are Helping Themselves', *New Britain*, 1 (14 June 1933), 126.

[96] Mairet, 'Cultural Integrity of the State'; also Robb, in H. L. Beales and R. S. Lambert (eds.), *I was One of the Unemployed* (London, 1934), 271–85.

[97] Inside back cover of *New Britain Quarterly*, 1/1 (Oct. 1932).

[98] G. Scott Williamson, 'The Scientist's Outlook', *New Britain Quarterly*, 1/2 (Jan.–March 1933), 44–6.   [99] Hughes, *Major Douglas*, 93–4.

exploring the relationship between psychology, the self, and the social world, Nicoll forged a more psycho-spiritual path. Born in 1884, he had gone into medical training alongside Kenneth Walker, who would also be associated with the *New Age* circle and who would take a similar subsequent medico-mystical route. Finding his duties light in his first practice, he took on supplementary work at Bowden House, one of the first medically-run psychotherapeutic clinics in the country, under the leadership of Dr Hugh Crichton Miller who would go on to set up the renowned Tavistock Clinic after the War.[100] With his appetite whetted, he travelled to Zurich in 1914 to meet Jung. A letter home to his parents recorded this as a sort of conversion experience. 'I have not the slightest doubt of the value of this line of work I am in', he wrote to his father, a former Free Church minister:

In fact, it is such a very extraordinary thing, so completely remarkable and curious that one finds it difficult to talk about and quite impossible to explain. It is an experience and not a teachable thing. For it ever to be accepted, either generally or popularly, would mean a complete social turnabout. But to me it seems a thing well worth devoting one's life to, whatever comment is made about the work. And I believe privately that it holds in some way that one cannot clearly see yet the key to the solution of a host of troubles that we comfortably think 'will always be with us'. I mean that out of it will arise that impulse that will give a universal newness as the impulse of Christianity gave a universal newness. And it is precisely because it is the last place that a man would look for such an impulse, because it is exactly where one would pour scorn and ridicule on such a possibility, that I feel confidence in the significance of it. So much for my confession of faith.[101]

Jung would also lead him to an interest in dreams, and in his *Dream Psychology* of 1917 he would present Jung as the successor in understanding of mind to Freud.[102] He also became increasingly dissatisfied with Crichton Miller's use of hypnotism as well as the sanatorium-like role of Bowden House, the First World War providing him with the opportunity to break free from this approach in his treatment of officers suffering from shellshock.[103] Here, the war may have not have been the spark for new ideas it is sometimes presented as being, but it was an important catalyst for the development of practice, and by 1918 Nicoll felt emboldened to announce that 'the orthodox medical reactionaries have been smashed and psychology has been born'.[104]

After the War, Nicoll shared a practice at 146 Harley Street with James Carruthers Young. Along with Young, he was drawn into Orage's discussion group on psychology, and he also had literary reasons for links to the *New Age*, writing a series of novels under the pseudonym of Martin Swayne. One of these books in particular, *The Blue Germ* of 1918, provided an alternative platform for thinking about the psychological subject, centring as it did on the psychological problems

[100] See pp. 186–8.   [101] B. Pogson, *Maurice Nicoll: A Portrait* (London, 1961), 22–3.
[102] As announced in the preface: Pogson, *Nicoll*, 51–2.   [103] Ibid. 50.
[104] Letter to his father, ibid. 57–8.

raised by the invention of a germ that killed all others in the body and in the process effectively eradicated death but also desire. Between 1920 and 1921, he was in close contact with Jung and attended his summer school at Sennen Cove in Cornwall.[105] However this tie was broken after he heard Ouspensky talk in the autumn of 1921. The seriousness of this new conversion is apparent in his decision to move with his wife and young baby to Gurdjieff's Fontainebleau Institute.[106] On his return to England, he rejoined the Ouspensky circle but also returned to his Harley Street practice where he integrated the insights of Ouspensky's 'System' into his own psychotherapeutic practice. In 1931, Ouspensky would publish his most influential book, *A New Model of the Universe*, which had at its centre his psychological method.[107] The book attracted considerable attention and Ouspensky began to recruit in droves. As a later reviewer recalled:

For quite a lot of people the years before Hitler's war were still dominated, not by the new Oxford communist poets, but by Central European mystagogues . . . In many a Garden Suburb sitting-room, beside the nature cure pamphlets and the outlines of Adlerian psychology, lay a copy of *Tertium Organum* or *A New Model of the Universe*. People were bent on awakening their higher centres, emerging from the prison of mechanicalness, being at One with the One, achieving synthesis and breathing correctly.[108]

Under Ouspensky's guidance, Nicoll emerged as a psycho-spiritual teacher, authorised to teach the 'System', with his group of followers, and own places of retreat, but also continuing to practice as a psychotherapist; indeed, the two roles were impossible to separate. He would be particularly valued both for his analysis of Christian values and his fundamental goodness in person. In his later life, he would publish a series of books that applied psychological and mystical insight to study of the Gospels.[109]

---

[105] As with Adler's visits, one is struck here by the fact that Britain was not as intellectually isolated as it sometimes appears in accounts of the period; but in breaking down such isolation there is a story to tell of the translation of ideas into a British idiom.   [106] Pogson, *Nicoll*, 61–77.

[107] Webb, *Harmonious Circle*, 393–411.

[108] Rayner Heppenstall reviewing Ouspensky's *The Fourth Way* in the *New Statesman*, cited in Webb, *Harmonious Circle*, 400. In relation to the contrast with the 'communist poets', Ouspensky as a Russian émigré was virulently anti-Soviet and demanded that his followers steered clear of association with political parties (a contrast to the Mitrinovic route). He prevented his other main lieutenant, J. G. Bennett, from taking up Labour Party leader Ramsay MacDonald's invitation to sit for a seat in Parliament. For more on the fascinating figure who had earlier been a spy for the British government in the Near East, and whose role in industrial research on fuel efficiency in the Second World War indicates another intriguing link between mysticism and the problems of industrial civilisation: J. G. Bennett, *Witness: The Autobiography of John G. Bennett* (London, 1974). Buchan, as already mentioned, would draw on Ouspensky in his portrayal of Professor Moe. He was also probably an influence on Aldous Huxley's portrayal of Mr Propter in *After Many a Summer* (London, 1939). Among his illustrious followers was Mrs Bernard Shaw and he was an influence on J. B. Priestley's explorations of ideas of time: Webb, *Harmonious Circle*, 400–3.

[109] Pogson, *Nicoll*, 92–108. At that date, there was still great secrecy about Gurdjieff's method. A prohibition on publication was not removed until 1949.

WALKER AND THE MEDICO-MYSTICAL PATH

Though Kenneth Walker did not follow Nicoll in becoming a kind of guru in his own right, his own 'venture with ideas' would mirror the way that psychological medicine and mysticism could be brought together.[110] Walker does not appear to have been present in the initial *New Age* psychoanalytic circle, but he followed his friend Nicoll's recommendation to come to one of Ouspensky's early lectures. Expecting to find a mystic, he was surprised to find what seemed more like a scientist, a good deal of common sense, and in fact something rather akin to the behaviourist psychology that was so in vogue in the United States. What also surprised him was that he had expected the audience to be looking for solace and some kind of comforting substitute for religion; what they received instead was a lack of directive teaching, a system challenging and even disturbing in the questions it forced individuals to ask about their own psychological subjectivity.[111] He was not alone in being struck by the rational style and absence of occult trappings: the audience saw in Ouspensky, with his model of different states of consciousness, another Freud.[112] Like Young, Alcock, and Nicoll, Walker was attracted as a doctor, both by the promise of practical therapeutic tools, and by the idea that negative emotions played a key part in the vast swathe of physical illness that showed no sign of fading away despite advances in biomedicine.[113] There was also a more personal attraction, with Walker for instance finding that the psychological principles of Ouspensky's system helped him conquer the debilitating problem of worry in his own everyday life.[114] Just as in the popular psychological movements of the period, such practical benefits were vital in the appeal and sheer excitement that surrounded psychology. It was the fact that psychology confirmed common sense that could be its greatest asset; the esoteric presentation obscured this, and was of secondary importance. Like Nicoll, Walker would remain a medical ally of Ouspensky and a visitor to his schools at Hayes and then Virginia Water throughout the interwar period. When the War, the split with Madame Ouspensky, and then the death of Ouspensky himself soon after his return to England following a wartime sojourn in the United States, broke the movement up, Walker was on hand to pick up some of the pieces as a key figure in setting up the Historico-Psychological Society.[115] Nicoll, too, would come to the fore in his own right. In the 1950s, he had an estimated six-hundred followers, who made pilgrimages to study at his Great Anwell House in Hertfordshire as others had come to the retreats of Ouspensky and Gurdjieff before the War.[116]

---

[110] The title of his memoir: *Venture with Ideas* (London, 1951). [111] Ibid. 15–28.
[112] Ibid. 50–1.
[113] Ibid. 35–6. M. Thomson, 'Neurasthenia in Britain', in M. Gijswijt-Hofstra and R. Porter (eds.), *Cultures of Neurasthenia: From Beard to the First World War* (Amsterdam, 2001), 77–96.
[114] Walker, *Venture with Ideas*, 90.
[115] Ibid. 99–136; Webb estimates about 300 followers: *Harmonious Circle*, 448.
[116] Webb, *Harmonious Circle*, 448.

EDER AND THE FREUDIAN PATH

Dr David Montague Eder provides us with a final Freudian route beyond the *New Age*. The fact that this was just one of a range of trajectories for the rethinking of the psychological subject in such intellectual circles is one of the central points of this chapter. Even Eder strayed from the path on the way, with Freud an end-point and development out of a series of earlier guides. Born in 1866, he was of a generation, as in the case of Orage, where this was always likely to be the case. In Eder's case, before Freud and alongside a medicine that, as in the other cases surveyed here, failed to excite, came literature, alongside cousin Israel Zangwill; the socialism of William Morris; anarchist Prince Kropotkin's call for a new politics of individual self-development; and a projection of New Life politics into a series of adventures overseas, where his search for places of settlement on the behalf of the Jewish Territorial Organisation would provide subsequent inspiration for his friend D. H. Lawrence's vision of 'Renamin' away from the repression and decay of old world England.[117] Alertness to Freud came on his return, via his friendship with Ernest Jones between 1904 and 1908.[118] It was also encouraged by his work in the emerging system of clinics for working-class schoolchildren.[119] His public expressions on childhood sexuality would court considerable controversy with much of the initial British reception of Freud descending into acrimony over what was regarded as gross exaggeration of the importance of sex to psychology.[120] The *New Age* provided a more conducive audience. The new psychology fitted in within Eder's circle in Hampstead Garden Suburb, alongside divorce (his own and remarriage to Edith, sister of Barbara Low, the future psychoanalyst, in 1909), sexual freedom (Edith having an affair with H. G. Wells), and a politics of individual self-realisation expressed through what one ate (vegetables), what one wore (flat heels and hatless), and how one moved; all countering the statist socialism of the Fabians.[121] By the outbreak of the War, Eder had met Jung and Freud, set up his own psychoanalytic clinic, translated Freud's work on dreams, and helped found the London Psycho-Analytic Society.[122] A key figure in setting up the institutional framework for psychoanalysis in Britain, he was also very important as a conduit into one of the most fashionable, metropolitan, intellectual circles of the day. Therefore, when the members of the *New Age* circle made their various

---

[117] Thomson, 'Psychology in Socialism'.

[118] T. G. Davies, *Ernest Jones, 1879–1958* (Cardiff, 1979), 29.

[119] C. Steedman, *Childhood, Culture and Class: Margaret McMillan, 1860–1931* (London, 1990).

[120] Hobman, *Eder*, 94.

[121] For the Hampstead Garden Suburb context: B. Maddox, *The Married Man: A History of D. H. Lawrence* (London, 1994), 197. For the socialist context: S. Yeo, 'Notes on Three Socialisms—Collectivism, Statism and Associationism—Mainly in Late-Nineteenth- and Early-Twentieth-Century Britain', in C. Levy (ed.), *Socialism and the Intelligentsia, 1880–1914* (London, 1974), 219–70; S. Yeo, 'The Religion of Socialism in Britain, 1883–1896', *History Workshop Journal*, 4 (1977), 5–56.

[122] C. G. Jung, *Studies in Word Association*, tr. M. D. Eder (London, 1918); Hobman, *Eder*, 94–8.

choices about the way forward in the early 1920s, it was not through any lack of a Freudian option. The intriguing thing, then, is the rejection of Freud and the enthusiasm for parallel paths. Perhaps it is significant that although Eder is recorded as being involved in the discussions, for most of the period 1918–1922 he was tied up in involvement in Palestine.[123] We also need to bear in mind that he was increasingly interested in Jung and that this open-mindedness became unacceptable to Ernest Jones who dissolved the London Psycho-Analytic Society and replaced it with the British Psycho-Analytic Society in 1919, leaving Eder in isolation.[124] It was therefore as something of a free spirit that Eder would arrive to hear Ouspensky.

Eder would become reconciled to the Freudian path by 1923. But, now an ageing man, and with broader political interests and commitments, his role in the heated interwar institutional politics of psychoanalysis would become less central.[125] With respect to the focus of this chapter, two features of his subsequent career are particularly significant. The first is the way that people would come to remember him in terms and images not so very far removed from the guru or sage. His position as the senior citizen in the new psychoanalytic world, his huge range of interests, his experience of travel, and his exotic Jewish origins may all have contributed to this. So too did the fact that, like the more mystical gurus of the era, he was seen as physically embodying and projecting to all who came into contact with him a wisdom about the self. In his case, this was an embodiment of genuine humanity and warmth—the spirit as it were of socialism—that contrasts to the more authoritarian and intimidating personal power of someone like Mitrinovic. Novelist Dorothy Richardson described him as literally radiating warmth and light.[126] Writer Ethel Mannin argued that Eder's wisdom went far beyond mere psychoanalysis, so much so that she had come to 'believe in David Eder as some people believe in God'.[127] Even psychoanalyst Edward Glover saw him as someone who had gained a rather unique inner serenity through psychoanalytic resolution of inner conflict.[128] Like the guru, he appears to have attained a meaning that transcended his own individual identity: in his apparent radiation of goodness and wisdom, he emerged as a symbol and prophecy of how the lessons of experience, socialism, and psychoanalysis might become naturalised, embedded in the self.

The second feature of his post-war career deserving particular attention in the context of this chapter is an increasing engagement in relating a psychology of the individual to the political and economic. What one sees in a series of essays over the next decade is not crude justification of his own beliefs through psychoanalysis, but instead an exploration of how psychoanalysis might lead to a rethinking of some of the essential categories of political ideology, political practice, and

---

[123] Hobman, *Eder*, 133–96.   [124] Brome, *Ernest Jones*, 121.
[125] Hobman, *Eder*, 100.   [126] Ibid. 16.
[127] E. Mannin, *Confessions and Impressions* (London, 1930), 223.   [128] Hobman, *Eder*, 104.

economics.[129] Again, the parallel to the guru's search for a path that lay beyond mere conventional politics is striking. Disillusionment with what had happened to the Labour movement, encouraged this reorientation, so too did economic crisis at the end of the 1920s, and before his death in 1936 the rise of the dictators would provide further reason. Progress—even in the form of socialism—emerged as a myth and psychological balm used by man to make sense of a life and world otherwise out of control. Eder put it starkly, in a manner that would shock his contemporaries:

We are born mad, acquire morality and become stupid and unhappy. Then we die. This, the natural history of man under domestication, is so rigid a sequence under a variety of forms and changes in the patterns of civilisation, that mankind has invariably found it helpful to find a refuge in myths to mitigate its unhappiness.[130]

With the advantage of so much more experience of politics and social deprivation behind him compared to the younger generation of Freudians, Eder was a pioneer in turning psychoanalysis in such directions. The mounting pessimism about human nature provoked by the international crisis would soon bring the psychoanalytic approach into the arena of the political in a way that the problems of industrial civilisation had earlier struggled to do.[131]

THE SEXUAL PATH

The psychoanalytic frame also tends to be associated with a preoccupation with sex and gender. In fact, neither theme attracted the central attention that one might have expected when it comes to the figures at the heart of this chapter. This is an appropriate place to comment on both issues. The main actors in the story have all been men. Women have been largely absent, appearing mainly in supporting roles such on that of the hostess, benefactor, or disciple. This has been no coincidence. With the exceptions of Madame Blavatsky and Madame Ouspensky, who both brought the added allure of an exotic foreignness, the guru had an almost exclusively male identity. With their charisma and supposed ability to project a natural truth about the self, these gurus also emerged as symbols of a new sort of masculinity among their followers. It is difficult to tell whether men also predominated when it came to followers. In the absence of any comment on this, and with both male and female disciples in evidence, it would be fairest to assume

[129] M. D. Eder, 'Psycho-Analysis and Politics', in E. Jones (ed.), *Social Aspects of Psycho-Analysis: Lectures Delivered under the Auspices of the Sociological Society* (London, 1924); M. D. Eder, 'On the Economics and the Future of the Super-Ego', *International Journal of Psycho-Analysis*, 10 (1929), 249–55; M. D. Eder, 'Psychology and Value', *British Journal of Medical Psychology*, 10 (1930), 175–85.
[130] M. D. Eder, 'The Myth of Progress', *British Journal of Medical Psychology*, 12 (1932), 1. For the contemporary response: Hobman (ed.), *Eder*, 30. Eder was influenced by Freud's *Civilisation and its Discontents*, published in England in 1930.   [131] See Ch. 7.

that the mix of the sexes was at least not grossly unequal.[132] This is not, however, to say that the sexes received equal treatment. The existence of separate groups for men and women in the Adlerian movement and then under Mitrinovic in the 1930s reflected belief that there were fundamental psychological differences between the sexes, and a desire to foster this in self-realisation.[133] This was not simply the path taken by conservative, male-led organisations. A stream of feminism in this era also turned to psychology as a way to emphasise the special qualities of its sex.[134] This is not to say that through psychology gender divisions necessarily sharpened in the aftermath of the Great War.[135] In fact, such thinking could exist alongside and interact in quite complex ways with a recently emphasised mutualism that downplayed difference.[136] Perhaps most significant, however, is the relatively marginal overall position of the issue of gender in the movements considered here.

When it came to the issue of sex, despite the fact that this was undoubtedly a significant period for the breaking of silences in advice literature, much of it led by doctors with an interest in psychology, popular ignorance and reticence remained a constraining factor.[137] Even the psychoanalysts in interwar Britain tended to downplay Freud's views on sex, some like Hadfield emphasising the compatibility with a new morality, and others shifting the focus to love and attachment.[138] Within the type of intellectual terrain surveyed in this chapter, there was another type of moralisation of sex, and this would spill over into what some have dismissed as the mystical side of an influential advice-writer on sex like Marie Stopes.[139] Here one would need to turn to figures like Edward Carpenter, Ouspensky, who would

[132] Dixon's study of the related Theosophical Society of England provides a picture of declining membership but of the majority of new members being women: *Divine Feminine*, 228.

[133] For brief mention of these groups: Rigby, *Initiation and Initiative*, 91, 103. Mitrinovic felt that modern life was distorting the male/female distinction and within his New Britain movement looked to set up a separate 'Senate' for women so as to benefit from their 'life-preserving' qualities: ibid. 158. On psychological differences between the sexes: A. T. Schofield, *The Mind of a Woman* (London, 1919); B. Kidd, *The Science of Power* (London, 1918).

[134] 'A Plea for Psychology', *The Freewoman*, 1 (1912), 181–2; J. M. Kennedy, 'The Psychology of Sex', *The Freewoman*, 1 (1911), 14–15. My thanks to Lucy Delap for these references, and see her article 'The Superwoman: Theories of Gender and Genius in Edwardian Britain', *Historical Journal*, 47 (2004), 101–26.

[135] As argued in S. K. Kent, *Making Peace: The Reconstruction of Gender in Interwar Britain* (Princeton, 1993).

[136] M. Collins, *Modern Love: An Intimate History of Men and Women in Twentieth-Century Britain* (London, 2003).

[137] Cook, *Long Sexual Revolution*, 167–8.

[138] Hadfield, *Psychology and Morals*. Also important in this respect was Suttie, *Origins of Love and Hate*. See pp. 71–2. Note the low profile of sex in what was one of the more significant early attempts at explaining psychoanalysis to the public, with the subject hidden away as a brief aside: B. Low, *Psychoanalysis: A Brief Account of the Freudian Theory* (London, 1920), 96–103. By contrast, see the ways in which she could speak in a language that appealed to the constituencies explored in this chapter, with psychoanalysis presented as 'harmonizing . . . psychic life' (p. 38); demonstrating 'the unity and continuity of all mental life' (p. 39); implying a 'creative force' akin to Bergson's *élan vital* (p. 44); and producing new individuals (p. 159).

[139] For instance, 'When two who are mated in every respect burn with the fire of the innumerable forces within them, which set their bodies longing towards each other with the desire to

write in a similar vein to Carpenter in his *Model of the Universe*, or the writing on
sex and mysticism of Kenneth Walker.[140] Such writers brought sex into the open,
not simply by emphasising the pathological consequences of not doing so, and not
by argument centred on selfish pleasure, but by presenting it as a key route to transcendence of individual consciousness and an outlet for the creative energies that
were central to the progress of civilisation. In the ecstasy of sex, the individual mind
could become at one with the sensations of the body, at one with another human
being, and ultimately at one with the consciousness of the race. Sex played a role,
like some of the other practical techniques explored in this chapter, in escaping the
limiting constraints of everyday consciousness. It became as much a mental and
spiritual act as a biological one and this moralised the separation of sex and reproduction that was a key challenge for this generation.[141] The implications of this
vision of sex were not altogether clear for gender. The emphasis on transcending
the individual mind and body could point to the ephemeral nature of individually

interpenetrate and to encompass one another, the fusion of joy and rapture is not purely physical. The
half swooning sense of flux which overtakes the spirit in that eternal moment at the apex of rapture
sweeps into its flaming tides the whole essence of the man and woman, and as it were the heat of the
contact vapourises their consciousness so that it fills the whole cosmic space. For the moment they are
identified with the divine thoughts, the waves of eternal force, which to the mystic often appear in
terms of golden light': M. Stopes, *Married Love* (London, 1918), 130. Historians have tended to note
such mysticism but have rarely paid it serious attention. See, for instance, J. Weeks, *Sex, Politics and
Society: The Regulation of Sexuality since 1800* (London, 1981), 148–9. Though, note the attention to
'psychic love' in work on feminism: L. Bland, *Banishing the Beast: English Feminism and Sexual
Morality, 1885–1914* (London, 1995), 267–96. The importance of the mystical in the popularity of
Married Love is suggested in A. C. T. Geppert, 'Divine Sex, Happy Marriage, Regenerated Nation:
Marie Stopes's Marital Manual *Married Love* and the Making of a Best-Seller, 1918–1955', *Journal of
the History of Sexuality*, 8 (1988), 433.

[140] It is recognised that sex is likely to have been downplayed in the memoir material. Carpenter
was of a slightly older generation than the gurus in this chapter, however he was a key influence on
radical opinion at the start of the period. His works would continue to sell in the interwar years and
he would be an important influence on writers such as Marie Stopes and D. H. Lawrence:
E. Devaleny, *D. H. Lawrence and Edward Carpenter: A Study in Edwardian Transition* (London, 1971).
Historians have tended to avoid serious consideration of the 'mystical' side of Carpenter. It is seen as
something of a distraction and embarrassment by those more interested in his role within socialism.
For instance, C. Tsuzuki, *Edward Carpenter, 1844–1929: Prophet of Human Fellowship* (Cambridge,
1980). Even a study that focuses on Carpenter's (and Havelock Ellis's) contribution to sex reform
skirts over the 'mysticism': S. Rowbotham and J. Weeks, *Socialism and the New Life: The Personal and
Sexual Politics of Edward Carpenter and Havelock Ellis* (London, 1977). For an account that considers
this side of Carpenter more seriously: S. Pierson, 'Edward Carpenter, Prophet of a Socialist
Millennium', *Victorian Studies*, 13 (1970), 301–18. Particularly relevant are Carpenter's *The Art of
Creation: Essays on the Self and its Powers* (London, 1904); and his *The Drama of Love and Death*
(London, 1912). Carpenter is a seminal figure in Collins' account of a new mutualism: *Modern Love*,
1–4. The attraction of Havelock Ellis also owed something to a more mystical side of his writing:
Nottingham, *The Pursuit of Serenity*. On Walker: H. Cook, 'Sex and the Doctors: The Medicalization
of Sexuality as a Two-way Process in Early to Mid-Twentieth-Century Britain', in W. de Blécourt and
C. Usborne (eds.), *Cultural Approaches to the History of Medicine: Mediating Medicine in Early Modern
and Modern Europe* (Basingstoke, 2004), 201–2.

[141] This view of the essential challenge and the solution in a moralisation of sex is in sympathy
with two important recent accounts that focus on writing on sex rather than psychology: Collins,
Modern Love; Cook, *Long Sexual Revolution*. In both cases, there is an overlap with some of the figures
considered here and in Ch. 6.

bound categories of man and woman. In the hands of someone like Carpenter, it provided the opportunity to present a transcendence of sex as a necessary feature of attaining a higher consciousness, with the homosexual thereby presented as perhaps the most highly evolved of individuals in this respect.[142] However, in tending to make the act of heterosexual union central, and in the emphasis on becoming at one with the body and even a history of race identity embedded within, it could equally easily lend itself to reinforcing ideas about difference. In the end, these ideas could be taken in either direction.[143] Neither, however, was as important as, and both ultimately were reconcilable with, the attempt to give sex a profound meaning beyond mere individual pleasure.

CONCLUSION

It has been a central proposition of this chapter that the interest in Freud and psychoanalysis among the British intelligentsia in the first decades of the twentieth century, which has attracted considerable attention elsewhere, was just one of several paths in a broader and more eclectic excitement about exploring psychological subjectivity. Inspiration was as likely to come from Adler and Jung. It also came from Eastern mystics and broad-ranging synthesisers. Although the chapter has traced a number of different trajectories from the initial *New Age* circle, one of the things that becomes apparent is the common threads that connected these, in terms of people, but also ideas, broader ambitions, and practices. As often as not, the psychological message was one of improving alertness, developing personality, and exploring new levels of consciousness through practical mental techniques: messages and methods that overlapped those of the more populist movements considered in the first chapter of this book. What also distinguishes these psychotherapeutic routes is their interest in problems of an industrial civilisation. Invariably, they looked outwards from the individual to address social, economic, and political issues. However, since mass society was something to escape from and set oneself above through advanced or even secret psychological understanding, there was also often an inclination towards elitism.

Such ambivalence about the democratisation of knowledge limited the influence of such movements. Depending so fundamentally on the force of individual personality and personal networks, they were also prone to a process of generational attrition, as both gurus and their disciples aged, moved on, and died. Orage and Eder were both dead by the time war broke out. The memorial volume to Eder of 1945 marked out the profound impact he had on his peers, but also made it very

[142] Carpenter, *Art of Creation*, 101.
[143] The new understanding of hormones could also both emphasise the distinctiveness of the sexes, and blur it by pointing to the way that these crossed the sex barrier. For an overview of the impact on understanding: L. Hall and R. Porter (eds.), *The Facts of Life: The Creation of Sexual Knowledge in Britain, 1650–1950* (New Haven and London, 1995), 169–77.

clear that this rested to a large extent extent on force of personality. His name there-fore gains honorary mention as an early Freudian, but since 1945 there has been lit-tle serious historical study of his ideas and life in their own right. Orage, on the other hand, has attracted considerable interest, but this is because of his involve-ment in the *New Age*, with his engagement with psychological subjectivity largely ignored. Young was never in the same league in terms of influence and followers—he was more an observer at the scene, interesting for the way that he rejected the role of disciple—and thus the same question hardly applies. But we can ask what happened to the Adlerian engagment with the problems of industrial civilisation that he and so many others in this story supported. Perhaps Adler's own death in 1937 robbed this movement of its own inspiration, particularly important since his writing on its own was regarded as a pale imitation of the man; in contrast, for instance, to the power of Freud's written legacy. In the local British context, the death of Crookshank and then Mitrinovic's shift of energies removed two of the key catalysts of the early years. The ideas also lost their purchase as circumstances changed. People abandoned the economics of Social Credit because of the way that the War changed the problem. The same was true of the odd mix of psychology, mysticism, and politics that so often ran alongside such an economics. War and the social and economic reconstruction that followed made the interwar concerns about industrial civilisation far less pressing and set new problems and new solu-tions in their place. The War's resuscitation of the economy and the post-war boom, guided now by the Freudian John Maynard Keynes (looking in psychoana-lytic fashion to manage an economy of desire), promoted full employment, a more self-confident and socially secure working class, and seemed to suggest that the Labour movement and the state now had answers that had appeared lacking several decades earlier. The earlier Adlerian focus on the problem of the inferiority com-plex, on class as a problem, and on the importance of an individual will to power and independence from the state all now found themselves out of step with new social, economic, and political realities. Likewise, the interwar psychological drive towards the development of personality and resulting individual power, which had found its full realisation in the figureheads and leader cults of the movements, now found an ideologically unacceptable mirror image in the dictator.

There were some links into the post-war era. Following the disruptions of the War, Mitrinovic set up his Anti-Barbarus Renaissance Club, but he died in 1953, any remnants of a movement passing away with him.[144] The other post-war survivor, Maurice Nicoll, would die in 1952, his legacy stronger because of the significance of his writing and the continued life within the broader Gurdjieff movement, whose more individualist emphasis made it easier to transcend interwar concerns.[145] In the

[144] For details: http://www.hlss.mmu.ac.uk/pap/politics/nafl.htm. Mitrinovic's large collection of books and pamphlets passed to the J. B. Priestley Library at the University of Bradford. A listing offers some idea of his range of interests: http://www.bradford.ac.uk/library/ special/mitrinovic.php

[145] For instance, B. Hunter, 'Combining Good and Truth, Now: An Homage to Dr Maurice Nicoll', *Gurdjieff International Review*: http://www.gurdjieff.org/hunter1.htm. He is also a key reference point for the Enneagram movement: http://www.hurleydonson.com/nicoll.htm

figure of Gerald Heard, who had been at the early Ouspensky meetings and whose ideas could easily be fitted within the framework set out in the paper, there is a more direct bridge between the one new age and the other. Though in this case, as in that of Alan Watts noted earlier, or that of Aldous Huxley, a first new age in Britain, with its location within Empire perhaps helping to situate it as a crossroads between East and West, would be followed by a second at the new centre of exchange on the West Coast of the United States.[146] In the idea of psycho-social evolution as the basis for a new humanism, Huxley and his brother, the biologist Julian, would also continue to advance that moralisation of character, sex, and biology that had been a feature of the interwar scene.[147] Evolution of individual consciousness as the key both to understanding the history of man and to breaking into a new age was also central in Gerald Heard's post-war pronouncements.[148] As these direct linkages across time and place suggest, one should be wary about drawing too sharp a contrast between the ideas of one age and the other.[149] At the very least, this chapter hopes to have reminded us that our new age follows or emerges out of another, and that this even reaches down to specific practices such as the encounter group. However, it also suggests that some of the qualities of the first new age—its engagement with the problem of industrial civilisation, its fascination with will, personality, and consequently the guru, as highlighted here in particular—may mark it out as distinct from the more individualist, emotionally introspective emphasis in the second half of the century. The final chapter of the book will have more to say on this issue.

[146] A. Watts, *Psychotherapy East and West* (London, 1961), 9. Watts had published a book before the Second World War that looked in this direction: *The Legacy of Asian and Western Man* (London, 1937). As well as his involvement with Mitrinovic he had been active within the early British Buddhist movement. Geraldine Coster's bringing together of Yoga and Psychotherapy similarly indicates that this marriage had interwar roots: her *Psycho-Analysis for Normal People* was in its third edition by 1932. She saw great similarities between the new psychological approaches to the self and those drawn from older Eastern systems of thought: *Yoga and Western Psychology: A Comparison* (London, 1934). During this period, Coster was Principal of Wychwood School, Oxford, opening up the possibility of a rather different social constituency to that explored in this paper.

[147] J. Huxley (ed.), *The Humanist Frame* (London, 1961), including an essay from his stepbrother Aldous on 'Human Potentialities'; J. Huxley (ed.), *Essays of a Humanist* (London, 1964). The Catholic theologian, Pierre Teillard de Chardin was also influential in this respect. Julian Huxley would write the introduction to his book *The Phenomenon of Man* (London, 1959). This book was already in its 6th impression by October 1960. The novelist Michel Houellbecq has used Aldous and Julian Huxley as a counterpoint but in some ways a bridge from rational enlightenment thought to his story of the shallow nature of late twentieth-century new age culture: *Atomised* (London, 2001). My thanks to Rhodri Hayward for pointing this out.

[148] For instance, G. Heard, *The Five Ages of Man: The Psychology of Human History* (New York, 1963); G. Heard, *The Third Morality* (London, 1937).

[149] For indications of a continuity of interest in creating a dialogue between the psychology of the West and the wisdom of the East as a way to transcend the ideological polarities of Cold War culture: E. Graham Howe, *A Psychologist at Work* (London, 1952); H. V. Dicks, *Mental Health in the Light of Ancient Wisdom* (London, 1959). For further thoughts on the ideological challenge for mental health after the Second World War, see pp. 231–41.

PART II

PROBLEMS AND PROSPECTS

4

Psychology and Education

The first chapters of this book made a case for reframing the prevailing view of lack of interest in and the backwardness of psychology in early-twentieth-century Britain, not just at a popular level, but also among intellectuals, and even among academics and professionals. In each instance, psychology, often of a rather different hue to that regarded as progressive in either disciplinary or Freudian narratives, was the source of considerable excitement and huge ambitions, appearing to offer systems of thought and practice for reinvigorating self-, social-, and even spiritual-development. For all the similarities, there were also notable tensions and differences. This was partly an issue of conflict over the necessity of expertise, partly too the reflection of an elite lack of confidence in the capacities of the mass to elevate themselves above the irrational, whether in the form of herd instincts or the suggestiveness of psychological charlatanism. Although the elite and popular shared much in common in terms of an ethical vision that helped to accommodate psychology within an existing framework of values, the similarity was not always apparent: one side's philosophy of mind could be the other's mysticism. Both sides were also ready to accuse the other of putting its material interest before higher ends. Thus, the populists and new age intellectuals could dismiss academic psychology as mechanistic or overly obsessed with controlling pathology. The elite, in turn, could portray populists as concerned with little more than practical but superficial techniques for self-advancement. For the emerging profession, this largely independent practical psychology, driven on by the power of the market and a rich associational life far more than influence from above, was only, if at all, a very flawed route to fulfilling the potential of psychology in developing better people and a better society. Instead, it turned to the new interventionism of the state, advancing itself through an ability to measure, classify, and offer apparently scientific evaluation of normality and abnormality. The next three chapters will reconsider this story of what Nikolas Rose has called the 'psychological complex' by setting it alongside that of excitement and popularisation.[1] The first aim is to put the scope of development in perspective. The second is to reappraise its character, in particular to draw out some similarities with the features highlighted in the first chapters.

[1] Rose, *Psychological Complex.*

For reasons of rights, responsibilities, and cost, the British state never, in fact, had either the will or the ability to apply psychology as a tool of effective regulation over a broad swathe of the adult population. Even when it came to those more exposed within an institutional setting, where such ideological and economic objections were weaker—the mental hospital, the prison, and the army—advances were slow.[2] The position of children, however, was fundamentally different. It was society's responsibility to provide them with care; it was not yet their right to resist. Moreover, the emergence of a universal elementary education system and an expanding secondary system provided what was a unique opportunity to reach out at a formative stage to a cross-section of the population as a whole. Unsurprisingly, work on the advance of psychological regulation leans heavily on the example of the child, drawing attention in particular to mental testing and child guidance. What this chapter aims to draw out instead, and by way of contrast, is a more romantic excitement about the implications of psychology for pedagogy as a whole. Here, the potential for influence was in fact greater, albeit more indirect. Psychology stood between 'what is and what might be', as one influential manifesto for change put it.[3] Utopian ambition was very different from reality on the ground, but elements did filter through.[4] One of the reasons for this was the ability to cohere with existing philosophies and values. Another was that the psychologically informed pedagogy was able to convince that it brought certain practical benefits. The attractions to some teachers—a form of popularisation rather neglected to date—was also a factor. However, a fully child-centred approach was always going to be hugely difficult if not impossible within the economic and conventionally academic straitjacket of state education. Besides, it pushed psychological consideration beyond the school to the home. Ultimately, then, psychology needed to reach out not just to the teachers but the parents. In doing so, it struggled because of its ambivalence about popularisation and had to accept that its message changed as it passed into the hands of those who took it up.

MENTAL TESTING

The mental test continues to attract more interest than any issue when it comes to the impact of psychology on education.[5] This is partly because it supports the thesis about psychology as a tool of regulation. It also reflects the fact that the

---

[2] M. Thomson, 'Constituting Citizenship: Mental Deficiency, Mental Health and Human Rights in Inter-War Britain', in C. Lawrence and A. Mayer (eds.), *Regenerating England: Medicine and Culture in Inter-War Britain* (Amsterdam, 2000), 231–50.

[3] E. Holmes, *What is and What Might Be* (London, 1911).

[4] George Walden highlights the extraordinary influence of an idealistic progressive pedagogy in a country normally so intellectually pragmatic: *We Should Know Better: Solving the Educational Crisis* (London, 1996).

[5] For instance, B. Evans and B. Waites, *IQ and Mental Testing: An Unnatural Science and its Social History* (London, 1981); Rose, *Psychological Complex*, 112–45; A. Wooldridge, *Measuring the*

mental test is integral to two of the central narratives about modern British history: on the one hand, a narrative about economic efficiency and economic decline; on the other, a narrative about social mobility, social justice, and class. In both instances, interest focuses on the contribution of mental testing in attempts to turn the education system into a 'ladder of opportunity'. This is terrain for heated debate. In terms of perceptions and intent, rather than actual results, what does seem clear is that the mental test emerged as a tool of social justice in the first half of the century. In the second, though supporters remained, critics would attack the test as reifying inborn inequality and thereby weakening the basis for tackling social causes of inequality. Neither side has been slow to claim that theirs is also the path of economic efficiency. The stakes have been high, with the basic organisation of the education system at issue for much of the century: a system graded according to ability in conflict with more comprehensive models.[6] In the case of this book, the dual themes of economic efficiency and social justice are less central. The question, instead, is whether the education system acted as arena for the construction of psychological subjects. In this respect, the mental test was in fact less pervasive or significant than psychology's influence on a new pedagogy.

As Nikolas Rose has explained, psychology had the potential to make the individual 'knowable, calculable and administrable', according to which mental tests were selected, the qualities they chose to address, and their positioning of the individual within the population.[7] As he also points out, mental tests for intelligence of the child or the mental defective were springboards for an expansion of this mode of 'governance' via norms, both to other invented capacities, such as attitudes and personality, and to other arenas such as the army or the factory.[8] This is a compelling thesis. Whether it stands up to scrutiny when the focus shifts from the potential of discourse to the reality of practice is another matter.

Take, for instance, the mental defective, the subject of major alarm, and the creation of a new system of segregation in 1913. Here, the category of the mental deficiency and its crude calibrations from 'high-' to 'low-grade' of 'feebleminded', 'imbecile', and 'idiot', emerged before psychological testing had any authority in Britain and certainly did not depend on this technology. Even over the next decades as use of the psychological test did spread in the practice of diagnosis, it was rarely as fundamental a trigger to action as was social inefficiency. In the case

---

Mind: Education and Psychology in England, c.1860–1990 (Cambridge, 1994); R. A. Lowe, 'Eugenicists, Doctors and the Quest for National Efficiency: An Educational Crusade, 1900–1939', *History of Education*, 8 (1979), 293–306. For a more cautious view of the impact of testing: G. Sutherland, *Ability, Merit and Measurement: Mental Testing and English Education, 1880–1940* (Oxford, 1994); D. Thom, 'The 1944 Education Act: The Art of the Possible?', in H. Smith (ed.), *War and Social Change* (Manchester, 1986), 101–28.

 [6] For the outstanding account of its politics: Wooldridge, *Measuring the Mind*.

 [7] Rose, *Psychological Complex*, 65.

 [8] The argument runs through his *Psychological Complex* and is developed in relation to the army and factory in his *Governing the Soul*.

of mentally defective children, the primary focus was educability rather than the results of any psychological tests.[9]

When it comes to the move towards selection in interwar secondary education, only around half of the local authorities went as far as introducing intelligence testing, and here practice was often inconsistent. Ultimately, existing attitudes towards ability were hard to dislodge.[10] Psychologists did have some influence on the rethinking of government policy in the period. Their vision of intellectual differences between children was a factor, for instance, in the recommendation of secondary education for all differentiated through selection at the age of eleven. Ultimately, however, the rationale was broader.[11] The key influence behind the 1944 Education Act, which eventually introduced a fully selective secondary system, was the Norwood Report, and this rested on a very traditional understanding of children's abilities and was sceptical about the insights of psychology.[12] Subsequently, it was as much the practical challenge of selection as conversion to psychological principles, that led nearly all authorities to adopt a standardised intelligence test by the early 1950s.[13] Even then, the intelligence test was just one part of a broader armoury that still rested much of its weight on tests of performance in traditional academic subjects. In fact, the period saw mounting criticism of the equity of the tests. In sum, reluctantly used in the first half of the century, under increasing egalitarian critique in the second, a picture emerges of a much more fragile achievement for psychology and its tests.

The same is true when one looks beyond policy to the professionals—psychologists, but also teachers—whose support was necessary for implementation. In the interwar period, teachers appear to have been often quite ill informed and sceptical about the tests. Not until the ninth print run of one typical popular textbook on educational psychology did the subject receive attention. Even then, the tone was cautious, with stress on the inability to measure some of the most important products of education such as character.[14] Research from the early 1930s on the attitudes of students in teacher training indicated that they saw mental testing as having little bearing upon their daily work.[15] It certainly did not fire the teachers' imagination in the way that other psychological ideas would. A survey of 1942 found that 73 per cent of teachers doubted that it was practicable to discover a child's special aptitudes or interests through testing between the ages of eleven and thirteen.[16] Psychologists were equally cautious, some questioning the value of

[9] Thomson, *Problem of Mental Deficiency*, 95, 231–3.

[10] Sutherland, *Ability, Merit and Measurement*, 191–270.

[11] Wooldridge, *Measuring the Mind*, 225–6.   [12] Ibid. 239–44.

[13] Thom, 'Art of the Possible', 117–23.

[14] B. Dumville, *Child Mind: An Introduction to Psychology for Teachers*, 2nd edn. (London, 1931), 305–35. Dumville was Late Master of Method and Lecturer on Education in the LCC Islington Day Training College.

[15] A. W. Wolters, 'Psychology in the Training of Teachers', *British Journal of Educational Psychology*, 5 (1935), 253.

[16] C. Burt, 'An Inquiry into Public Opinion Regarding Educational Reforms Part II', *Occupational Psychology*, 18 (1944), 13–23.

tests for intelligence, and many uncertain about what intelligence actually was.[17] Those who did support the tests did so invariably as a means towards a more fundamental primary objective of placing the needs of the individual child at the heart of the educational process.[18]

It is also relevant to consider the views of the public on this issue. Evans and Waites have claimed that the 'gospel' of psychometrics was inscribed on the social consciousness of the period, through the role of testing in schools and in the extension beyond in vocational testing, and in the way that this role was now promoted through the radio and popular press.[19] This is a fascinating suggestion, though unfortunately their own study makes little attempt to back it up and no one else has followed their lead. Cyril Burt, by contrast, claimed that 'intelligence' was not common in everyday discourse, let alone understood in the way that it was by psychologists.[20] In this regard, it is quite striking that intelligence gains scarcely a mention in the popular psychological literature, surveyed at the start of this book. The view that intelligence was innate and therefore fixed would certainly have been out of step with the self-improving thrust of this culture, and this may help to explain its absence. A focus on intelligence would also have led to a self-limiting elitism. Significantly, the interwar intelligence testing literature that did reach beyond its main audience of educators to the public often assumed both a value of practice, and a potential for improvement, that were wholly inconsistent with the vision of intelligence that was being propagated by psychologists. Even when this more popular testing literature did distinguish intelligence or an ability to think from mere knowledge or memory, the very act of consuming such material in order to gain advantage undermined the psychologists' aim of testing for something uncontaminated by culture.[21] Asked to comment on the 1942 Ministry of Information survey of opinion regarding post-war reconstruction, Burt would note the apparent lack of appreciation among the public of any need to differentiate education according to ability.[22] Once such a selective system was in place, one finds greater interest among parents in intelligence, though it is still clear that this carried multiple and overlapping meanings and could refer to level of education or social refinement as well as native wit.[23]

---

[17] Wooldridge, *Measuring the Mind*, 221–4, 285–93.   [18] Ibid. 208.

[19] Evans and Waites, *IQ and Mental Testing*, 78–9.

[20] Ibid. 35; Hearnshaw, *Cyril Burt*, 48.

[21] For instance, Anon., *Test Yourself: Intelligence Quizzes based on Official Tests and Arranged as Party Games* (London, 1951). For a recognition that intelligence was not the same as knowledge: H. W. Haggard, *T'isn't What you Know But are You Intelligent?* (London, 1927). For a test resting on general knowledge: Pallas Publishing Company, *Test your Intelligence: Questions and Replies from General Knowledge* (London, 1940). Pelmanism, discussed in Ch. 1, emphasised strengthening memory, not intelligence.

[22] C. Burt, 'An Inquiry into Public Opinion Regarding Educational Reforms', Part I, *Occupational Psychology*, 17 (1943), 157–67.

[23] B. Jackson and D. Marsden, *Education and the Working Class* (London, 1966).

CHILD GUIDANCE

If mental testing forms one central pillar of the case for this period being one in which psychology was imposed from above as a tool of normalisation, the emergence of a system of child guidance clinics acts as the other. Rose describes the former as a 'psycho-eugenic' path, the latter as one of 'neo-hygienism'.[24] Emerging as a project of marking out the pathological mental defective, 'psycho-eugenics' was limited in its range and, with its emphasis on restriction of rights, difficult to extend within a liberal political climate.[25] In the long term, 'neo-hygienism' would prove more successful. In shifting the emphasis to prevention of illness, adjustment of behaviour, and the construction of mental health, its scope was much greater, while in proffering its service as a right of the citizen, but also as a necessity for the production of democratic subjects, it aimed to overcome ideological objections yet still served the interests of the social order. During the interwar period, the child guidance clinic was at the cutting edge of this strategic shift. Staffed by teams combining the expertise of psychologists and psychiatric social workers under psychiatric direction, the clinic in theory would enable the imposition and dissemination of psychological 'norms for happy families and contented children'.[26]

In practice, the command of psychological 'neo-hygienism' and its norms was far less secure and more limited in scope. The emergence of forty-six clinics between 1927 and 1938 may be significant in the way that any pioneering venture is, but they were often part-time, their geographic distribution was uneven, and they treated no more than 3,000–4,000 children a year, the majority with minor behavioural problems.[27] There was no single model for the way forward. Divisions existed over both whom to treat and who should be doing this. There were major differences in the sources of funding and the way clinics aligned themselves as a result: as part of the local education services, tied to a mental hospital, linked to the courts, or in a more independent position. A mere seventeen of the established clinics which existed by 1938 were staffed by what was regarded as a complete team of at least one psychiatrist, psychologist, and psychiatric social worker.[28] As this indicates, it is certainly too simplistic to regard the clinics as little more than an extension of the established American model, even if the influence of the American example was undoubtedly extremely important from the mid-1920s. From 1927 onwards, the financial support of the American Commonwealth Fund was

---

[24] Rose, *Psychological Complex*, 85.

[25] A conclusion broadly shared in Thomson, *Problem of Mental Deficiency*.

[26] Rose, *The Psychological Complex*, 203.

[27] D. Thom, 'Wishes, Anxieties, Play and Gestures', in R. Cooter (ed.), *In the Name of the Child Health and Welfare, 1880–1940* (London, 1992), 215–16; O. Sampson, *Child Guidance: Its History, Provenance and Future* (London, 1980), 65.

[28] W. Moodie, 'The Child Guidance Council' unpublished report, (Dec. 1938), 4–6, Rockefeller Foundation Archive, Commonwealth Fund, Box 3, Folder 32.

certainly important in sustaining the scale of development and shaping its evolution. It sponsored visits of practitioners to the United States, funded the London Child Guidance Clinic in Islington as a model from 1928, and then supported the Child Guidance Council as an organising body to provide direction to the spread of clinical work. However, indigenous clinics for children had also emerged by the mid-1920s and continued alongside the Commonwealth Fund-backed activity, not always in complete harmony. The East London Child Guidance Clinic in Spitalfields, run by the Jewish Health Organisation and under Medical Director Emanuel Miller, often takes the credit for being the first British clinic. However, depending on how one defines the child guidance clinic, there are earlier examples. Cyril Burt claimed that he regularly saw children in his work at the London County Council from 1913 onwards. It is likely that he was not alone. For instance, Birmingham School Medical Officer, George Auden (father of the poet W. H. Auden) had some kind of child guidance clinic. The Tavistock Clinic set up a clinic for children in 1920, though this was within a psychiatric setting. The founding of the Child Guidance Council in 1927 at a meeting of the London Day Training Council may better be seen, then, as an attempt to rationalise a process of development that was already active within Britain, rather than as a platform to import a model from outside.[29] Indeed, one of the main concerns of the Commonwealth Fund sponsors and its professional supporters during the 1930s was that growth was out of control, threatening both standards and the professional reputation of such work. Some within the movement seemed to be fuelling a popular demand for the service by lectures and broadcasts to the lay public. As a result, clinics emerged without sufficient trained personnel, and lay enthusiasts infiltrated the organisational structures of the movement.[30] Clearly, there was an excitement about child guidance during these early years, which was not fully under professional control: a kind of missionary zeal and 'mystic' attraction to the strange new promise of psychotherapy.[31]

The 'consumer' also had a role in shaping provision. The fact that such a large proportion of cases were bed-wetters, hardly a threat to the social order, exemplifies the way that clinics responded to the needs and concerns of parents. The fact that demand regularly exceeded supply, evident in waiting lists, also indicates that we need to take seriously this factor of demand from below. Thom suggests three reasons: the lack of connection to punitive officials; the targeting of publicity to mothers and their acclimatisation to such an appeal through a broader culture of child-rearing advice literature; and the fact that the clinics generally distanced themselves from psychoanalysis—which remained suspect among the public because of its associations with sexuality.[32]

[29] Sampson, *Child Guidance*, 3; Thom, 'Wishes, Anxieties, Play and Gestures', 203–5, 208.
[30] Moodie, 'Child Guidance Council', 1.
[31] The first chapter of an account written by practitioners captures this flavour in its title 'Bliss was it in that dawn': Sampson, *Child Guidance*, 2–13, 48.
[32] Thom, 'Wishes, Anxieties, Play and Gestures', 209.

Although the number of clinics rose to ninety-five through the temporary needs of dislocation and evacuation in the Second World War, this also encouraged a re-evaluation of the estimated demand for the service, raising it from one in every thousand to one per cent of the child population, leaving provision further behind the ideal than ever.[33] Expansion proved unrealistic in a situation of stretched resources and at a time when mental health services were a low priority compared to the challenge of rescuing a collapsing hospital service and catering to the physical needs of a population after years of neglect. Calls for a two-tier service, split between child guidance centres under psychologists dealing with largely educational problems, and child guidance clinics under doctors dealing with psychiatric problems, brought to the surface the movement's inherent professional rivalries and lack of unified direction.[34] The Ministry of Education's *Report of the Committee on Maladjusted Children* of 1955 under Chairman Dr J. E. A. Underwood would make the challenge even greater, suggesting that at least eight per cent of the child population needed help.[35]

With severe shortages in the number of trained personnel, it was proving impossible to satisfy such rising expectations. The model of having psychiatrists, psychologists, and psychiatric social workers in a team was highly ambitious but hugely difficult to realise in practice. The Underwood Report estimated that there was a need for 280 psychologists, with only 141 currently filling these posts; and an even greater shortfall both among psychiatrists, with 56 filling 140 posts, and among psychiatric social workers, with 109 filling 420 posts.[36] There were two potential solutions. The first was to co-opt and incorporate other groups—social workers or teachers—into child guidance work. The second was to relocate limited expertise from the isolation of the clinic to the proximity of the school. Both were to some extent taken, and both modified the nature of the encounter between psychology and its subjects.

In relocating the site of intervention from the clinic to the school, the problem shifted from mental ill health and its prevention to educational maladjustment. In fact, this alternative strategy had origins in the interwar period, emerging alongside or as part of the child guidance system. This reflected that broader ambivalence alluded to in relation to diagnosing children as mental defective, which here extended to any sense that children might be 'mental', and a preference for pursuing educational channels instead. By 1939, there were forty-six schools for 'nervous, difficult and retarded' children recognised by the Child Guidance Council.[37] A number of child guidance clinics had also been set up under local education authorities—notably the influential Birmingham Clinic in 1932—and

---

[33] Sampson, *Child Guidance*, 54.

[34] See, for instance, the heated debates from a symposium of psychologists and psychiatrists on child guidance services, *British Journal of Educational Psychology*, 21–3 (1951–3).

[35] Ministry of Education, *Report of the Committee on Maladjusted Children (Underwood Report)* (London, 1955), 171–2.   [36] Ibid. 102–14.

[37] Ibid. 12.

this was to be important in facilitating a transition from voluntary to statutory funding. From 1945, special schools for 'maladjusted pupils' received statutory funding.[38]

What this summary of the history of child guidance indicates is that 'neo-hygienism' was not without its own limitations. Resting still on a central medical model, there was an ongoing struggle for resources and personnel, and the public remained wary. Further expansion depended on the compromise, translation and indeed popularisation of ideas and practices involved in co-opting psychologists, social workers and even teachers, as well as attracting parents. We need to study these groups if we are fully to appreciate the nature of any imposition of psychology. The second half of this chapter offers a start in this respect. More fundamentally, this brief analysis of limitations and necessary dialogue at the heart of child guidance aims to suggest that we should be cautious about accepting this arena as the most potent example of psychological intervention in shaping the modern British child. Instead, the chapter will now shift to an area of psychological influence, very different in character, which had the potential to reach all schoolchildren, affecting what they studied and how they were to learn.

PEDAGOGY, PSYCHOLOGY, AND THE NEW ERA

In eighteenth- and nineteenth-century Britain, literature played an important role in the 'discovery' and romanticising of childhood as a separate stage of human development. An interest in applying enlightenment and post-enlightenment theories of child development to education, by contrast, came comparatively late.[39] However, by the late-nineteenth century, there was considerable excitement about this possibility and the formation of several movements for study and reform. In particular, two decades after his own death, Friedrich Froebel became influential in spawning a kindergarten movement, with the Froebel Society set up in 1875, followed by the Froebel Educational Institute for Training Teachers in 1894, and the Froebel-inspired Norland Institute for the Training of Ladies as Childrens' Nurses in 1892. The Froebelian approach centred on three ideas: play was crucial in child development; words should be connected to the things that the child could touch and see; and that in the discovery of the unity of self and nature through education, the child could discover the divine.[40] The period also saw the development of the Child Study movement.[41] Here the roots went back to no single figure, and mounting anxieties about children as an element of

[38] Under the Handicapped Pupils and School Health Service Regulations: ibid. 13.

[39] Steedman, *Childhood, Culture and Class*, 81–2.

[40] N. Whitbread, *The Evolution of the Nursery-Infant School* (London, 1972), 37.

[41] H. Hendrick, *Images of Youth: Age, Class and the Male Youth Problem, 1880–1920* (Oxford, 1990), 111–18.

national efficiency was more of a factor.[42] Both movements benefited from a lay energy that saw the future as lying in discovery of and fulfilment of the child's potential.

There has been a tendency to assume that such amateur enthusiasm and romantic idealism fell away rapidly in the twentieth century, replaced in part by a new science of psychology.[43] This probably overestimates the extent of change. The basic Froebelian orientatation remained influential: the emphasis on play, learning by doing, and on teaching by things, rather than words, increasingly accepted as the natural and therefore best way when it came to young children. It was a message inherited by a new generation of educational reformers, like Britain's own Margaret McMillan or the Italian Maria Montessori.[44] Child Study, likewise, maintained a presence. There was a weekly column in the *Times Educational Supplement* written by Thomas George Tibby, Vice-President of the Child Study Society.[45] Although national membership of the Child Study Society fell from 1908, the figure for London rose, from 303 in 1908, to 608 in 1922, with popular lectures and a journal throughout the 1920s.[46] As organised movements, both were on the retreat, but this is not necessarily indicative of a decline in enthusiasm for the projects themselves: they had helped to create an appetite and audience among both teachers and parents.[47] Rather than seeing retreat as a response to rejection, it is closer to the truth that these ideas no longer needed such support since to some extent they were now becoming part of the mainstream of educational theory and even to some extent practice.

Britain was in fact unusually open to new ideas in education in the early twentieth century.[48] There was greater room for experimentation than within more centralised state education systems, and much of the most experimental work went on within the strong independent sector.[49] However, there were also broader ideological and cultural dimensions at work. New departures in education were perhaps the most important and lasting legacy of a utopian impulse in the early twentieth century.[50] The promise of remaking man through a new education, epitomised by Edmond Holmes' *What is and What Might Be* of 1911, was attractive to those disenchanted by a socialism that was losing such a dimension, increasingly characterised as it was by Fabian intellectual detachment and an emphasis on public corporatism.[51] Holmes is an intriguing figure, indicative of

---

[42] See the essays emerging from a conference on childhood and national efficiency in M. Gijswijt-Hofstra and H. Marland (eds.), *Cultures of Child Health in Britain and the Netherlands in the Twentieth Century* (Amsterdam, 2003).   [43] Wooldridge, *Measuring the Mind*, 44–5.

[44] Whitbread, *Evolution of the Nursery-Infant School*; R. J. W. Selleck, *The New Education, 1870–1914* (London, 1965), 203.

[45] P. G. Ballard, *Thomas George Tibby: A Lecture in his Memory* (London, 1936).

[46] Wooldridge, *Measuring the Mind*, 40–1.   [47] Ibid. 47.

[48] R. Skidelsky, *English Progressive Schools* (London, 1969), 243.

[49] W. Boyd and W. Dawson, *The Story of the New Education* (London, 1965), 62.

[50] W. H. G. Armytage, *Heavens Below: Utopian Experiments in England, 1560–1960* (London, 1961), 438.   [51] Ibid. 375–6, 433–4. See also Ch. 3.

the ties between educational reform and the broader new age idealism of the period. What makes his contribution more significant is that he was very much an insider: a government inspector of schools and examiner since the 1870s. Yet he was a disillusioned insider, increasingly aware that the system lacked any real interest in the minds or the inner life of the working-class child. During this period, he became interested in the psychic and psychological world, first through spiritualism, and then in Theosophy, and this reorientation away from material-ism helped him to recognise what was wrong with existing educational practice.[52] *What is and What Might Be*, as the title suggested, was a book of two parts: the first, setting out 'What Is'—'The Path of Mechanical Obedience'; the second, set-ting out a vision of 'What Might Be', including his vision of 'A School in Utopia'. At the heart of this new education was the process of self-realization. '[T]he self of each of us', he argued, 'is waiting, not to be asserted against all other selves': this was the fallacy at the heart of a system centred on examination. 'It is waiting to be brought into actual existence, to be endowed with reality, to become what its nature predestined it to be. The real self is not there. Or rather, it is there, but it is hidden from us by our own immaturity. Its existence is potential. It is waiting for us to make it actual.'[53] This self-realization, he was keen to emphasise, had nothing at all in common with egotism, it was ultimately dependent upon going beyond the individual self as normally understood:[54] 'one must empty oneself of "self" '.[55]

Holmes was widely influential. He was also not alone among Theosophists in his interest in a reorientation of education from mechanical learning to a more holistic mission of self-development. Such interest led to the formation of the Theosophical Fraternity in Education in 1915. The driving force behind this group was another educational insider, Beatrice Ensor, who in 1910 had been the first woman school inspector for Glamorgan County Council and who later became an inspector for the Board of Education. Like Holmes, who was clearly an influence, she had become increasingly critical of the current system through direct experience. Towards the end of the war, she resigned her official post and became Managing Director of the Theosophical Educational Trust, which went on to found a series of schools, the first in Letchworth.[56] After the war, she would play a key role in spreading the net of this movement much further. She would be a founding editor of the journal *New Era* and a pioneer of the New Education Fellowship, tying the vision of a new education to the mission of securing interna-tional peace through a reformation of human character. The reach of such vehicles went far beyond their narrower Theosophical origins, aiming not only to bring together pioneers and supporters of reform in private and state schools alike, but

[52] E. Holmes, *In Quest of an Ideal: An Autobiography* (London, 1920).
[53] E. Holmes, 'The Meaning of Self-Realization', *New Ideals Quarterly*, 1/3 (Sept. 1925), 6–7.
[54] Ibid. 9.   [55] Holmes, *In Quest of an Ideal*, 143.
[56] M. D. Lawson, 'The New Education Fellowship: The Formative Years', *Journal of Educational Administration and History*, 13 (1981), 24–8; Boyd and Rawson, *The New Education*, 65–7.

also via the Fellowship forging international links through a series of conferences over the next three decades. The Fellowship supported the substitution of cooperation for competition and of discipline from within for discipline from without. It stressed the importance of spiritual development. And with a mind to the problem of the herd instinct, which many now associated with the descent into war, it aimed to cultivate the power to think for oneself rather than to be swayed by mass emotion.[57] At the first international conference at Montreux in 1923, 100 British delegates attended out of a total of 370 and were exposed to papers on the psychological ideas of Badouin, Coué, and Jung.[58] Attendance of British delegates at these meetings increased steadily over the interwar period, peaking in the meeting at Cheltenham in 1936. The vibrancy of the movement was evident in the founding of a series of local groups in the 1920s, with twenty-three branches by the end of the Second World War. The Theosophical origins of the British movement became less significant as it expanded and matured. Ensor departed to South Africa in the early 1930s, and leading educationalists like Sir Michael Sadler, Percy Nunn, Cyril Burt, and R. H. Tawney all began to support its work. The essential aims of the movement remained, as now it marshalled the language and theory of psychology to provide continued support for the vision of education as self-realization.[59] Like the mysticism of Theosophy before it, psychology offered a path to evolution that lay within. Both were now moving to the position that, not only was self-realization necessary for the pupils, but, in order for this to be possible, it was essential for their teachers as well.[60] Ensor could move from one language to the other in supporting a common purpose.[61] Indeed, with the profusion of competing psychological theories by the late 1920s, the unique authority of any one was undermined, suggesting that it was possible to present them as on a par with less orthodox and more mystical disciplines of the self. People should not be in awe of psychology, they should think for themselves and use the various tools available to get at underlying principles—the importance of wholeness, for instance—that tied these different philosophies together in their approach to the reform of education.[62]

The idea that a new education was the key to a new era was also at the heart of a number of other remarkable independent ventures in this period. Though the psychological inspiration was often more secular than in the Theosophist case, there was still a deeply romantic dimension, both in the goal of liberating individual development, and in the vision of a self-realization that transcended the materialist, atomised individualism of industrial civilisation. Two of the most

---

[57] Rawson and Boyd, *The New Education*, 68–73.   [58] Ibid. 77–8. On Coué, see Ch. 1.
[59] Ibid. 77–128.
[60] Boyd and Rawson, *The New Education*, 81; W. Boyd (ed.), *Towards a New Education: Based on the Fifth World Conference of the New Education Fellowship at Elsinore, Denmark* (London, 1930), 352–3.
[61] B. Ensor, 'Crusades in the Realm of *Education*', in Boyd, *Towards a New Education*, 1–5.
[62] Boyd and Rawson, *The New Education*, 86; Boyd, *Towards a New Education*, 435, 446–7.

notable were the schools set up by Bertrand and Dora Russell and by A. S. Neill.[63] The Russells were hardly experts in psychology, and would be criticised as amateurs in their attempts to defend their Beacon Hill School, opened in 1927 in response to what they found to be the deficiencies of the existing system when looking for an education for their own children. Nevertheless, they would claim that their study of psychology, whether amateur or not, had been a central guide and inspiration. Dora Russell took it upon herself to set out the basis for the project in *The Right to be Happy* of 1927, which she described as her 'manifesto against that religion of the machine age'—the dualism of mind and matter. Happiness had emerged as the fundamental problem within industrial civilisation. The solution was to educate people to be free and to recognise the wholeness of their humanity. She was typically eclectic in her taste, setting Freud alongside Adler, Piaget, Froebel, Montessori, and especially McMillan as influences. Unusually within the British context, the Russells were also enthusiasts for the behaviourism of American psychologist W. F. Watson. One must assume that the emphasis on environment, carrying with it the idea of elevating man through control of his surroundings, appealed to their socialist sensibilities.[64] They were also excited that Watson's work seemed to parallel that of the Soviet psychologist Pavlov, suggesting a synthesis in the central vision of human development between the communist East and the capitalist West. Their sympathy for behaviourism helps to explain why *The Right to be Happy* was particularly successful in the United States.[65] Generally, however, there is little sign that the British warmed to the behaviourism that swept the United States during this period. Indeed, more often than not one finds criticism, and it is possible that there was an element of this in suspicions of Beacon Hill. Behaviourism, essentially a psychology of control, was too markedly out of line with the British attraction to a psychological subjectivity of self-realization; its determinism and materialism were also out of line with the idea that there were important spiritual and moral dimensions to psychological development that was so strong in Britain in this period.[66]

A. S. Neill's Summerhill School would become even more notorious than Beacon Hill. Alongside Beatrice Ensor, Neill was one of the original editors of the *New Era*. Again, he had taken the path from practical experience of 'what is', as a schoolteacher in Scotland, to rejecting this for a vision of 'what might be'.[67] As such, psychological theory once again came second to the cause of changing humanity at an ideological level. Indeed, in typically provocative and anti-authoritarian style, he pointed to the danger of a progressive education that bowed down in homage to the new psychology. Many of its core ideas—release of

---

[63] For details on another important pioneer in this area: W. D. Wills, *Homer Lane: A Biography* (London, 1964).   [64] See also the discussion of the Plebs League in Ch. 5.

[65] D. Russell, *The Tamarisk Tree*, 2 (London, 1980), 193–200; B. and D. Russell, *The Right to be Happy* (London, 1927).

[66] For the latter criticism: Board Of Education, *Report of the Consultative Committee on Infant and Nursery Schools* (London, 1933), 244.

[67] He was also a contributor to the *New Age* and on the fringes of the circle explored in Ch. 3.

pent-up emotion, for instance—were essential. Yet a figure like Charlie Chaplin, he only half jested, had done more in this respect than Freud, Jung, and Adler together. There was a danger of marginalising progressive education by pinning it to any dogma. 'The crank school', he argued, oblivious to the way that his own Summerhill would gain just this type of reputation, 'must come down to earth. It must cease making a song about its ideals. Today the crank school is producing a new crowd, partly shy, partly superior. That is wrong; its job is to produce boys and girls who will fit into the Bottomley crowd and help it to reach a higher level.'[68] Certainly, at Summerhill and also in his successful advice writing for a general audience over the next half century, he would attempt to follow his own admonition, developing a bluff, no-nonsense style which though deeply informed by the new psychology served no obvious master and distanced itself from the obfuscations of professional language.

FREEDOM WITH DISCIPLINE

Though figures like Neill, Lane, and the Russells were undoubtedly significant when it came to the public reputation of progressive education, a focus on their eccentricities can obscure the fact that the progressive mood had a much broader and subtly different influence. The lasting picture may have been one of children left to do whatever they wanted at Beaconhill, or taking over the running of a school at Summerhill, and in general of study being rejected for play, but in practice the integration of a vision of individual freedom with one of an enhanced social order was equally if not more influential.

Montessori teaching would attract considerable criticism, both from those like Neill who wanted to push freedom and self-government of the child towards complete realisation, and from the Froebelians in nursery teaching who opposed the emphasis on sense training and the neglect of imagination.[69] However, its supporters asserted that freedom was exactly what it did provide, but that finding freedom involved some kind of relationship of order with the broader world: harmony to its supporters, discipline to its detractors. What we have here is different visions of freedom. In fact, it was the vision that looked beyond individualism that was more characteristic of this period. Neill's vision would have more in common with the ideology of the second half of the century, which perhaps helps to explain why his writing and Summerhill itself straddled the period as a whole more easily.

The Montessori approach presented itself as offering an ideologically progressive freedom, but one that did not degenerate into socially unacceptable disorder.

---

[68] 'The Outlook Tower', *New Era*, 1/3 (1920), 63. As a notorious journalist for the tabloid *John Bull*, Horatio Bottomley emerged in the First World War as a symbol of the way mass society was in danger of manipulation through the force of herd instinct and appeal to lower instincts. See for instance the description in D. H. Lawrence's 'nightmare' vision of the war in his 1923 novel *Kangaroo*.   [69] Whitbread, *The Nursery-Infant School*, 59.

Real freedom, whether for children or teachers, meant ridding oneself 'of vain preoccupations and of vain complacencies' and thus depended on a degree of discipline.[70] The latter could be something that became 'entirely forgotten', naturalised, expressed in the very movements and tranquillity of the children.[71] Psychological theory was important but hidden by the emphasis on concrete activities.[72] There were objections from those who found such prescription authoritarian and overly rigid, with too little freedom for either students or teachers.[73] However, interest was considerable. Between 1909 and 1914, some two hundred books and articles appeared in English inspired by her work.[74] The message also spread through bi-annual training courses introduced after Montessori's visit in 1919.[75] To its supporters, Montessori brought the best of both worlds: the allure of being progressive and of a new focus on the mind of the child; yet also order in the classroom and efficiency. As one contemporary advocate put it, the Montessori approach was to the existing education system what the Hampstead Garden Suburb was to the sprawl of development on the outskirts of London. If a Montessori approach could bring freedom but discipline—and well behaved children—it could be genuinely practical for implementation in the large classes of the state system.[76] Of course, in practice, teachers in state schools lacked either the resources or the freedom to take on a strict Montessori approach. But there was a section of this broader community of elementary teachers who were both alert to the new ideas and keen to modify current practice accordingly even if only in a small way.[77] Thus, the influence of Montessori, like other pioneers of the new pedagogy, could be surprisingly broad even if it was diffuse and diluted. Probably a better way of looking at it is that such ideas were attractive because these changes—towards the individual focus, an interest in the education of the senses, and the new balance between freedom and discipline—were already taking place.[78]

Though psychoanalysis was becoming increasingly influential, it did not fundamentally challenge or add to the new pedagogic agenda. The most influential figure in this field, Susan Isaacs, acknowledged this.[79] She also generally accepted the compromise between freedom and discipline. For although the psychoanalytic school did support greater openness about sexuality, when it came to pedagogy more generally a figure like Isaacs expressed concern about too much freedom within the school: the child needed a sense of order if he or she was to

---

[70] Ibid. 37.

[71] A. Machermi, 'The Opening of a Montessori School', *New Era*, 1/2 (1920), 36.

[72] M. Drummond, 'The Psychological Bases of the Montessori Method', *New Era*, 2, 6 (1921), 189.

[73] For criticisms: Russell, *The Tamarisk Tree*, 2, p. 13.

[74] V. Babini, 'Science, Feminism and Education: The Early Work of Maria Montessori', *History Workshop Journal*, 49 (2000), 44–67.

[75] *New Era*, 1/1(1920), 25; Whitbread, *The Nursery-Infant School*, 59.

[76] C. A. Claremont, 'Montessori and the New Era', *New Era*, 1/1 (1920), 11–16.

[77] This is evident in letters to the *New Era*.

[78] K. J. Brehony, 'Montessori, Individual Work and Individuality in the Elementary School Classroom', *History of Education*, 29 (2000), 115–28.

[79] S. Isaacs, *Social Development in Young Children: A Study of Beginnings* (London, 1933), 416.

feel secure. In fact, even when it came to sexuality itself, Isaacs would acknowledge that it was better to accept repression—after all, this was part of normal development within the culture—than to attempt thrusting any deeper understanding on the child: again, protection was just as important as freedom.[80] Likewise, in the leading progressive journal of the era, the *New Statesman*, psychoanalyst Barbara Low took issue with Bertrand Russell's support of free speech for children, arguing that children were not capable of knowing their own thoughts and feelings.[81] Freedom, as the psychoanalysts recognised, was difficult and potentially dangerous.

As this indicates, there was a potential for critics, who felt that a progressive pedagogy—in particular, the emphasis on freedom—had gone too far, to claim that the authority of psychology was in fact on their side. Writing in F. R. Leavis's culturally conservative journal *Scrutiny*, Alan Keith-Lucas argued that it was disingenuous to claim that the progressive route was a natural rather than an ideological one. There was a constant process of moral and idealistic suggestion at work in such schools. Free expression was an illusion; children, instead, were acting as objects for the free expression of the teachers. Given apparent free rein, moreover, the children ended up emotionally exhausted, for it was far harder to be left to one's own devices in using free time (which often descended into fighting in the advanced school) than to fill this time constructively with hobbies guided by teachers. In positing an idealised natural culture, rather than accepting the value of one based on civilisation and its culture, the progressives were both blinding themselves to their own role in creating the 'natural' and abdicating from the educator's proper responsibility of guiding the organisation of the emotions in the child and thus fostering real mental health.[82]

Psychology, then, did not necessarily line up on the side of a radical experiment like Summerhill. Instead, it could point to a middle way between discipline and freedom. A focus on Neill and his like has made the phenomenon appear more marginal, and radical in its nature, than it really was. When one turns to state elementary education, there is general agreement that this period did see some fundamental changes, and it is clear that psychology and its challenge to thinking about pedagogy was an important element here. In the words of one historian, elementary education was 'made in the progressive image' in the period from 1914 to 1939.[83] For another, there was a 'silent revolution in teaching methods'.[84] Such a shift in practice is also apparent in the government reports on elementary as well as infant and nursery education in the early 1930s. 'The old idea that intellectual exercises, however dull and incomprehensible, may nevertheless provide a wholesome mental gymnastic, has long ago been exploded', argued the report on elementary schools.[85] As the report

---

[80] S. Isaacs, *Social Development in Young Children: A Study of Beginnings* (London, 1933), 424, 428–9.   [81] J. Park, *Bertrand Russell on Education* (London, 1964), 119–22.

[82] A. Keith-Lucas, 'Enlightened Education: A Discussion of the Young Child and Cultural Problems', *Scrutiny*, 1 (1932), 96–101.

[83] R. J. W. Selleck, *English Primary Education and the Progressives 1914–1939* (London, 1972), 32.

[84] Lowndes, *The Silent Social Revolution*, p. 161.

[85] Board of Education, *Report of the Consultative Committee on the Primary School* (London, 1931), 164.

on infant and nursery schools put it, education was moving from an instructional mode towards one in which each child under sympathetic guidance might 'cultivate his own garden'.[86] Here, the contribution of psychologists like Cyril Burt and Susan Isaacs was clearly influential. However, as early as 1902, there had been talk of a 'profound revolution in method' in the best schools.[87] Looking back from the mid-1930s, Ruth Thomas, Lecturer in Education, felt that the impact of the new psychology on school teaching had already been 'almost revolutionary'. It guided teachers away from being moralists; or, as she recognised, it was perhaps more accurate to say that it guided them towards a 'new morality' in which the teacher balanced discipline and psychologically informed guidance and cooperated with children in addressing their problems. Learning had become an issue of addressing the interests and appetite for play of the child. Dry academic textbooks were falling out of favour. Nature study, pre-history (the child's interests recapitulating those of the race), craftwork, and the project were all in favour instead. The daily routine of the school was also transforming, with timetables and physical space becoming far more flexible in order to follow the expansion of consciousness of the child.[88] Critics shared the view that such an advance was taking place.[89] So did an early history of elementary education written in 1925.[90] Even if some of these commentators may have overestimated the real extent of any advance, it does indicate at the very least a strong contemporary belief that something profoundly important had happened. To pursue further the question of whether education really did take a psychological turn, the chapter will turn to those who did the teaching.

TEACHER TRAINING

Lecturing on the legacy of fellow educationalist John Adams in the mid-1930s, Sir Michael Sadler suggested that

[T]he very look of the word Psychology, with its superfluous P, has done something to render it unpopular. Used as an adjective, it is now enough of itself to condemn any novel. It suggests everything that is dull and unreadable. Behind it all, too, there is an underlying

---

[86] Board of Education, *Report of the Consultative Comittee on Infant and Nursery Schools* (London, 1933), xviii.

[87] R. E. Hughes, *The Making of Citizens* (London, 1902), quoted in Whitbread, *The Nursery-Infant School*, 86.

[88] R. Thomas, 'The New Psychology at Work in the School', *The New Era in Home and School*, 17, 1 (1936), 185–8. On the Dalton Plan, which originated in the USA: A. J. Lynch, *Individual Work and the Dalton Plan* (London, 1924); C. W. Kimmins and B. Rennie, *The Triumph of the Dalton Plan* (London, 1932); L. F. Lee, 'The Dalton Plan and the Loyal, Capable Intelligent Citizen', *History of Education*, 29 (2000), 129–38.

[89] A. Keith-Lucas, 'Enlightened Education: A Discussion of the Young Child and Cultural Problems', *Scrutiny*, 1 (1932), 96–101; L. C. Knights, 'Will Training Colleges Bear Scrutiny?', *Scrutiny*, 1 (1932), 247–63.

[90] C. Birchenough, *History of Elementary Education in England and Wales from 1800 to the Present Day* (London, 1925), 352–411.

idea of a pompous assumption of special knowledge. To begin with, there is a difficulty knowing exactly what it is.[91]

Teachers, he argued, had little interest in theory; they just wanted to know Jack or Jill. 'Wherever Psychology differs from common sense, in the popular meaning of that term, the teacher naturally abides by common sense.'[92] Another contemporary commentator shared the concern about psychology's relationship to common sense, though in this case adopted a position that was more critically sceptical, suggesting that the 'new psychology has merely put into words—sometimes rather more elaborate than were strictly necessary—what understanding and observant teachers know already about the different stages of child development.'[93] There is inevitably an element of truth in this. Though teachers were now almost certain to encounter the ideas of McDougall, Freud, and other representatives of the new psychology, their understanding was of course often superficial, modified to accommodate existing values, and shaped to suit their own practical purposes: as at the popular level, this is what gave it its appeal.[94] Behind Sadler's dismissal, is the frustration of someone who lamented the difficulty of extending the influence of psychology with a capital P. Yet, hidden here, is also the recognition that a significant shift in mood—psychological without a capital—had taken place: Jack and Jill—the individuality of the pupils—not Mathematics, English, or Science, were the subjects in a new era of education. 'Common sense', not psychological theory, may have guided the teacher, but common sense had changed and psychology had played a crucial role in this.

Teachers trained to staff the expanding state education system of the early-twentieth century would in fact have found it very difficult to avoid exposure to the new psychology. Adams, the subject of Sadler's lecture, had wanted to publish a book under the title of 'Psychology with the Chill Off', though his publishers and fellow academics objected to the populist tone and he retreated to a more staid title.[95] As this tension suggests, teacher training was located at a crossroads between popularisation and professionalisation. It was integral to turning teaching into a science. But it was also the most crucial of state and institutional sites for extending the influence of psychology to the lives of the public, and to do so depended on exciting the new generation of teachers, translating dry, off-putting theory into a more popular, accessible, and practical idiom. The tension was resolved, to some degree, by the emergence of a psychology that was visionary, in many ways utopian, but also practical in that it directed attention towards the activities and individuality of the child rather than abstract, introspective speculation.

[91] Sir M. Sadler, *John Adams: A Lecture in his Memory. The Second John Adams Lecture* (London, 1935), 17.   [92] Ibid. 18.

[93] L. B. Pekin, *Progressive Schools: Their Principles and Practice* (London, 1934), 44.

[94] Selleck, *English Primary Education and the Progressives*, 106–7; Knights, 'Will Training Colleges Bear Scrutiny?', 253–4.

[95] Sadler, *Adams*, 8–9. The book was published as *The Herbartian Psychology Applied to Education* (London, 1897).

In thus turning the child rather than the academic syllabus into its main subject, and in the process emphasising the value of freedom in development to mirror the broader cult of self-realisation of the period, this education aligned itself with two powerful currents of thought which brought with them a powerful moral justification and inspiration. The first was the idea that in its understanding of human nature, the new psychology could make education natural: a powerful argument in favour in a culture so aware and generally ambivalent if not negative about the unnatural character of modernity and one romantic since the early nineteenth century about rescuing the still innocent child from such degradation. The second was that the new education would foster democratic values. In learning by doing, and in the exercise of the imagination, education would cultivate subjects in their own right: subjects responsible for their own actions; subjects who could decide for themselves; subjects, therefore, naturally developed and fit for the political challenges of the age. Psychological theory portrayed the existing educational emphasis on memory as abstract, tyrannical, and unnatural. Instead, it supported the 'emancipation' and cultivation of the reasoning child mind.[96] In doing so, a set of ideological values at the heart of the British liberal polity were naturalised and fostered. Presented, then, as natural and ideologically normative, and grounded in practical, concrete activity, the new pedagogy could readily appear to offer little more than common sense. This was important to its success, for, as Sadler's remarks suggest, to have presented it as based on psychological theory alone would have been to undermine it on those very grounds of pragmatism upon which much of its potential appeal rested.

Given that the first decades of the century were crucial, both in the expansion of teacher training courses, and in a new excitement about psychology, it is unsurprising that the two should have come together. In 1895, under half of the teachers in elementary schools had a training certificate; but by 1935, the figure had soared to five out of six.[97] As early as 1894, academic psychologists were lecturing to teachers.[98] At least as important, however, and indicative of the problems with a notion of popularisation that assumes a single level of knowledge exchange, were intermediary channels of communication linking academic psychology with the teaching profession on the one hand and parents on the other.[99]

In the twentieth century, expansion of teacher training would take on the mantle from child study as the key channel for disseminating a psychological approach to education. Women like Catherine Dodd, 'Mistresses of Method', emerged as influential figures in the day training colleges that were springing up—eighteen of them between 1890 and 1902. Dodd, a socialist, a feminist, and active in the

---

[96] The language of tyranny and emancipation is drawn from Margaret McMillan's, *Education through the Imagination* (London, 1904), 21–4.

[97] Lowndes, *Silent Social Revolution*, 155–6.

[98] C. M. Fleming, 'The Place of Psychology in the Training of Teachers, *British Journal of Educational Studies*, 3 (1954), 18–19: L. Morgan, *Psychology for Teachers* (London, 1894).

[99] On the problems with the idea of popularisation: D. Riley, *War in the Nursery: Theories of the Child and Mother* (London, 1983), 84–5.

Manchester Child Study Association, found initial inspiration in Froebel and other romantic visions of the potential of the child. For Dodd and others like her, including most famously Margaret McMillan, education bore the promise of rescuing the working class child and remaking society.[100] Dodd would be prolific in spreading such ideas to teachers. She also reached out to children more directly through stories inspired by these theorists.[101] Women like Dodd may not have held the reins of power in teacher-training institutions, but they were an inspiration to the ranks of young women entering the profession, marking out teaching as a vital mission.

The importance of psychology is equally apparent if one turns to one of the central texts of teacher training in the period: Percy Nunn's *Education: Its Data and First Principles*, first published in 1920, with numerous further editions over the next two decades. Nunn positioned a psychological understanding of life as literally the first principle of education and as the basis for a defence of individualism therein. Whether students warmed to this complex model of individuals as purposive, instinct-driven psychological subjects (the central influence of McDougall is very apparent here as elsewhere) is another matter. Brian Simon, the leftwing historian of education, who had first-hand experience of the teacher training in the late 1930s, recalled that *First Principles* 'epitomised yesterday's thinking' and 'insofar as it could be understood, seemed to offer a dusty answer to most of our questions'.[102] Another student would share this lack of enthusiasm, but more because of Nunn's dry and theoretical style than because of objections to psychology. 'Squirrel Blurt's' lectures, by contrast, were recalled as offering 'never a dull moment'. A figure like Burt, perhaps partly because his mannerisms made him an easy object of fun as suggested here, but also because of the emphasis on practice and individual cases that established the popularity of his books on delinquent and backward children, showed that '[p]sychology was a live subject.' Psychology could be fun (the mental test—applied to child or teacher—seems to have included this kind of appeal), and it could be practically relevant.[103] A contemporary survey of teacher training lends further support to the idea that students resisted the more theoretical side of

---

[100] Steedman, *Childhood, Culture and Class*. For the parallel radicalisation in Germany, with an emphasis on the seeds of this process coming from below from teachers excited, among other things, by the discovery of a new psychology: M. Lambert, 'Radical Schoolteachers and the Origins of the Progressive Movement in Germany, 1900–1914', *History of Education Quarterly*, 40 (2000), 22–48.

[101] J. B. Thomas, 'Mistresses of Method: Women Academics in the Day Training Colleges 1890–1914', *Journal of Education and Administrative History*, 29 (1997), 93–107. See also E. C. Wilson, *Catherine Isabella Dodd, 1860–1932: A Memorial Sketch by her Friend and Colleague* (London, 1936).

[102] As a consequence of his battles against mental testing and as an early advocate for putting social circumstances at the forefront of the educational problem, he was in general no supporter of psychology: B. Simon, *A Life in Education* (London, 1998), 20. He did, however, become interested in Soviet psychology, with a lecture on the subject published as *Educational Psychology in the USSR* (London, 1952); and he edited and introduced *Psychology in the Soviet Union* (London, 1957).

[103] University of London, Institute of Education, *Studies and Impressions, 1902–1952* (London, 1952), 72–3.

psychology but welcomed the shift, epitomised by Burt, towards practical situations, with many still believing that the best way to gain psychological understanding was through the experience of teaching.[104]

It seems clear, therefore, that the position of psychology within teacher training, though fundamentally important in this period, did remain a subject of tension and a struggle for its supporters. A manual of 1949 still had to make a defence of taking the subject seriously.[105] Indeed, a survey in the 1950s argued that psychology had not yet gained universal acceptance in training, despite its now foundational position within education theory:

The subject has in some places been despised, in others feared, in others misunderstood; and while there are substantial grounds for the claim that psychology has been, and still is, the basic discipline of the training course, the word appears relatively rarely in the lists of examinable subjects in the curriculum.[106]

However, the position of psychology was in fact less beleaguered than this suggests. There may have been a radical shift away from the idea that introspection could be the basis for psychological understanding, but critics failed to acknowledge that the new psychology, with its emphasis on looking at individuals and real situations, had itself been in the vanguard of this critique. Exam questions such as 'Distinguish between instincts and capacities' (1911) might have fallen away, to be replaced by others along the lines of 'To what extent may the social climate of the classroom affect children? How can the teacher influence that social climate?' (1953), but the latter question, in its interest in affect, the social situation, and relationships, had itself been provoked and framed by the new psychology, even if the new sociological interest in 'social climate' of the 1950s now obscured this line of descent.[107] It seems reasonable to accept the idea that the rather cerebral and to some extent still introspective psychology of someone like Nunn may have left many students cold, but what is striking is that when one looks at textbooks from less celebrated authorities one finds, albeit in a diluted form, very much the same message. 'No teacher', asserted the ninth impression of one of these texts in typical fashion 'can now be considered fully qualifiable who is totally unfamiliar with these recent [psychological] developments.'[108] It is both the ubiquity and enthusiasm of such intermediary channels—after all these writers were hardly leading, or necessarily even academic, psychologists—that leads one to question the idea that there had been a wholesale shift from the amateur, the popular, and the enthusiastic, to the dry, the abstract and the professional.

---

[104] L. G. E. Jones, *The Training of Teachers in England and Wales* (London, 1924), 138. For further sources on this neglected subject: M. Berry, *Teacher Training Institutions in England and Wales: A Bibliographical Guide to their History* (London, 1973).

[105] W. T. Davies and T. B. Shepherd, *Teacher Training: Begin Here* (London, 1949), chs. 11 and 13.

[106] C. M. Fleming, 'The Place of Psychology in the Training of Teachers', *British Journal of Educational Studies*, 3 (1954), 18.

[107] Ibid. 22–3. Fleming was a Reader in Education at the University of London.

[108] Dumville, *Child Mind* (1931).

Of course, just because psychology made such a significant entry into the training curriculum does not mean that the future teachers accepted it or that it influenced them in practice. Further insight on this emerges from a series of surveys undertaken in the 1930s asking teachers to reflect on the psychological element of their teacher training.[109] Here, despite the potential bias of the samples (focusing on the newly trained) and of the investigators (in most cases, clearly keen to defend the importance of psychology), the fact that the findings were so consistent does suggest that they merit serious consideration.

All four surveys were on the side of psychology: reporting criticisms from some teachers but outweighing these with a common series of perceived benefits. Those with greater experience tended to be more critical, suggesting that practice was a better guide than theory and that psychology was no more than fancy common sense.[110] Elsewhere, there was clear excitement about psychology, not just as something that would reshape teaching, but also as a source for personal growth and revelation.[111] Undoubtedly, this was an important element in the general view that one of the great values of a psychological dimension was that it made training, and then teaching, so much more interesting.[112] Many of the trainees were very young and would have been inexperienced in life as well as in work. They appear to have been attracted by psychology because it offered guidance to overcome such inexperience, but in their own lives, as much as in their need to understand the child, helping them to grapple with personal relations.[113] Undoubtedly, the increasing influence of psychoanalysis contributed both to the potential attraction of psychology as a guide in personal and even sexual relations, but also to anxieties about the potential psychological damage of taking the introspective psychological route.

Susan Isaacs, though more influential than any other figure in bringing a psychoanalytic perspective to teachers in this period, and in that sense a key populariser, recognised that such ideas were both difficult and disturbing, particularly since so many of the trainees were 'themselves not yet out of the wood with regard to their own emotional conflicts'.[114] It had led some of these teachers down the path of 'morbid introspection' and 'unhealthy self-analysis'. There was also a real danger in confusing the roles of the analyst and the teacher. The latter depended not only upon real expertise (this was 'a spring from which one must drink deeply or not at all'), but also on an emotional transference that was simply incompatible with the teacher–pupil relationship. Isaacs warned against 'quasi-educators going

---

[109] M. Phillips, 'Professional Courses in the Training of Teachers: A Report on an Enquiry into Values', *British Journal of Educational Psychology (BJEP)*, 1 (1931), 225–44; A. W. Wolters, 'Psychology in the Training of Teachers', *BJEP*, 5 (1935), 250–5; A. Lloyd-Evans, 'The Place of Psychology in the Training of Teachers', *BJEP*, 5 (1935), 257–64; H. R. Hamley, 'The Place of Psychology in the Training of Teachers', *BJEP*, 6 (1936), 1–7.

[110] Phillips, 'Professional Courses', 235, 237.

[111] Ibid. 231–2; Hamley, 'The Place of Psychology', 4.

[112] Phillips, 'Professional Courses', 234; Wolters, 'Psychology in Training', 251–2.

[113] Phillips, 'Professional Courses', 231–2.

[114] Isaacs, *Social Development*, 415.

about who do attempt to educate by a sort of analysis, as well as to analyse by a sort of education'.[115] The ranks of psychology's supporters within teaching rarely did go this far: though a few notorious figures like Neill and Homer Lane clearly had. It landed Lane in considerable trouble, with accusations of abuse relating to his 'Little Colony' forcing its closure.[116] Neill too had initially offered psychotherapeutic sessions to Summerhill pupils, seeing the uncovering of the unconscious as a panacea. However, it gradually became clear that cure was just as likely in its absence, and that the nature of the school regime—its fostering of freedom and love—was far more important. Therapy could even be harmful if the doctors—Freudians, for instance, towards whom he felt an increasing disenchantment—were opposed to freedom.[117] In Neill's view, a therapeutic approach was ultimately too obsessed with the pathological, not interested enough in life.[118] It was not in fact until the 1960s that there was a serious attempt to extend a psychotherapeutic 'counselling' role to teachers, the heightened level of anxiety about the adolescent, the inadequacy of the home environment, and the changing relationship between pupils and teachers helping to overcome resistance from the experts.[119]

Nevertheless, teachers well before this did see in psychology, if not therapeutic tools, at least some basic insight that would help in dealing with personal relations and problems, and this was important in reshaping attitudes to teaching more generally. There was a great deal of interest, for instance, in what psychology had to reveal about the abnormal child.[120] This, in turn, fostered alertness, a genuine interest in, and a tolerance towards individual difference in all children. The focus of teaching shifted as a result, from instructing students about subjects, to recognising the students as subjects—indeed, psychological subjects—in their own right. What psychology brought was not definite pedagogic practices—this was what was wrong with the 'Masters of Method' approach of the past; rather, method had to adapt itself to mind. Just as in the world of industrial psychology,

---

[115] Wolters, 'Psychology in Training', 254; Lloyd-Evans, 'The Place of Psychology', 261; Hamley, 'The Place of Psychology', 1.

[116] H. Lane, *Talks to Parents and Teachers* (London, 1928), 8–14.

[117] A. S. Neill, *'Neill! Neill! Orange Peel': A Personal View of Ninety Years* (London, 1972), 210.

[118] Hence his attraction to Wilhelm Reich, to whom he wrote of Melanie Klein: 'To read her is like being in a graveyard with open putrefying bodies': Neill to Reich, 5 Feb. 1949, in B. R. Placzek, *Record of a Friendship: The Correspondence between Wilhelm Reich and A. S. Neill, 1936–1957* (London, 1982).

[119] A. Holden, *Teachers as Counsellors* (London, 1969). In 1965, the National Association for Mental Health began to organise courses in school counselling for experienced teachers. Initial opposition came from psychiatrists and psychologists. Supporters defended that counselling was not the same as therapy: it was preventive rather than remedial, educational rather than clinical. However, by 1973, the founding of a professional journal would announce the birth of a 'counselling movement'. In the face of shortages of expertise and the problems of at least 5 per cent of their pupils, there was a new assertiveness about the need of teachers to play a psychotherapeutic role: Editorial, *British Journal of Guidance and Counselling*, 1 (1973), 2; U. Maguire, 'The School Counsellor as Therapist', *British Journal of Guidance and Counselling*, 3 (1975), 160–71. For more on the post-war counselling movement, see Ch. 8.   [120] Hamley, 'The Place of Psychology', 6–7.

there was no 'one best way'.[121] Such teachers were rarely that excited by abstract psychology—lists of instincts and faculties of mind, or models of perception and memory—or even by so-called 'laws of learning'.[122] Neither did they particularly warm to the mental test.[123] What did animate them was any demonstration of how psychological understanding could help in the school situation, sometimes in the form of practical teaching methods, but most often in dealing with the child as an individual.[124] Psychology, therefore, was partly attractive as an aid to help the often inexperienced, childless, and young teacher cope with the daunting challenge of managing children, and for this reason one of the surveys called for training to pay more attention to the psychology of discipline and freedom.[125] More fundamentally and more idealistically, it appealed as a way to humanise and individualise education.

Women appear to have been keenest on the promise of psychology as a tool of both management and humanisation.[126] Men were either more likely to focus on its use in techniques of learning, or were sceptical about whether it was of any use at all. This was partly because most of the men in this survey worked in secondary schools, where the examination system meant that there was more pressure for teaching to centre on subjects of knowledge. Women were perhaps predisposed because they were in general less approving of disciplinary modes of management, including the still prevalent corporal punishment—which was itself heavily gendered in its focus on boys.[127] The admonition for education to be a source of love and security from a figure like Isaacs, and for a resulting quite radical shift in the recommended emotional style of teaching, may also have found more sympathy from women, who were already culturally located as more naturally equipped for a mothering role.[128] A relationship between gender and professionalisation was also at work, with psychology, as a new and lower status area than subject-specific educational studies, providing opportunities for women in the first place and in doing so marking itself out as a feminised sphere for other women to follow.[129]

THE CHILD'S PERSPECTIVE

If teaching really did become more child-centred then one might hope to find validation of this in first hand accounts of childhood. However, there are some fundamental difficulties when it comes to addressing such a question. There is in

---

[121] See Ch. 5.   [122] Hamley, 'The Place of Psychology', 4.
[123] Wolters, 'Psychology in Training', 253.   [124] Hamley, 'The Place of Psychology', 2–3.
[125] Ibid. 5.   [126] Phillips, 'Professional Courses', 238.   [127] Ibid. 234.
[128] On the persistence of corporal punishment (mainly for boys): D. Thom, 'The Healthy Citizen of Empire or Juvenile Delinquent? Beating and Mental Health in the UK', in Gijswijt-Hofstra and Marland (eds.), *Cultures of Child Health in Britain and the Netherlands*, 189–212. On the relationship between mothering and educating: C. Steedman, ' "The Mother Made Conscious": The Historical Development of a Primary School Pedagogy', *History Workshop Journal*, 20 (1985), 149–63.
[129] Lloyd-Evans, 'The Place of Psychology', 257–60.

particular the problem of the reliability of memories of childhood.[130] Whether written or oral, such accounts are invariably those of adults looking back: the adult's view of the child mind. There may be a tendency to fit personal memories of education into well-established public narratives. In particular, the powerful image of nineteenth-century education centred on discipline and rote learning may have influenced the view of schooling well after such a style was breaking down in practice. Moreover, without something to compare with, children were not in a strong position to recognise shifts. If we accept the psychologists' arguments about what was natural and what unnatural, they were probably more likely to recollect the 'unnatural' discipline that remained.

Adults looking back may not have been aware of what was progressive in the context of the time. Jeremy Seabrook's autobiographical study of childhood in the 1950s, for instance, dismisses the impact of new educational ideas because the driving assumption was that a working-class mind was incapable of dealing with abstract ideas.[131] However, this fails to recognise that the new educational ideas encouraged such a position, suggesting that abstraction was artificial, and that children responded better to the concrete, as it was both more natural and more interesting. The new education embraced the challenge of reaching out to a working-class child population at a time when these minds were in many ways alien to the middle-class reformers, and consequently assumptions about class pervaded the era's idea of the child mind. By the last decades of the century, that concrete mind and the suspicion towards abstraction could appear to have nothing to do with new educational ideas; in fact, it had everything to do with them, except that these ideas now came from another time. A new set of more individualist values were now driving concern about liberating the child.

Although autobiographical material is unlikely to be that directly revealing about the influence of psychology on pedagogy, some insight may emerge from attention to underlying assumptions. For instance, autobiographies of childhood before the pedagogic shifts of the twentieth century highlight the central position of memory work at school. Daisy Cowper, recalling her working-class childhood in Liverpool where she was born in 1890, seemed to have accepted the model of the child mind as an essentially empty vessel: 'Children's minds are so receptive, so unconcerned with matters that call for much thought that oft repetition seems to make impressions that are altogether indelible.'[132] Though this is Daisy the adult's point of view, it does suggest the influence of a particular psychological view of the child mind, perhaps outside as well as within the school, and the way that this could be inscribed in the consciousness of the child and future adult.

Most historians have accepted that children did not like the dominant nineteenth-century instructional and disciplinary approach in schooling. However,

130 Steedman, *Childhood, Culture and Class*, 71.
131 J. Seabrook, *Working-Class Childhood* (London, 1982), 48.
132 J. Burnett (ed.), *Destiny Obscure: Autobiographies of Childhood, Education and Family from 1820 to the 1920s* (London, 1982), 204.

there has been little direct attention to whether attitudes changed as a new pedagogy emerged. In his oral history of working-class childhood in the period 1889–1939, Stephen Humphries regards children as consistent in their hostility to school and their subversion of the syllabus, whether it be of a more liberal variant or not.[133] Such hostility has been put in question by Jonathan Rose through his own analysis of oral histories recalling childhood from 1875 to 1918—a slightly earlier period than that of Humphries.[134] If one accepts that progressivism would go on to push schooling even further away from the disciplinary approach that Rose already questions as something of a caricature at the start of the century, then one might expect his picture of an enthusiasm for education to have become stronger still in the decades that followed.

On the other hand, whether children went to school more willingly or not, does not help us that much with the question of whether and how this schooling may have shaped them as psychological subjects. Contemporary psychological research would offer a potential source, but this remains a completely neglected subject among historians.[135] However, as Britain faced the rise of political extremism and violence in the middle of the century there seemed more reason than ever to take seriously the argument that education could be a crucial arena for the making of psychological subjects fit for a world of peace, tolerance, and freedom.[136] By the 1960s, as anxieties emerged about the permissiveness of the new generation, critics too rounded on the influence of psychology in education, with its emphasis on free expression, as a key to the changing of the psychological subject.[137] In short, even though historians have been wary of engaging with its psycho-historical assumptions, the idea that psychology could be a vehicle within the education system for changing human nature would be of crucial importance for much of the century.

BEYOND THE SCHOOL

If the role of the teacher was one way in which the psychology of the child mind could hugely extend its influence, the other was the channel of the parent. At the start of the century, 600,000 children under five years of age—a remarkable 43 per cent of the age cohort—were being educated in infant schools. The figure had risen dramatically from 1870, as non-fee paying, state elementary provision expanded, and as fewer older siblings remained at home to help with care of the very young. The presence in school of such a high number of very young children

---

[133] S. Humphries, *Hooligans or Rebels: An Oral History of Working-Class Childhood and Youth, 1889–1939* (Oxford, 1981), 28–61.

[134] J. Rose, *The Intellectual Life of the British Working Classes* (New Haven and London, 2001), 146–86.

[135] For instance, a study based on interviews and drawings of five-year-old children in London and Brisbane, Australia: R. Griffiths, *A Study in Imagination in Early Childhood* (London, 1935).

[136] See Ch. 7.   [137] See Ch. 8.

must have been a significant factor in encouraging the rethinking of pedagogy that was taking place. However, the combined effect of rising consciousness about the special needs of very young children and stretched resources would soon put the system under pressure. Local Education Authorities began to exclude the under fives from infant schools. By the mid-1930s, the number of children under five years of age in the infant classes of the state elementary system had fallen dramatically, now just 155,000. Specialist nursery provision had expanded, but it only made up for a small part of the shortfall, with just fifty-nine schools serving 4,446 children by 1934; though this was rising quite rapidly, and doing so within the context of a falling birth-rate, to reach 5,666 children in around a hundred nurseries by 1938. The main trend, nevertheless, and a very striking one, was a move away from school, to home care, for the under fives.[138] If educationalists and psychologists were going to make their ideas about this group count, they would have to reach out to parents rather than teachers.

This was not the only factor behind such a reorientation. Parents themselves were becoming more interested in what went on in schools. In the 1940s, when Lowndes wrote of a 'silent social revolution' having taken place in education since the late-nineteenth century, he was making the point that change came about because of pressure bubbling up from below. A significant indicator was the growth of parents' associations.[139] One of the things that such parents became concerned about was psychology. In 1932, the *New Era* began to publish a supplement, *Parents and Children*, which also incorporated the *Bulletin of the Home and School Council of Great Britain*. Here, parents encountered articles on child rearing, many from the leading psychologists of the day. Consciousness also spread through study circles and discussion groups. The supplement proved so successful that from 1936 it became a separate publication under the new title *Home and School*.

Psychologists themselves were increasingly likely to point out that the problems of the child within the school did not exist in isolation from those of home life. The growing influence of psychoanalytical thought encouraged this reorientation. Teachers also became more aware of having to think about the individuality of the child as something that necessitated looking well beyond the classroom.[140] However, once again psychologists faced a dilemma over popularisation: recognising its necessity if influence was to reach the home, but with serious misgivings about encouraging amateur dabbling in the potentially dangerous territory of psychoanalysis. Thus, Susan Isaacs reached out to parents in *Highway*, the journal of the Workers' Education Association, as well as *Home and School*, and published a highly influential popular book, *The Nursery Years*, in 1929. She recognised that it was undoubtedly useful for parents, like teachers, to have a basic understanding

---

[138] F. Hawtrey, 'The Nursery School and its Future', *The New Era in Home and School*, 17/5 (1936), 200–7; Whitbread, *The Nursery-Infant School*, 42–6.

[139] Lowndes, *Silent Social Revolution*, 128–9, 181.

[140] Hamley, 'The Place of Psychology', 6–7.

of psychoanalysis. However, she also believed that it was inappropriate and potentially very harmful for them to use psychoanalysis in practice, their parental role incompatible with the emotional transference—of hate, as well as love—at the heart of analysis.[141] As she put it:

> The serious risk when any person, with an active real relation to the child, makes attempts to get below the surface of the child's mind in pursuit of his ordinary relation is that it is really impossible to know what the effect may be, what immense conflicts he may be stimulating, and what immense changes of feeling, positive and negative, he may be drawing to his person, without ever being able to dispense these again by tracing them to their sources in the real experiences of infancy.[142]

The best that the psychoanalyst could hope to do was to reach out with general advice on behaviour, informed by psychoanalysis but in non-technical language and with no encouragement to the parents to act as their child's own analyst. Symbolising this dilemma and the desire to translate psychoanalysis into a tamer, practical, common sense for popular consumption, she adopted the pseudonym Ursula Wise in her advice column in *Nursery World*.[143]

This ambivalence about the popularisation of a psychology of intimacy may help to account for the apparent discrepancy between what the leading child psychologists of the day believed in, on the one hand, and what existing histories of childcare literature claim was dominant practice, on the other. To some extent, such surveys make a mistake in assuming that what was happening in the United States (where behaviourism did have considerable popular appeal) tells us about views on the other side of the Atlantic. When one turns to British publications, it is difficult to find direct validation for the claim that J. B. Watson was an important, let alone a dominant influence, in the British context.[144] There may have been suspicion of the Freudian position on sex, but this did not mean rejection of the broader implications of the new psychology. The picture of a behaviourist obsession with habit training or of a taboo on love sits very strangely alongside the popular appeal of a psychoanalytic psychology filtered of its most controversial and potentially upsetting dimension.[145]

In her study of childcare advice, Christina Hardyment locates the 1939 publication of American couple Anderson and Mary Aldrich's *Babies are Human Beings* as a turning point between a behaviourist and psychoanalytic emphasis in Britain. Even then, she notes that because of the war it took a while for the new approach to work its way into social life. It is really the affluence of the post-war

---

[141] Isaacs, *Social Development*, 403–13.   [142] Ibid. 412–13.

[143] Some of this correspondence was republished, now under Isaacs' own name in *Children and Parents: Their Problems and Difficulties* (London, 1948). Her most noted venture in popularisation was *The Nursery Years: The Mind of the Child from Birth to Six Years*, first published in 1929 and in its seventeenth print run by 1960. Ursula was the name of one of the central children in Isaacs' Malting House studies.

[144] C. Hardyment, *Dream Babies: Child Care from Locke to Spock* (London, 1983), 164–5, 173.

[145] See the discussion of the shift in popular taste in the 1930s in Ch. 1.

era that she regards as most crucial, freeing up time, for instance through the spread of domestic appliances, for unprecedented parental attention. Ideologically, the interwar emphasis on control was also out of step with a cold war emphasis on the value of freedom. The new common sense, epitomised by the American Dr Benjamin Spock, was one of enjoying babies and children rather than worrying about them. Again, in the emphasis on labour-saving devices, the cold war context, even Spock, she may rather too readily have assumed that what mattered in the United States did so in the same way in Britain.

In the early 1960s, John and Elizabeth Newson had interviewed 700 working-class British mothers of one-year-olds about childcare practice.[146] They found that the keynote of childcare advice was flexibility: general principles, rather than prescriptions. Spock, they point out, had his British counterparts in psychologist Donald Winnicott, with his lectures on the BBC, and Dr Hugh Jolly, with his column in *The Times*.[147] The key was to enjoy parenting—a 'fun morality' as the Newsons called it, borrowing from an American study a decade earlier.[148] Like Hardyment, they contrasted post-war childcare to the more authoritarian 'hygienist' style of the interwar period, suggesting that the latter had emerged out of a longer prescriptive tradition with science now replacing the authority of religion.[149] The figure of the New Zealand-born Truby King, both here and in Hardyment's account, looms large in the characterisation of the interwar period, because of the influence of his highly regimented vision of baby care, with strict patterns for feeding and sleeping. Whether historians have too readily accepted that mothers really did follow such an extraordinarily rigid regime should remain open to debate. It certainly does not represent or reflect what was happening within mental hygiene. In the British context, the psychological advice offered to mothers in the post-war decades was a development out of interwar mental hygiene, not a reaction against it.

At the heart of Hardyment's history of childcare advice is the view that the expert does not necessarily know best. It is a picture of the ephemeral nature of expert theory, of ideas running back and forth, and of medical fashion rather than progress. One of the reasons why the early twentieth century is viewed so negatively is that this was the era of the expert coming to the fore: by contrast, her chapter on the preceding period 1820–1870 takes the title 'mothers in command'.[150] The shift of power from mothers to experts brought with it, she argues, a loss of affection. Instead, what we see is an attempt 'to produce well-behaved, polite children, with regular habits, who could easily be disciplined to fit into the assembly-line culture of the new metropolis'.[151] However, it is difficult to see why

[146] J. and E. Newson, *Patterns of Infant Care in an Urban Community* (London, 1963).
[147] D.W. Winnicott, *Getting to Know your Baby: Six Broadcast Talks* (London, 1944).
[148] M. Wolfenstein, 'Fun Morality: An Analysis of Recent American Child-Training Literature', in M. Mead and M. Wolfenstein (eds.), *Childhood in Contemporary Cultures* (Chicago, 1955).
[149] J. and E. Newson, 'Cultural Aspects of Childrearing in the English-Speaking World', in M. Richards (eds.), *The Integration of a Child into a Social World* (Cambridge, 1974), 53–82.
[150] Ibid. 86.   [151] Hardyment, *Dream Babies*, 229.

middle-class families would have wanted or accepted such an industrialised vision of the child. And though it might have fitted some middle-class assumptions about the working-class child, the parents of such children were far less likely to be reached by such advice in the first place. What we do know about the middle-class family during this period is that it was likely to contain significantly fewer children than in the mid-nineteenth century. This major shift in patterns of fertility was also spreading down the social scale. Improvements in hygiene, medicine, and standards of living meant that children were also more likely to survive, and these were the demographic conditions to foster a greater prizing of the child. Some of the cultural conditions have already been noted: the romanticisation in literature and the popularisation of child study among them.[152] The acute loss—demographic and psychological—of the First World War experienced in Britain may have added to this prizing and fostered a particular psychological culture as a result. Here we may find something that helps to explain the contrast to the behaviourist emphasis in the United States, where the First World War was a less traumatic experience for the majority of the population. In Britain, the war had two profoundly significant psychological legacies. Firstly, in its shattering of optimism about human nature, it promoted the new psychology's concern about man's hidden drives and in so doing drew attention to the importance of attending to the healthy development of these drives in the child.[153] Secondly, it directed a generation of psychologists who had gone through this experience to explore the psychology of loss and attachment.[154] Out of the war, therefore, there came an interest in the psychological origins in the child of both love and hate. The new psychology would cater to such interests; behaviourism did not. The second problem with the idea of experts imposing authoritarian behaviourism is that, although this was undoubtedly a key era in the emergence of the psychological expert, it also saw the emergence of a popular psychological culture. Characteristic of this culture, particularly in the first decades of the century, was scepticism about the expert and an emphasis on self-realisation: both acted as brakes on hygienism.

CONCLUSION

This chapter has highlighted some of the limitations to the spread of psychology's influence on mental testing, child guidance, and behaviourism. It has argued that the influence on pedagogy was at least as important and its potential far greater.

---

[152] V. Zelizer, *Pricing the Priceless Child: The Changing Social Value of Children* (New York, 1985); R. Cooter, 'Introduction', in R. Cooter (ed.), *In the Name of the Child: Health and Welfare, 1880–1940* (London, 1992), 1–18.

[153] P. Crook, *Darwinism, War and History: The Debate over the Biology of War from the 'Origin of Species' to the First World War* (Cambridge, 1994).

[154] J. C. Lerner and N. Newcombe, 'Britain between the Wars: The Historical Context of Bowlby's Theory of Attachment', *Psychiatry*, 45 (1982), 1–12; P. Halmos, *The Ability to Mourn: Disillusionment and the Social Origins of Psychoanalysis* (Chicago, 1989). For further discussion, see Ch. 7.

Here, its character was also markedly different. Rather than a tool for regulation and normalisation, it was attractive as a way to realise the full and hidden nature of the child and reshape education accordingly. Particularly at the start of the period, Psychology had a utopian and romantic quality. This could inspire broader popular support, evident for instance in the Froebel and Child Study movements, the involvement of Theosophists, and the enthusiasm for nursery schools. It also, however, had important supporters at the heart of the educational establishment, and in modified form (with a balance between freedom and discipline), it did help to reshape practice in state elementary education. The focus on a small number of more radical independent schools has obscured this more important story. Whether this had much impact on children themselves is another matter and awaits further study, though the fact that those looking back failed to appreciate this needs cautious interpretation. Gradually, during the interwar period, a psychoanalytic approach also became more important. It appears that many teachers, particularly new teachers, and particularly women, were excited about how this psychology helped them to think about themselves as well as their children: an idealistic but also a practical issue. This approach also exposed the limitation of focusing on school life alone, and thus the focus of popularisation turned to reaching out to parents. As already apparent from the opening chapter of the book, it found a ready audience. However, in the case of parents, as in that of teachers, popularisation of psychoanalysis faced the dilemma that the demand for knowledge was always in danger of spilling over into a desire for tools of practice that were not clinically appropriate and were even dangerous. Practice on the ground therefore tended to reflect, as in the culture of practical psychology, processes of translation and accommodation with local needs and existing values. Ultimately, just because the psychological experts may have been dismissive about what went on in the classroom or the home does not mean that a version of psychological thought and practice was not important. This chapter has attempted to open these areas for exploration.

5

Psychology and the Problem of Industrial Civilisation

In Britain, the rise of psychology took place in a society with an acute consciousness of the problems of industrial civilisation. It would come to both reflect this context and provide a new tool for understanding and even defining it. Indeed, in setting the mental and thereby the ethical alongside the economic, psychology was one of those forces that could help to frame the situation as one of industrial civilisation, not just industrial society. A historiography that focuses on class politics tends to overlook this mental and ethical dimension.[1] The third chapter of this book has already highlighted the relationship between this context and currents of psychological thought and activity within interwar intellectual circles. This chapter looks at thinking about the relationship between industrial civilisation and the psychological within the discipline itself, but also among employers, advertisers and managers, on the one hand, and within the working classes and among their representatives, on the other. To date, only the first of these—and then only with respect to psychology's role in industrial psychology and in attempts to enhance productivity, rather than in its input to a rethinking of advertising and consumption—has attracted much attention. When it comes to industrial psychology, this chapter will suggest that, despite an excitement about the potential of psychology to transform economic thinking and practice, in particular to rescue man from the tyranny of the machine, the practical achievement was narrow and largely technical. At best, industrial psychology was a valuable, though relatively minor, contribution to industrial welfare; at worst, it would struggle to prove itself as much more than Taylorism in new humanist guise. The chapter also, however, sets out to demonstrate the existence of a psychological dialogue with the problems of industrial civilisation that reached well beyond the confines of the profession itself. In both respects—the limitations of industrial

---

[1] Bertrand and Dora Russell used the term to suggest that the key problem of such an age was its challenge to the mental freedom of humanity: *The Prospects of Industrial Civilisation* (London, 1923). Psychology would also be central in the ethical analysis of C. Delisle Burns: *Industry and Civilisation* (London, 1925). See also J. H. Blaksely, 'Some Problems of an Industrial Civilisation', *Human Factor*, 10 (1936), 322–9. Typical of the historical focus on class politics, and the frame of 'industrial society' rather than civilisation: K. Middlemas, *Politics in Industrial Society* (London, 1979).

psychology, and the broader nature of interest—we see some of the problems of a model of the worker's psychological subjectivity that centres too exclusively on the ambitions of the psychologists.[2] Instead, in highlighting the different ways that psychologists, employers and managers, and workers approached the psychological problems of industrial civilisation, the importance of class in mediating psychological thinking becomes apparent. However, in each case, we also see the attraction of psychology as a system of thought that could offer an ethical appeal to positions that might otherwise have rested on the economics and politics of class alone. Sometimes, as with industrial psychology, the hope was to obscure class or economic interest. In other instances, psychology was attractive as a tool to crystallise and further a consciousness both of class and of the ills of an industrial civilisation.

It is worth pointing out some of the potential implications of the themes explored in this chapter when set against the account of popular and practical psychology that has preceded it. Firstly, the earlier account pointed to a vibrant culture of psychological self-realisation, which envisaged its subjects as free agents, open to self-improvement, rather than trapped by the social, economic, and psychological conditions of an industrial society. Both the practical psychologists and the intellectuals of the *New Age* circle positioned themselves against the mechanising threat of an industrial civilisation. This chapter provides the opportunity to examine whether those who faced more directly the problem of industrial society embraced psychology when it was applied from above, resisted it, or appropriated it in making sense of their own positions and in fashioning an independent response. In doing so, it will explore the potential of psychology as a tool of critique and complaint, to be wielded against the existing economic system, rather than something that was passively accepted in its support. Secondly, this chapter sets out to demonstrate that for workers, but also their employers and managers, the appeal of something more akin to the practical psychology explored in the first chapter was at least as significant in guiding them in relation to the problems of industrial civilisation, as was industrial psychology. The suggestion here is that we have paid too much attention to the efforts of a rather insecure industrial psychology concerned with increasing productivity and need to pay more to the ways in which psychology intersected with thinking about consumption, the health of the worker, and thinking about class relations. Finally, in comparison to the earlier account of popular psychology, the focus in this chapter shifts more to the working class and to men. Indeed, it was partly because of the high profile of the problem of industrial society that the working class and men began to move to the forefront of concern about mental health, and this would contribute to the emergence of psychology as an issue of national, not merely private, importance by the Second World War.

---

[2] Rose, *Governing the Soul*, 55–118.

INDUSTRIAL PSYCHOLOGY

The new psychology exposed the inadequacy of an economics that assumed humans behaved according to rational decisions about the balance between pleasure and pain.[3] It was suggested that the persistence of such thinking might be an object for psychological inquiry, the reflection of 'a psychological "complex" peculiar to those who organise modern industry'.[4] The new psychology shifted the focus of attention to a much broader set of instincts and drives that through civilisation came to be organised around goals. It suggested a new economic subject, more potentially irrational but at the same time more constrained and channelled by values, and moved out of an artificial, individualist isolation to be recognised as an unavoidably social animal. Such insight had potential implications far beyond mere organisation of the workplace. It pointed to a new understanding, not only of the worker and the working class, of unions and organised labour, but of employers, owners of companies and investors, and the middle classes. It had implications, not only for the problem of production, but for selling and advertising, as well as labour relations and class politics.[5] What made all of this so important was that the new psychology revealed the economic system as a whole as being, if not in terminal crisis, then in need of radical reform. In particular, approaching the worker as a psychological subject provided a case for replacing a mechanistic approach to the industrial system that overlooked workers' needs and interests by a humanist system that did not. Focusing so much on industrial psychology, with its limited and technical deployment of a psychological view of the worker, historians have overlooked this much broader moment of opportunity and excitement, which casts light on the idealism that accompanied the initial industrial psychology project but also highlights how disappointingly narrow the remit of industrial psychology became in practice.

Attempts to extend mental health care for adults into the community in the first decades of the century would face some fundamental barriers, including limited resources in terms of personnel and finance, and resistance from a culture of rights and responsibilities.[6] Because of this, the workplace became the most important early site, other than the army in temporary circumstances of war, for the discipline of psychology to access the adult British subject. In confined sites,

---

[3] McDougall, *Social Psychology*, 9. See also Ch. 2. Recently, some economists, such as Amartya Sen, have become more concerned about the 'anti-psychological' attitude of their discipline and have looked back with interest to the way that instinct theory fundamentally challenged an economics based on a hedonistic view of human nature at the start of the century. It is suggested that this fell away because of the rising influence of behaviourism (but in doing so, this overestimates the hold of the latter in the British interwar context): S. Lewin, 'Economics and Psychology: Lessons for Our Own Day from the Early Twentieth Century', *Journal of Economic Literature*, 34 (1996), 1293–1323.

[4] Burns, *Industry and Civilisation*, 140–3.

[5] M. Freeden, *Liberalism Divided: A Study in British Political Thought, 1914–1939* (Oxford, 1986), 228–46.   [6] Thomson, 'Constituting Citizenship'.

such as the mental hospital and the prison, a minority of adults were in addition potentially exposed to constant psychological intervention; but because of the shift of concern from policing mental abnormality to monitoring and shaping mental health, this intervention was regarded by professionals within the relevant fields as too little and too late. The workplace was important because it offered something midway between the total institution and the community. A difficult process of negotiation would be necessary, but access was feasible. The workplace, as such, was of similar potential importance to the education system in the case of the child, hence its importance in a body of work that explores the imposition from above of psychology as a tool of governance.[7]

Industrial psychology has also attracted attention among labour historians. Here, the tendency has been to position it alongside scientific management as a way to squeeze more production out of the labour force under the screen of welfare and as a way to wrest control at the point of production from workers to managers. It is portrayed as a tool which came to the fore because the increased power of labour demanded strategies of appeasement, but which still ultimately served the economic interests of capital rather than labour.[8] There is much to say for this interpretation. However, the scientific and ethical rationales do merit consideration, particularly since they could be in tension with the economic interests of the employers. Indeed, as a tool for raising efficiency and profit it had only limited success, struggling both to satisfy the interests of labour and to overcome the suspicions of employers. Nevertheless, for all its original idealism, industrial psychology would prove unable either to distance itself in practice from the mechanism of an efficiency engineering that broke the worker up into parts, or to position itself as being equally interested in the welfare of the worker as the profits of the employer. It wanted to reveal the worker as a real human individual, but its tools of measurement, abstraction and generalisation, and its focus on work in isolation, made this very difficult. Such a psychology was in stark contrast to that of knowing oneself, and of bettering, expanding, and even liberating oneself that had such popular appeal in the same years. It is no surprise to find that those involved in this culture were keen to contrast their own holistic approach to that of the industrial psychologists.[9]

Work on scientific management before the First World War suggests that it had made little progress in Britain, particularly if set against developments in the United States. This reflected both a general reluctance to innovate within a conservative

[7] Its central position, for instance, in Rose's, *Governing the Soul*, 55–118. Questioning its central position in defining the subjectivity of the worker: B. Whitelaw, 'Industry and the Interior Life: Industrial 'Experts' and the Mental World of Workers in Twentieth Century Britain', Ph.D. thesis in progress (University of Warwick).

[8] A. McIvor, *A History of Work in Britain, 1880–1950* (Basingstoke, 2001), 95, 93–109; K. Whitson, 'Scientific Management and Production Management Practice in Britain between the Wars', *Historical Studies in Industrial Relations*, 1 (1996), 47–76.

[9] For instance, W. Myddleton, 'Mental Stature', *Practical Psychology*, 1/3 (1924), 18–21; J. A. M. Alcock, *New Age*, 27 (20 May 1920), 42–3.

industrial culture, and the continuing hold of what the new psychologists dismissed as 'the cynicism of a purely hedonistic economics' as well as a habit of laissez-faire.[10] On the eve of the First World War, there was a brief spell of interest in the ideas of the American guru of scientific management and time and motion study, Frederick Winslow Taylor, but otherwise, argue the historians of this subject, 'British interest remained vague, cool and distant'.[11] British management was still primarily interested in the technical side of production. Thus, there was initially more interest in Taylor as an expert on high-speed steel manufacturing than in his broader ideas about a new approach to management. Although interest in management was growing by the second decade of the century, this centred on the practical issues of costing and cost control. Few in fact had read Taylor.[12]

Most accounts of this subject agree that the First World War was a key event in the introduction and spread of scientific management within Britain. However, the war also provided the circumstances for an 'Anglicisation', with British industrial psychology emerging to soften the crude profit-drive of American scientific management. The demands of industrialised warfare turned effective use of available labour into an issue of national importance, and the government responded by setting up the Health of Munitions Workers Committee and promoted the importance of this work through the propaganda of the Munitions Ministry's Welfare Department. Such conditions also offered new opportunities for workers to gain more power within industry, and war saw the development of a shop steward's movement and new demands for worker control and industrial democracy. One immediate result was the post-war experimentation with Whitleyism and joint councils between employers and workers. However, this petered out as the economic slump setting in from 1920 weakened the power of the trade unions. Instead, the Health of Munitions Workers experiment heralded an increasingly prevalent strategy in addressing the industrial problems of the interwar period.

The exceptional demands of economic mobilisation for a national war effort had been crucial in bringing to the fore an interest in the psychology of work. Full employment directed attention towards physical but also psychological constraints on productivity that the elasticity of the labour market usually obscured. The Health of Munitions Workers Committee, set up in 1915, was particularly concerned with fatigue and took an increasingly psychological view of the problem. However, with the return of peace, the propitious circumstances soon disappeared. The government retreated from its interventionist role. Employers had less need to worry about finessing the output of the worker when work once again became cheap and readily available, and in particular as demand slumped. The unions, meanwhile, were preoccupied with a fight to find and secure work, and in such an environment were inclined to be suspicious of employers' motivations in using experts to advise on work.[13] In short, economic circumstances were

---

[10] L. Urwick and E. F. L. Brech, *The Making of Scientific Management*, 2 (London, 1957), 202.
[11] Ibid. 88.   [12] Ibid. 89–102.
[13] M. Rose, *Industrial Behaviour: Theoretical Development since Taylor* (London, 1975), 99.

far from favourable for the establishment of industrial psychology in interwar Britain. The fact that it both came to the fore with considerable initial enthusiasm and then survived in a reasonable state of health suggests that at least part of its appeal did lie elsewhere.

At the centre of the history of British interest in the field, the National Institute for Industrial Psychology opened in March 1921. At the helm throughout the period was psychologist C. S. Myers. Although important early support came from philanthropy and government as well as industry, it would be securing the latter that was crucial for survival in the long term. The worsening economic situation meant that this was no easy task. In order to create a market, the Institute had to overcome widespread public ignorance. It sent representatives around the country, lecturing and organising conferences, broadcasts, and exhibitions at trade shows.[14] Meanwhile, a meeting took place at the Mansion House in 1922 to emphasise the national importance of industrial psychology at a time of industrial and economic crisis.[15] Excitement that this project would address some of the central problems of industrial civilisation helps to make sense of the decision of Myers to give up his prestigious position at Cambridge University to become full-time Director in June 1922.[16] In a radio broadcast of 1923, he would herald industrial psychology as key in the transition between an 'age of mechanism' and a new 'age of humanism'.[17] The actual achievements would be far narrower, more technical, and mundane.

A typical early investigation looked at workers in the tin-box industry, recognised as having jobs with a very high level of strain and repetition. A time and motion study suggested some small changes, such as altering the height of the bench, which resulted in a 9 per cent saving in production time. Other recommendations were the result of more general observations about the workplace, such as those concerning use of ventilation and reduction of heat.[18] The key psychological element of this early work was the insight, inherited from wartime work on 'fatigue', that the way people responded to work was as much mental as physical. Thus, breaking up work into a complex series of actions for short-term gain might seem like a good idea from the perspective of the stopwatch, but in fact placed long-term mental strain on the worker. The psychologist's solution was to replace fatiguing voluntary decision-making by rhythm: conscious by unconscious action.[19]

---

[14] Anon., 'The Early History of the NIIP', *JNIIP*, 1 (1922), 2; and G. H. Miles, 'An Autobiography Part I', *Occupational Psychology*, 23 (1949), 208–11.

[15] 'Mansion House Meeting', *JNIIP*, 2 (1922), 59–60.   [16] Miles, 'Autobiography', 209.

[17] C. S. Myers, 'The Human Side of Industry', *JNIIP*, 1, 8 (1923), 309.

[18] E. Farmer and S. C. Brooke, 'An Investigation into the Tin-Box Industry', *JNIIP*, 1 (1922), 9–11.

[19] See for instance an early report that claimed a 35 per cent increase in productivity following this strategy: E. Farmer and A. B. B. Eyre, 'An Investigation into the Packing of Chocolates', *JNIIP*, 1 (1922), 12–14; E. Farmer, 'The Economy of Human Effort in Industry', *JNIIP*, 1 (1922), 18–22.

A second 'psychological' element was the Institute's interest in utilising tests for vocational guidance.[20] There was always tension over the extent to which vocational work should figure in the Institute's work, with many feeling that moving industrial psychology beyond the workplace threatened the distinctiveness that was vital in establishing its claims as constituting some kind of scientific discipline in its own right.[21] However, vocational guidance was clearly a crucial component of the psychological vision for industrial civilisation, and one that at the time attracted considerable public excitement.[22] In its emphasis on measuring difference, it might appear to critics as a crude attempt to turn complex human character into little more than calculable numbers. Yet in truth, it aimed far beyond the snapshot of the test to take into account medical, parental, and home background, and, as such, it could present itself as a humanising influence: finding suitable work for all, and fitting the organisation of the workshop or office to the feelings, suitability, and individual psychology of the worker. Whereas economic conditions—the excess capacity of the labour market in particular—were unfavourable for an emphasis on raising productivity, they did encourage vocational guidance. Therefore, despite the misgivings from the perspective of the coherence of the field, this would be a key element in survival.[23]

Taylor's efficiency engineer provided an obvious target for industrial psychology to identify against: useful not only in attempts to highlight its supposedly more humane position, but also in defending its scientific credentials within the emerging discipline of psychology. Take, for instance, the concerted attack on the efficiency engineer's view that there was 'one best way' to do work.[24] Such a mantra ignored the importance of individual difference. In compounding a series of isolated actions from a variety of individuals to find the 'one best way', it failed to appreciate that living organisms were far more than the sum of their parts thrown together. It also made the crucial mistake of ignoring the fact that the feelings of the worker—who would inevitably be suspicious that the 'one best way' was seeking to undermine the craft basis of work—were as crucial to efficiency as mere mechanical speed.[25] Ultimately, like the psychology of an older era, efficiency engineering made the fundamental mistake of basing its 'one best way' on

[20] For instance, C. Burt, 'Tests for Clerical Occupations', *JNIIP*, 1 (1922), 23–7.

[21] Miles, 'Autobiography—Part I', 209; Miles, 'An Autobiography—Part II', *Occupational Psychology*, 24 (1950), 38–9.

[22] Evans and Waites, *IQ and Mental Testing*, 78. The NIIP claimed to receive frequent letters from parents thanking them for the vocational guidance offered to their children: 'Evidence on the Value of Psychology Applied to Vocational Guidance', *JNIIP*, 4 (1929), 295–301.

[23] Evans and Waites, *IQ and Mental Testing*, 78–9. For instance, E. P. Allen, 'Vocational Guidance: The Birmingham Experiment', *Human Factor*, 6 (1932), 170–3; C. A. Parkinson, 'Vocational Guidance for Secondary Schools', *Human Factor*, 6 (1932), 198–208; A. Macrae, 'Vocational Guidance and the Health of the Industrial Worker', *Human Factor*, 6 (1932), 369–81; F. M. Earle, 'Factory, School and Home', *JNIIP*, 3 (1927), 320.

[24] C. S. Myers, 'The Efficiency Engineer and the Industrial Psychologist', *JNIIP*, 3 (1927), 168–72.   [25] Ibid. 170–1.

an idealised individual worker who existed nowhere else other than in the laboratory.[26] Not only would learning the lessons of the new psychology lead to an approach that was more scientific, but in the long term it would be more efficient too, and crucially it would be more humane.

The Institute was keen to defend its humanist credentials by pointing out at every available opportunity that the subjects of its investigations both willingly accepted the industrial psychologist into the workplace and welcomed the results. Of course, it would be naive to take such reports at face value. Dependence on the finance of the employers inevitably complicated and compromised the relationship between the psychologists and their working-class subjects. If they really were welcomed, this may have been because the workers at these sites either had little choice or were so insecure that their conditions could only have improved. In this respect, it may be telling that a high proportion of these early investigations concentrated on female workers. Even here, however, where trade union organisation was weaker, recent research has suggested resistance leading to modification of plans for scientific management that were sometimes supported by reformist male union leaders.[27]

If the low prestige and limited authority of industrial psychology meant that the subjects of study were often women, it also led to a high number of women within the field itself. Like others in the new sector, May Smith had become interested in psychology through teaching and teacher training. However, in 1920, the government-funded Industrial Fatigue Research Board took her on to study hours of work and fatigue in the laundry trade. The first step was to take up a job in a laundry for several weeks to gain experience. This proved invaluable in gaining the confidence of the workers when she moved on to the investigation itself:

When a factory where I was investigating found itself rushed, or had to work on Sunday, I could help with the actual work, and in return all kinds of unusual facilities for research were willingly granted, even to the length of being allowed to give psychological tests which took workers away from their work for considerable periods.[28]

She painted a picture of the workers being more bemused by her presence, than disturbed: 'we were considered a little mad, but amiable and good listeners.'[29] In close contact with the workforce, Smith came to recognise, not only that the observer's point of view was often wrong, but also how faintly ridiculous her own efforts may have appeared from the perspective of the worker:

I was timing the hourly output of an old hand-ironer at one period and asked her if she found the work monotonous. 'Not at all,' she said, 'every shirt is different', and then she looked at my notebook and said, 'What are you going to do with all them figgers when

---

[26] Miles, 'Autobiography—Part II', 37–8.
[27] J. Cronin, *Labour and Society in Britain, 1918–1979* (London, 1984), 67; S. Todd, '"Boisterous Workers": Young Women, Industrial Rationalization and Workplace Militancy in Interwar England', *Labour History Review*, 68 (2003), 293–310.
[28] M. Smith, 'An Autobiography', *Occupational Psychology*, 24 (1950), 79.   [29] Ibid.

you've got em?' This was a little difficult to explain, but I did my best. 'And you talk to me about monotony! They've fair got you this time'.[30]

It is tempting to tie such a collapse of boundaries to a process of feminisation. Smith's own views may also have played a part: at university, she had been a member of a suffrage society and interested in social reform.[31] She was concerned to bring a humanising influence into a key area of women's work that had a reputation as being nasty, dirty, and unhealthy.[32] Thus, her continuing focus on the relationship between women and work—for instance, in studies of telegraphists cramp and unemployed girls—may have reflected the restrictions imposed by ideas about gender, but also probably developed out of a commitment to improve the circumstances of her sex.[33] The relationship between such an investigator and her subjects was clearly an unequal one, but here and elsewhere we do see a dialogue that began to challenge such inequality and we do see investigators who firmly believed that they were attempting to put both welfare and the advance of science ahead of mere profit.

Women working in a chocolate-packing factory or laundry may have been easy to coerce and convince about the benefits of changing their work pattern. It was likely to have been far harder to gain such influence when it came to men in a heavily unionised, proudly traditional sector such as mining, particularly in an era of industrial tension like the 1920s. Even here, however, the Institute reported a remarkable degree of acceptance when it proposed changing the technique used by miners when swinging their picks:

the miners' confidence was so completely won that they allowed themselves to be trained in the use of the pick by improved methods involving the employment of a metronome and the wielding of a pick in a continuous path. A noteworthy increase in output is recorded, and the men unanimously expressed their approval of the new methods.[34]

This rather extraordinary claim of cooperation appeared again in evidence to the Royal Commission on the Coal Industry in 1925.[35] Here, it was not workers but the employers who objected to the idea that psychologists had the expertise to dictate work practices.[36] Evan Williams, President of the Mining Association of Great Britain, which had funded a psychological study of the industry, now attempted to dismiss its conclusions about inefficiency, particularly the claim that idle time amounted to about 80 per cent of the working time at the coalface. Such a figure would seem a powerful vantage point for undermining the position of the

[30] M. Smith, 'An Autobiography', *Occupational Psychology*, 80.
[31] Ibid. 76.
[32] M. Smith and H. G. Maule, *Industrial Psychology and the Laundry Trade* (London, 1947), iii.
[33] M. Smith, M. Culpin and E. Farmer, 'A Study of Telegraphists' Cramp', *Industrial Health Research Board Report No. 43* (London, 1927).
[34] E. Farmer, S. Adams, and A. Stephenson, 'An Investigation in a Coal Mine', *JNIIP*, 4 (1922), 125.
[35] 'The Institute's Evidence before the Royal Commission on the Coal Industry (1925)', *JNIIP*, 3 (1926–7), 34.
[36] By the 1930s, Myers also believed that the employers and managers were far more likely than the worker to resist the industrial psychologist: C. S. Myers, *Industrial Psychology in Great Britain*, 2nd edn. (London, 1933), 27–36.

miner. Yet, at no point had the investigation cast blame in this direction. Rather, it suggested that the main causes of idle time were the inadequate transport system to the coalface, and the system of a common penalty for 'dirt'—which meant that a miner working a clean seam had no incentive to avoid sending up an unnecessary amount of dirt. Such structural problems had further unfortunate psychological effects on the worker—idleness encouraging inertia or irritation, and the penalty for dirt undermining pride in the job—but here again the individual worker was absolved of any personal responsibility.[37] Thus, psychology had the potential to turn the actions of the worker into a mere effect of the broader situation. In this particular situation, such logic could have unattractive implications for the employers. The episode also, however, indicates a potential of industrial psychology to turn the worker into a passive object trapped within a broader system that sits uneasily with its self-proclaimed humanising principles.

THE WORKER'S VIEW OF INDUSTRIAL PSYCHOLOGY

Unsurprisingly, the workers' views displayed in the industrial psychology literature were overwhelmingly sympathetic, tending to reiterate the industrial psychologists' own claim of a clear distinction between their own humane ambitions, and the autocratic, profit-driven character of efficiency engineering. For W. F. Watson, a mechanic with thirty years' experience:

The finest compliment that can be paid to the National Institute of Industrial Psychology is that at the very outset it recognized that there is something innate in the British temperament—a traditional love of sport, fairplay, freedom and independence—which makes it impossible for the average British workman to submit to robotic influences. Basing its work on recognition of the human factor, realizing that every worker, no matter the occupation, has a mind and an individuality, the Institute seeks to adapt the job to the individual.[38]

Watson, in short, recognising the limited ambitions and common sense of this psychology, regarded it as no threat to the worker. He also questioned the threat of mechanisation; indeed, he felt that the industrial psychologists were guilty of exaggeration on this count. For men like Watson, it could actually mean new opportunities in controlling increasingly sophisticated machinery; while for the unskilled, it could mean a lessening of human effort and liberation from the work process, which fostered, rather than crushed, individuality. Relieving mental effort and worry, industrial psychology simply brought this process one stage further: rather than turning men into automata, it helped to release them from the tyranny of the machine to express their individuality and to direct their energy towards 'higher

---

[37] 'Institute's Evidence before the Royal Commission on the Coal Industry', *JNIIP*, 3 (1926–7), 34–9.
[38] W. F. Watson, 'The Machine and the Individual', *Human Factor*, 7 (1933), 271. Also: W. F. Watson, *Machines and Man: An Autobiography of an Itinerant Mechanic* (London, 1935).

things'.[39] Clearly, this had much to do with Watson's own success in responding to the challenge of mechanisation. However, we find a similar sentiment elsewhere. J. H. Mitchell, a worker now training as an investigator for the NIIP, criticised employers for their lack of interest in psychology and emphasised its potential for the unions in adding scientific weight to their demands.[40] John Gibson, a plasterer, suggested that the trade depression would make workers more open to industrial psychology.[41] Alfred Barratt Brown, the Principal of Ruskin College, in his *The Machine and the Worker* of 1934, drew both on first hand impressions from work-ing-class students and his own survey of workers' views to add weight to the idea that mechanisation was not crushing individuality.[42] He was nevertheless alert to a series of new strains experienced. For although mechanisation had the potential to lessen rather than increase the number of purely routine jobs, the close attention demanded by fast and regimented machinery could result in nervous fatigue since it left little opportunity for the sustained thinking that had accompanied older craft-based work.[43] As to scientific management, Brown noted its dangers in exac-erbating the strains of mechanisation but again pointed to the way that industrial psychology had humanised scientific management in its British form.[44]

In 1931, the NIIP even consulted the TUC over whether it might change its name to the 'Workers' Research Institute'.[45] The change never took place. For all those who embraced or more cautiously accepted industrial psychology as trying to make things better for the worker, many others remained suspicious if not hos-tile. It does seem that those actively involved tended to be more favourable, per-haps because industrial psychology was indeed less threatening than it appeared from afar. However, the majority of workers never had this proximity. They were far too preoccupied with the pressing economic and political problems that arose in relation to work to be that concerned about industrial psychology. Ultimately, industrial psychology may have gone some way in humanising scientific manage-ment, but it never found the channels, the language, or the ideas to capture the imagination or enthusiasm of the worker.

PLEBIAN PSYCHOLOGY

An excitement about psychology and an interest in its relationship to the problems of industrial civilisation did exist, but unsurprisingly it surfaced well away from an industrial psychology that had such limited potential appeal for the

---

[39] W. F. Watson, *Human Factor*, 266–73. Some of the *Human Factor* contributions were collected for the book *The Worker's Point of View: A Symposium* (London, 1933).

[40] NIIP, *The Worker's Point of View*, 48, 64.   [41] Ibid. 109–13.

[42] A. Barratt Brown, *The Machine and the Worker* (London, 1934). Cronin highlights the book's ambivalent conclusions about the developing relationship between worker and machine: *Work and Society*, 63–4.   [43] Brown, *Machine and Worker*, 76–7, 80.

[44] Ibid. 138–40.

[45] Henry Ward (secretary of the NIIP) to Walter Citrine, 11 Sept. 1931: Modern Records Centre, MSS 292/570–65/2.

individual subject. At its peak in 1926–7, some 31,000 working-class students, the vast majority of them men, enrolled for courses of study within the National Council of Labour Colleges, coordinated by the Plebs League.[46] Here, the growing interest in psychology in the 1920s was partly the result of the difficulty in popularising a more philosophical Marxism and the search for something more accessible. Thus, when the Plebs published their *Outline of Psychology*, it took the place of a planned book on the philosophy of Dietzgenism—itself soon to be repackaged as a 'technology of brainwork' that would empower workers to take control of their minds. Indeed, it was an important enough subject to be the very first in a series of 'outlines'.[47] The *Outline of Psychology* went into multiple editions, and its influence was greater still through teaching.[48]

Having been introduced to the subject, the worker was directed towards more advanced psychological texts. The *Plebs* journal encouraged 'all Plebians who beg, borrow, or steal a copy' to study Tansley's *The New Psychology*.[49] Even the general pamphlet on *What to Read* now included psychology as one of its key categories.[50] The recommended reading list of the *Outline* in the early 1920s placed emphasis on Freud, but also directed plebians towards other figureheads of the new psychology like Adler and William James, though not Jung. An orientation toward native writers is also evident: William McDougall, Eden and Cedar Paul, W. H. R. Rivers, Bertrand Russell, Tansley, and Wilfred Trotter all received recommendation. Henri Bergson also broke into the list; an interesting inclusion, in terms of his rethinking of the nature of time having possible implications for

[46] The Plebs League originated in a dispute between Ruskin College, Oxford and the Workers' Education Association in 1908. The Central Labour College was set up to provide training for tutors for the Independent Workers' Education Association (IWEA), followed in 1921 by the National Council of Labour Colleges to coordinate expansion around the country. The IWEA had support from several unions and early links with the communist movement. By 1937–8, enrolments had slumped to 13,000: L. Goldman, *Dons and Workers: Oxford and Adult Education since 1850* (Oxford, 1995), 165–79; A. Miles, 'Workers' Education: The Communist Party and the Plebs League in the 1920s', *History Workshop Journal*, 18 (1984), 102–14. Men outnumbered women by a ratio of eight to one: J. Rée, *Proletarian Philosophers: Problems in Socialist Culture in Britain, 1900–1940* (Oxford, 1984), 20–2.

[47] Rée, *Proletarian Philosophers*, 34–7, 127; F. Casey, *Method in Thinking* (Manchester, 1933). For the view that the emphasis on Marxist philosophy lay behind the League's struggle for popularity: Goldman, *Dons and Workers*, 179.

[48] For instance, the 1923 Plebs Summer School at Scarborough had a session on 'Modern Workshop Methods', led by future Labour MP Ellen Wilkinson, which covered industrial psychology: 'Plebs Summer School—Programme and Particulars', *The Plebs*, 15 (1923), 234–5. By 1947, the *Outline of Psychology* was in its 10th edition. The first edition is credited to H. Lyster Jameson, but it was subsequently completely revised by Eden and Cedar Paul. One historian of the movement does briefly acknowledge the 'strenuous attempts of Lyster Jameson and the Pauls to develop psychology', which he sees as faltering by the mid-1920s, and shares the conclusion of this chapter that this reflected an attempt to address the nature of proletarian education as a whole: J. McIlroy, 'Independent Working Class Education and Trade Union Education and Training', in R. Fieldhouse (ed.), *A History of Modern British Adult Education* (Leicester, 1996), 271–3.

[49] Tansley, *The New Psychology and its Relation to Life*; E. and C. Paul, 'The New Psychology', *The Plebs*, 12 (1920), 222–4.

[50] It was available at 7*d*. It also sold in batches of 12 or 25. Both points indicate a likely large circulation: *The Plebs*, 16 (1924), 39.

conceptualisation of work.[51] Also included was Charles Badouin, who brought autosuggestion—that most do-it-yourself, and in that respect most potentially democratic, of the era's psychotherapies—to Britain. Unusually in the British context, J. B. Watson and his *Psychology from the Standpoint of a Behaviourist* was another key authority.[52] As already noted, it seems that in Britain behaviourism may have had its greatest appeal in radical circles like this: its assumptions about the malleability of human nature, and the emphasis on nurture rather than nature, lending itself to a marriage with the historical and economic determinism of Marxism.[53] By contrast, with the Plebs having forged their version of a practical psychology, the psychoanalytic determinism and pessimism of Freud was increasingly problematic, as it was elsewhere on the left.

It is difficult to assess how many of these working-class readers and students ventured beyond the clear messages of the *Outline* to this more advanced psychological territory. The reader who complained of struggling when he ventured into even the introductory reading recommended in *What to Read* would clearly not have been alone.[54] As such, it is best to base our understanding of a Plebian psychology on the more general literature published by the League itself. Carefully pared of technical language, and designed and revised with teaching in mind to reflect working-class concerns, we can assume that a book like the *Outline of Psychology* offers us some indication of the readers' appreciation of the subject.[55] The same is true for the dialogue in the *Plebs* journal. Even in this left-wing forum, we find a more muted critique of industrial psychology than we might have expected: acceptance that industrial psychology was sometimes used to exploit the worker, but recognition that this did not have to be the case, and sympathy for its potential to improve working conditions, to fit the job to the man, and to increase efficiency in the interests of all.[56] Industrial psychology could serve the interests of communism, just as well as capitalism: it was not inherently a bad thing. More importantly, however, psychology provided a way to frame discontent. The psychological effects of mechanisation were to be regarded as 'not less portentous' than the economic. The speed of work was liable to cause injury to 'nerve and mind'. And the threat and experience of unemployment was recognised as a source of constant 'mental anxiety'.[57] Psychology also offered a tool for socialist analysis. Indeed, the *Outline* presented psychology as being as important as economics in the class war. An understanding

[51] On the link in the French context: A. Rabinbach, *The Human Motor: Energy, Fatigue and the Origins of Modernity* (Berkeley and Los Angeles, 1992), 110–14.

[52] Plebs League, *An Outline of Psychology*, 2nd edn. (London, 1921), 139.

[53] See Ch. 4 in relation to education. There are parallels here with the attraction of radicals to both phrenology and spiritualism in the nineteenth century: Barrow, *Independent Spirits;* Cooter, *Cultural Meaning of Popular Science.*

[54] Letter to Editor from Ben Davies and response from Member of the Textbook Committee: *The Plebs*, 16 (1924), 80.

[55] 'R. W. P.' suggested that 'Nordicus' had managed to rescue the *Outline* from the excesses of Eden and Cedar Paul: R. W. P. response to letter from E. and C. Paul, *The Plebs*, 16 (1924), 397.

[56] E. and C. Paul, 'Robots Once More', *The Plebs*, 16 (1924), 355.

[57] T. Ashcroft, 'The Machine Age', *The Plebs*, 20 (1928), 155.

of the subconscious and of the herd instinct could give class-consciousness a new dimension. One reason for the strong recommendation of Tansley was that he had psychologically diagnosed the working class as 'the most intensely class conscious of all the social classes'.[58] Class-consciousness and class conflict became psychological complexes: the result of an encounter between subconscious drives and the economic environment of capitalism. As such, they were naturalised. This meant that when such complexes did not come to the fore—when the drives did not find release in class consciousness and conflict—it could now be diagnosed as a psychological problem that needed to be remedied for health, rather than attributed to inherent working-class apathy, or regarded as disproving Marxist analysis. A Marxist education that took into account such a psychology would equip proletarians with an ability to ensure that the complexes that built up around subconscious drives were a 'true picture' of the economic environment and its relations: class-consciousness was essential for self-realisation among the working class, and psychology would show the way.[59]

Key figures in this translation of the new psychology to reinforce and reinvigorate a Plebian ideology were, husband and wife, Eden and Cedar Paul. Concerned that there was little in practice to distinguish working-class from bourgeois education, they now also looked to psychology for guidance in developing a uniquely proletarian pedagogy. Because of the psychology of class consciousness, an education based on telling proletarians what to do—the existing bourgeois approach— would never succeed; hence, the failure of proletarians within current systems. The working class would only fulfil their potential when education began to harmonize with their own interests. The lessons of psychology were transforming children's education; now was the time to extend them to the proletarian adult. Child-centred education had shown the way. Now adult education would become proletarian-centred education, with discussion-classes and student-led teaching replacing the authoritarianism of bourgeois education. In revealing the power of suggestion and autosuggestion, psychology had opened up the possibility that education could transform from a process of dictation, into one of liberation. The suggestion of Marxist economics and history would now arouse latent trends in the proletarian subconscious, and autosuggestion would place the individual student at the helm in discovering a consciousness of class.[60] The emancipation of proletarian thought would be the key to later action.[61]

---

[58] From Tansley, *The New Psychology*, 213, cited in E. and C. Paul, *Proletcult* (London, 1921), 123.

[59] Ibid. 93, 131–41; E. and C. Paul, *Creative Revolution: A Study of Communist Ergatocracy* (London, 1920). Interest among communists had been spread by a 'comrade named Jameson' who had died prematurely in 1922: E. and C. Paul, 'Revolutionary Education in Britain', *The Plebs*, 15 (1923), 305–8.　　[60] On education, see Ch. 4.

[61] E. and C. Paul, *Proletcult*, 123–32. The Pauls were also important in bringing autosuggestion to Britain, translating the works of Charles Badouin. Their total list of translations of the period is extensive. This role as intermediaries between British socialism and continental thought would deserve further attention. Of significance here, it also included the work of Paul de Man on the psychology of socialism: *The Psychology of Socialism* (London, 1928); and *Joy in Work* (London, 1929).

Those within the mainstream of the labour movement were far more reluctant to engage with the idea of the unconscious as a potentially creative force. Concerned about the fragility of working-class consciousness, figures such as Ramsay MacDonald had tended to blame this on minds being unable to resist the control of the capitalist class over the instruments of public opinion. It was socialism's role to educate, elevate, and turn the working class into rational agents of their own destiny; however, its struggle to do so would tend to reinforce the negative stereotype.[62] At the Marxist fringe of the expanding workers' education movement of this era, the Plebs League may therefore have been rather exceptional in the way that it explored the relationship between psychology and class. The less radical but numerically more significant Workers' Education Association—by 1948–9, it had enrolled 111,351 students since its foundation in 1903—offers us a more typical picture; though this was still a 'motivated minority' spending on average, it has been suggested, over forty hours on reading every week.[63] There is nothing to suggest that in this arena the subject of psychology possessed the kind of revolutionary significance found in the Plebs movement of the early 1920s. However, it did establish itself as one of the leading subjects of study. By the end of the 1930s, psychology accounted for 9.8 per cent of all classes: more than natural science at 7.5 per cent, and approaching the numbers attracted to the most popular subjects of literature (14.9 per cent) and history (12 per cent).[64] This is even more remarkable when one considers the limited number of qualified teachers in the subject.[65] The slump to 4.5 per cent by 1957–8 suggests that the interwar period had seen a peak of enthusiasm for the subject. However, with the total number of classes rising significantly, even this masks a continuing appeal.[66] Indeed, in the late 1940s, psychology accounted for nearly a fifth of the correspondence courses arranged by the Educational Trade Union Committee, including a course on industrial psychology and others on general psychology, social psychology, criminal psychology, and child psychology.[67] It also needs to be borne in mind that many other working-class students encountered the new psychology through its emerging influence in the teaching of subjects such as English Literature.[68]

[62] On the problem of class consciousness within the movement: S. MacIntyre, *A Proletarian Science: Marxism in Great Britain, 1917–1933* (London, 1980), 198–218.

[63] Rose, *Intellectual Life of the British Working Classes*, 236, 265, 290. For those not able to avail themselves of such courses there was always the public library where writers like Freud and Jung appear to have been available, though not universally so: Ibid. 162, 246; A. Rodaway, *A London Childhood* (Bath, 1985), 230.

[64] The total number of classes this year was 3,219: D. B. Halpern, 'A Table Showing the Balance of Subjects in WEA Classes, 1913–58', *Rewley House Papers*, 3 (1959–60), 23–5.

[65] O. L. Zangwill, 'Doubts and Queries about Psychology', *Rewley House Papers*, 3 (1953), 38–43. Leading psychologists like Susan Isaacs, who lectured to the WEA on 'Psychology and Life' in the 1920s, were not averse to spreading the message, but it must be assumed that the majority of teachers were far less eminent: D. E. M. Gardner, *Susan Isaacs* (London, 1969), 48.

[66] Halpern, 'Balance of Subjects in WEA Classes'.

[67] In total, 28 courses were on offer either free to union members or at subsidised rates, as advertised inside the cover of the December 1947 edition of the WEA journal *Highway*.

[68] Rose, *Intellectual Life of the British Working Classes*, 138–9.

Why were these students drawn to psychology? Some did recognise the relevance of psychology to their own work, as the provision of courses in industrial psychology highlights. George Morris was one of these. He claimed that his experience on such a course had the benefit of making his employers far more cautious when they attempted to introduce the findings of a time and motion study.[69] However, a survey undertaken by educational psychologists in 1947, with information from 190 WEA psychology students (with women outnumbering men by 105 to 85), found that the most common origin of interest was the reading of books and magazines and the influence of friends. Most strikingly, nearly half had practical (though non-vocational) motives, hoping to gain knowledge that would help them in understanding and influencing other people and themselves.[70] More generally, a survey of WEA education in 1936 found that a key motivation was a desire for self-realisation—'to provide for the fullest expression of the faculties of the individual, and to direct energy towards the realisation of individual happiness through those faculties'.[71] In that respect, the appeal to the majority of workers was not so different from others who turned to practical psychology in this period.

THE PSYCHOLOGY OF SELLING

By the 1930s, industrial psychology occupied a very different position to that of national saviour set out in the Mansion House meeting a decade earlier. It was difficult to convince firms already struggling to sell that they should invest in increasing productivity. Unsurprisingly, the National Institute struggled to attract new companies to take on its services and even to hold on to those investigations it had already secured. The continuing predominance of small companies without the will or the means to support employment of expert investigators did not help matters.[72] In such circumstances, a cruder and cheaper emphasis on raising productivity by linking payment to targets was more attractive, as is evident in the spread of the Bedaux system, which reached at least two hundred and fifty firms but probably had a wider influence in practice and was a serious enough threat to provoke a TUC inquiry in 1933.[73]

One area with better prospects was market research. Selling, after all, was the main economic problem of the day. Though some within the Institute looked down on the commercialism of this work, it would emerge as an increasingly

[69] G. Morris, 'The Testament of a Trade Unionist', *Highway*, 39 (1948), 158–9.

[70] W. E. Flood and R. W. Crossland, 'The Origin of Interest and Motives for Study of Natural Sciences and Psychology among Adult Students in Voluntary Courses', *British Journal of Educational Psychology*, 18 (1948), 105–11.

[71] Cited in Rose, *Intellectual Life of the British Working Classes*, 282; W. E. Williams and A. E. Heath, *Learn and Live: The Consumer's View of Adult Education* (London, 1936).

[72] Cronin, *Labour and Society*, 52–3.   [73] Ibid. 61.

important arena for the application of psychological expertise.[74] Investigations into the marketing of tobacco and confectionery, most notably work on Black Magic chocolates for Rowntree, began a refashioning of the British consumer as a psychological subject, which has attracted far less attention than that of the working subject but was almost as significant.[75] As with the worker, we see both an attribution of psychological agency, partly based on hidden drives, and a search to understand and respond to the interests of this subject. Thus, this consuming psychological subject might be open to new forms of management and manipulation, but the assertion of the consumer's individuality, preferences, and needs also helped to give the consumer power within the commodity relationship.

By the eve of the First World War, annual expenditure on advertising was £80–100 million.[76] With the price of advertising in a newspaper like the *Daily Mail* soaring to £1,400 as readership rose to 1.7 million, there was a strong incentive to ensure that the message to the consumer was as effective as possible.[77] Although the American psychologist Walter Dill Scott published his seminal book on *The Psychology of Advertising* in Britain in 1909, it was not until the 1920s that psychological theory was being widely disseminated to the expanding advertising industry.[78] The demonstration of the value of psychological insight within wartime propaganda may have been a factor, but its significance has probably been overplayed. At least as significant was the public excitement about psychology that came to the fore in these decades. Advertisers now also began to take practical action to push their understanding further. For instance, the Regent Advertising Club invited members of the NIIP to lecture on the subject in 1924 and 1925, and the success of this venture led to the formation of a class in the Psychology of Advertising at King's College London.[79]

British advertisers, however, were reticent about the acceptability of following the Americans in using psychology to appeal to the base instincts of the consumer.[80] The findings of psychology had to be an essential element in any modernisation of advertising; yet the advertiser needed to be aware that this psychology indicated that consumers would object if they felt any sense of

[74] Miles, 'Autobiography—Part II', 33.

[75] By contrast, the subject has attracted serious attention in the American and French contexts, suggesting directions for research on Britain: T. J. Jackson Lears, *Fables of Abundance: A Cultural History of Advertising in America* (New York, 1994); M. Beale, *The Modernist Experience: French Elites and the Threat of Modernity, 1900–1940* (Stanford, Calif., 1999), 11–47.

[76] Sir C. Higham, *Advertising: Its Use and Abuse* (London, 1925), 8. The nineteenth century has received more attention from historians: T. Richards, *The Commodity Culture of Victorian England: Advertising and Spectacle, 1851–1914* (London, 1991); R. Church, 'Advertising Consumer Goods in Nineteenth-Century Britain: Reinterpretations', *Economic History Review*, 53 (2000), 621–45.

[77] Higham, *Advertising*, 63.

[78] E. S. Turner, *A Shocking History of Advertising* (London, 1952), 166. For a picture of the advertising agency: D. L. Sayers, *Murder Must Advertise* (London, 1933).

[79] R. J. Bartlett, 'The Judgement of the Value of Advertisements and the Construction of Rating Scales', *JNIIP*, 3 (1927), 252.   [80] Turner, *Shocking History*, 189.

manipulation. Writing for the Library of Advertising, A. P. Braddock highlighted the dilemma:

The use of 'psychology' and its correlative 'to psychologise' has become increasingly common in every phrase of modern life; people acquiesce quite willingly in experimental investigations and afford stores of valuable information, but they do not as a rule like to feel they are being made the subjects of experiment without their permission being first sought. Ill-considered attempts on the part of salesmen to psychologise their customers may result in arousing contra-suggestions, leading to very different results from those desired.[81]

Thus, as with the psychology of work, there was an inherent tension at the heart of this agenda: psychology had exciting potential as a tool for understanding and manipulating its subjects; yet the power of these subjects in the relationship, that was partly an effect of psychology, meant that evidence of such manipulation would largely undermine success. The psychology of work found a compromise in the 'human factor'; that of advertising sought one in 'truth'.[82] In both cases, psychology attempted to advance itself on ethical as well as economic grounds.

Psychology, in short, bore the promise not only of more effective selling, but also of turning buying into a need and advertising into a service. 'Good advertisement', argued psychologist R. J. Bartlett, would understand the psychology of its subjects, 'correct any bias of the salesman', and thereby help to moralise the market. It would 'give precision to the indefinite want' of people whose needs were not currently being satisfied, and it would help spread the 'pleasure in spending'.[83] Sir Charles Higham, author of one of the more authoritative guides on the rights and wrongs of advertising, agreed: 'the advertisement that is psychologically perfect has stimulated and reinforced the onlooker's attention to his or her own latent wishes, and at the same time associated the goods that are advertised with those wishes latent in his or her own mind.'[84] The sheer ubiquity, confusion, and clutter of printed advertising by this date—festooning roadsides as well as dominating the pages of the press—meant that modern advertising was 'largely dependent on the casual glance'.[85] In such circumstances, the psychologist could market an ability to attract attention but in doing so also present this as an exercise in clarification and thus as a service to the public. The advertiser, therefore, was to use the insights of psychology to manipulate the consumer towards purchase, but had to recognise that this would only be successful if advertising was also a tool for making the market more truthful. Without truth, the victory of the initial purchase would not convert into a psychological habit and long-term profit; without truth, advertising would flounder under public scepticism.[86]

---

81 A. P. Braddock, *Applied Psychology for Advertisers* (London, 1933), 183.
82 R. J. Bartlett, 'Advertising and the Will to Buy', *JNIIP*, 4 (1928), 25.
83 Ibid. 18.   84 Higham, *Advertising: Its Use and Abuse*, 58.
85 R. J. Bartlett, 'Psychology and Advertising', *JNIIP*, 2 (1925), 378.
86 Bartlett, 'Advertising and the Will to Buy', 25.

PSYCHOLOGY AND BUSINESS

When it came to psychological thinking in business, the type of practical psychology considered in the opening chapter was as important as anything offered by the industrial psychologists. This is evident in the popularity of efficiency entrepreneur, Herbert Newton Casson.[87] With an English father, but born in Ontario, Canada in 1869, Casson had been an active socialist in his youth, but then living in the United States turned via journalism to writing best-sellers about the romance of business.[88] By 1908, he was presenting himself as an expert in this field. He became involved in the founding of the American efficiency movement and was author of an early study of efficiency in advertising.[89] On the eve of the First World War, he moved to Britain, with plans to retire. However, he soon became embroiled in efforts to bring efficiency to wartime Britain. He was involved in the spread of the telephone, with Britain at the time having fewer than New York on its own; he would see it as establishing a nervous system for the country.[90] He also headed a mass meeting at the Queen's Hall in London in 1915, attracting over 3,000—said to be the largest business meeting ever in Britain at that time. Casson collaborated with the government in a number of schemes in which he spoke to British businessmen about the merits of efficiency, and here found an ally in Lord Northcliffe. However, his brief experience with bureaucracy and politics left him disillusioned with any strategy that depended upon the state. Instead, he launched his own *Efficiency Magazine* in 1915, which served as a forum for his increasingly right-wing economic and political vision of efficiency as the key to national salvation. Democracy had failed. Now was the time for the 'Efficient Few' to come forward. There was an urgent need to develop 'a British type of Efficiency'; he had already come to accept that it was not possible to translate the more materialist American model—there was 'a higher quality of human nature in Great Britain than there was in the United States'.[91] If Britain was to recover her position in the world and spread the internationalism that was necessary for peace, she needed to make better use of her Empire and even extend it to China. However, to do so she needed first to address her ailing domestic economy. The key problem was over-production, and the solution was to replace existing amateurism with new ranks of efficiency-minded sales people and advertisers.

[87] The account which follows is based on Casson's own autobiography and supplemented by the biography written by his son Edward, who inherited the publishing business, which follows his father's account closely but provides supplementary material on the final two decades of his life: H. N. Casson, *The Story of My Life* (London, 1931); E. E. Casson, *Postscript: The Life and Thoughts of Herbert N. Casson* (London, 1952).

[88] For the claim that on early trips to England he was involved in the formation of not only Ruskin College but also the Independent Labour Party: Casson, *Postscript*, 26.

[89] *Ads and Sales: A Study of Advertising and Selling from the Standpoint of Scientific Management* (London, 1911).   [90] Casson, *Postscript*, 67.

[91] Casson, *Story of My Life*, 187–9.

Casson also addressed productivity, directing his message at managers and fore-men in a new type of business book that was clear, practical, and cheap. Over the interwar decades, a seemingly endless series of books would roll off his Efficiency Magazine production line right up to his death in 1951.[92] Circulation of his *Efficiency Magazine*, if we are to believe his claims, soon reached 24,000, despite the difficult wartime circumstances. In 1930, it was selling 50,000 copies each month. By 1950, circulation had become international, soaring to 200,000, with editions in six languages.

For Casson, the pathway to efficiency and economic growth lay in personality. An age of democracy had made way for an age of socialism, which now in turn was to make way for an age of 'new and higher individualism'.[93] He accepted the importance of the academic psychology but considered it a failure in terms of reaching people. His role would be to translate such theory into the language of common sense and then to demonstrate its relationship to practical problems:

The New Psychology teaches us to know more about the ideas, motives and feelings of our-selves and others. It concentrates attention on the inner life—on the mental and emotional causes of action. And its most valuable service is this—that it helps people to develop their own mental powers and to control the feelings that weaken them.[94]

The dynamic nature of the new psychology, set against the static nature of the 'Old', fitted it to Casson's own dynamic agenda for the remaking of the business self.[95] The mind, like the business, became something that was open to adaptation and improvement. In his language, the issue was one of 'brain-making'. This meant learning how to exercise the mind. Here, although he believed that the pro-fessional psychologists had achieved little themselves, he acknowledged the value of something like the Pelman system in popularising an understanding about mental development and helping 'hundreds of thousands' to cultivate a 'working brain'.[96] He translated the division between conscious and subconscious mind, which was so central to the new psychology, into a much more pessimistic 'Front-Brain'/ 'Back-Brain' dichotomy. In doing so, he recast the story of civilisation as one of the gradual taming of the instinctive 'Back-Brain', with this clash continuing within the mind of every individual. Without active 'brain-making', brain dereliction, and 'Back-Brain' dominance threatened. Indeed, he painted a gloomy picture of the current situation:

It is a tragic fact that in the streets of our proudest cities there are thousands of Back-Brain people. They are the Goths, Huns and Vandals of our times . . . The fact is that the man who is dominated by his Back-Brain is a brute. He may degenerate into a wild beast—a murderer. Our prisons are filled with Back-Brain people. If a man's Front-Brain loses

---

[92] He would publish over 100 titles, with the majority concentrated into this last stage of his career.
[93] Casson, *The Story of My Life*, 216.
[94] H. N. Casson, *Twenty Tips in Psychology* (London, 1936), 1.   [95] Ibid. 6.
[96] H. N. Casson, *Twelve Tips of Brain-Making* (London, 1935), 35. For more on Pelmanism, see pp. 23–6.

control, he may become an ape man. He may become an enemy of society—an outlaw unfit for liberty and perhaps unfit to live.[97]

Academic psychology had little to offer in combating this threat of the Back-Brain (indeed, Casson would have objected to the way that it was much more open-minded about the need to accept Back-Brain impulses). Far more attractive was practical psychology's tool of autosuggestion, but perhaps best of all was simply to build up the strength of the Front-Brain through regular mental exercise.[98]

The promise of financial success but also psychological happiness, as indicated by the sheer volume of circulation for the *Efficiency Magazine* and his numerous books, clearly did have considerable appeal. Yet, Casson always claimed that 'efficiency' could be like a red rag to a bull in Britain, resisted by virtually all sections of society. In that sense, his co-opting of the psychological to moralise efficiency into a state of mind—an issue of character and personality—was important.[99] Analysis of Casson's appeal also, however, highlights that when psychology was being used to address the economic challenge of industrial civilisation it reflected and rearticulated the different class concerns of its audiences; in this instance, a concern about elevating oneself from a brutal mass. Once again—and here the contrast might be with the struggle of industrial psychology, while the parallel would be practical or even Plebian psychology—in order for such a literature to have popular appeal, it had to be one in which psychological subjects were at the helm in their own making. And once again, we see psychology playing a role in giving moral sanction to economic identities and practices that remained uncomfortable within a culture of character: here efficiency became personality; elsewhere, as we have seen, scientific management was recast as humanism, advertising as truth, and even class conflict was offered reassurance in its recasting as a natural psychological need.

INDUSTRY AND THE PSYCHOLOGY OF
HUMAN RELATIONS

Alongside this story of the businessman and practical psychology, there is another of the growing appeal of a more academic psychology within such circles. Here, news of the work of Elton Mayo in the United States, particularly his famous Hawthorne experiment, helped to steer British management towards an interest in 'human relations', though in fact such a reorientation was already in the air. It was evident, not only in the excitement surrounding the NIIP, but also in references to the new psychology in the literature of industrial administration.[100] It was one thing, however,

---

[97] Casson, *Twelve Tips*, 96.
[98] Ibid. 99; H. N. Casson, *Efficiency Mentality* (London, 1933).   [99] Ibid. 15.
[100] See for instance the interest in McDougall and Jung in J. Lee (ed.), *Pitman's Dictionary of Industrial Administration*, 2 vols. (London, 1928); and J. Lee, *Management: A Study of Industrial Organisation* (London, 1921).

to write about the value of bringing the 'human factor' to British management, another altogether to convince British employers of this in practice or to reach the majority of managers. Even in the period from the outbreak of the Second World War to the mid-1950s, when the human relations approach was at its strongest, employers and managers did often remain ignorant of the most basic research in the field.[101] Yet conditions were favourable. Wartime economic mobilisation had led to the appointment of personnel officers to improve working conditions and efficiency in all but the smallest of factories. Full employment and high demand on the one hand, a socialist government willing to intervene at a micro-economic level on the other, meant that both economic and political circumstances remained far more propitious for such a psychology in the aftermath of this war than they had been in 1918.[102] The new climate of social solidarity and the growing strength of the trade unions placed managers—as representatives of the polarised labour relations of the interwar period—in a difficult situation, and the hope was that an emphasis on their interest in human relations might allay the problem. The economic crises that followed the War kept up the momentum and encouraged managers to present good human relations with a panacea. With management reframed with a task of satisfying the social needs of workers in order to ensure high productivity, it also proved possible to gain support from some leading members of the labour movement.[103] High-profile coverage in widely read journals like *Industry Illustrated* and in semi-popular books like J. A. C. Brown's *The Social Psychology of Industry*, published by Penguin in 1954, and entering ten editions over the next decade, fostered the message.[104] Membership of the Institute of Personnel Management shot up from 760 in 1939, to 5,730 by 1963, and that of the Institute of Industrial Administration saw a wartime rise from 517 to 2,508. However, this was still a small minority of managers in the country as a whole. The majority remained either unconvinced or ignorant.[105] Moreover, by the mid-1950s, a critique of human relations was emerging from within. There was an increasing emphasis, in particular, on the effect of broader social structures and forces. The individualist focus and consensual ambition of human relations would come to be criticised by a new generation of left-inclined academics in the field as depoliticising the position of the worker and as colluding with the employers in offsetting the challenge of industrial action.[106] The ethical appeal of psychology, that had been such an essential part of its attraction at the start of the century, had largely disappeared.

War also provided work for industrial psychology, leaving it in a much more secure economic position. However, there was uncertainty about the future identity and purpose of the vocation. In the interwar period, it had drawn on the

---

[101] The account that follows draws on J. Child, *British Management Thought: A Critical Analysis* (London, 1969), 111–21.

[102] J. Tomlinson, 'Mr Attlee's Supply-Side Socialism', *Economic History Review*, 46 (1993), 1–22.

[103] Child, *British Management Thought*, 121, 135–6.   [104] Ibid. 114.

[105] Ibid. 113–14.

[106] For instance, Child, *British Management Thought*; Rose, *Industrial Relations*.

strong sense of purpose and excitement that came from the faith of bringing a new understanding of human nature to the problems of industrial civilisation. However, a process of specialisation had been set in motion that broke down the focus of industrial psychology into separate studies and tests of attitudes, skills, motivation, fatigue, accidents, and the working environment. Writing at the end of the 1940s, British psychologist Leslie Hearnshaw felt that the relationship between the parts, and thereby the whole human situation, was being lost sight of. Likewise, with the psychological problems of work coming to centre on the role of the managers who were to institute changes, the worker as human being was drifting out of focus. There was a danger that industrial psychology would become 'a kind of psychological engineering or psychotechnology', drifting away from the 'person-centred' aims of psychology.[107] Hearnshaw was scathing about the coverage of the subject in recent textbooks: 'One finds virtually no reference to real people. The industrial psychologist is dealing apparently with strange, abstract human beings, in some ways almost as bloodless as the economic man of the economists.'[108] The abstract approach had been less problematic when the main subject of the industrial psychologists had been the physical conditions of the workplace in relation to the mechanics of work, but as this focus had shifted to attitudes and motivation, it became crucial to understand the whole person. This meant, for instance, bringing to the study of the working subject an understanding of 'the environment in which it has been moulded, the anxieties and irritations to which working-class people have been subjected, their loyalties, traditions and ideologies—many of them . . . so different from those of the managerial class.'[109] Even if attention remained focused on the mechanics of work, the very process of industrialisation itself—the formation of an attitude of acceptance of the obligation to work—had to be recognised as a psychological issue. As an inherently psychological issue, work needed to be reframed in relation to the individual personality: something which could bring satisfaction in assuaging guilt and in integrating the personality; but also something that was an inevitable source of conflict in demanding the control of personal psychological needs and desires.[110] In opting for the path of studying the human condition of work, rather than accepting industrial psychology's fate as a tool of psychotechnology, Hearnshaw recognised what had in fact always been a dual vision within the field. His lament was for the ethical vision of humanisation that had been a key element in inspiring work within the field.[111]

THE HEALTH OF THE WORKER

In the 1930s, some extraordinary claims began to emerge about the extent of psychoneuroses within Britain's working population, with the idea that as much as a third of all absence through sickness from work had a psychoneurotic dimension

[107] L. S. Hearnshaw, 'What is Industrial Psychology', *Occupational Psychology*, 23 (1949), 3.
[108] Ibid. 4.   [109] Ibid. 5.   [110] Ibid. 7.   [111] Ibid. 8.

attracting particularly widespread attention.[112] The dilemmas of shellshock were returning, transported from the battlefields of the Western Front to the factories, mines, buses, and building sites of what was now a peacetime nation, though one in the midst of economic depression that was very obviously far from having peace of mind. This rather significant episode of social alarm, connecting so intriguingly contemporary anxieties about economic and mental depression, has attracted very little scrutiny from historians of either health or labour. In the few instances where contemporary interest in the relationship between social conditions and mental health has attracted attention, there is a tendency to highlight the ways in which psychological diagnoses combined with class prejudice to turn lower-class behaviour into signs of pathology.[113] What follows is an attempt, instead, to explore whether this literature offers insight into how those who experienced these circumstances thought about it and expressed it in psychological terms.

Books like Beales' and Lambert's *Memoirs of the Unemployed* gained much of their appeal from the impression that one was listening to voices of authentic experience.[114] Of course, such voices in reality also reflected the underlying orientation of the investigators. As Ross McKibbin has suggested, interviewees faced leading questions about their pessimism and optimism that reflected a model of mental deterioration drawn from social psychology. Nevertheless, such memoirs remain in some ways revealing about the psychological views of the unemployed themselves.[115] It may have been the editors who framed the story of an unmarried engineer as one of 'My Inferiority Complex', but this title did echo both the sentiment and the language of the engineer himself. It also makes sense in terms of that broader anxiety about inferiority and the Adlerian psychology that emerged to address it noted elsewhere in this book.[116] Likewise, very apparent in these accounts is the persistence of a language of 'nerves', 'nervous strain', and 'nervous breakdown', which, in its out-datedness as far as medical theory goes, can hardly be attributed to those conducting the surveys.[117] Again, this indicates something about the view from below. The nervous discourse was not only still popular, but here it also provided a material basis for mental deterioration, lack of food literally draining the nerves, that helped to turn the focus from personal responsibility to social inequity. As such, it enabled the unemployed to articulate their emotional experience in strikingly open terms.[118]

[112] 'Psychoneurosis and Incapacity', *British Medical Journal*, (16 March 1935), 533.

[113] The most important study is R. McKibbin, 'The "Social Psychology" of Unemployment in Interwar Britain', in Mckibbin, *The Ideologies of Class: Social Relations in Britain, 1880–1950* (Oxford, 1991), 228–58. Briefer commentaries on Stephen Taylor's 'Suburban Neurosis' article in *The Lancet* (26 March 1938) also take this type of position, for instance, Giles, *Women, Identity and Private Life*, 78–85. For more on Taylor, see pp. 202–4.

[114] Beales and Lambert (eds.), *Memoirs of the Unemployed*, 13. Extracts were also published in the BBC's *Listener* magazine.   [115] Beales and Lambert (eds.), *Memoirs of the Unemployed*, 11–12.

[116] Ibid. 149–55. On Adler, see Ch. 3.

[117] See also: 'Unemployment and Nerves—A Skilled Letterpress Printer', in Beales and Lambert, *Memoirs of the Unemployed*, 230–6.

[118] Thomson, 'Neurasthenia in Britain', 77–95. See also Ch. 6.

Max Cohen, a carpenter by trade and a communist by the 1930s when he was in and out of unemployment, made his name after the Second World War when he wrote a series of first-hand accounts of his experiences in the first half of the century. The best known of these was his *I Was One of the Unemployed*, written during the Second World War and published to widespread acclaim in 1945 with extracts even broadcast on the BBC.[119] It offers an alternative insight into the mental effects of unemployment, without the problem of editorial control, but with some significant complicating factors of its own: not least, the fact that Cohen was a radical and unusually well read, but also that he wrote with some novelistic license, and after a further decade and a half of shifting attitudes. Accepting that unemployment had a seriously debilitating affect on mental health, here was a defence of the sick role from the inside and from experience. Unemployment, argued Cohen, brought worry from all directions: about a man's past, his present, and his future; and about himself, his wife, his children, and his parents. The cumulative effect was intolerable: the 'psychological suffering or instability' was difficult for the lay observer to recognise, but thousands had experienced 'excruciating mental tortures'.[120] The psychological provided a terrain for the articulation of invisible pain, grievance, and the claim for redress.

His account is at its most compelling when it comes to charting his own descent from unemployment to psychological breakdown. Already sunk in a state of 'depression', waiting in the Labour Exchange queue one day Cohen was suddenly 'catapulted' into a far more extreme state of mental instability in which he questioned his grasp on reality. 'I could not shake off a nightmarish sense that it was all unreal', he recalled, 'everything was unreal: the Labour Exchange was unreal; the clerks were unreal; the notices were unreal; I was unreal. Terror smote me like a blow.' The drama of this collapse evokes that other popular expression of mental breakdown, 'shellshock'. However, the physical expression of breakdown was now far less central. Cohen dramatised the collapse in terms of an internal psychological struggle, with mind out of control and its delusions eating away at a consciousness of the physical self:

A grey mist was descending before my eyes. There was a sinister roar in my ears. The walls of the Labour Exchange seemed to crowd around me, threatening to shut me tightly in narrow confines. The crowd clamoured from far away. I was weak, my knees were as water, the blood was perceptibly draining from my face. 'Am I going to faint?' The thought boomed in the huge, hollow emptiness of my brain.[121]

The fact that he found it possible and appropriate to describe himself, and implicitly unemployed man, in such terms suggests that a space was being eased open between madness and sanity for thinking about psychological subjectivity and for dramatising the self's relation to the social.

---

[119] J. Saville and J. Bellamy (eds.), *Dictionary of Labour Biography*, 9 (London, 1993), 50–1. His brother Jack was a leading communist.
[120] M. Cohen, *I was one of the Unemployed* (Wakefield, 1978), 159.   [121] Ibid. 163.

Even if Cohen is a useful indicator of how things were changing, we should not of course assume that the average worker of the 1930s would have felt as comfortable in such emotional exposure. Indeed, even Cohen recalled his acute, unbearable self-consciousness, and intense shame in the public exposure of his mental collapse. 'E's feeling queer', the onlookers said. Cohen, himself, recognised his problem in terms of an emotion of fear out of control:

an unwelcome visitor began to insinuate himself gradually but persistently into my being. At first he was unnoticed. When I became aware of his presence I tried to dismiss him with increasing anger. Then perforce I accepted his presence. Then I became his slave, and the thought of banishing him from me became as the thought of some unattainable hope. The name of this visitor?—Fear.[122]

The account picks out key symbols of urban, industrial life in describing the 'vortex of fear, depression, [and] despair' that follows. Walking the streets, he feels swamped by the cityscape of thousands and thousands of people, but they seem purposeless and this turns Cohen to a morbid fear about why he is alive and why he should care about being alive. The crowds shuttling between home and factory are in turn transformed into an unthinking and frightened mass, people living their lives like 'robots'. He feels under attack from the clamouring voices of the advertisements that bombard his senses as he walks the city:

'Buy Gloops' Gaspers and Don't Suffer from Sore Throat!' howled one. 'Buy Floops' Face Powder, and be Alluring!' shrieked another. 'Buy me! that I might make more profit than my neighbour!' 'No! Buy me, that I might make more profit than my competitor!' 'Buy all of us; buy everything under the sun; buy, buy, buy!' they all shrieked in a maddening, tumultuous chorus. And I saw all the voracious advertisements, and I was afraid.[123]

This was no ordinary fear. It was uncontrollable, 'a mental distress so acute as to be well-nigh indistinguishable from physical pain'.[124] There are two key messages in the narrative: firstly, such invisible psychological suffering was a painful reality; secondly, it was a product of the social situation, not simply an individual failing. Cohen's framing of the vortex in terms of a landscape of faceless crowds, robotic industrial lives, and vulgar consumerism, and his focus on the Labour Exchange as the catalyst for a disintegration of the self, turn this into a narrative not only of compassion but also of complaint. There is an acceptance of a psychological subjectivity here, but also a critique of the way that industrial civilisation impinged on the economy of the emotions. Cohen's readiness to put the narrative in such open and painful psychological terms was almost certainly partly a consequence of the aim of critique. It would be rash to assume that his ease in framing the self in psychological terms was representative of the working man. To deny any such possibility, however, would be equally unsatisfactory. In its very act of demotic communication, Cohen's narrative does imply the existence of an understanding of and a popular language for psychological and emotional breakdown among

---

[122] Ibid. 164.   [123] Ibid. 165.   [124] Ibid. 165.

workers themselves. At the very least, this kind of narrative read by other workers would have helped to open up such a way of seeing the self. It may be right that social psychologists misinterpreted working-class behaviour when they pathologised the unemployed as being in a situation of psychological depression, but the significance of Cohen's account is that it opens up the possibility that workers themselves may have drawn on the psychological in imagining their positions within industrial society. Cohen, like others however, did not simply accept what an orthodox psychology told him to think, particularly when it seemed as ridiculous to him as psychoanalysis: he co-opted its apparatus where useful to create his own.[125] Indeed, despite poking fun at psychoanalysis in his *What Nobody Told the Foreman* of 1953, he would nevertheless go on to highlight how the interwar depression had 'profound psychological effects' for those in work just as much as those without. A constant insecurity and resulting loss of respect became internalised in individuals who unconsciously came to blame themselves for their problems. For a skilled cabinetmaker like himself, a sense of social identity forged in the solidarity of the small workshop of the craftsman was torn apart as the individual came unconsciously to see his fellow workmates as rivals, while those on the production line similarly found themselves becoming rivals in mind with their fellow workers.[126] In sum, Cohen, like the Plebs before him, had found in the territory of the psychological a way to attack but also comprehend the very personal inhumanity of capitalism.

THE WORKING CLASS AND THE PROBLEM OF PSYCHOLOGICAL FIRST AID

Given the cultural suspicion of psychological illness as well as the fraught class relations of the period after the First World War, it was a hugely sensitive issue for doctors to be suggesting that this was a serious problem among workers. On the other hand, as already suggested, this was also a period in which not only medical attitudes but also those of the public were gradually shifting. These tensions emerged as industrial psychology moved beyond time and motion study and vocational testing to highlight psychological predisposition to fatigue and sick leave. Here, psychologist Millais Culpin found himself attacked on both fronts, accused by organised labour of libelling innocent people as neurotic, but on the other hand seen by employers as abetting the malingerer in suggesting that people without any physical disease might be justifiably ill or fatigued.[127] However, he also recognised a growing emotional openness among his subjects. He was amazed

---

[125] M. Cohen, *What Nobody Told the Foreman* (London, 1953), 28.

[126] Ibid. 44–6, 57–69.

[127] M. Culpin, 'A Study of the Incidence of the Minor Psychoses: Their Clinical and Industrial Importance', *The Lancet*, (4 Feb. 1928), 220–4; M. Culpin, 'The Need for Psychopathology, *The Lancet* (4 Oct. 1928), 725–6.

by the willingness to 'pour out to a total stranger a mass of emotionally charged symptoms which have never been previously confessed'. He noted how often he was thanked for listening to them. He even found it unnecessary to approach the subject obliquely, finding that most people would respond to the question of whether they saw themselves as nervous types.[128] This included men who had gone through the war and who proved in fact far more willing to talk about this and were less 'suppressed' than he had expected.[129]

The issue of psychoneurosis among the working population shot to the fore of public attention in 1935 when the *British Medical Journal* published the research of James L. Halliday, Regional Medical Officer of the Department of Health for Scotland, and a Medical Referee under the National Insurance Act. Officially, only 2 per cent of those claiming National Insurance benefit due to incapacity to work in Scotland were suffering from psychoneuroses, but Halliday's research suggested that the true level was as high as 33 per cent. Moreover, this figure increased with the length of unemployment: for those claiming benefits for less than three months it was just 25.7 per cent; but for those out of work for between six and twelve months it rose to 41.5 per cent. Halliday argued that a very considerable proportion of illness through conditions such as stomach and gastric problems, anaemia, and rheumatism was in fact partly or wholly psychological.[130] Work like Halliday's looked well beyond the technical fix that tended to emerge when the industrial psychologists cast their attention to such problems. As he was keen to point out, when the industrial psychologists' advice of tackling Miner's Nystagmus by improving lighting had been taken up in Scotland it had done nothing to hold back a further fivefold increase in the condition between 1922 and 1930.[131] Lighting was only part of the problem, there were also clear psychological roots: the effect of unemployment, falling wages, and mechanisation, on the one hand; and the 'advertisement and suggestion' provided by the *Nystagmus Report* of 1922, on the other.[132]

What Halliday was revealing here had radical implications for understanding of sickness, and this will be more fully considered in the next chapter.[133] Relevant here are the consequences for the workforce, which were potentially acute. If his figures were even remotely correct, it raised the hugely sensitive issues of whether such psychological illness was a valid illness under the insurance system.[134] There had been some debate in the early 1930s as to whether psychotherapy should be available as a treatment under National Insurance, the view emerging that panel

---

[128] Culpin, 'Study of the Incidence of Minor Psychoses', 221.   [129] Ibid. 222.

[130] 'Psychoneuroses as a Cause of Incapacity among Insured Persons', *BMJ Supplement* (9 March 1935), 85–8; *BMJ Supplement* (16 March 1935), 99–102.

[131] J. L. Halliday, *Psychosocial Medicine: A Study of the Sick Society* (London, 1948), 37–8. See also 'Challenge on Cause of Eye Disease', *Daily Herald* (4 Nov. 1936).   [132] Ibid. 38.

[133] See especially pp. 200–2.

[134] See for instance the unease within the TUC about accepting the psychological view of Miners' Nystagmus: MRC MSS 292/144.6/3.

doctors could not provide what was a specialist skill.[135] However, in practice if a psychological basis was ever recognised it tended to be pigeonholed as having some kind of nervous organic basis, even if nobody could really demonstrate this: 'neurasthenia', 'nervous debility', 'nervous exhaustion', were all convenient labels that satisfied a laity and medical profession neither of which was fully comfortable with a psychological reorientation. It was also fortunate, pointed out Henry Dicks of the Tavistock Clinic, that the approved societies were 'not yet so advanced in psychotherapy as to quarrel with it'.[136] Halliday was not one of those who set out to attack the authenticity of claims on sickness benefit: psychoneurotic illness, in his view, was just as real as illness with an organic origin; there could be rare cases of malingering, but there could not be imaginary illness. Others were less sympathetic, more eager to see such studies as evidence of malingering or of innate constitutional and mental debility, and more likely to question whether a psychological condition was covered by the insurance system. Such concern came together with a related debate over workmen's compensation. In the interwar period, some 5–6.5 percent of the workforce annually made successful claims under this scheme, with nearly half a million cases in 1938 for instance.[137] What were the implications for claims of compensation if emerging medical research was correct in arguing that the original injury, let alone the ongoing problem, was so often psychological, and that the claim itself often resulted in a psychological complex that held back recovery and indeed 'sedulously fostered' others to follow suit?[138] Understandably, against such a background, workers and their representatives could have mixed views about an argument that such a high proportion of illness lacked a real organic basis. Not only were there vital economic interests at stake here, but there was also continuing sensitivity about being publicly recognised as a 'mental case'. Many of those workers who did obtain psychotherapeutic treatment continued to secure this on a private basis and remained very anxious that their employers should not find out.[139]

By the 1930s, the silence and deliberate confusion or evasion surrounding the issue was under challenge from new medical thinking, and this would force organised labour to address the subject more directly. In the mid-1930s, Dr M. Rosenfield, employed by the TUC at their Manor House Hospital and a psychiatrist to the East London Child Guidance Clinic, put forward a case for the organised labour movement to take far more seriously the mental effects of industrial life. In his view, there should have been a system of specialised industrial psychological clinics to parallel the child guidance clinics now emerging for children. Instead, there was a situation in which workers were so afraid of being accused of malingering that they would not face up to the often psychological roots of their

---

[135] 'Psychotherapy', *The Lancet*, (29 July 1933), 262.
[136] H.V. Dicks, 'Neurasthenia: Toxic and Traumatic', *The Lancet*, (23 Sept. 1933), 683.
[137] P. Barttrip, *Workmen's Compensation in Twentieth-Century Britain* (Aldershot, 1987), x, 121.
[138] T. A. Ross, 'Some Evils of Compensation', *Mental Hygiene*, 3, 4 (1937), 143.
[139] J. R. Rees, 'Neurotic Disorder and Mental Efficiency', 8–9: MRC MSS 292/140.1/2.

illnesses, and without this there was little hope of proper cure. Despite some sympathy for Rosenfield's case, officials at the TUC held back support because of concern that they would end up having to fund such clinics.[140] There were also tensions over Rosenfield's adamant view that a political bias in favour of the worker had to be central in addressing the problem. In Rosenfield's view, such psychological clinics needed to be run by workers and workers' organisations if they were to recognise and successfully tackle the economic basis of mental problems: 'clinics run in accordance with orthodox teaching', he argued, 'will only be able to help a class whose mental troubles are not due to economic causes.'[141] Existing psychiatry was 'class psychiatry'.[142] Currently, the psychological casualties of industry, unrecognised as such, ended up mired within the complex legalism and class politics of the compensation system. Spied upon by employers, confused and obsessed by the legal struggles that ensued, the compensation issue rapidly became part of the worker's underlying neurosis. If it did result in a pay-off, the long-term result was unemployability, a loss of self-respect, and a persistent psychological malaise that now found itself further cemented by economic and legal circumstances. Mental disorder, argued Rosenfield, was a social rather than a personal problem. Solutions had to be too. This would mean going beyond the provision of special worker-run clinics to address the working environment as a whole: 'An adequate psychotherapy', he argued, 'is one that can interfere decisively in factories, workshops, and all work environments. It must be able, as far as possible, to control the workers' environment.'[143] This did not mean simply going down the industrial psychology route of adjusting the worker: as Rosenfield scathingly put it, there were 'factors in industry to which only mental defectives are able to adapt'.[144] It meant instead adjusting work to the worker.

Exasperated by the lukewarm reception within the bureaucracy of the TUC, and almost certainly not helping his cause, Rosenfield fired off that he considered it to be a reactionary body. Instead, he set out to appeal to the workforce directly, as he had already attempted through the Journal of the Omnibus Employees and the *Daily Herald*.[145] Nevertheless, the TUC did continue cautiously to explore the issue. Its Medical Adviser, Dr Hyacinth Morgan, would even claim that the 'indictment of the present organisation of Society as it mentally affects workers' was also generally the view of the Trades Union movement.[146] In reality, the problem of cost remained a fundamental deterrent to any independent or radical

---

[140] Memo from H. B. Morgan to J. L. Smyth (undated, *c*.May 1935): MRC MSS 292/140.1/2.

[141] Rosenfield to J. L. Smyth (Social Insurance Department), 28 May 1935: MRC MSS 292/140.1/2.

[142] Rosenfield, 'Memorandum on the Organisation of Mental Hygiene Clinics for Industrial Workers' (May 1935), 6–7: MRC MSS 292/140.1/2.　　　　　　　　　　　[143] Ibid. 1.

[144] Ibid. 5.

[145] Report on the Meeting of Dr M. Rosenfield and Dr H. B. Morgan to discuss Mental Health Clinics, 14 May 1935: MRC MSS 292/140.1/2.See also M. Rosenfield, 'Industrial Psychotherapy', *Human Factor*, 10 (1936), 360–5.

[146] Memo from Morgan to J. L. Smyth (undated, *c*.May 1935): MRC MSS 292/140.1/2.

strategy. Instead, the mental hygienists and insurance companies set the agenda: the former, looking to save money for the nation by keeping down the 'burden' of missing work through psychological illness; the latter, keen to keep down costs for their own financial reasons.[147]

With the pressure mounting, Morgan turned to an old acquaintance, Dr E. N. Snowden, who he had worked alongside at the Queen Alexander Military Hospital in the First World War when dealing with shellshocked officers—an experience that is also significant in helping to explain Morgan's own interest and sympathy in this field. Snowden, now Psychologist to the Hospital for Nervous Diseases at Maida Vale, had gone on to serve for eighteen years in the Psychotherapy Department at St Bartholomew's Hospital in London. However, he had recently resigned in pique after losing out to a younger man for a senior post in his department. Morgan was of the opinion that his passing over had at least something to do with his leftward sympathies. His resignation appears to have freed him to become more open in this respect.[148] With Morgan's guidance, Snowden wrote a long memorandum on the subject. This was considered by the General Council of the TUC and passed on to the Mental Health Committee of the British Medical Association. The internal debates offer an insight into the continuing sensitivity surrounding the issue. There was uncertainty, for instance about whether to present this in public as an issue of 'mental rehabilitation' or 'injury psychoneurosis', with the movement keen to dissociate it from the taint of insanity but nevertheless wanting to emphasise its serious nature.[149] The paper also had the hard task of reconciling the conflicting financial interests of the worker and the approved societies. Finally, there was the tendency of medical men to class a psychoneurosis as less than full disablement, or even to turn it down completely. In advancing the case for justice and sympathy for the psychoneurotic worker, Snowden drew a direct parallel with the shellshock victim of the Great War, where a similar struggle over rights had been fought over pensions in the aftermath of war.[150] However, this was not simply a problem of the struggle to recognise the validity of psychoneurotic injury. Through neglect of the latter, the whole system was under threat; hence the concern of the approved societies. The current system focused resources towards workers with the more serious physical injuries, who were also often among the easiest to rehabilitate. It neglected, through a combination of suspicion, priorities, and limited resources, those with the less serious physical problems; but, since these were often cases with a

---

[147] J. R. Rees, 'Neurotic Disorder and Industrial Efficiency'; R. D. Gillespie, 'Mental Hygiene as a National Problem', *Mental Hygiene*, 4 (Dec. 1931), 1–9; *National Insurance Gazette* (9 June 1938); *Manchester Guardian* (11 Nov. 1937): MRC MSS 292/140.1/2.

[148] Memo of interview between Dr H. B. Morgan and Dr E. N. Snowden, 1 March 1938: MRC MSS 292/140.1/2.

[149] Letter, Morgan to Snowden, 2 May 1934: MRC MSS 292/140.1/2.

[150] Snowden, Paper to Workmen's Compensation and Factory Committee, 15 June 1938: MRC MSS 292/140.1/2. On the pensions issue in relation to shellshock: P. Barham, *Forgotten Lunatics of the Great War* (New Haven and London, 2004).

psychoneurotic dimension, they were also in reality the hardest to solve. Indeed, the worker whose injury was a psychological response to an accident at work would resist cure indefinitely if that meant a return to the original source of danger. The result was a gradual clogging up of the system as a whole, as well as on an individual level a growing number of workers left in a limbo of mental torment, compounded by legal and financial anxiety. Snowden, like Rosenfield before him, concluded that specialist mental clinics for workers were a necessity. The busy psychologist attached to a general hospital could do little more than hand out sedatives or send the patient to massage or exercise departments. Effective treatment meant not just specialist clinics but tackling the originating and complicating causes: the fear of the workplace and compensation, respectively.[151]

CONCLUSION

By the end of the 1930s, the labour movement was taking seriously the idea that work, and more generally industrial life, could be the cause of mental ill health. Encouragement did come from outside groups because of their own interests, whether the approved societies, psychologists, or the medical profession, but a narrative of psychological complaint against the industrial system was also emerging from below. Indeed, one of the central propositions of this chapter has been that if we want to understand the relationship between psychology and the problem of industrial civilisation, we need to consider the availability of this knowledge and its practices by those who have figured thus far merely as objects of expert inquiry.

In the language of the neuroses and psychoneuroses, we do see a breakdown of a stark division between the normal and the insane, and we see space opening up for understanding the worker as an emotional, psychological subject. However, there were serious tensions over moving in this direction. There was concern about any model that might be seen as blaming psychological conditions on the individual; hence the focus on psychoneurosis as an injury. This reflected the problematic status of psychoneurosis in claims for compensation and sickness insurance on the one hand, and a persistent reluctance to accept a diagnosis that put in question a sense of character and manhood on the other. The latter was an increasingly sensitive issue. This was partly because of the way that unemployment challenged a concept of manhood that centred on work.[152] The sexual dimension to this problem was also difficult to ignore within a culture that was both more aware of Freud and now becoming alarmed about what seemed to be a dangerous collapse in the birth rate.[153] According to Adlerian psychologist

---

[151] Dr E. N. Snowden, 'Replacing in Industry the Workmen Suffering from Injury Psychoneurosis', May/June 1938: MRC MSS 292/140.1/2.

[152] Suggestive in this regard: S. Alexander, 'Men's Fears and Women's Work: Responses to Unemployment in London between the Wars', *Gender and History*, 12 (2000), 401–25.

[153] On the birth rate and 'race suicide': E. Charles, *The Twilight of Parenthood* (London, 1934).

Maurice Robb, a vicious circle was at work when it came to many working-class men: economic insecurity leading to pragmatic *coitus interuptus* to keep down family size, this exacerbating a nervous strain that was a product of the inferiority complex associated with job insecurity, and this in turn resulting in an emerging problem of male impotence.[154] As Halliday pointed out, the rise of psychoneurosis among the working-class male was taking place as levels of female hysteria were collapsing, and this further emphasised the fact that working-class manhood was emerging as a key psychological problem.[155] As already noted, the practical psychology of self-realisation examined earlier in this book tended to offer a path of self-elevation that transcended sex and thus de-emphasised gender as a problem, hence perhaps its reluctance to fully embrace Freud. When the organised working class turned to psychology, they too were likely to look to its positive potential for the self or for class, or if not to use it as a tool for attacking social and economic injustice. However, when outside commentators viewed the situation, the anxieties about masculinity apparent in relation to shellshock in the First World War now resurfaced.[156] Because of the politics of class, this remained far too sensitive a territory to do much about, even if the resources had been available. It would take not only the renewed economic challenge of war, but also, and more crucially, the mounting anxiety about psychological roots of the mid-century ideological crisis—again a problem that centred on men—to make the problem of the psychological subject a public and state issue.[157]

---

[154] M. Robb, 'The Psychology of the Unemployed from the Medical Point of View', in Beales and Lambert (eds.), *Memoirs of the Unemployed*, 271–85. Robb was on the fringes of the Adler circle examined in Ch. 3.   [155] Halliday, *Psychosocial Medicine*, 60–70, 130–7.
[156] E. Showalter, *The Female Malady: Women, Madness and English Culture, 1830–1980* (London, 1987), 167–94; J. Bourke, *Dismembering the Male: Men's Bodies, Britain and the Great War* (London, 1996).   [157] See Ch. 7.

6

Medicine and the Psychological

This chapter reflects on the problems of British medicine in coming to understand illness and health as psychological subjects in the period from the start of the century until around 1960. The limitations of the profession in this regard help to account for the active and eclectic, popular and practical psychological culture of the period. However, the medical profession was neither wholly immune from the broader cultural influences that promoted enthusiasm and shaped psychological culture and practice at the popular level, nor was it ready to cede control over the psycho-medical territory to popular competitors. In the past, histories of this subject have focused on two stories: on the one hand, the emergence of an often narrowly defined psychoanalytic psychology, painting a picture of slow, embattled progress by pioneers; on the other, the translation of psychodynamic assumptions into the prescriptions of mental hygiene for adjustment in conformity with psychological norms. If the former has tended to be very cautious about broader influence, the latter, albeit through a focus on rhetoric more than actual practice, has veered in the opposite direction. This chapter will briefly consider both stories, and highlight certain limitations in both cases. It will also argue this is not the whole story. In particular, it will explore the ways in which a Victorian medicine, not in fact without its own psychological tactics, could accommodate aspects of the new psychology by casting it in more pragmatic, more culturally traditional idiom. It will also argue that we should pay more attention to the way that psychology could act as space for bringing values into medicine.

The first framework for telling the story of psychology's relationship with British medicine reflects powerful assumptions about both the progressive nature of Freudian theory and practice and the conservative nature of the surrounding culture. In such a history, David Eder's presentation on the treatment of hysteria by psychoanalysis to the British Medical Association in 1911, the first Freudian paper delivered in this setting, is both an important landmark and a highly symbolic event. 'We are surely on the threshold of discoveries in the psychic region comparable with the gift of the new world', he pronounced, in words befitting a man who would come to be seen, by no less a figure than Freud himself, as the pioneer of the subject in Britain.[1] The audience is reported as having demonstrated

---

[1] J. B. Hobman, (ed.), *David Eder: Memoirs of a Modern Pioneer* (London, 1945), 94.

its own view on the subject by following the Chairman out of the room in an act of silent censure. The episode epitomises the story of psychology's entry to British medicine. It situates the importation of Freud and psychoanalysis as central; it implies a radical break with the past; and it portrays the British as unwilling to listen—offering in their resistance, what can be presented as, ironic, confirmation of the very Freudian account that they were at the same time objecting to. It sees the entry of a dramatic external pressure, in the form of 'shellshock' in the First World War as an important event in forcing a partial retreat from such resistance. However, it sees the decades that followed as still ones of isolation or at best pioneering activity within a hostile environment, defence of truth against misinterpretation and bastardisation, and internal division, more than expansion, acceptance, and diffusion.[2] The ongoing importance of such internal disputes, but also the assumption that the broader culture was hostile territory for psychoanalysis, particularly when set against a history of popularisation in the United States, has until very recently discouraged historians of the movement from looking much beyond its own narrow boundaries.[3]

For a long time, a bleak picture of psychiatry, centred on the dominance of a custodial role and a therapeutic nihilism that had become such characteristic features of the asylum by the end of the nineteenth century, did little to jolt this story of an isolated island of Freudian insight from its narrow horizons.[4] Psychoanalysis has been, though as a silent presence, an almost impossible to avoid filter for historical judgement, and an unspoken model of what should have been: there, in particular, at the back of the historian's mind in the attack on alienists who refused to talk to the mad.[5] Unsurprisingly, such historians have found it rather irresistible to cast late-Victorian psychiatrists as leading villains in the conservative resistance to Freud.[6] However, a new body of research has begun to highlight some of the ways in which the gloomy picture of early-twentieth-century psychiatry changes in light of moves towards outpatients, community care, an interest in mental health as well as illness, and a greater open-mindedness about the use, not only of new physical treatments, but also psychotherapy. 'Two

[2] G. Kohon (ed.), *The British School of Psychoanalysis: The Independent Tradition* (London, 1986); E. Jones, *Free Associations: Memories of a Psycho-Analyst* (London, 1959); J. A .C. Brown, *Freud and the Post-Freudians* (London, 1961).

[3] On the United States: Hale, *Rise and Crisis of Psychoanalysis*. For a shift towards looking outwards from psychoanalysis: D. Pick, 'The Id Comes to Bloomsbury', *Guardian* (16 Aug. 2003). Over the last decade, there have been some other historicist moves, albeit very sketchy, from within the psychotherapeutic movement, for instance: Hinshelwood, 'Psychodynamic Psychiatry before the World War I'; Pines, 'The Development of the Psychodynamic Movement'.

[4] The picture for the nineteenth century was dominated by Andrew Scull's *Museums of Madness: The Social Organisation of Insanity in Nineteenth-Century England* (London, 1970), revised as *The Most Solitary of Afflictions: Madness and Society in Britain, 1700–1900* (New Haven, 1993).

[5] Not only in Scull's picture of asylumdom, but in Roy Porter's project of retrieving the patient's voice: R. Porter, *Mind Forg'd Manacles: A History of Madness in England from the Restoration to the Regency* (London, 1987), 229–73.

[6] T. Turner, 'James Crichton Browne and the Anti-Psycho-Analysts', in G. Berrios and H. Freeman (eds.), *150 Years of British Psychiatry*, 2 (London, 1996), 144–55.

cheers' for psychiatry, suggested Roy Porter, half-hearted praise maybe, but praise nevertheless that signals a significant turn in the sympathies of the historian.[7] Set alongside new findings about the existence of popular psychotherapeutic cultures, this suggests that it is time to look hard at the narrative of failure and resistance that has come from writing in an age when historians were too exclusively preoccupied with the acceptance of Freud.

This chapter will argue that the emergence of a psychological dimension to British medicine needs to be set within the context of a much broader terrain of available psychological ideas and practices.[8] Much of what went on in the name of psychology in medicine, just like what went on at a popular level, and sometimes even what went on in the name of Freud, was viewed as theoretically wrong and even dangerous by those within the Freudian fold. What made the Freudian approach hard to accept for the majority, and in turn often attractive for a self-inquiring minority, was its emphasis, initially on sex, and subsequently and in the long term just as fundamentally on love, open discussion about relationships and emotions, and a private self that found comfort in this state of privacy.[9] Far more conducive to the majority—both doctors and patients, though for rather different reasons—was a psychology which centred on and fostered, rather than under-mined in acts of exposure, the power of the self. The reasons for such attraction will be at the heart of the analysis that follows.

The second framework for psychology's relation with early twentieth-century British medicine has moved in the opposite direction: it is an account, not of resis-tance, but of imposition from above. It has emerged most influentially in the work of sociologists David Armstrong and Nikolas Rose, both of whom have under-taken path-breaking historical studies of the subject in support of theoretical posi-tions inspired by the work of Michel Foucault. In their willingness to go beyond both Freud and the asylum to a broader discourse of mental hygiene, they portray psychology emerging as a powerful and pervasive tool for defining and governing not just illness, but health, and ultimately subjectivity.[10] The new history of

[7] For a summary of the case: R. Porter, 'Two Cheers for Psychiatry!: The Social History of Mental Disorder in Twentieth Century Britain', in ibid. 2, pp. 383–406. Informed by this shift in mood, and with an interest in 'care in the community' pushed back to revise our view of the earlier period: P. Bartlett and D. Wright (eds.), *Outside the Walls of the Asylum: The History of Care in the Community, 1750–2000* (London, 1999). Much of the most significant recent research on the twentieth century remains unpublished, notably: L. Westwood, 'Avoiding the Asylum: Pioneering Work in Mental Health Care, 1890–1939', Ph.D. thesis (University of Sussex, 1999); and V. Long, 'Changing Public Representations of Mental Illness in Britain 1870–1970', Ph.D. thesis (University of Warwick, 2004). For an insight into therapeutic advance, even at an asylum in provincial north Wales: P. Michael, *Care and Treatment of the Mentally Ill in North Wales, 1800–2000* (Cardiff, 2000).

[8] For criticism of the 'persistent Freudian legend' about the origins of psychotherapy: S. Shamdasani, 'Claire, Lise, Jean, Nadia, and Gisèle: Preliminary Notes towards a Characterisation of Pierre Janet's Psychasthenia', in Gijswijt-Hofstra and Porter (eds.), *Cultures of Neurasthenia*, 364.

[9] On the primary importance of the latter: N. Spice, 'I Must be Mad', *London Review, of Books* (8 Jan. 2004), 11–15.

[10] Rose, *The Psychological Complex*; Rose, *Governing the Soul*; Armstrong, *The Political Anatomy of the Body*. For criticism of the failure to attend to modification of the mental hygiene through growing

psychiatry has more often been of the 'two cheers' school, nevertheless it does offer indirect support through a picture of psychiatric power spreading beyond the narrow realm of the asylum into the community and to borderline conditions such as feeble-mindedness and the neuroses. Yet, such detailed research also invariably indicates the difficulties in escaping the asylum and in translating ambition into practice; difficulties that the schematic Foucauldian approach tends to underplay.[11] The one study thus far to attend in detail to the subject of mental hygiene, shares the focus on discourse rather than practice, and this holds back a more measured picture of limitations of influence and modification in the messy business of practice. It does however make important qualifications concerning modification of ambition over time, particularly as relationships became a focus of attention and in due course encouraged a more self-critical stance from the professionals.[12] What follows will support some of these reservations. It also points to the greater variety of options in terms of psychological thought and practice that were available for early-twentieth-century medicine. When it comes to studies of psychology within general medicine—the subject pioneered by Armstrong—historians, rather surprisingly bearing in mind the potential scope of such influence, have had less to contribute.[13] Development of this dimension will therefore constitute a significant element within the analysis that follows.

THE NERVE DOCTOR AS PSYCHOTHERAPIST

Although the emergence of a popular psychotherapeutic culture in early twentieth-century Britain was encouraged by lack of provision from orthodox medicine, and sometimes even by hostility towards the medicine that was on offer, the relationship was not exclusively one of opposition. The medical profession had its own internal divisions over orthodoxy, and from the start there were qualified doctors who were active and influential within the popular psychotherapeutic sphere. During the interwar period, though severe tensions remained, there was a gradual breakdown of the initially sharp divisions, with the popular audience increasingly likely to feed on a diet of advice literature coming from members of the medical profession. The first chapter of this book explored this from the perspective of popular psychology; this chapter turns to the medical side of the

appreciation of the importance of relationships, including that between observer and observed: J. Toms, 'Mental Hygiene to Civil Rights: MIND and the Problematic of Personhood, *c.*1900 to *c.*1980', Ph.D. thesis (University of London, 2005).

   [11] For instance, on child guidance clinics: Thom, 'Wishes, Anxieties, Play and Gestures', in Cooter (ed.), *In the Name of the Child*; and on feeble-mindedness: P. Dale, 'Implementing the 1913 Mental Deficiency Act: Competing Priorities and Resource Constraint Evident in the South West of England before 1948', *Social History of Medicine*, 16 (2003), 403–18.

   [12] Toms, 'Mental Hygiene to Civil Rights'.

   [13] A notable exception is Lawrence, 'Still Incommunicable: Clinical Holism and Medical Knowledge in Interwar Britain', 94–111.

relationship. In due course, it will examine the profession's shifting position regarding popular psychology over the first decades of the century.[14] To start with, it considers three doctors whose activities transcended such a barrier. In doing so, it suggests that we would benefit from looking beyond the two frameworks that have dominated the historiography to date.

Before turning to the case studies, it is necessary to say something about historical understanding of medicine's relationship with psychology in the late nineteenth century. We have come to accept that Victorian medicine rejected a psychological approach.[15] However, such a truism needs qualification. Medicine rejected a certain sort of psychological approach: one which explicitly focused on mind, rather than body; one which accepted the irrational as inherent and central to human nature and so challenged the primacy of the will; and one which thereby questioned the idea of a distinct boundary between insanity and normality. To say that a psychological approach was rejected, and to leave it at that, assumes, in short, a post-Freudian perspective about what we mean by the psychological. In turn, it is to overlook a different type of psychological subjectivity: one which centred on channelling the powers of the conscious mind, even if this was articulated in terms of a language of the body; and one which would come to integrate the irrational side as something to be managed and harnessed by the self. In the mid-nineteenth century, all medicine was in fact necessarily psychosomatic.[16] By the turn of the century, such a medicine was becoming increasingly interested in and ambitious regarding the unconscious and would find a route through the British version of the new psychology to turn itself into a more self-conscious psychotherapy—a therapy openly focused on mind just as much as body. The road from nerves to the psychoneuroses, in short, was one with its route of evolution as well as celebrated revolution; indeed, the former may even have been the more common of the two routes.

The popular physiological model of the nerves had provided Victorians with a culturally-acceptable way to frame much of what we now commonly understand in mental and emotional terms; in fact, the continuing use of a language of nervous breakdown highlights that there may be more continuities than we would at first imagine.[17] Location of unhappiness in bodily condition had advantages, both in terms of explaining causation, and in the nature of the curative regimes

[14] Thomson, 'The Popular, the Practical and the Professional', in Bunn et al. (eds.), *Psychology in Britain*, 115–32.

[15] M. Clark, 'The Rejection of Psychological Approaches to Mental Disorder in Late Nineteenth-Century British Psychiatry', in A. Scull (ed.), *Madhouses, Mad-Doctors and Madmen* (London, 1981), 271–312.

[16] C. Rosenberg, 'Body and Mind in Nineteenth-Century Medicine: Some Clinical Origins of the Neurosis Construct', *Bulletin of the History of Medicine*, 63 (1989), 187–8.

[17] Oppenheim, *Shattered Nerves*; E. Shorter, *Paralysis to Fatigue: A History of Psychosomatic Illness in the Modern Era* (New York, 1992). The argument that follows is developed in Thomson, 'Neurasthenia in Britain', in Gijswijt-Hofstra and Porter (eds.), *Cultures of Neurasthenia*, 77–95. On language: M. Barke, R. Fribush, & P. Stearns, 'Nervous Breakdown in Twentieth-Century American Culture', *Social History*, 33 (2000), 565–84.

that emerged in response.[18] It suited the patients: something that we should regard as a more important factor before 1900 than after it, when the relationship to medicine began to move from that of consumer to state subject. If debilitating unhappiness was rooted in the condition of the nerve fibres, it was not the fault of the patient, nor was it a sign of mental imbalance; to have said as much in the period would have shamefully questioned the sanity of the patient. It also suited the doctors, not least because they depended on the market of patients. And with the germ of illness located in the nerves, curative regimes of feeding, rest, and other forms of lifestyle management were the order of the day, all not only relatively acceptable to patients and their families but readily accommodated within the physiological framework of medicine.

In practice, however, there was a significant psychotherapeutic dimension to such regimes. Restricting the intake of food, imposing rest, or prescribing drugs, the doctor was mastering a will that had given way and psychologically restoring it to self-command. Alert to some of the new psychological currents of the day, towards the end of the century such doctors would be increasingly open about the psychotherapeutic dimension of their role, albeit in a fashion that accommodated itself to the prevailing culture of character and the primacy of will.

Alfred Taylor Schofield was one of these doctors and the author of some sixty books, a great many of which addressed the nerves. Like many of those of his generation who turned to psychology, within medicine just as without, Schofield saw in the exploration of mind some meeting point for his interests in the bodily and the spiritual: a route away from the poverty of meaning and ambition of a purely materialist medicine.[19] Writing in 1906, he pointed out that 'psycho-therapy' was in fact 'universally used', even if it was 'seldom spoken of or studied scientifically by the profession'.[20] Indeed, it was little more than a further development and theorisation of the doctor's traditional interpersonal skill in understanding and managing the patient: 'the moment the eye of the patient meets the eye of the physician, psychological action influencing the course of the disease at once takes place through the patient's unconscious mind.'[21] Hiding from this reality was simply to cede the territory of medicine to a host of quacks, mystics, and 'psycho-cults' who were in the process of taking the psychotherapeutic vanguard, meeting considerable popular demand.[22] The unconscious, sometimes seen as hostile

[18] B. Sicherman, 'The Uses of Diagnosis: Doctors, Patients and Neurasthenia', *Journal of the History of Medicine*, 32 (1977), 33–54.

[19] Schofield wrote numerous books on religion as well as medicine. In a memoir he recalled his childhood conversion in terms that reflected the power of the mind over body: *A Harley Street Doctor's Story* (London, 1930). For the points of contact between psychiatry and demonology in a figure like Schofield: R. Hayward, 'Demonology, Neurology, and Medicine in Edwardian Britain', *Bulletin of the History of Medicine*, 78 (2004), 49–50. Interwar writer on medical psychology, Francis Crookshank, who would come from a similar religious background to Schofield, would recall the influence of Schofield through his writing on faith healing in *The Sunday at Home* and other popular Christian journals of the period: F. G. Crookshank (ed.), *Anorexia Nervosa*, Individual Psychology Pamphlet 2 (London, 1931), 19–20.

[20] A.T. Schofield, *The Management of a Nerve Patient* (London, 1906), 110.   [21] Ibid. 133.
[22] Ibid. 32.

territory when it came to the Victorian medical profession, could be embraced by a doctor like Schofield in terms of its potential power over the body. Absent, however, is direct engagement with internal psychological and emotional conflicts. The language may have been changing. There may have been a greater sense of urgency, fuelled sometimes as in this case by religion, to think more self-consciously about the psychological interaction of the doctor–patient encounter and of the power of mind over body. However, in many respects this was the older model of an economy of nervous energy in new psychological clothes.

Edwin Lancelot Hopewell Ash provides a second example of this type of psychotherapeutic tradition within British general practice, and an even stronger indication of continuities reaching into the interwar period. His first publication on the use of hypnosis and suggestion came in 1906. Over the next three decades, a plethora of titles would follow. Ash was one of many who attempted to bring together psychotherapy and Christianity.[23] New understanding about the power of the subconscious mind over the body via suggestion pointed to a way in which religious accounts of the role of faith in healing might be consistent with a medical framework.[24] However, there was a tension here: an emphasis on suggestion might appear to support the dismissal of religion as little more than delusion. Ash was therefore not alone in arguing that the power of the subconscious mind helped to keep the door open both for the possibility of a spiritual force within life and for religion as a positive influence on health.[25] On the eve of the War, Ash explored this in relation to the sudden cure of Dorothy Kerin, bed-ridden with tuberculosis for five years: the 'Herne Hill Miracle'.[26] He also suggested that the wave of nervousness sweeping the country might be due to a weakening of faith, and he would reiterate this idea about spirituality as mental nourishment in the context of war two years later.[27]

Though many of the initial publications were aimed at the popular market, by the 1930s his audience included not only general practitioners but also mental nurses.[28] Ash offered a psychotherapy which would increase the personal

---

[23] Richards, 'Psychology and the Churches', 57–84. See also Ch. 2.
[24] E. L. H. Ash, *Faith and Suggestion* (London, 1912).   [25] Ibid. x.
[26] Ibid. xii, 17–19.   [27] Ibid. ix; E. L. H. Ash, *Nerves in War-Time* (London, 1914).
[28] It is not always possible to distinguish the popular from the professional market when it comes to Ash, and this is of particular interest. However, those books that more clearly fall into the former category included a series published by Mills & Boon: *Nerves and the Nervous* (London, 1911, 1921); *Nerves in War-Time* (London, 1914); *Mental Self-Help: A Practical Handbook* (London, 1912, 1920); *'Can't Waiters' Or How You Waste Your Energy* (London, 1913); *Stammering and Successful Control in Speech and Action* (London, 1916); *Middle Age Health and Fitness* (London, 1922); *I Am and I Will: Twelve Practical Lessons in Mental Science* (London, 1924); *Facts about Stammering* (London, 1925); *On Keeping Our Nerves in Order* (London, 1928). Those directed at general practitioners included: *How to Treat by Suggestion, with and without Hypnosis: A Notebook for Practitioners* (London, 1914); *Melancholia in Everyday Practice* (London, 1934); *Manipulative Methods in the Treatment of Functional Disease* (London, 1935); *Diagnosis of Some Delusional Types in General Practice* (London, 1936). Books directed at nurses included: *The Nursing of Nervous Patients* (London, 1913); *The Mental Nurses Dictionary* (London, 1942, 1952). More generally on personal influence: *Therapy of Personal Influence* (London, 1929).

influence of the practitioner over the patient. Its tools were hypnosis, suggestion, and psycho-magnetism; psychoanalysis did not enter the picture. Writing in 1929, he regretted the fact that medical practitioners had so little opportunity to learn about such techniques; though the very fact that he was able to sell a series of guidebooks which were explicitly directed at this market suggests at least some, and probably a growing, appeal and awareness.[29] In his case, the interest in personal influence, mind-healing and also spiritual healing had again been there since his schooldays and it had actually been what encouraged him to turn to medicine as a career: he hoped that medicine might further an approach to healing that he was already developing.[30] Medical training did not turn him away from his existing beliefs; indeed, it uncovered new areas of mystery to explore, and fellow students were keen to join him. Such students, he recalled, were alarmingly relaxed about using psychotherapy when they went into practice, despite the complete lack of effective training within the medical curriculum.[31] By 1929, he was accepting that a form of psychotherapy was making an advance within medicine, but he was evidently rather unhappy about the route it was now threatening to take. In its emphasis on ideas, complexes, and repressions, there was a danger of minimising the personal factor; theory and its world of feelings and relationships, studiously avoided by Ash and his like, was in danger of swamping the more crucial issue of the power of practice.[32]

Addressing his profession in the mid-1930s, Ash would emphasise both the physiological basis to his form of psychotherapy and its applicability within everyday practice. In touching the body, all doctors were touching the nervous system, and in doing so they were literally touching the mind. Modern understanding, not only of the nervous system, but of the influence of the body's release of chemicals on emotion, gave authority to such a position; no longer was there any need to talk in vague terms of the force of 'psychomagnetism'. A psychotherapy that did not recognise this value of touch would leave patients only partly satisfied. It would also be confined in its use. Ash offered a vision of general medicine, armed with 'neurotherapy'. The general practitioner would be a surgeon of psycho-physical touch, satisfying body and mind, equipped to tackle the vast range of medical problems encountered in everyday practice.[33]

Born in 1864, and publishing an account of 'Advanced Suggestion' for the first time in 1918 with a second edition in 1921, Haydn Brown, a Fellow of the Royal Society of Medicine, provides a third example of the persistence of such alternative routes in psychotherapy. In popular books on sexual matters, sleep, and vitality, he would continue to promote his message regarding mind's relation to

---

[29] *Therapy of Personal Influence: An ABC of Treatment by Personal Influence, Suggestion, Medical Hypnosis, and Psychomagnetic Methods* (London, 1929).   [30] Ash, *An ABC*, 16–17.
   [31] Ibid. 19–21.   [32] Ibid. 93–4.
   [33] E. L. H. Ash, *Manipulative Methods in the Treatment of Functional Disease* (London, 1935). A medicalisation of massage was also taking place and this also raised interest in and went some way towards legitimating touching the body to reach the mind: S. Root, 'Healing, Touch and Medicine, c.1890–1950', Ph.D. thesis (University of Warwick, 2006).

body until his death in 1936. Defending such populist efforts, he would point out that the rising consciousness about preventive health care in the lay press, despite the suspicions of the profession, was in fact one of the most crucial of all factors in the dramatically rising standard of health of the period.[34] Brown had been interested in hypnotism and suggestion since the 1890s. By 1918, he was aware, though critical, of the psychoanalytic ideas of Freud and Jung. He had developed his own form of 'psychotherapy' in his general practice and now hoped to overcome suspicion within the profession and thereby deal a blow to the charlatanry that this had encouraged.[35] His strategy was one of presenting a psychological approach as common sense rather than mystery, convincing through the results of numerous cases ranging across virtually all the conditions a consultant was likely to meet: addressing his profession in terms of its familiar daily experience, rather than attempting to convince via abstract theory. However, he did co-opt the fashionable idea of a 'vicious circle', to support the proposition that apparently unrelated nervous symptoms might actually provide an effective point of treatment for physical symptoms connected in a circle of responses.[36] Psychotherapy was thus something that was relevant to all medicine, and something moreover that needed to be applied at an early stage rather than as a last resort when all else failed. Although he called his approach 'neuroinduction' and rooted it in the induction of neurones, offering an impression that this was still a therapeutic approach that had a physiological basis, it was basically a development of the practices of mental suggestion and relaxation allied to sensible advice on personal psychological technique in the management of patients. Nevertheless, he argued that there was a fundamental difference between this and earlier forms of psychotherapy, such as hypnosis: here, the patient was to remain in full control of his reasoning powers. Suggestion, too, he recast as a process that encouraged the conscious self, rather than exploited its weakness and suggestibility: one of teaching, advising, and induction.[37] He was also keen to highlight a fundamental difference to psychoanalysis (though he rejected the latter term, in a gesture of 1918 anti-Germanism, replacing it with 'thought-analysis'): neuroinduction helped the patient to analyse himself.[38] Indeed, as long as a patient was showing some sign of responding to treatment, there was no need at all to 'grope amongst a person's private affairs'; the latter something that was not only potentially dangerous, but also distasteful.[39]

Figures like Schofield, Ash, and Brown provide a bridge between the nineteenth-century medical discourse on nerves and the psychodynamic psychology

---

[34] H. Brown, *Modern Medical Methods* (London and New York, 1925), 9.

[35] H. Brown, *Advanced Suggestion (Neuroinduction)* (London, 1918), 1–3.

[36] Ibid. 5, 24. The idea was particularly promoted by J. B. Hurry. For instance, 'The Vicious Circle of Neurasthenia', *BMJ* (27 June, 1914), 1404–6; *The Vicious Circles of Neurasthenia and their Treatments* (London, 1915); *Vicious Circles of Disease*, 3rd edn. (London, 1919). He also projected the idea to sociological issues: *The Vicious Circles of Sociology and their Treatment* (London, 1915); *Poverty and its Vicious Circles* (London, 1917, 1921).   [37] Brown, *Advanced Suggestion*, 274.

[38] Ibid. 290–301.   [39] Ibid. 28.

of the twentieth century. Reaching out to the latter in terms of their acceptance of the psychological roots of illness, they nevertheless held back from turning doctors into analysts of emotions and relationships, let alone emancipators for repressed feelings—projects for which the majority of doctors, let alone the public, were both ill-equipped and had little enthusiasm. Instead, theirs was the psychotherapy of the conscious mind on the one hand, and of the embodied mind on the other: both visions were essentially pragmatic rather than introspective, optimistic rather than pessimistic, and both pointed the way to mastering the psychological subject. Such figures were clearly aware of a dual challenge: on one side, from the charlatans; on the other, from 'thought analysis'. On the basis of the popularity of their work, and, it would surely be fair to assume, that of others who have similarly been lost from historical sight, a case emerges for thinking rather differently about the nature of medical psychotherapy in the first decades of the twentieth century. Standard accounts already accept that Britain saw an eclectic tradition in psychotherapy; adding the Schofields, Ashes, and Browns to the mix pushes this much further.[40] It suggests that there may be a hidden history of this type of psychotherapeutic practice and thought within everyday medicine. It highlights the need to pay more attention to continuities, including the persistence of attention to body and spirit within psychotherapy. In doing so, it also begins to collapse the boundaries with the type of practical psychological culture explored at the start of this book.

SHELLSHOCK

The shellshock episode of the First World War has often been seen as a watershed for Freud and psychoanalysis in Britain, or at least for the advance of a psychodynamic psychology. In light of recent research, the former is difficult to sustain, and even the latter is in need of some revision.[41] The episode makes at least as much sense in terms of the frame of evolution just outlined, as it does in terms of the rather romantic narrative of revolution that has come to capture the public imagination.[42] There are two main problems with accepting shellshock as pivotal in such a story of mental illness. Firstly, it underestimates the willingness of pre-war medicine to think about psychological breakdown, albeit partly within a somatic framework of the nerves. Secondly, it overplays the promotion of Freudian and

---

[40] On the eclectic style of British psychotherapy, for instance: Brown, *Freud and the Post-Freudians*, 56–87.

[41] P. Leese, *Shell Shock: Traumatic Neurosis and the British Soldiers of the First World War* (Basingstoke, 2002); Shephard, *War of Nerves*; Barham, *Forgotten Lunatics of the Great War*.

[42] There has been a recent tendency to emphasise the antecedents of shellshock in railway spine and in the problems of trauma in relation to industrial work: Leese, *Shell Shock*, 15–17; W. Schivelbusch, *The Railway Journey: The Industrialization of Time and Space in the Nineteenth Century* (Berkeley and Los Angeles, 1986); A. Rabinbach, *The Human Motor: Energy, Fatigue and the Origins of Modernity* (New York, 1990).

psychodynamic medicine, and underplays the way that war gave new legs to an existing psychotherapeutic orientation.[43]

The attraction of seeing shellshock as a turning point has undoubtedly had much to do with a broader need of the British to regard the First World War as a cultural rupture: their moment of modernity; a harsh mirror of reality, in which Victorian values were shattered.[44] Undoubtedly, the very term 'shellshock' leant itself to this reading. Initially, it had a literal meaning, referring to the internal damage to the nervous system through shell explosion. As cases multiplied, many of them with no direct contact with an explosion, this physiological explanation faded away. Nor, in the face of many of Britain's finest young men breaking down, was it possible to sustain a belief that insanity was due to hereditary and constitutional weakness. In two fundamental respects, then, the shellshock story appears to present us with a fundamental shift from the organic to the psychological as the primary focus for explaining mental breakdown.

Scratch at the surface of this traditional interpretation, however, and problems emerge. Why, if 'shellshock' was so theoretically redundant—indeed, it was outlawed by the medico-military authorities by the end of the war—was the term so hard to dislodge within popular discourse? Why, if this was a turning point for attitudes, was the reframing of mental breakdown as something less organically definite and fixed than insanity (a term and a legal status studiously avoided when it came to the troops), not also extended to the civilian population? Scratch deeper still, as archival research on patients' records is at last beginning to do, and one finds continuing attitudes about degeneration, diagnostic inconsistency, and suspicions that a psychological explanation simply let malingerers off the hook.[45] Such scholarship is beginning to deconstruct the myth of shellshock at a time when the broader interpretation of the War as a fundamental break within British culture also finds itself on the wane.[46]

When it comes to the thesis of a retreat from the organic, we need to ask whether our developing understanding of what came before and after the war makes it still feasible to draw broader conclusions from the particular and exceptional circumstances of 1914–18. This is not easy, because the focus on shellshock has so overshadowed and coloured our picture of longer-term development that research on the period before and after is not as strong as it might have been. Nevertheless, there is enough to suggest that change was both less unexpected and

---

[43] Similar misgivings, it is worth pointing out, have recently been expressed about the tendency to read railway spine as an earlier episode on the path of psychodynamic progress: R. Harrington, 'On the Tracks of Trauma: Railway Spine Reconsidered', *Social History of Medicine*, 16 (2003), 209–24.

[44] On this mythologisation of rupture: P. Fussell, *The Great War and Modern Memory* (Oxford, 1975); S. Hynes, *A War Imagined: The First World War and English Culture* (London, 1990). The most recent cultural history has tended to highlight the way that the war could encourage a reassertion of the traditional in response to collective suffering and loss: J. Winter, *Sites of Memory, Sites of Mourning: The Great War in European Cultural History* (Cambridge, 1995).

[45] Leese, *Shell Shock*; Barham, *Forgotten Lunatics*.

[46] Winter, *Sites of Memory*; G. De Groot, *Blighty: British Society in the Era of the Great War* (London, 1996).

more partial than in the dominant, rather romanticised picture that came to capture the imaginations of historians and the public alike by the end of the century.[47] Rather than a story of its fall in the context of war, it might be better to highlight the ongoing weakness of the organicist position. The difficulty of finding a physical injury behind incapacitation due to shock in railway and industrial injury, meant that the shellshock, or at least the idea of functional neuroses (physical incapacitation unrelated to a specific organic lesion), had already been well rehearsed.[48] When it came to the problem of insanity, a project of locating a demonstrable organic cause had little success and meagre respect within the medical profession as a whole: in terms of laying the ground for regimes of cure, it remained, as virtually all agreed, a spectacular failure. Through the physiological screen of the nerves, a realm had already been opened up that was separate from the gloom of insanity, where a mix of physical and psychotherapeutic explanation and cure, rather inconsistently but in a cultural sense successfully, operated. This school of thought and practice was common within everyday medical practice. It now extended into tackling the shellshock problem. It would, after all, have been just as unacceptable to have dealt with soldiers as insane, as it had been with the private patients of the pre-war era. In sum, the idea that war shattered either organicism or harsh attitudes towards insanity is misleading: shellshock came to inhabit an existing borderline territory, which had found a practical way of sidestepping these paradigms.

Looking forwards, the War's impact on an organicist approach to insanity was also limited. The story, instead, was of a very gradual advance. The few areas of excellence before the war—the research headed by F. W. Mott at the London County Council's pathological laboratory at Claybury, and the Queen Square Neurological Hospital in London—did not benefit greatly, certainly not in the way that a psychotherapeutic approach did, but neither did they find themselves discredited. Figures like Mott, or Gordon Holmes of Queen Square, remained hugely respected and influential. The sleight of hand of representing the organicists by the bullishness of a single, young, Queen Square doctor, Lewis Yealland, has been misleading.[49] In fact, such organicists complemented rather than opposed what went on under a more overtly psychotherapeutic mantle; indeed, the psychological was integral to their therapeutic strategies. It is also worth noting that they were likely to be dealing with more intractable and more seriously dysfunctional cases. When it came to treatment of mental illness, the war was followed—though as no direct consequence—by a revival of fortunes. The

[47] The issue was brought to public attention in Pat Barker's critically acclaimed and popular trilogy of novels centring on the work of the psychoanalytically-orientated W. H. R. Rivers in treating shellshocked soldiers in the war: *Regeneration* (London, 1992); *The Eye in the Door* (London, 1993); *The Ghost Road* (London, 1995). For criticism that Barker offers a rather romanticised vision of psychoanalytic progress: B. Shephard, 'Digging up the Past', *Times Literary Supplement* (22 March 1996).

[48] Schivelbusch, *The Railway Journey*; Rabinbach, *The Human Motor*.

[49] Typically: Showalter, *Female Malady*, 167–94. For a defence of Yealland: Shephard, *War of Nerves*, 76–8; Leese, *Shell Shock*, 73–81.

first signs of results from organic therapies emerged in the use of malaria, insulin, and electric shock to treat the insane. The opening of the Maudsley Clinic in 1923 provided the British with an organically-orientated research centre to parallel the progress seen in Germany and the United States, and with the opportunity to reach out to cases in their earliest stages.[50] Indeed, up and down the country, asylums were seeing renewed vigour in scientific research into the organic basis of mental illness.[51] The rejection of insanity for 'mental illness' under the Mental Treatment Act of 1930 was itself indicative to some extent of this reorientation.

All this is not to say that we are wrong to view the shellshock episode as hugely important. It did encourage three linked processes: a breakdown of existing assumptions about a polarity between insanity and health; the move towards acceptance that mental collapse was an issue of the emotions; and the spread of treatment, accordingly, by psychotherapy directed at mental and emotional cause.[52] However, it was still only a catalyst for what was taking place independently. The three changes were processes, and thus partial rather than complete. The idea that mind, and in particular an emotion such as fear, could cause mental and physical breakdown became not only obvious (for the more progressive it probably already was), but a compelling issue when tied to the human tragedy and national emergency of war. But a shift in attitudes was by no means total. There were those who continued to suspect, and in some cases to argue, that a good portion of this breakdown was also related to a weak mental or physical constitution.[53] There were also those who felt that attributing it to fear, meant that it became indistinguishable from cowardice or malingering; and without wishing to question the suffering experienced, recent historical research certainly highlights that such sceptics had good reason for such concern.[54] Undoubtedly, considerable confusion surrounded the condition during the War, and was still evident when the government reported on it four years later.[55] Recent work has also highlighted that although their identity as soldiers who had risked life and mind for the nation meant that there was a considerable moral, public, and even political pressure to treat the shellshocked as different to the insane, this very act of differentiation highlights that the plight of the civilian remained relatively untouched by the

[50] E. Jones, 'Aubrey Lewis, Edward Mapother and the Maudsley', in K. Angel, E. Jones, and M. Neve (eds.), *European Psychiatry on the Eve of War: Aubrey Lewis, the Maudsley Hospital and the Rockefeller Foundation in the 1930s*, Medical History Supplement, 22 (London, 2003), 3–38.

[51] For one example: Michael, *Care and Treatment of the Mentally Ill in North Wales*.

[52] The case for change is neatly summarised in M. Stone, 'Shellshock and the Psychologists', in W. Bynum, R. Porter, and M. Shepherd (eds.), *The Anatomy of Madness*, 2 (London, 1985), 242–71.

[53] A large number of cases were attributed to mental deficiency: M. Thomson, 'Status, Manpower and Mental Fitness: Mental Deficiency in the First World War', in R. Cooter, M. Harrison, and S. Sturdy (eds.), *War, Medicine and Society* (Stroud, 1998), 149–66.

[54] J. Bourke, *Dismembering the Male: Men's Bodies, Britain and the Great War* (London, 1996), 76–123; R. Cooter, 'Malingering and Modernity', in Cooter, Harrison, and Sturdy (eds.), *War, Medicine and Society*, 125–48.

[55] *Report of the War Office Committee of Enquiry into 'Shell-Shock'* (London, 1922); T. Bogacz, 'War Neurosis and Cultural Change in England 1914–1922: The Work of the War Office Committee of Enquiry into "Shell-Shock" ', *Journal of Contemporary History*, 24 (1989), 227–56.

progressive mood. Moreover, once the War was over, it was a long, hard struggle to defend the rather exceptional status achieved by the insane soldier.[56] So, a story of progressive new psychotherapeutic methods and a breakdown in stigma, which has focused on the less severe mental problems of figures like Siegfried Sassoon and Wilfred Owen, and in general on the officer class, rather than the ranks, sits alongside another of what Peter Barham has called the 'forgotten lunatics' of the Great War. The latter forces us to think rather less romantically or dramatically about the nature of the shifts in attitudes and therapy that took place. In the hands of Ben Shephard, even the story of psychotherapeutic advance is subject to revision. Shellshock was ultimately a military problem, he reminds us.[57] It has been romanticised by the centrality of atypical figures like W. H. R. Rivers, with his sympathies for psychoanalysis. The psychotherapy that made an advance was of a much more pragmatic nature. Psychoanalysis was too time-consuming a method when faced by the scale of shellshock. War, anyway, steered even the relatively few sympathetic doctors like Rivers to look at fear rather than sex as a source of mental conflict. More commonly, the blunter and quicker tools of suggestion, persuasion, and education would come into their own, alongside massage, rest cure, and faradisation. It was these tools, then, just as much if not more than the more eye-catching but rarely used talking cure that demonstrated their practical value as an adjunct to the personal influence of the doctor.

INTERWAR PSYCHOTHERAPY

Conventionally, the First World War has been seen as a crucial influence on the emergence of a new form of mental health care: treatment through psychodynamic psychotherapy, available to people in the early stages of mental disorder or with neuroses rather than psychoses, and delivered on an outpatient basis from clinics located within the community. As already indicated, there may be more continuity than this suggests. Pressure to move away from the strict legalism of the lunacy system, which prevented treatment of anyone not already in a severe enough state to be certifiable, was very evident in the late-nineteenth century. Indeed, it was this longer term pressure from within the asylum system that was the major factor behind the eventual reform of the system with the introduction of new possibilities for voluntary and temporary treatment under the 1930 Mental Treatment Act. And as already noted, within private medicine, under the rubric of treatment for nervous conditions, such 'borderline' cases were already receiving some form of mixed psychotherapeutic and physical treatment. The idea that the war was a springboard for psychotherapeutic clinics also needs qualification.

The Tavistock Clinic was, in terms of scale, the most significant of these ventures. Often attributed like others of its generation to the influence of shellshock,

---

[56] Barham, *Forgotten Lunatics*.   [57] Shephard, *War of Nerves*.

it had its origins in Hugh Crichton Miller's Bowden House nursing home for functional nervous diseases, set up in 1912. Miller had read Freud and Jung, again before the War, though he was not a strict theoretical follower. In part, it was as a Christian that he looked to bring together psychology with medicine. He regarded the pre-war explosion of public interest in psychic phenomena as something of a threat to traditional Christianity, encouraging a move to religious movements that accommodated the new thinking more readily, such as 'new thought', Theosophy, and Buddhism. However, he was equally worried about the way that psychology had the potential to dismiss Christian experience as a product of auto-suggestion or self-hypnotism. Instead, he looked towards a reconciliation in which psychology could indeed help in understanding Christian experience but would lead to a reconfiguring, rather than the dismissal, of an underlying reality.[58] It could also contribute to a mission of healing, and do so in such a way as to humanise medicine in line with Christian values. Unsurprisingly, this background had an important influence on the type of psychotherapy that emerged. Miller's was to be a psychotherapy of liberating the self from bondage—whether of drugs, alcohol, or a one-sided attitude to life—and opening the path to fulfilment of God-given potential.[59] The fostering of individual responsibility and self-government was therefore fundamentally important: psychotherapy was to be a tool for individual emancipation and a renewal of consciousness. By the 1930s, he would come to believe that this emphasis on self-regulation was in danger from a psychotherapy that was increasingly inclined to impose regulation from outside. Whether such a dichotomy stands up to scrutiny is another matter altogether. Others might suggest that Miller's use of hypnotism and suggestion, rather than the psychoanalysis that gradually replaced it, was more characteristically a form of imposed control.[60] In the 1920s, Miller's was still the dominant vision. Centred on individual responsibility, the preservation and cultivation of character, and with its Christian sympathies, this was hardly a psychotherapy to challenge the moral status quo.[61] It also maintained an interest in the bodily origins of behaviour: alert to the potential implications of the new endocrinology; with a continuing belief in the role of focal sepsis; and forthright about the role of heredity.[62] Miller had seen the Tavistock as playing an experimental role, which others with more resources would then follow up, rather than as offering a solution in its own right.[63] The situation began to change at the end of the 1920s, as the Tavistock

---

[58] R. Rouse and H. Crichton Miller, *Christian Experiences and Psychological Processes* (London, 1917), 2–4. The book was published by the Student Christian Movement and Ruth Rouse was Travelling Secretary of the World's Student Christian Federation. At Edinburgh University, Miller had been President of the Christian Union.

[59] E. F. Irvine, *A Pioneer of the New Psychology, Hugh Crichton Miller, 1877–1959* (Chatham, 1963), 29, 37.

[60] H. Crichton Miller, *Hypnotism and Disease: A Plea for Rational Psychotherapy* (London, 1912).

[61] Irvine, *Pioneer of the New Psychology*.

[62] H.V. Dicks, *Fifty Years of the Tavistock Clinic* (London, 1970), 52; H. Crichton Miller, 'Mental Hygiene and Preventive Medicine', *Mental Hygiene*, 2 (1936), 160.

[63] Dicks, *Fifty Years of the Tavistock*, 34.

began its own training courses and moved to larger premises. By the time Miller resigned in 1933 there were around twenty-five doctors attached to the Clinic.[64] Yet, for all its achievements, he had been right to recognise limitations. When the succeeding Director, J. R. Rees, looked for funds to support expansion in the 1930s he would find that the Tavistock, with the eccentric image of the 'parson's clinic' because of its Christian associations, still had a long way to go before convincing the broader medical and scientific community of its worth. In particular, it compared unfavourably in the assessment of key funding agencies such as the Rockefeller Foundation to the more organicist orientation of the Maudsley Hospital, south of the River.[65] Looking back on this situation from 1970, Henry Dicks, who had worked at the Tavistock in the interwar period and now became its historian, would point out that it had performed an important role as a mediator between psychoanalysis and British medicine. In its eclecticism, its emphasis on the whole person, on body as well as mind, it had gone some way in making the 'British psychiatric world safe for psychoanalysis'.[66] Even so, this was only a partial victory: the change in medicine was very slow. Indeed, for all its eclecticism, even the Tavistock struggled to escape being, as Dicks put it, 'tarred with the Freudian brush'.[67]

The Lady Chichester Hospital in Sussex, another innovator in the provision of psychotherapy, also had pre-war roots. Here, the driving force was Helen Boyle, a doctor whose interest in providing for people in the early stages of mental disorder went back to her experiences working in the East End of London in the 1890s and took institutional form at the Lady Chichester Hospital in the decade before the War. At first, her emphasis was on providing an option of in-patient care and aftercare beyond the stigmatised lunacy legislation. By 1920, Boyle was also emerging as a public supporter of psychotherapy.[68] However, adamant that this type of care needed to remain separate from the lunacy legislation because of its associated stigma, the potential scope of any such activities remained limited.

Another pre-war experiment was the Medico-Psychological Clinic, also known as the Brunswick Square Clinic, which opened in London in 1913, and ran until 1922. The clinic has attracted attention partly because of the central role of women (including the novelist Katherine Mansfield), suggesting, as did Boyle, a link between gender and this reorientation in psychological medicine; it was also a pioneer, though often in 'maverick' form, in the use of psychoanalysis, and

[64] Dicks, *Fifty Years of the Tavistock*, 50.

[65] The papers of the Rockefeller Foundation are revealing for the interwar rivalry between the Maudsley and the Tavistock and the preference for the science of the former. This is considered in Thomson, 'Mental Hygiene as an International Movement', 292–4; and K. Angel, 'Defining Psychiatry', in Angel, Jones, and Neve (eds.), *European Psychiatry on the Eve of War*, 54–6. See also: Dicks, *Fifty Years of the Tavistock*, 315.   [66] Dicks, *Fifty Years of the Tavistock*, 299.

[67] Ibid. p. 315.

[68] L. Westwood, 'A Quiet Revolution in Brighton: Dr Helen Boyle's Pioneering Approach to Mental Health Care, 1899–1939', *Social History of Medicine*, 14 (2001), 439–57.

included a training programme.[69] Initially, it was highly eclectic. The Society for the Study of Orthopsychics, which was associated with the clinic, introduced a very broad programme of study, including philosophy, anthropology, comparative religion, and mythology, suggesting parallels to the kind of culture explored elsewhere in this book in relation to the interwar guru. However, psychoanalysis gained ground, with most of those involved eventually going on to be absorbed by the British Psycho-Analytical Society after the War. In 1918, it treated 189 outpatients and 36 inpatients, with an average of 20 sessions each.[70]

Lesser known is the even earlier British Hospital for Functional Nervous Disorders, an outpatient clinic set up in the 1890s by Forbes Winslow, a doctor who was in fact on the fringes of the kind of alternative psychotherapeutic scene explored in the opening chapter. This clinic would go through a series of transitions and changes of name to survive as the Paddington Centre for Psychotherapy under the NHS.[71]

The one example that did emerge more directly out of the shellshock episode was also in fact rather traditional in psychotherapeutic style: the Cassel Hospital, founded in 1919, and opened in 1921 in a large country house near Penshurst in Kent, with the financial support of businessman Sir Ernest Cassel. Here, the aim was to offer treatment for problems similar to shellshock among the civilian population, particularly educated people of slender means. The Medical Director, T. A. Ross, drew on the French psychiatrist Déjerine and his work on suggestion.[72] In its early days, the Cassel provided a kind of rest cure. Ross noted that following Weir Mitchell's real method resulted in something close to the psychological approach of persuasion, providing the doctor with a powerful 'moral' role over his patients to steer them towards recovery.[73] With separate rooms for the majority of what was initially a total of about fifty patients, with a ratio of one doctor to a dozen patients, and with its private golf course, tennis courts, and cricket field, it represented the extension of an existing style of private asylum care to the middling sort, albeit on a subsidised and voluntary basis, rather than anything fundamentally new.[74] Gradually, a more explicit psychotherapy emerged alongside this. It took the form of persuasion: a strategy of leading patients to understand and accept the real cause of their condition. However, there was little sympathy towards psychoanalysis, which was regarded as too time-consuming, encouraging dependence, and actually holding back patients from full recovery. The aim was to

[69] S. Rait, 'Early British Psychoanalysis and the Medico-Psychological Clinic', *History Workshop Journal*, 58 (2004), 63–85. For analysis of the relationship with gender: Westwood, 'Quiet Revolution'; and C. Mackenzie, 'Women and Psychiatric Professionalization, 1780–1914', in London Feminist History Collective (eds.), *The Sexual Dynamics of History* (London, 1983), 107–19. Brief mention of Boyle's work is to be found in Hinshelwood, 'Psychodynamic Psychiatry before World War I', 203; and Pines, 'Development of the Psychodynamic Movement', 212–13.

[70] Rait, 'Early British Psychoanalysis', 69.

[71] Pines, 'Development of the Psychodynamic Movement', 208.

[72] T. A. Ross, *The Common Neuroses: Their Functional Treatment by Psychotherapy* (London, 1923).

[73] T. A. Ross, *An Enquiry into Prognosis in the Neuroses* (Cambridge, 1936), 9–10.

[74] Ibid. 6–7.

ensure that patients were cured before they became dependent on the institution itself, and Ross was able to claim some success in this respect, with an average stay for neurotic cases of just over four months, nearly half reporting themselves as well a year after admission, with a further quarter as improved.[75] Taking in a total of 2,270 patients up to 1934, the Cassel was undoubtedly one of the signs that a more humane, and perhaps too a more successful, approach to the treatment of mental disorder was emerging in the interwar period. Yet, its limited scale and its far from radical approach again highlight the piecemeal, tentative, and evolutionary nature of such a transition.

The child guidance clinics of the era constitute an important additional example of the emergence of outpatient mental health services. On the other hand, they were not, of course, an alternative to the asylum. Moreover, although some of these clinics adhered to the new psychodynamic agenda, others sprang up in response to the concerns of educationalists, and as often as not clinics found themselves dealing with the practical behavioural concerns of parents. By the end of the 1930s, there were around forty of these clinics, though less than half were equipped with a team of a psychologist and psychological social worker under a Medical Director as recommended by the Child Guidance Council that had brought this model from the United States.[76] For all its significance in terms of innovation, the movement offered the average British child no more chance than their parents had of finding readily available psychotherapeutic care for their mental problems.

To this list of experiments in circumventing the lunacy legislation to provide psychotherapy for people in the early stages of mental disorder, a final significant entry would be the Maudsley Hospital. In this case, the war delayed the opening, which eventually took place in 1923. However, the Maudsley was most important as a pioneer in physical therapies, and its director Edward Mapother was deeply suspicious of the kind of psychotherapy going on elsewhere, particularly at the Tavistock.[77]

The differences between these examples of interwar psychotherapeutic clinics are striking, indicating the problems of regarding them as constituting a single movement. Even if one ignores this, the total reach of the phenomenon was very limited: no more than several thousand individuals a year, compared both to the numbers languishing in mental hospitals—some 120,000 by 1930—and to the emerging estimate that something like a third of the total population would benefit from this type of assistance.

Addressing the second of these problems—the mental health of the majority—demanded very different types of solution: either reaching out to re-educate the public in living in a mentally healthy way, or convincing general medicine to change. The chapter will consider this in due course. Addressing the first—the

[75] T. A. Ross, *An Enquiry into Prognosis*, 78–80.

[76] Thom, 'Wishes, Anxieties, Play and Gestures', 200–19. See Ch. 4.

[77] E. Jones, 'Aubrey Lewis, Edward Mapother and the Maudsley', in Angel, Jones and Neve (eds.), *European Psychiatry on the Eve of War*, 3–38; P. Allderidge, 'The Foundation of the Maudsley Hospital', in Berrios and Freeman (eds.), *150 Years of British Psychiatry*, 1, pp. 79–88.

ongoing problem of the asylum—meant overcoming the legal hurdle that excluded early cases of mental illness. Superficially, the Mental Treatment Act of 1930 solved this by permitting voluntary and temporary treatment. In reality, a considerable cultural barrier remained to deter people from coming forward unless as a last resort. Institutions therefore remained shackled by the role they had inherited as custodians of vast populations of chronic, long-term 'incurables'. There was little incentive to foster psychotherapy in such circumstances. It was easier to develop psychotherapy outside the home that psychiatry itself had inherited. Thus, sometimes on the perimeters of the mental hospital, though increasingly attached instead to the general hospital or separately under municipal control, facilities did emerge to provide the voluntary and temporary treatment possible under the 1930 Act. In terms of scale, this was a far more significant development than that of the clinics that have tended to dominate the story of reform to date. This was the reason there were 167 psychiatric clinics by 1937, rising to 229 by 1941.[78] The vast majority—around 83 per cent—had emerged in response to the 1930 Act. Only 7 per cent were in mental hospitals, and these were far more likely to deal with psychotic than neurotic conditions. The majority, over 70 per cent, were attached to voluntary hospitals. A further 14 per cent operated under municipal auspices.[79] Such figures suggest that if there was a significant reorientation of psychiatric care in the interwar period, much of it was taking place, not just outside the traditional orbit of psychiatry itself, but also beyond the pioneer clinics. It leads us towards a story of how the subject of medicine itself was coming to be recognised as embracing the psychological.

MENTAL HYGIENE

Addressing the mental health of the population as a whole demanded a very different type of therapeutic solution to either the asylum or the clinic. British medical psychologists faced a dilemma. The emergence of a popular psychological culture indicated the public's interest in practical advice on psychological management of their problems and prospects. Clearly, there was a case for arguing that this route of proffering advice was the one way for the medical profession itself to reach a much more significant proportion of the population. It also offered the prospect of putting mental health on the kind of preventive basis that had been of fundamental importance in recent advances in the physical health of the population. The defence for such a populist strategy was that it could only be safer if doctors participated and thereby defended the population from the potentially dangerous advice of the non-medically qualified. On the other hand, to do so effectively would have demanded a leap of faith about the abilities of the popular

---

[78] Westwood, 'A Quiet Revolution', 450.
[79] C. P. Blacker, *Neurosis and the Mental Health Services* (London, 1946), 9–10.

audience. Thus, although a section of the British medical profession would enter the fray in the interwar years, their reach would be handicapped compared to their popular competitors by an unwillingness to move beyond advising on behaviour from a position of psychological authority to popularising psychological understanding and practice.[80]

Talk of 'mental hygiene' was encouraged by the activities of the mental hygiene movement in the United States, and the mission to turn this into an international movement inspired by its founder Clifford Beers, self-proclaimed 'advocate for the insane'.[81] In the British context, it also grew out of the activities of several voluntary groups, which together looked to extend provision beyond serious mental illness to borderline conditions and beyond the asylum to the community. It took on a specific institutional identity, with the formation of the National Council for Mental Hygiene in 1922 and the publication of its journal, *Mental Hygiene*.[82] This body developed as a vehicle for the voice of medical interest. By contrast, other groups in this field did more to mobilise and express the views of voluntary and amateur as well as professional social workers, most of them women. The Mental After Care Association, offering support to deserving types to assist adjustment to life outside the asylum, had roots that went back to the 1870s.[83] The Central Association for Mental Welfare emerged out of the campaign to provide care and control for mental defectives.[84] Both these groups had strong indigenous origins. The Child Guidance Council, by contrast, drew inspiration and depended on financial support from the United States.[85] Helen Boyle was one of the early driving forces on the National Council. Another was J. R. Lord, superintendent at Horton, one of the London County Council's huge asylums, who found encouragement in the activities of volunteer social workers as well as examples of practice in the United States. Such figures were sympathetic towards the introduction of early treatment, aftercare, and the use of social workers to supplement medical care, not only within the hospital, but also to extend it into the community.[86] However, slow progress and the problems of limited resources and expertise forced consideration of other strategies.

[80] Thomson, 'The Popular, The Practical and Professional'.

[81] J. Pols, 'Managing the Mind: The Culture of American Mental Hygiene, 1910–1950', Ph.D. thesis (University of Pennsylvania, 1997).

[82] On the relationship to the American and international movement: M. Thomson, 'Mental Hygiene as an International Movement', in P. Weindling (ed.), *International Health Organisations and Movements, 1919–1939* (Cambridge, 1995), 283–304. Also: K. Angel, 'Defining Psychiatry: Aubrey Lewis's 1938 Report and the Rockefeller Foundation', in Angel, Jones, and Neve (eds.), *European Psychiatry on the Eve of War*, 57–63.

[83] Long, 'Changing Public Representations of Mental Illness', 178–232.

[84] Thomson, *Problem of Mental Deficiency*, 149–79.

[85] Apart from the MACA, these groups would amalgamate in 1942 to form the National Association for Mental Health, the predecessor of MIND. For details on the interwar provision: *Report of the Feversham Committee: The Voluntary Mental Health Services* (London, 1939): Thomson, *Problem of Mental Deficiency*, 149–79.

[86] J. R. Lord, *Mental Hospitals and the Public* (London, 1927); J. R. Lord, 'American Psychiatry', *Journal of Mental Science*, 76 (1930), 456–95.

Eugenic concern was, initially at least, an integral dimension of mental hygiene. Although the campaign for the 1913 Mental Deficiency Act came before it was fashionable to talk in this language, it was still British mental hygiene's most substantial concrete achievement. This legislation extended the ambitions of segregation from the 'idiots' and 'imbeciles', already covered by the lunacy legislation, to those on the borderline of normal intelligence, the 'feeble-minded'. In doing so, it aimed to remove from society what was, in the view of a large section of the educated public at this time, one of the main sources of pauperism and crime, likely to breed future generations of its kind, and in its sexual profligacy threatening to drag down the general mental fitness of the nation. The Eugenics Society would be keen supporters of the legislation and would go on to lobby for its full implementation, and many of these eugenicists would be drawn into the mental hygiene movement as it emerged after the War. In light of the partial success of the 1913 legislation, support would emerge for sexual sterilisation of the 'feeble-minded', but this campaign fell away for politi-cal as well as practical reasons (science played a part, but a subsidiary one, with many remaining sympathetic to the eugenic case if not because of conviction about the hereditary basis of mental disorder then because of a moral and social case for the inadequacy of the feeble-minded and backward as parents). As much as anything, focusing on this small group was only ever going to be a partial solu-tion to the broad concern that had now emerged about the mental health of the population as a whole.[87]

With the expansion of a system of clinics such a gradual process, and with the knife of eugenics both too fine a tool to cope with the perceived breadth of the problem and too illiberal for the politico-legal climate of the era, mental hygiene fell back on aspiration, education, and exhortation: a suitably liberal route, but one with little real power. Never attempting to spread its wings as a movement, the National Council remained, as its title suggested, a meeting place for the psy-cho-medical elite. As well as publishing articles, members offered lectures to soci-eties of the learned, professional, and public-spirited. As such, they contributed to a shift in medical and also educated opinion, though in truth these shifts were already taking place. But they had little chance through such channels, and indeed little inclination, of reaching out to the majority, particularly not that vast terri-tory towards the bottom of the social scale which was in their view such a mental health risk for the nation. When it came to such a constituency, their inclinations remained authoritarian. Here, freedom, in the view of Crichton Miller, could actually be a problem, and he looked with interest and some admiration to political developments elsewhere:

Only a sense of social responsibility can save civilised man from himself. I find confirmation for this belief in the spectacle of the 'dictator' countries, where man's freedom of choice is largely restricted. He may resent such restrictions, but they make for an

[87] Thomson, *Problem of Mental Deficiency*, especially Ch. 1 and 5.

ultimate simplification of life that is nearer to mental health than the freedom which only accentuates embarrassment of choice. I believe that these countries will presently show a reduced incidence of insanity and psychoneuroses, while the free countries will gradually deteriorate.[88]

If eugenic solutions were on the wane, the stratagems of social engineering that emerged in their place would tend to reflect Miller's view that one could not rely upon such individuals to change themselves. It is impossible to ignore the tone of hostility when mental hygienists noted the existence of a popular psychology that lay beyond their own authority. 'There is nothing more inimical to mental hygiene', argued Henry Yellowlees, as late as the 1940s, when psychiatrists like this were still very concerned about the existence of a mix of ideas about psychic power and more orthodox psychology in popular circles, 'than this utterly vicious principle "every man his own psychologist", or rather "every man his own psychological broadcaster". The extent to which we aid and abet the public in this game of fads, slogans, and short cuts, is a blot on our profession.'[89] Therefore, when psychological advice was proffered, it tended to be in the form of accessible but anodyne common sense. Where such professional advice was most successful was in more specialist channels addressing particular practical problems and audiences. The obvious example is in the psychological advice offered to parents on child rearing, an issue which is considered in more depth elsewhere in this book.[90] The continuing anxiety about unorthodox competition suggests, however, that the often prosaic and prescriptive message of mental hygiene struggled to capture the popular imagination.

It would be wrong to lose sight of how remarkably socially ambitious the mental hygiene message was in some respects. Psychiatry had been a hidden, closed domain. Mental hygiene turned everyday life into a potential subject of psychological medicine. In this sense, mental hygiene mirrored practical psychology; the difference being that it tended to offer a vision of changing or managing its subject, rather than of subjects changing or managing themselves. It also tended to frame the psychological subject in social terms. Mental health was not simply an issue of the individual; it was about how the individual operated within society. Tackling the challenges of mental health could therefore mean going beyond a psychological medicine of the isolated individual to a psychologically informed programme of social policy, even to a new view of healthy politics.[91] On the other hand, if one wants to understand what medicine actually achieved in terms of taking on a psychological perspective in the interwar period, one has to look beyond the grand ambitions but still relatively limited practical reach of the mental hygienists.

[88] H. Crichton Miller, 'Mental Hygiene and Preventive Medicine', 160.
[89] H. Yellowlees, 'Mental Hygiene in Modern Life', in *Out of Working Hours: Medical Psychology on Special Occasions* (London, 1943), 77.   [90] See pp. 134–8.
[91] See Ch. 7.

MEDICINE TURNS TO PSYCHOLOGY

By the late 1920s, a more tolerant attitude was emerging within the British medical establishment towards psychoanalysis. The BMA had set up a committee to consider the subject in 1927, reporting in 1929. Gone, certainly, was the mixture of distaste, shock, and ridicule that had greeted Eder. But recognising the importance of Freud for modern thought was not the same as accepting his importance for medicine as a whole. The psychoanalytic assertion that it was the one method that worked was particularly out of step in this climate of attempted open-mindedness and there were ongoing concerns about whether there was the evidence to back up its therapeutic claims.[92]

By the 1930s, knowledge of psychology was becoming a valid, and for some an essential part, of every doctor's equipment. There was a growing tendency to criticise the neglect of the subject in medical training. Students were more likely to come in to contact with mental cases, now that out-patient work in this field had become increasingly common in general hospitals. But they were most likely to gain this experience in relation to cases of severe mental disorder, and because of this their view that this was a field that was very different to general medicine and largely segregated from it tended to be confirmed. Specialist training was increasingly available to those doctors working in mental hospitals, with seven university diplomas in psychological medicine available by this time as well as courses of instruction at leading institutions, though it was still not compulsory; and arguably this very specialisation again acted against proper integration with medicine as a whole.[93] But we should not simply regard such criticism as a sign of backwardness: the very fact that psychological training was now recognised as a problem, and that some began to question the value of separating off psychiatry from medicine, indicates how far attitudes and ambitions, if not yet practice, had actually moved.[94]

An excitement about the potential for a reinvigoration of general medicine through psychology was also emerging in some circles. This is apparent, for instance, in the Medical Society for Individual Psychology, an organisation discussed earlier.[95] Chris Lawrence has argued that this interest reflected a crisis of confidence in a materialist medicine among elite practitioners and an attempt to find in psychology a way of reinvigorating a more traditional, personal form of

[92] 'Psycho-Analytic Treatment', *BMJ* (23 Dec. 1933), 1,175–6.

[93] 'Psychological Medicine', *BMJ*, ii (1933), 455–7. Diplomas were offered by the Universities of London, Edinburgh, Leeds, Manchester, Durham, Dublin, and by the Conjoint Board of England. Courses of instruction were available at the Maudsley Hospital, the Institute of Medical Psychology (Tavistock Clinic), the National Hospital Queen Square, and the Bethlem Royal Hospital. On psychiatric training: J. Crammer, 'Training and Education in British Psychiatry 1770–1970', in Berrios and Freeman (eds.), *150 Years of British Psychiatry*, 2, pp. 209–36.

[94] 'Teaching of Medical Psychology', *The Lancet* (23 Nov. 1935), 1,185.   [95] See p. 90.

authority: one that lay in the general practitioner's special ability to know a person in the round. Specialisation within medicine had led to a focus on disease; individual psychology called for a return to the focus on the particular patient.[96] The driving force behind the Society, Francis Crookshank, argued that attention to the psychological called for a radical rethinking of the focus on disease within modern medicine: 'Diseases exist, not as real external things, but as concepts which we find useful as a means of classifying the ways in which patients—who are the only real clinical entities—are ill.'[97] Disease, he provocatively suggested, was a 'fiction', the dominant school of modern medicine, 'necrological'.[98] 'Organic is what we say we cure, but don't; whilst functional disease is what the quacks cure and we wish we could.'[99] Inspired by Crookshank, the Society grew to 120 members by 1934, the year after his death.[100] But what is particularly significant about the movement is that it drew in some of the leading British medical figures of the day, including Sir Walter Langdon Brown, Regius Professor of Physic at the University of Cambridge, Chairman of the Society from 1931 to 1933, and President after Adler's death in 1937. Such figures saw in psychology a return to a more holistic approach within medicine, and though such an attraction may have been particularly marked among the elite because it responded both to their professional and broader cultural anxieties, their endorsement of taking psychology seriously had influence within British medicine as a whole.[101]

In the 1930s, there was a strong sense among doctors sympathetic to psychotherapy that alternative practitioners were threatening to outflank them.[102] Since there was no prerequisite for practising as a psychologist, it was difficult to regulate practice, apart from ensuring that practitioners did not falsely claim to be medically qualified.[103] Psychology, in this respect, was little different to alternative practices such as bone setting or nature cure.[104] Yet, unlike these other areas, there was a growing body of doctors who would practice as psychologists, and a growing body too who would come to regard psychology as an integral part of medicine as a whole.

Indicative of such transition, the British Medical Association accepted the creation of a section concerned with psychological medicine in 1937, following the petition of 180 of its members.[105] The establishment of this group reflected a

[96] C. Lawrence, 'Still Incommunicable', 94–111.

[97] F. G. Crookshank, *Individual Psychology, Medicine, and the Bases of Science*, Individual Psychology Pamphlet 3a (London, 1932), 12.   [98] Ibid. 10–12.

[99] Quoted in Sir W. Langdon Brown, *Thus We are Men* (London, 1938), 92.

[100] O. H. Woodcock, 'The History of the Medical Society of Individual Psychology of London', in Sir W. Langdon Brown et al., *Early Phases of Medical Psychology*, Individual Psychology Pamphlet 23 (London, 1943), 11–16.

[101] W. Langdon Brown, 'The Return to Aesculapius', *The Lancet* (7 Oct.1933), 821–2; Langdon Brown, *Thus We Are Men*, 72–92. H. Brackenbury, *Patient and Doctor* (London, 1935), 55–63.

[102] F. G. Crookshank, 'Types of Personality with Special Reference to Individual Psychology', *The Lancet* (8 Mar.1930), 546.

[103] Contemporary Medical Archives Centre (CMAC), SA/BMA C 378.

[104] See for instance the investigation of the problem: *Report as to the Practice of Medicine and Surgery by Unqualified Persons in the United Kingdom* (London, 1910), 3.

[105] CMAC, SA/BMA/B.83, Psychological Medicine Group Minutes; *BMJ* (30 Jan. 1937), 58.

strengthening consciousness about the need to defend psychology as medical territory and to counter the still vibrant popular psychological culture.[106] It also now drew on the emerging belief, propagated by the mental hygienists, that the nerves were an issue of increasing national importance within an industrial civilisation. Sir Farquhar Buzzard, one of the most respected doctors of his day, warned leading businessmen that nerve trouble in industry accounted for the loss of at least ten million weeks of work every year.[107] Equally alarmist were reports of figures in the Feversham Report on the voluntary mental health services, claiming that only 43 per cent of the population were wholly unaffected by mental problems. The popular response was mixed, the *Evening News* headlining this as 'Nonsense about Nerves', and arguing that psychologists were becoming obsessed with abnormality and overlooking the fact that a certain level of depression was just a normal feature of human nature; while the *Daily Mail* less critically concluded, 'Britons Need "Mind Doctoring" '.[108]

Advocates of a psychological approach within medicine used such prominence to campaign for the spread of training within the profession and for more funding to support the provision that was already in place. The problem with such an agenda was that it coincided with the coming to the fore of a psychological medicine that was increasingly analytical and personal. Such an approach was both more time-consuming and more theoretically challenging than the psychotherapies of mind over body and body over mind that had been such a feature of the first decades of the century. It was also far from clear whether the public would be comfortable in approaching doctors about such issues. In short, the ambition of the strategy exposed the huge gap between consciousness of the problem and basis for practice and in doing so raised further questions as to whether the answer lay with the medical profession itself.

Calling for financial support to assist the expansion of his own clinic, J. R. Rees, who had replaced Crichton Miller as Director at the Tavistock, estimated that only one doctor in a hundred and fifty across the country as a whole had the necessary experience to deal properly with psychoneuroses.[109] In shifting psychological medicine towards psychoanalysis, the problem of resources had become far more acute. One possible way forward was to reappraise the strategy of drawing such a sharp line between medical and lay practitioners; the latter, after all, might well have something closer to the necessary analytical training than the former. Thus, in 1938 we find the Tavistock Clinic actively seeking guidance over whether it could overcome its own limitations by collaborating with lay practitioners. The particular group in mind was the growing body within the clergy practising forms of psychotherapy. What would happen, for instance, if the

[106] For instance, Psychological Medicine Group member Millais Culpin: *Daily Herald* (22 Oct. 1937); 'Scope for Quacks—Psychology's Popularity', *Belfast Telegraph* (26 Jan. 1938).
[107] Sir F. Buzzard, 'Nerves', *Evening News* (28 Oct. 1937).
[108] *Evening News* (10 May 1938); *Daily Mail* (10 May 1938).
[109] 'Mental Illness', *Manchester Guardian* (10 May 1938).

Tavistock recommended such a practitioner to a patient who then went on to commit suicide? The case of the Revd Nelson of Eastbourne was brought before the BMA. Nelson was proposing to devote himself full-time to psychology and had the support of the Bishop of Chichester, but he had no medical training, and though he had studied psychology he had no qualification. He was willing to cooperate with the medical profession, and a case was made for such cooperation to be forthcoming in return, not only because of the lack of doctors to perform the role, but because of belief that many patients would be more likely to discuss their personal problems with their minister than a doctor.[110] Indeed, when it came to patients who were religious, there was a case for arguing that the minister was better fitted for the role than the doctor: psychotherapy touched on questions of the value of life that were inevitably religious in nature when it came to such patients, and there was concern that the non-religious doctor might deal with this in a cavalier fashion when in fact it was central to the process of adjustment and cure.[111] Indicative of the profession's weak position, the BMA's Central Ethical Committee ruled that a doctor could recommend treatment with a lay therapist if they were satisfied that this would be both responsible and in the interests of the patient.[112] Free from implications of faith healing, the way was now clear for an accommodation between the church and medicine, with the relationship now variously presented as one of cooperation rather than competition.[113] The Guild of Pastoral Psychology, for instance, emphasised that its work was continuous with, rather than overlapping with, that of medical psychology, that it was against accepting any case that a doctor had not first medically examined and approved, and that its work was educational rather than a form of treatment.

FROM CONSUMERS TO SUBJECTS OF MEDICINE

Whether much was to result from this growing openness of medicine towards a psychological dimension in health was another matter altogether. For when it came to practice, the doctors of the interwar era were operating within an environment that was becoming fundamentally different to that which had encouraged the Victorian medical establishment to branch into the lucrative business of pandering to the nerves. Under the National Insurance Scheme of 1911, it was no longer in the interests of the doctor to spin out the lengthy treatments associated with conditions like neurasthenia. Neither was it as important to satisfy the feelings of patients in the hope of attracting further custom. The physiological

---

[110] CMAC, SA/BMA/B 89, Mental Health Committee, 29 Nov. 1938.

[111] CMAC, SA/BMA B 89, Rev. England, Memorandum on the Practice of Psychotherapy by Non-Medical Persons, 31 Jan. 1939.

[112] CMAC, SA/BMA/B 89, Central Ethical Committee, 20 Dec. 1938.

[113] H. Crichton Miller, 'The Priest and the Doctor in the Treatment of Nervous and Mental Disorder', *Mental Hygiene*, 2 (1936), 23–9.

diagnosis of the nerves, which had saved private patients from the stigma of personal responsibility, or even madness, no longer had such a compelling financial logic to help overcome its waning theoretical authority. Of course, the doctor–patient relationship did not change overnight: the shift had already begun in the doctor's role of gatekeeper in relation to railway spine and industrial compensation; besides, much general practice remained on a private basis, and there are indications that the nervous diagnosis remained more prevalent among such patients.[114] But the financial difficulties of the interwar medical system did encourage the change of attitude. Voluntary hospitals, in particular, were in crisis by the 1930s, and had good reason to turn with frustration on the irritant of the 'bottle of medicine' patient—constantly reappearing to be palmed off with precious time, waning sympathy, and a placebo, but with no obvious organic problem.[115]

In such circumstances, and increasingly alert to the more overtly psychological perspective, doctors had further reason to lose patience with the nervous diagnosis. Millais Culpin, Professor of Medical Industrial Psychology at the London School of Hygiene and Tropical Medicine, was outspoken in his frustration about the continued use of a language of the 'neuroses', and called for a reframing of such conditions in purely psychological terms.[116] Farquhar Buzzard attacked neurasthenia—still a popular diagnostic catchall—as a 'dumping ground' for anything that doctors were unable to cure or to explain, a diagnosis that misleadingly, and potentially dangerously, conflated distinct psychological conditions.[117] Ross, of the Cassel Hospital, suggested that it would be better to acknowledge that most of those claiming compensation for nervous shock relating to workplace injury were suffering from purely psychological 'compensation neuroses'.[118]

Given the ambiguity about qualification for treatment under the National Insurance Scheme, but also the greater sensitivity over being seen as 'mental', doctors had a number of reasons for being reluctant to give a psychological diagnosis.[119] It was not simply an issue of ignorance or conservatism. They were now encountering more people coming forward hoping for psychological treatment, and with preconceptions about this involving lengthy and private consultation.[120] Some no doubt shared the view that recognition of the psychological was a good reason to offload this difficult and unrewarding work to psychiatrists. But the facilities simply did not exist to make this possible.[121] Instead, compromises

[114] A. Digby, *The Evolution of British General Practice, 1850–1948* (Oxford, 1997), 211.

[115] S. Taylor, 'The Suburban Neurosis', *The Lancet* (26 Mar. 1938), 759–61.

[116] M. Culpin, 'Some Cases of "Traumatic Neurasthenia"', *The Lancet* (1 Aug. 1931), 233–7.

[117] E. F. Buzzard, 'The Dumping Ground of Neurasthenia', *The Lancet* (4 Jan. 1930), 1–4.

[118] T. A. Ross, 'Some Evils of Compensation', *Mental Hygiene*, 3, 4 (1937), 141–5.

[119] H. V. Dicks, 'Neurasthenia: Toxic and Traumatic', *The Lancet* (23 Sept. 1933), 683–6; 'Psychotherapy', *The Lancet* (29 July 1933), 262: 'Psychotherapy and National Health Insurance', *Mental Hygiene*, 5, 3 (July 1939), 73–4.

[120] E. N. Snowden, 'Mass Psychotherapy', *The Lancet*, (21 Dec. 1940), 769–70.

[121] Report on the Section of Neurology and Psychological Medicine at the BMA Annual Meeting, *BMJ* (5 Aug. 1933), 257–8.

emerged. It may not have been possible, or indeed helpful in the view of many doctors, to provide lengthy psychotherapy, but it was possible to present much of what the doctor had traditionally done, in terms of talking through problems, as a psychotherapeutic alternative—through 'explanation' and 're-education'—to offset demand. In nearly all cases of anxiety and loss of physical function, the patient knew of the underlying psychological problem, even if he or she failed to associate it with the symptom. What the doctor needed to do was to expose this with a few basic, direct questions, thus removing much of the anxiety that stemmed from lack of understanding of the symptoms, and then guide the patient towards an active role in changing habits of thinking. There was even doubt about this method though, given what it could entail in terms of individual attention and time, and this encouraged experiment with a group approach in the stretched circumstances of war.[122]

THE SICK SOCIETY

By the mid-1930s, there was a stark gulf between, on the hand, the achievements of mental hygiene to date and the capacity of the medical profession to integrate psychology, and on the other, a chorus of pronouncements claiming that as much as a third of all illness in Britain had psychological roots. Such headline figures, like calculations of the economic cost of all mental ill health to the nation, had their polemical role: they aimed to capture the attention of the public, but per-haps more crucially the State. The case for action, for so long supported by a focus on the dangers of ill health to the nation, particularly its eugenic implications, an argument that for all the attention it has received from historians largely failed to convince, now turned to the spectre of the 'sick society'. In diagnosing society itself as sick in psychological terms, the scalpel of eugenic engineering, by now anyway a clearly unacceptable solution in political terms, emerged as also largely redundant because of its limited scope and its misreading of the problem as one of biology rather than environment and values. A solution of mental hygiene, for reasons of limited resources and ongoing suspicion both of and from the public in return, as already considered, remained an ambition but one that was very far from realisable on the scale that was now proposed. Another possibility therefore raised its head. Turning the whole population into vulnerable psychological subjects provided a powerful case for wholesale social and political action. The economic insecurity of the 1930s, heightened still further by the prospect and onset of a war of national survival, provided an environment in which the type of psychological social diagnosis, recommended by figures like McDougall from the start of the century, would at last have a real opportunity of influencing those in

[122] Snowden, 'Mass Psychotherapy'. On the openness of patients to direct questions: M. Culpin, 'A Study of the Incidence of the Minor Psychoses: Their Clinical and Industrial Importance', *The Lancet* (4 Feb. 1928), 221.

power. Full exploration of this issue will follow in the next chapter in relation to the Second World War, but some preliminary observations in relation to sickness as a psychological subject will follow here.

One of the most significant contributions came from Halliday in response to his findings about the high proportion of psychological illness in sickness claims under the National Insurance Scheme, developed most fully in a book published after the Second World War.[123] He had come to realise that telling such patients that they were suffering from physical disease simply helped to fix the symptom.[124] Denying the reality of the condition was not an option either: illness was no less real for being the result of anxiety.[125] Nor was the provision of specialist psychological care yet a viable solution: it ignored both the lack of specialist resources and the cultural and ensuing political barriers in redefining illness in this way. Halliday looked instead to a medicine that appreciated the psychosomatic basis of illness, on the one hand, and a solution that went beyond the limited capacity of medicine altogether, on the other.

Epidemiological evidence suggested that this was ultimately a problem of values: society itself was sick. Changing child-rearing practices had played a part: hence an epidemiological shift to younger age groups. Smaller, more affectionate, less patriarchal families, and earlier schooling encouraged dependency and left hostility more likely to be repressed which encouraged obsessive behaviour.[126] The problem was also more acute in urban areas. Here a number of damaging features of modern life were at their most acute: separation from nature and cosmic and biological rhythm, frustration at the lack of opportunities for creative activity, the standardisation and repression of individual expression, and an absence of aim and direction.[127] Arising mental problems were compounded as 'inner security', already fostered by the changes in childcare, was encouraged further as a defensive response to increasing 'outer insecurity' in a more transient society. Resulting emotional tensions that might earlier have found opportunities for liberation through creative activities and belief, now found themselves trapped.[128] Some fell into a resulting state of dependency and helplessness, others into a state of compulsive over-independence. If the rise of psychosomatic illness was a necessary response to the first of these, the rise of the market for popular psychology was a direct result of the second.[129] Like others, Halliday suggested that the recent fall in fertility, for many a very serious trend for the future of the nation, was due to this broad psychological malaise, with men—particularly prone to these conditions— the primary subject of concern.[130] Eugenic anxieties about fertility thus evolved into psychosexual ones, and in doing so attention shifted from the pathological few to the pathological strain at the heart of all British social life in the period. Integration—the key as we have seen to the idea of the healthy personality—now emerged as a dual solution for the mental health of the individual and for that of

[123] J. L. Halliday, *Psychosocial Medicine: A Study of the Sick Society* (London, 1948).
[124] Ibid. 86–7.   [125] Ibid. 83.   [126] Ibid. 115–18.   [127] Ibid. 121–4.
[128] Ibid. 125.   [129] Ibid. 126.   [130] Ibid. 130–40.

society as a whole. An 'integrated medicine' was needed: not psychiatry, which falsely separated off the problem of mental illness from that of the general health of the population; and not the 'false logic' of the 'healthy mind in a healthy body' (how, after all, could the two be separated?). But a fully integrated medicine also called for situating the healthy person in a healthy society.[131] It was a medicine that had to reshape, not only how the individual was understood and treated, but how politicians understood and treated society. Such a vision would capture the imagination of others within British medicine, some even within its establishment, as the idea of Social Medicine had its heyday in the aftermath of the Second World War.[132] Halliday's work indicates that one of the roots of this phenomenon was the gap that emerged in the interwar period between a growing sense of the importance of psychology to general medicine, and the practical means to tackle this through a specialist route.

Stephen Taylor, a resident medical officer at the Royal Free Hospital in London in the late 1930s, would be another to conclude that the scale of the problem pointed the way to social rather than merely medical solutions. Taylor's 1938 article in the *Lancet* on the 'Suburban Neurosis' has recently attracted attention because of more general interest in its subject of a suburban, middle-class, domestic, feminised England, and because it highlights a contemporary social snobbery towards such an Englishness.[133] The medical context, however, attracts little attention. Here was a doctor who accepted that psychological conflict was one of the most important present-day factors behind illness. More importantly, here was a doctor who recognised that any answer lay not in medicine, not even in the expansion of psychoanalytic therapy, but in social reconstruction, lest the alternative of the psychic salve of totalitarianism emerge here, as it had on the continent. Such concerns would lead Taylor into politics in the Second World War, successfully standing for Labour in the election of 1945 and contributing to its thinking on the issues of health and public opinion. On the other hand, Taylor was also speaking from the perspective of a medical profession struggling to cope with huge demand and thus exasperated by and intuitively unsympathetic towards the neurotic.

PSYCHOLOGICAL MEDICINE UNDER THE NHS

The National Health Service, making health care free at the point of delivery available to the whole population, struggled to make psychotherapeutic services more readily available. Utopian visions floated briefly in the aftermath of war, in

---

[131] J. L. Halliday, *Psychosocial Medicine: A Study of the Sick Society* (London, 1948). 209.

[132] D. Porter (ed.), *Social Medicine and Medical Sociology in the Twentieth Century* (Amsterdam, 1997); D. Porter, 'John Ryle: Doctor of Revolution', in D. and R. Porter (eds.), *Doctors, Patients and Society: Historical Essays* (Amsterdam, 1993), 247–74; and Porter, 'Changing Disciplines: John Ryle and the Making of Social Medicine in Britain in the 1940s', *History of Science*, 30 (1992), 137–64.

[133] Taylor, 'Suburban Neurosis', 759–61: Giles, *Women, Identity and Private Life in Britain*, 79–85.

which psychological medicine would be at the heart of the new service, offering prevention, not just cure, had little chance of realisation.[134] They floundered, not only because of the ongoing lack of specialists, but also because of the deeply entrenched attitude that psychiatry was a specialist service rather than integral to general medicine.[135] Exacerbating the situation further, psychiatry found new optimism in physical treatments and this strengthened those hostile towards psychotherapy and dubious about its therapeutic claims.[136]

This was the context for Halliday's call to look, not to specialist psychotherapy, but to a vision of changing social life and the causes of mental ill health. Even here, however, confidence faded. Taylor's post-war research into mental health in the new towns set up to alleviate the expanding population of London found little evidence for his earlier hypothesis about the relationship between a more carefully planned environment and levels of neurosis. Instead, his suspicions of the neurotic came to the fore again. With neurosis reframed as a normal part of everyday life, the real issue was whether to make a fuss about it—thereby turning it into a problem—or not.[137] Thus, Taylor's influential vision of 'good general practice', disseminated both in his book of that title in 1954, and in the government report that incorporated its findings, to a large proportion of the country's GPs, was less one of extending psychotherapy than of preventing the population from calling on such medicine in the first place.[138]

Taylor's research revealed that in the early 1950s, even in an area like London where services were more readily available, only one case of neurosis in one hundred and forty actually received any psychological treatment.[139] Psychotherapy was still something almost exclusively for the rich. In Taylor's own survey of general practice, diagnosis of neurotic illness was rare; though he estimated that it actually accounted for between five and ten per cent of all new cases, with the compensation neurosis of the first half of the century making way for the 'sickness-with-pay' neurosis of the second.[140] He remained unconvinced, however, that simply reframing the problem in psychological terms would have done much to prevent this. Here, an 'over-enthusiastic approach' could actually exacerbate the situation.[141] Indeed, he suggested that there was 'a substantial element of truth in the hypothesis that the better the clinician, the less often does he diagnose neurosis'.[142] What was needed was good common sense in general practice, informed by the kind of psychology which had been closer than the more celebrated psychoanalysis to the heart of everyday medical practice throughout the period: the key

---

[134] For instance, Blacker, *Neurosis.*   [135] Ibid. 40.

[136] M. Balint, *The Doctor, the Patient and the Illness,* 2nd edn. (London, 1964), 282; W. Sargant, *The Unquiet Mind: The Autobiography of a Physician in Psychological Medicine* (London, 1967); Dicks, *Fifty Years of the Tavistock,* 317.

[137] S. Taylor, *A Natural History of Everyday Life: A Biographical Guide for Would-be Doctors of Society* (Cambridge, 1988), 443–4.

[138] S. Taylor, *Good General Practice* (London, 1954). The book sold 12,000 copies and in Taylor's view 'helped to change for the better the whole pattern of British medical practice': Taylor, *Natural History of Everyday Life,* 219.   [139] Taylor, *Good General Practice,* 418.

[140] Ibid. 415–18, 541.   [141] Ibid. 420.   [142] Ibid. 416.

thing, as ever, was not to confirm the patient's false idea that he or she was suffering from a real physical illness. Sympathy was dangerous; patients needed good humour, firmness, and sanctions.[143]

Such pragmatism and bloody-minded scepticism from a doctor who recognised the psychological dimension of illness is important to note, lest we believe that Michael Balint's celebrated post-war psychotherapeutic overture towards general medicine swept all aside. Balint recognised this himself.[144] 'It is no exaggeration' he admitted 'to say that to obtain psychotherapy for an adult under the National Health Service is nearly as difficult as winning a treble chance in a football pool.'[145] Born in Hungary, a student of the eminent psychoanalyst Sandor Ferenczi, Balint had immigrated to Britain in 1939. Based at the Tavistock after the war, he was involved in a group approach to psychotherapy, explored first in relation to marriage guidance, and in the 1950s in relation to general practice. Group discussion with doctors and their patients aimed to encourage a reorientation from a focus on diagnosis, to a focus instead on the meaning of illness, the patient, and most crucially the patient–doctor relationship. Changing the general practitioner was the key to changing medicine as a whole. Taking on psychotherapeutic responsibility, rather than evading this in the doling out of drugs, would help to change the personality of the doctor, making him less distant and more understanding, more conscious of his own personal influence and attitudes to health and illness, turning him into a comforter rather than a priest. This was the only way to overcome the inadequacies of psychiatry. The doctor could be the wonder drug of the coming age.[146] Balint's publications on the subject attracted considerable attention.[147] A flavour of the excitement about changing general practice is captured in a book of 1960 that was part novel, part polemic in favour of a Balintian turn in general practice. Here, the number of patients in need of psychiatry leapt, further than ever, to three quarters of the population. Recognising that such a challenge would be impossible to overcome through current training facilities, the turn became at heart one of values: the doctor was to 'become a good mother to his patients'.[148] This seemed radical, and, in its psychoanalytic sophistication, it was, but it also echoed earlier developments. The idea that illness was something to be understood and addressed, not just in physical, but in psychological and social terms had been prominent since the 1930s. The emphasis on the importance of the doctor–patient relationship had been a theme within general practice throughout the period, albeit from a very different and ultimately more authoritarian theoretical perspective. Even the group approach had been rehearsed, not just in the war, but also in the 1930s, encouraged by an ideological mood as a way to offer a democratic therapy, but also and more crucially as a way to stretch limited resources. Balint's own experiments could only

[143] Taylor, *Good General Practice*, 449–61.
[144] Balint, The Doctor, *his Patient and the Illness*, 282   [145] Ibid.
[146] Ibid. 215–38, 289–92.   [147] Dicks, *Fifty Years of the Tavistock*, 237.
[148] A. Mitchell, *Harley Street Psychiatrist* (London, 1960), 181–7.

directly reach a minority; ultimately, the theoretical sophistication of the message and its potential implications for the authority of medicine may have made it unattractive for the majority. Reporting in 1968, the Royal Commission on Medical Education would still complain about the need for more psychological training and note that things had progressed little over the last decade.[149] By the 1970s, the concern about the psychological was being translated back into the more nebulous but also realisable emphasis on allying general practice to an interest in human values and in the patient as a person.[150] Once again, we are reminded of the way in which throughout the century, though there may have been persistent barriers to the advance of psychological technique within general medicine, psychology could still have an importance as a vessel for bringing values into medicine. This will become even more apparent when the Second World War is considered in the next chapter.

Ultimately, Balint's solution of lengthy dialogue, with all it depended on in terms of time, patience, and training, would prove almost as difficult for post-war medicine to realise as the vision of solving problems at their social roots. Within a field of medicine that was without its own firm claims to specialist knowledge and continued to be highly conscious of the vast terrain of ill health that had more to do with unhappiness and social deprivation than physical illness, the psychological had great potential attractions for general practitioners struggling for prestige. It would therefore remain an aspiration; as, in truth, it was already becoming in the interwar period. But with practice continuing to lag so far behind ideals, what had been created was a climate in which general practice was increasingly alert to the way that modern life placed real psychological strain on health, and was also more likely to be sympathetic, but was without the tools to do much about this. Faced with the resulting dilemma, many general practitioners would turn to the modern equivalent of the pre-war 'bottle of medicine': the sedative and the tranquilliser.[151] The patients, in turn, would be as open as ever to outside alternatives.[152]

CONCLUSION

Recent work in the history of psychiatry has indicated the need to look beyond the institutional setting of the asylum, particularly when it comes to the twentieth century, with a growing body of work on the emergence of outpatient psychotherapy and mental hygiene. In both cases, this chapter has suggested that we need to be cautious about their reach and practical influence. We have also probably been

[149] *Report of the Royal Commission on Medical Education, 1965–1968* (London, 1968), 104–7.

[150] M. Marinker, 'Medical Education and Human Values', *Journal of the Royal College of General Practitioners*, 24 (1974), 445–62; I. Tait, 'Person-Centred Perspectives in Medicine', *Journal of the Royal College of General Practitioners*, 24 (1974), 151–60; Royal College of General Practitioners, *The Future General Practitioner—Learning and Teaching* (London, 1972).

[151] Sir R. Gibson, *The Family Doctor: His Life and History* (London, 1981), 120–1.

[152] See Ch. 8.

too ready to recognise their novelty, overlooking aspects that are more traditional: the interplay of mind and body, the centrality of self-responsibility, and a practical concern with managing the patient. The chapter has also attempted to cast light on the challenge of integrating a psychological approach within general medicine. Here, a vast terrain of common but stubbornly persistent sickness would gradually emerge as a psychological as much as a physical subject, though this had considerable obstacles to overcome: not just cultural but economic. Much of what went on in everyday general practice was nevertheless inescapably tied to this grey area, and there is a hidden history here of often rather pragmatic psychological advice and practice that this chapter has begun to uncover. This indeterminacy of illness proved a huge dilemma for medicine. The psychological diagnosis responded to but also helped to expose insecurities about the inadequacy of medicine, as traditionally conceived, to do its job. By mid-century, it forced consideration of subordinating or allying medicine to a broader programme of social change. Here, as in the rhetoric of mental hygiene, there was a huge gap between vision and reality. It would be wrong, however, to conclude on this basis that the real story is one of how psychology failed to gain a foothold in twentieth-century medicine. The constant complaints to this effect are as much an indicator of a radically changed landscape for imagining sickness and health as they are of the undoubted barriers and limits to practice that remained. Ultimately, we need to look beyond the use of specific psychological tools or languages. The psychological problem of medicine was close to the forefront of consciousness, even if it was very far from being adequately addressed, and this was already the case in the first half of the century. Even if medicine was slow to do much about this in terms of psychological training, funding, and practice, we still need to recognise that psychology's influence went beyond acting as a vanguard for psychology itself. The fact is that the encounter with psychology helped to bring values into medicine. In the first decades of the century, this was particularly significant in the realm of Christianity and a holistic orientation, in mid-century it took the form of a turn towards thinking about the relationship between individual and social health, and thereafter it emerged as an amalgam of all three in a sense of the importance of humanising medicine. In each of those stories, psychology, for all its practical difficulties, did play an important role in shaping the subject of twentieth-century British medicine.

PART III

ENDS

7

Psychology and the Mid-Century Crisis

This book has argued that the early twentieth century was a period of considerable and underestimated excitement about the potential of psychology. It was also, however, a period of institutional weakness. Visions of reorganising society according to the insights of psychology struggled for influence. Even in psychology's less ambitious guise as a tool of governance in education, industry, and medicine, its achievements were limited. Two consequences flowed from this. First, development was often at least as significant at a popular level. Secondly, psychology invariably advanced through a process of accommodation with existing values. Consequently, psychologies of putting oneself together, of improving oneself, and of connecting oneself to a broader whole all had a generally unrecognised appeal. By contrast, a psychology of breaking oneself down, such as psychoanalysis, met cultural resistance. This chapter considers the extent to which the mid-century national, political, and ideological crisis centring on the Second World War destabilised this situation. It provides an opportunity for exploring the psychological subjects of both politics and war.

The problem of human nature was at the very heart of a crisis of values, which centred on the Second World War, but which went back to the First World War, and which had gained increasing urgency with the rise of political extremism and the prospect of another war in the 1930s. Because of this, a history of the psychological subject in this period can contribute to our understanding of what remains the seminal historical episode of our time. Detailed analysis of psychology within the military—a key element in the wartime story—has not been included. This is partly because, as with the First World War, this is now one of the areas best served by historical study. It also reflects the aim of situating the conflict as part of a longer crisis of confidence in human nature, which centred on the psychology of peace as much as war.[1] Many of the threads of development in previous chapters come together in relation to the crisis. In areas like health, education, and industry, the Second World War provided potential circumstances of national emergency to advance psychology as a tool of social engineering. In reality, it also highlighted and left a legacy of shortages in terms of trained personnel and funds. Because of raised expectations, one might even suggest that it left the gap between

---

[1] For an excellent survey of military psychiatry in both wars: Shephard, *War of Nerves*.

psychological ambition and reality wider than ever. There were also heightened ideological grounds to be suspicious of policies with authoritarian undertones. Ambitions for psychology had to accommodate themselves with this ideological mood. The crisis, in short, brought psychological subjectivity face-to-face with social and democratic subjectivity. This encounter is at the heart of the analysis that follows.[2]

POPULAR PSYCHOLOGY AND THE WAR

Because this chapter focuses on the opportunities offered by an expanding sphere of state responsibility, it pays less attention to a popular psychological culture, whose pre-war history was the subject of the first chapter of the book, and whose post-war history will be one of the main subjects of the next. Where the chapter will contribute to the book's analysis of the relationship with the popular is in its argument that in several respects the elite perspective was democratised: first, in its acceptance of the mental fortitude of the masses; secondly, in its interest in the psychological roots of democratic, tolerant, and non-aggressive subjectivity; and finally, in its turn to the psychology of everyday life. Here, however, it is worth briefly noting that the popular psychological culture, explored earlier, did not find itself wholly ill-equipped to adapt to the wartime ideological mood. 'The real enemy is not without but within . . . more than ever, during war-time, will thousands need the inspiring and practical psychological teachings of this Magazine', trumpeted the popular magazine *Psychology*, never slow to see a new opportunity for self-promotion. Ann Temple, an advice columnist at the *Daily Mail*, and a critic of this sort of popular psychology, which she regarded as cause, rather than cure, for the problems of many of her correspondents, accounted for the appeal of this literature through the 'flat tenor of mechanized life'. She hoped that the heightening intensity of emotional life in war would undercut the popular enthusiasm for such nonsense.[3] However, contrary to what most psychologists had expected, certain contemporary survey material suggests that a stoic normality—of getting on and making do—was just as common.[4] Even if Temple was right in certain respects about a heightened intensity of emotional life, this was something that affected some far more than others, differentiated between war and home fronts, between men and women, between young and old, between those in the

---

[2] In his exploration of the 'narrativisation' of democratic subjectivity in the nineteenth century, Patrick Joyce suggests that a 'realist' psychological notion of the self would be one of those things that displaced the Victorian 'romance' of character: *Democratic Subjects*, 223. This chapter will again argue that there could be continuity between the two.

[3] A. Temple, *Good or Bad—It's Life* (London, 1944), 26. She also lamented the decline of older forms of advice provided by the pastor or family doctor.

[4] A picture of greater psychological normality emerged in Mass-Observation's wartime surveys, for instance; T. Harrisson (ed.), *War Factory: A Survey by Mass-Observation* (London, 1943).

blitzed city and those in the relative calm of the countryside. Nor does it necessarily follow that any such excitement would have turned people away from the distractions of a popular psychology. The emerging coverage of the psychology of beauty and glamour in a popular magazine like *Psychology* may have brought relief from stress, or it may just show that psychology could be attractive as a way to equip oneself for wartime excitement.[5] The popularisation of Waddington's new game of character analysis, 'Physogs', reportedly sweeping the country in 1939, may also have come down to its appeal as a distraction, though it too hints at a curiosity about the psychological that may have been heightened by international events and their personalities.[6] Some people may have turned away from psychology as an indulgence in a context of daily and national struggle, but others turned to it for answers. The War, it was suggested at the time, left the British, a 'puzzled people'. Their traditional faith undermined by the War, with the values wrought by war not enough or not with the endurance to compensate for this, and with new anxieties arising from the peace, many people found themselves looking for something to believe in: conditions that may have made them ripe for the attractions of psychology.[7] In sum, although this chapter focuses on a psychological vision that came largely from above, it does not suggest in doing so that the popular died away. The conditions favouring the top–down vision were temporary, and although psychologists had new opportunities to access those with power, it is less clear that their message had any significant popular purchase. Even in wartime, contradictions in psychology's relationship with democratic politics would be exposed and in the longer term would emerge as weaknesses or lead to modification. By contrast, the conditions favouring continued expansion of a popular market were in most respects more deeply rooted.[8]

THE FIRST WORLD WAR

This book has chosen to pay more attention to the second than the first of the century's world wars. This is partly because, in the British context at least, the shell-shock phenomenon of 1914–18 has already attracted so much attention. But it is also because the book has attempted to downplay this episode and emphasise,

---

[5] P. Kirkham, 'Beauty and Duty: Keeping up the Home Front', in P. Kirkham and D. Thoms (eds.), *War Culture: Social Change and Changing Experience in World War Two Britain* (London, 1995), 13–28. Generally on wartime leisure: N. Hayes and J. Hill (eds.), *'Millions Like Us'? British Culture in the Second World War* (Liverpool, 1999). For post-war escapism: A. Medhurst, 'Myths of Consensus and Fables of Escape: British Cinema, 1945–51', in J. Fryth (ed.), *Labour's Promised Land: Culture and Society in Labour Britain, 1945–51* (London, 1995), 289–301.

[6] Advertisement in *Psychology* (January 1939), 16–17.

[7] Mass-Observation, *Puzzled People: A Study in Popular Attitudes to Religion, Ethics, Progress and Politics in a London Borough* (London, 1947).

[8] M. Thomson, 'Before Anti-Psychiatry: "Mental Health" in Wartime Britain', in M. Gijswijt-Hofstra and R. Porter (eds.), *Cultures of Psychiatry in Postwar Britain and the Netherlands* (Amsterdam, 1998), 43–60. For post-war development, see Ch. 8.

instead, certain processes that were already well in place before 1914. The war was clearly a catalyst when it came to the emergence of a mental hygiene movement and clinics for civilians suffering from something comparable to shellshock. The emergence of industrial psychology also had roots in the war, in particular through the work on fatigue but also in heightening awareness about the value of psychology in managing morale. In education, progressives mobilised to fashion new approaches which might help foster future generations more immune to the psychological seductions that had made it so easy to lead civilised populations into such slaughter. But in each of these areas, there is a good case for arguing that something similar would have emerged without going through the experience of war. When it came to propaganda, the War would be a spur to development but the extent to which this was directly informed by psychological theory remained very limited and tended to be overestimated in the following decades.[9] In all of these areas, major development was handicapped by the primitive nature of the profession and consequent severe limitations of resources.

In another sense, however, the psychological impact of the War was perhaps more profound, yet also more intangible: it exposed human irrationality, re-orientated psychological theory as a result, and provided a compelling reason for a much broader audience to listen, if not actively respond. Of course, as recent work has reminded us, responses to the War were varied, and its trauma was just as likely, probably more likely in the short term, to lead to a reassertion, than a rejection, of traditional values.[10] Nevertheless, it was clearly a crucial springboard in putting human nature more firmly on the stage of public concern.[11] As J. A. Hobson, the leading liberal political scientist would recall, 'the belief in man as a rational and thoughtful being was shaken almost to destruction by the war . . . Formerly we thought of civilised man as eighty percent rational. We have now halved the percentage.'[12] Once there, alongside a peace settlement that destabilised international politics, this problem of human nature festered as part of the unfinished business of war. By the late 1930s, psychological reading of the international situation was attracting interest among an influential section of the population as vital for statecraft.

Many of the concerns that came to the fore about human nature, politics, and war in the interwar years had already been raised in the conflict of 1914–18, most notably by Wilfred Trotter, in his *Instincts of the Herd in Peace and War*. Bringing together his pre-war views, with those from the first half of the War in the first edition of 1916, and those from the end of the War in subsequent editions, he offers a commentary on how thinking about psychological subjectivity interacted with

[9] M. Balfour, *Propaganda in War, 1939–45: Organisation, Policies and Publics in Britain and Germany* (London, 1979), 3–10.   [10] Winter, *Sites of Memory, Sites of Mourning*.
[11] This is of course not to say that an interest in the relationship between war and human nature was new: D. Pick, *War Machine: The Rationalisation of Slaughter in the Modern Age* (London, 1993).
[12] J. A. Hobson, *Confessions of an Economic Heretic* (London, 1976; 1st edn. 1938), 96.

the ongoing experience of war.[13] In this regard, one of the important things demonstrated is that Trotter's most fundamental insights did not actually depend on the War itself. War swept him away as part of the 'herd', as he himself would come to recognise by its end, and in this sense the book serves as further evidence for its own argument. However, its foundations emerged out of that pre-war dialogue between the new psychology, anthropology, and sociology discussed in the second chapter of this book. Trotter had come to accept the significance of Freud well before war broke out, having been introduced to him by his own friend, psychoanalyst Ernest Jones. He went on to place a conflict between unconscious instinct and social convention at the heart of his political analysis, bringing this together with the interest of pre-war psychologists such as McDougall in the modification of individual behaviour by social and cultural context.[14] Writing in the midst of war, he would come to adopt a crude biological analogy to contrast the social psychology of Britain and Germany: the spirit of the hive, opposed to that of the wolf. But such language has perhaps led to an underestimation of the psychological sophistication of his analysis. In fact, the setting up of such a contrast enabled him to move beyond a position of simply attacking the irrationality of mass society, towards instead harnessing its force as something that could be vital in the successful modernisation of Britain as a democratic society. Though Trotter would move on from the subject after the War, to an illustrious surgical career, his book would be in its eleventh impression by 1930, suggesting ongoing influence. The model of a British counter-posed to a German social psychology would re-emerge in the 1930s to play a role in understanding the challenge of cultivating a democratic subjectivity.[15]

SOCIAL DEMOCRATIC SUBJECTS AND PSYCHOLOGY BEFORE NAZISM

With his language of the herd and his recommendation that psychology be taken on as a key tool in the statecraft of the future, Trotter has been seen as representative of a new elitism in which social science unsuccessfully advanced itself on the basis of an authoritarian ability to engineer society.[16] But the young Trotter was also in many respects a radical.[17] He was critical of a society in which the force of

[13] R. W. Chapman, 'Wilfred Trotter's "Instincts of the Herd in Peace and War" ', *Sociological Review*, 35 (1943), 44–7. The initial papers were published in the *Sociological Review* in 1908 and 1909. The first edition of *Instincts of the Herd* came out in February 1916, the second in November 1919. [14] Brome, *Ernest Jones*, 26–9, 45, 78–9.

[15] Trotter would briefly return to the subject in the Second World War: 'Panic', *BMJ* (17 Feb. 1940), 270.

[16] Soffer, 'The New Elitism'. Soffer's view may be coloured by the fact that it is based on Trotter's pre-war writing. See also Ch. 2.

[17] He was described by Ernest Jones as an 'extreme and bloodthirsty revolutionary': Brome, *Ernest Jones*, 26.

social convention gave no freedom for the expression of primitive drives. Like others of his generation, he turned to psychology for a vision of the ideal democratic subject as one whose democratic character rested, both in a freedom of instinctive spirit, and in the channelling of the energies thereby released in responsible and sympathetic harmony with fellow citizens: the latter making possible the former. This, then, was a vision of democratic subjectivity that had some room for elitism.[18] To a considerable extent, it was the elitism that would be eased out over subsequent decades.[19] By 1950, psychoanalyst Donald Winnicott would be suggesting that the psychology of democracy was rooted in the 'ordinary good home': the argument for a unique fit between British culture and a psychological predisposition towards democracy remaining remarkably consistent. However, the ordinariness of this notion of democracy separated it by some considerable distance from the thinking of four decades earlier.[20]

In the early decades of the century, voices like Trotter's giving psychological advice to politics fell on largely deaf ears. Within a political culture which has been accepted, albeit sometimes rather too readily, as notoriously resistant to being swept away by ideas, this should come as no surprise.[21] The most open-minded section of the political spectrum was the progressive left, incorporating sections of the new Labour party, smaller groups on the left, as well as some Liberals.[22] As Michael Freeden has shown, there was serious interest within interwar Liberalism, attracted by using psychology's 'scientifically based conception of community as a formidable weapon against the vociferous forces of doctrinaire individualism'.[23] As already noted, further to the left, within the radical circle of the Plebs League and to some extent within the broader workers' education movement, there was interest in the new psychology, both in its own right and in relation to a dominant approach of economic analysis of society.[24] The driving force of the Social

[18] On elitism, see Ch. 3.

[19] On the persistence of an elitist strain of thought struggling for survival in the interwar period: Stone, *Breeding Superman*.

[20] D.W. Winnicott, 'Some Thoughts on the Meaning of the Word Democracy', *Human Relations*, 3 (1950), 175–86.

[21] For instance, on the left: D. Martin and D. Rubinstein (eds.), *Ideology and the Labour Movement* (London, 1979); R. McKibbin, 'Why was there no Marxism in Great Britain?', *English Historical Review*, 99 (1984), 297–331.

[22] Here, a number of studies adopting a broader view of ideas do point to a greater significance for ideology: D. Tanner, 'Ideological Debate in Edwardian Labour Politics', in E. Biagini and A. Reid (eds.), *Currents of Radicalism: Popular Radicalism, Organised Labour, and Party Politics in Britain, 1850–1914* (Cambridge, 1991); I. Brittain, *Fabianism and Culture: A Study in British Socialism and the Arts, c.1884–1918* (Cambridge, 1982); Yeo, 'The Religion of Socialism in Britain'. For suggestions on the influence of psychology across the political spectrum: W. Greenleaf, *The British Political Tradition. Volume I: The Rise of Collectivism* (London, 1983), 273–86.

[23] M. Freeden, *Liberalism Divided: A Study in British Political Thought 1914–1939* (Oxford, 1986), 233, 228–46.

[24] See Ch. 5. The theme of thinking about mind within socialism is also highlighted in J. Nuttall, 'Psychological Socialism, Tony Crosland, and the Politics of Mind', D.Phil. thesis (Oxford, 2001); J. Nuttall, 'Psychological Socialist; Militant Moderate: Evan Durbin and the Politics of Synthesis',

Democratic Federation, H. M. Hyndman, likewise acknowledged that a problem with materialist Marxism was that it ignored the psychological dimension.[25] Attracted more by an earlier socio-biological framing of social problems, Ramsay MacDonald was perhaps too embroiled in the practical politics of the Labour Party by this stage of his career to take on board in a serious way the findings of the new psychology.[26] Having come to object to a psychology that he assumed necessarily emphasised the individual, he would fail to appreciate the increasingly social turn that the discipline would take in years to come; in fact, some of his ideas in respect of the diffusion of consciousness within society could have found support in the psychology of the new era.[27] Psychological assumptions both about differences in ability and about the suggestibility of mass society were clearly influential in informing this generation's ambivalence about the potential of the working class as democratic subjects.[28] More positively, the Labour movement would also prove highly receptive to the psychology of individual difference as a basis for turning the education system into a ladder of opportunity, though in truth this only partly overcame, indeed for some it more clearly defined, the problem of a psychological underclass.[29]

Despite such instances of politicians and political scientists who were considering more seriously the implications of psychology, there was little sign of such an interest becoming sustained, general among the political class, or genuinely influential.[30] It is striking, for instance, how little interest there appears to have been in drawing insight from psychology when it came to the economic crash at the end of the 1920s, even though this event would have so readily lent itself to diagnosis in terms of mass psychology and irrationality. The one economic diagnosis that did take such forces more seriously was that of John Maynard Keynes, exposed to psychology and psychoanalysis at Cambridge and within the Bloomsbury circle, but at this time his influence was marginal to classical economics, on the one hand, and to Marxist analysis, on the other.[31] As already

Labour History Review, 68 (2003), 235–52; J. Nuttall 'The Labour Party and the Improvement of Minds: The Case of Tony Crosland', *The Historical Journal*, 46 (2003), 133–53.

[25] H. M. Hyndman, *The Future of Democracy* (London, 1915), 31–4.

[26] On the nature of this politics: R. McKibbin, *The Evolution of the Labour Party, 1910–1924* (Oxford, 1975).   [27] J. R. MacDonald, *Socialism and Society* (London, 1905), 13–15.

[28] S. MacIntyre, 'British Labour, Marxism and Working Class Apathy in the Nineteen Twenties', *Historical Journal*, 20 (1977), 479–96; S. MacIntyre, *A Proletarian Science: Marxism in Great Britain, 1917–1933* (London, 1980), 198–218; B. Barker (ed.), *Ramsay MacDonald's Political Writing* (London, 1972), 4–5.

[29] On Labour and the attractions of mental testing in the period: Wooldridge, *Measuring the Mind*, 182–9. On anxieties about a mental 'underclass': Thomson, *Problem of Mental Deficiency*, 36–76.

[30] For instance, Freeden suggests that other than in the case of Leonard Hobhouse—himself a psychologist—the New Liberal interest struggled to get beyond 'dilettante dabbling': *Liberalism Divided*, 245.

[31] R. Skidelsky, *John Maynard Keynes: The Economist as Saviour*, 2 (London, 1991), 234–7; T. Winslow, 'Keynes and Freud: Psychoanalysis and Keynes's Account of the "Animal Spirits of Capitalism"', *Social Research*, 53 (1986), 549–78; P. Mini, *Keynes, Bloomsbury and the 'General Theory'* (London, 1991), 152–8.

noted, there was a serious interest in exploiting the new psychology to find answers to social and political questions, but this tended to be secondary to its implications for personal and spiritual development and fell well outside the mainstream of politics.[32]

THE MASS PSYCHOLOGY OF DEMOCRACY
IN PEACE AND WAR

It took the rise of political extremism, the prospect of war, and changing attitudes towards the last conflict, to achieve what the experience of economic chaos and the vogue for planning had not: bring the psychological problem of human nature towards the fore of public attention.[33] By the early 1930s, the real shellshocked soldier had become largely hidden away from public view, but in his place was emerging a symbolic figure, representative of a growing cultural critique of the war.[34] What Samuel Hynes has called the 'War Myth' took time to emerge, perhaps because it was too traumatic to recall this side of war in its immediate aftermath.[35] Instead, the relief of victory and pride of sacrifice were powerful immediate responses and found an avenue for emotional release in supporting the rights of the shellshocked soldier, rather than in romanticising him.[36] It was only gradually that the dilemma of Siegfried Sassoon's George Sherston—mad, or just caught in madness—or the pity of Wilfred Owen's 'minds whom death has ravished' and the lunacy of his world of 'Dulce et decorum est' began to turn war itself into the subject for diagnosis.[37] Meanwhile, recalling her own experiences as civilian and nurse, Vera Brittain brought the role of irrationality and trauma to the home front.[38] Figures like Sassoon and Brittain were writing from a situation in which it was increasingly apparent that this had not been the war to end all wars. In both cases, their memoirs were also to some extent exercises in rewriting from this new perspective.[39] Brittain would be an active member of the peace movement,

[32] See Ch. 3.

[33] This is not to say that an attempt to address the latter could not run alongside that of the former. See for instance the new journal *Human Affairs* launched in 1937.

[34] Pointing to the contrast between this situation and that in nations where the veteran, instead, came to occupy a comparable symbolic position: J. Winter, 'Shell-Shock and the Cultural History of the Great War', *Journal of Contemporary History*, 35 (2000), 7–12.

[35] Hynes, *A War Imagined*, 423–63.   [36] Barham, *Forgotten Lunatics*, 112–27.

[37] It was not until 1928 that Sassoon published the first volume of his semi-autobiographical study of George Sherston: *Memoirs of a Fox-Hunting Man*. Owen's poetry only slowly gained critical approval or public recognition. Recent criticism has shifted away from the portrayal of such poets and writers as falling into an anti-war camp, to emphasise instead a more complicated ambivalence to war, sanity, and their own psychological subjectivity. See, for instance, A. Caesar, *Taking it Like a Man: Suffering, Sexuality and the War Poets* (London, 1993).

[38] V. Brittain, *Testament of Youth: An Autobiographical Study of the Years 1900–1925* (London, 1933).

[39] T. Mallon, 'The Great War and Sassoon's Memory', in J. Hildebidle and R. Kiely (eds.), *Modernism Reconsidered* (Cambridge, Mass. and London, 1983), 81–99; L. Layton, 'Vera Brittain's

which emerged in response to this situation.[40] It is surely no coincidence that she should contribute a preface to the memoirs of John Vincent, himself both self-confessed mental patient and peace activist.[41] She was making a point: the causes of peace and mental health were inseparable. The same concern was evident in proposals to establish a Pacifist Organisation for Psychological Research within the Peace Pledge Union in the later 1930s.[42] Europe, with its merry-go-round of seemingly irrational politics had become the 'insanity fair'.[43] It would be against such a cultural background that people would begin to expect mass civilian mental breakdown in any future war; a fear further fuelled to unrealistic levels by the publicity attending bombing in the Spanish Civil War.[44] And it would be against this background that psychological diagnosis of national and international politics began to gain a voice.

Such psychological diagnosis would come from what might be called a conservative as well as a radical wing of the psychotherapeutic movement, from psychologists who felt so strongly about the matter that they dedicated themselves to working for peace, and also from a new generation of politicians born into a world of the new psychology. A case study will follow a figure from each of these groups: respectively, the psychiatrist and peace activist Ranyard West; the Oxford academic psychologist and psychotherapist William Brown, discussed earlier in relation to the new psychology; the psychoanalyst Edward Glover; and the young Labour politician Evan Durbin. As in the case of Trotter before them, a vision of psychological subjectivity tended to be framed, not just in relation to the prospect and then reality of war, but in relation to an ideological other, particularly that of Nazism, though to a certain extent also that of political extremism more generally and thus of communism too. Through psychology, the problems of war and political extremism were thus neatly coupled, both regarded as exploiting a potential for violence towards others that lay at the heart of human nature.

Ranyard West was a leading medical activist in the interwar peace movement. He would draw on psychological theory to justify the need for international codes of law and systems of government. As the work of figures like McDougall had demonstrated, unconscious forces such as aggression functioned at the national as well as the individual level: man was a group animal with a 'group mind'.[45] Driven

Testaments(s)', in M. Higgonet et al. (eds.), *Behind the Lines: Gender and the Two World Wars* (New Haven and London, 1987), 70–83; A. Bishop, 'The Battle of the Somme and Vera Brittain', in M. Roucoux (ed.), *English Literature of the Great War Revisited* (Amiens, 1987), 125–42.

[40] P. Berry and M. Bostridge, *Vera Brittain: A Life* (London, 2001).

[41] J. Vincent, *Inside the Asylum* (London, 1948). See also the interplay between a career as mental patient and peace activist in E. Raymond (ed.), *The Autobiography of David* (London, 1946). Both cases are considered in Long, 'Changing Public Representations of Mental Illness in Britain', 276–87.

[42] See the correspondence on this issue: *Peace News* (22 Jan. 1938), 4; *Peace News* (18 Dec. 1937), 4.

[43] D. Reed, *Insanity Fair* (London, 1938). See also 'It's a Mad World', *Peace News*, (12 Feb. 1938), 8; and Falby, 'Gerald Heard'.

[44] B. Nichols, *Cry Havoc!* (London, 1933). On the alarmist response to the Spanish Civil War: Shephard, *War of Nerves*, 175.   [45] R. West, *Psychology and World Order* (London, 1945).

by this concern, West would be involved in a series of schemes to enhance world government over the interwar years, including plans for a European union and for an international police force.[46] It is not clear, however, that contemporary psychological theory gave much hope to West's preferred solution of international government, even if it did point to the dangers inherent in a system of competing nations. His vision appears ultimately much more optimistic about the potential for human rationality to prevail than in those cases where a more sophisticated understanding of the new psychology was involved.

William Brown had served as a shellshock doctor in the First World War, and writing in 1939 acknowledged that the problem of war had preoccupied him ever since.[47] Like many of this generation, he was adamant that another war should not take place and critical of the peace settlement in giving Germany grievance. He set about using his psychological insight in defending this position, studying the personality of Hitler, receiving daily reports of his speeches from 1933, monitoring both these and the pronouncements of other Nazis, and visiting Germany in 1936 'meeting and talking with important people'.[48] Though critics of appeasement would subsequently come to attack the character of Prime Minister Neville Chamberlain, Brown saw what he regarded as an ability not to be swayed by emotionalism as a great strength.[49] Meeting him in the Commons for an hour-long meeting in February 1939 to discuss Hitler's personality confirmed this view.[50] The wild swing of popular opinion over Munich, moving so rapidly from a mood of relief to revulsion, was a good indication of how the British public, by contrast, was out of control in terms of either rationally understanding its own situation or recognising the way that it was being led by the hidden forces of the mind.[51] The rest of the population was not as immune to being swept away by a tide of emotion as their prime minister.

Looking to Germany, Brown admitted his admiration for Hitler as 'the greatest psychotherapist of a nation', even if he also recognised that the Nazi leader was emerging as a subject for diagnosis.[52] Brown was not alone in casting Hitler as master of psychology. Reviewing *Mein Kampf* in 1940, George Orwell would point to Hitler's astuteness in psychological manipulation and describe Nazism as 'psychologically far sounder than any hedonistic conception of

---

[46] CMAC, PP/ E1, and E4–8.

[47] W. Brown, *War and Peace: Essays in Psychological Analysis* (London, 1939), xv.

[48] W. Brown, 'The Psychology of Modern Germany', *British Journal of Psychology*, 34 (1944), 49, 54.

[49] Chamberlain has suffered because of the contrast with the less emotionally restrained Winston Churchill whose style of leadership has been regarded as necessary for the mobilisation of the population in war. However, it has been suggested that such emotional control continued to be a feature of leadership and manliness in the 1950s and was, indeed, encouraged by the apparently dangerous example of unrestrained human nature in the context of the Second World War: M. Francis, 'Tears, Tantrums, and Bared Teeth: The Emotional Economy of Three Conservative Prime Ministers, 1951–1963', *Journal of British Studies*, 41 (2002), 354–87.

[50] Brown, *War and Peace*, 4; Brown, 'Psychology of Modern Germany', 52.

[51] Brown, *War and Peace*, 2.   [52] Ibid. 5.

life'.[53] For someone like Brown, highlighting Hitler's powers as psychological manipulator was another way of saying that Britain needed to turn to its own experts in the field. Unsurprisingly, writing in the *Times* about Hitler's virtues as a psychologist or of *Mein Kampf* revealing 'great psychological acumen' attracted some hostile response. Brown defended that this was a psychological rather than ethical judgement.[54] But it is revealing that even the appeasement-friendly *Times* balked at publication of a second letter of defence that acknowledged sympathies for some of Hitler's policies.[55] However, until that time Brown had made regular contributions on the issue through the correspondence pages of this influential forum. The strength of his sympathies towards the position of Germany and admiration for Hitler may have set him apart, but many of his psychological arguments were representative of the way that the discipline was forcing its way into the debate. The most fundamental point was that the unconscious, and through this aggression, was integral to human nature. It was therefore psychologically unrealistic to believe that a policy such as disarmament could work: the best that could be hoped for was that aggressive instincts might be sublimated in the development of defensive force, or that self-assertive tendencies might be sublimated in the promotion of supra-national institutions. The unconscious needed to be worked with; simply to ignore it could be fatal.[56] Something could undoubtedly be achieved in a preventive sense through education: the reduction of levels of repression, the cultivation of sympathy for other nations. But 'a mere orgy of pacifist sentiment' was not going to achieve anything, resting as it did on a fundamental psychological misapprehension.[57] Neither did he see any hope in treating figures like Hitler as if they were dictators over submissive populations: expressing and liberating the repressed unconscious desires of their people, they needed to be handled in international diplomacy and political decision-making as leaders with genuine mass support.[58]

It should come as no surprise that Brown's tone and emphases should have changed quite radically when he came to write about the psychology of Germany in the very different circumstances of wartime. Gone largely was the open admiration of Hitler (though he still saw some truth in Jung's 1936 paper 'Wotan' which compared Hitler to the medicine man of primitive tribes, with an ability to get hold of the unconscious minds of his people to recall and stimulate deeply embedded archetypes).[59] In its place is a much more fully developed psychopathology, not only of Hitler (a 'hysterical paranoiac') but of Germany ('a sick nation').[60] To be fair to Brown, it appears that his view had begun to shift further in this

[53] *New English Weekly*, (21 Mar. 1940), in G. Orwell, *Collected Essays, Journalism and Letters*, 3 (London, 1968), 29.   [54] *The Times* (23 Sept. 1937).
[55] Unpublished letter, 6 Oct. 1937: Brown, *War and Peace*, 45–6.
[56] Letters in *The Times* (23 Nov. 1934) and (11 Dec. 1934): Brown, *War and Peace*, 22–3.
[57] Letter in *The Times* (21 Dec. 1934): Brown, *War and Peace*, 23.
[58] *The Times* (15 Sept. 1937): Brown, *War and Peace*, 43–6.
[59] Brown, 'Psychology of Modern Germany', 55.   [60] Ibid. 50.

direction in the late 1930s, though looking back on this from the war he tended to make it far more definite than it actually emerges in his writing of the time where it was toned down by his sympathy towards appeasement. His wartime criticism of German psychiatrists for failing to sound a warning in this respect—he recalled his horror on visiting Oswald Bumke, to find a picture on his wall of the 'greatest paranoiac in history'—is surely a little hypocritical considering his own pronouncements at the time from a safe distance.[61]

The move towards a psychopathology of Germany was a comfortable position for British psychologists as part of a nation at war. A far more challenging picture was offered by psychoanalyst Edward Glover, developing once again in relation to the changing situation in the three editions of his *War, Sadism and Pacifism* of 1933, 1935, and 1946.[62] Glover went much further than Brown in casting light on the psychopathology of peace as well as war, and, as such, in shifting attention to the British population itself. Pacifism was now not only misguided in its psychological understanding of the situation, but was portrayed as resulting from the very same drives of destructiveness and love, sadism and masochism, as the urge for war.[63] Indeed, his writing on the subject began with an engagement with pacifism, in a lecture to the Federation of League of Nations Societies in Geneva in 1931, where his views on the unconscious aggression behind peace attracted widespread objection. He was particularly interested in studying the response of the British population to episodes such as the Munich Crisis. Drawing on a survey undertaken by twenty analysts and covering a hundred cases, he found that many people were actually relieved by the Crisis itself, just as they would be by the outbreak of war, but found themselves depressed and anxious in response to the peace: the opposite of what one might have expected following the standard peace–sanity equation.[64] It was becoming apparent that psychological problems associated with war in fact spilled over into peace. Direct experience of war was not a necessary precondition for the experience of war neuroses. Indeed, civilians either in war, or in the peace that lived in the shadow of war, were particularly liable to breakdown, since mitigating group bonds were likely to be less strong than in the closely-knit confines of the armed services.[65] In sum, not only did Glover show how psychoanalytic theory might destabilise the comfortable verities of the advocates of peace, but he relocated the psychopathology of war, both to the civilian population and to peacetime itself. This was a message that was far less ideologically comfortable than that of either West or Brown. But like them, perhaps even more so, it thereby offered up a powerful case for both the expansion

---

[61] Brown was told that if he let it be known that he was a mental specialist he would have no chance of meeting Hitler: 'Psychology of Modern Germany', 54.

[62] Essays from earlier editions were collected in the edition of 1946. Like Trotter's *Instincts of the Herd* this therefore offers his views in serial perspective. References will be to this later edition: E. Glover, *War, Sadism and Pacifism* (London, 1946). Where appropriate, there will also be an indication [in square brackets] of the date at which this part of the book was written.

[63] Glover, *War, Sadism and Pacifism* [1933], 51.   [64] Ibid. [1938–40], 97–111.

[65] Ibid. [1938–40], 112–25.

of psychotherapeutic services and the role of the psychologist in guiding international relations.

That such concerns were beginning to resonate beyond the professional psychological community and even seeped into the political arena is indicated by the case of the young Labour politician, Evan Durbin.[66] Like others of his generation—he was born in 1906—he would come of age within a society that was increasingly viewing the First World War in terms of loss, rather than victory. However, special circumstances also played a role, with his father, a Baptist Minister, becoming a pacifist in the course of the conflict.[67] He was encouraged to think biologically about the problem through a first degree in Zoology, and then through his close friendship with psychologist, John Bowlby.[68] The two men were keen walking as well as intellectual companions, and they would share a house for a time.[69] Together, they would write a long essay on personal aggressiveness and war that dominated a left-leaning collection of essays on war and democracy of 1938, with other contributors including future Labour luminaries Douglas Jay and Richard Crossman. The essay, with a first section attributed to Durbin and a second to Bowlby, brought the latest psychological ideas on innate aggression to the book's left-wing audience, and included extracts from Glover's work, as well as Susan Isaacs on the psychological development of children, and Solly Zuckerman's study of *The Social Life of Monkeys and Apes*.[70] One of the main aims was to counter the prevailing Marxist view on the left that the international situation could be accounted for by a purely economic analysis. 'Simple economic motives', argued Bowlby, 'are as out of place in the explanation of the Jewish persecutions in Germany as they are in explaining the violence with which the natives of the Gold Coast drive off the cholera demons.'[71] Attacks on Jews and Communists both stemmed from a 'scapegoat motive'. There was also a process of projecting guilt over Nazi atrocities onto the Bolsheviks. Hostility, in sum, went well beyond mere economics or ideology. Hitler played a key role in awakening and exploiting such popular feelings, but he did not create them. In a lesser-developed form, the same attitudes were at work in Britain, found for instance in the hostility between the Labour Party and the Communists. Aggression was an integral part of human nature, and it would tend to find release in scapegoats, whether domestic or foreign, so that it could find self-righteous expression. It was

[66] Stephen Brooke suggests that the psychological dimension may actually have been at 'the ethical heart' of Durbin's vision: 'Evan Durbin: Reassessing a Labour "Revisionist"', *Twentieth Century British History*, 7 (1996), 40–2. It is largely ignored in the main study of Durbin written by his daughter Elizabeth Durbin: *New Jerusalems: The Labour Party and the Economics of Democratic Socialism* (London, 1985).

[67] Extract from Diary of Beatrice Webb (July 15 1937): CMAC, PP/BOW/J.9/54.

[68] CMAC, PP/BOW/A.6/1: obituaries.

[69] J. Holmes, *John Bowlby and Attachment Theory* (London, 1993), 22–5.

[70] 'Personal Aggressiveness and War', in E. F. Durbin, J. Bowlby, I. Thomas, D. Jay, R. Fraser, R. Crossman, and G. Catlin (eds.), *War and Democracy: Essays on the Causes and Prevention of War* (London, 1938), 3–150. Fellow editor George Catlin was married to Vera Brittain.

[71] 'Personal Aggressiveness and War', 139.

only by recognising and controlling this—hence the central importance of the psychotherapist—that society might be purged of the need for war.[72] The essay was considered important enough for publication its own right later that year.[73]

The extent to which the argument depended upon the psychological half of the partnership is not completely clear. By the end of the 1930s, Durbin appears to have taken the initiative in developing the implications of the position, not just for international relations, but also for the future of socialism itself. Bowlby was involved in bringing together psychologists to research into the causes of war and the ways that psychology could help prevent conflict. In 1937–8, he participated in an attempt to establish a Psychologists' War Prevention Society, linked to the Medical Peace Campaign and the International Peace Congress, and he gained the support of other noted British psychotherapists, including William Brown, Edward Glover, Ernest Jones, Hugh Crichton Miller, Emmanuel Miller, J. R. Rees, and John Rickman.[74] Thereafter, record of such activities is harder to locate. In the post-war period, he would publish his influential work on the importance of attachment between mothers and young children, which has often been seen as part of a new maternalism arising from war, but in fact also drew on his pre-war research and thinking.[75] Indeed, there is a case for suggesting that the prominence of attachment in British psychological thought was encouraged by the longer-term perceived crisis in human nature, going back to the trauma of the Great War, with emphasis on the maternal bond as a further strategy for turning the child into a subject fit for democracy.[76]

When it came to Durbin, the main response of the left-wing press was one of hostility towards his displacement of the economic by the psychological. 'This book makes no contribution to the understanding of war', argued *Tribune*. 'Ban this Book Today', proclaimed the *Daily Mirror*. 'Floundering Psychologists', wrote the *Daily Worker*, objecting to the attempt to dissociate the problem of international aggression from the capitalist system.[77] In a second review in the paper, unease is also evident towards the inherently pessimistic diagnosis of human nature which was so difficult to reconcile with a socialist faith in the power of environment.[78] What added to the force of such concerns was the feeling that the contributors to *War and Democracy* were likely future leaders of the Labour Party. Durbin stood, unsuccessfully in the 1931 and 1935 elections, but would win the Edmonton seat in 1945 and was making a name as a rising star when he drowned off the coast of Cornwall in 1948 at the age of just forty-two.[79] Beatrice Webb met

   [72] 'Personal Aggressiveness and War', 149.
   [73] *Personal Aggressiveness and War* (London, 1939).   [74] CMAC, PP/BOW/G.3/1.
   [75] J. Bowlby, *Maternal Care and Mental Health* (Geneva, 1952); J. Bowlby, *Child Care and the Growth of Love* (London, 1953); Riley, *War in the Nursery*.
   [76] J. C. Lerner and N. Newcombe, 'Britain between the Wars: The Historical Context of Bowlby's Theory of Attachment', *Psychiatry*, 45 (1982), 1–12.
   [77] *Tribune* (31 Mar. 1938); *Daily Mirror*, n.d.; *Daily Worker* (31 May 1938): clippings in CMAC, PP/BOW/K.1/2.   [78]*Daily Worker* (8 June 1938): clipping in CMAC, PP/BOW/K.1/2.
   [79] Biographical material drawn from obituaries: CMAC, PP/BOW/A.6/1.

him in 1937 and described him as being on the extreme right of the party, seeing little difference between fascists and communists (clearly his psychological theory lent itself to this), and as 'more of a politician with his eyes on the front bench, than an investigator'.[80] However, the response was not wholly negative. The *New Statesman and Nation* would describe the new psychological perspective as being 'of an importance that it is difficult to recognise'.[81] Durbin would receive an eleven-page letter of congratulation from intellectual elder statesman of the movement R. H. Tawney, and others from influential Fabian Barbara Wootton and future Chancellor Hugh Dalton.[82] The issue touched on a nerve within the movement, bringing to the fore a broader emerging rift between those who wanted to adhere strictly to an economic model of social explanation and those who were looking to modify this through a more complex appreciation of human nature.[83] Figures within the academic community also took notice and plans developed for collaborative, interdisciplinary research on the way that psychological, but also anthropological, sociological, and historical research might inform policy making in international relations. Durbin received Rockefeller Foundation money to assist his own ongoing research, and Arnold Toynbee and T. H. Marshall were involved in further developing the scheme at the London School of Economics.[84]

Durbin developed his dialogue between psychology and socialism in *The Politics of Democratic Socialism* of 1940. The influence of psychological research on animals and children was again very apparent. But now the problem of aggression was translated from the domain of international relations to that of making man sociable—fit for democratic socialism—in the domestic context. Indeed, once the significance of the irrational and unconscious side of human nature was accepted—and it had to be given the state of modern understanding of the mind—then 'nothing is the same as it was before'.[85] This was a manifesto for a new way of analysing and therefore tackling the problems of society:

> The social scientist must look through the psychological microscope; so must the politician. They will see the real, but macroscopic institutions of government and property, party and revolution, with which they deal and must continue to deal, dissolve into a thousand fragments of personal ambition and patriotism, of secret love and hatred, unconscious purpose and need.[86]

The excitement of the convert is palpable, reminiscent of so many others who saw in the new psychology a doorway to a new age: '[w]e do not know ourselves. We are not the creatures of rational purpose that we think we are. The springs of our

---

[80] From Webb's diary, 15 July 1937: copy in CMAC, PP/BOPW/J.9/54.

[81] *New Statesman and Nation* (25 Mar. 1939).

[82] The letters were written in May and June 1938: CMAC, PP/BOW/K.1/2.

[83] For the fuller dimensions of this tension, both in relation to Durbin and Labour more generally: Nuttall: 'Psychological Socialist'.

[84] British Library of Political and Economic Science (BLPES), Durbin Papers, 4/4.

[85] E. Durbin, *The Politics of Democratic Socialism: An Essay in Social Policy* (London, 1940), 70.

[86] Ibid. 71.

action lie hidden, like corpuscles and phagocytes, secret but dominant, in our spiritual blood.'[87] Situating his own conversion, he cited three main factors: the collapse of social hope experienced in the depression of the interwar period; a growing certainty that a new politics had to address not only these failures but the history of human atrocity that had formed a backdrop over the past four decades; and a need to take account of the revolution in social science that had taken place since the start of the century.[88] Psychology, 'the greatest achievement of the scientific method in this century', pointed the way forward.[89] Alongside its role in providing therapy, it had profound implications for guiding education in the cultivation of healthy and democratic psychological subjects. It was crucial, in particular, to offer children outlets to release their aggressive impulse; repression was likely to lead to the release of aggression when circumstances allowed it in adulthood.[90] Democracy, Durbin was suggesting, was as an issue, not just of political culture or even economics, but also of psychological health and emotional development.

Partly because the state could provide such solutions, partly because peaceful cooperation was another innate human tendency and one which largely prevailed in Britain, cemented in the culture through the force of history and tradition, Durbin's vision was nowhere near as pessimistic as Glover's.[91] His confidence in the inherent psychological health of British national character also meant that he could still believe in the virtue of pacifism in a way that Glover could not. Psychology offered up a new way of demarcating the right political path from the wrong. There was a direct correlation between democracy, peace, and mental health: the political culture was necessary for the health; and the health in turn was a prerequisite for the culture.[92] Based on a long history of peace, toleration, and democracy, British national character emerged, implicitly if not explicitly, as the embodiment of psychological health. Some nations, by contrast, had reached a state where internal aggression and war became 'a psychological necessity'.[93]

Despite such predictable ideological dichotomies, the encounter with human violence and aggression, provoked initially by the First World War and then re-emerging with the rise of fascism and the descent into another world war, was forcing not just psychologists but here a politician of the new era to revise quite fundamentally his view of Britain's own political health and of the way to defend this. As a significant political figure, Durbin was exceptional in his degree of engagement with psychological theory, for some of the reasons of personal cir-cumstance already outlined; though as Jeremy Nuttall's work now indicates, he was not alone among Labour politicians in exploring the importance of the 'improvement of minds'.[94] Certainly, this issue of the influence of psychological

---

[87] E. Durbin, *The Politics of Democratic Socialism: An Essay in Social Policy* (London, 1940), 72.
[88] Ibid. 21–6.   [89] Ibid. 331.   [90] Ibid. 66, 263–6.   [91] Ibid. 41–8.
[92] Ibid. 49.   [93] Ibid. 28.
[94] This will be developed in his forthcoming book, *Psychological Socialism: The Labour Party and Qualities of Mind and Character since 1931* (Manchester, 2005).

thought, not just on the left, but also across the political spectrum, is a subject that deserves far more attention.

THE PSYCHOLOGICAL SUBJECT IN WARTIME

By 1939, the stage was set for concern over psychological subjectivity to step out of the private arena or the specialist environments of the clinic or schoolroom onto the very public stage of national and ideological warfare. Influential figures were well aware that civilians would be psychological targets of the enemy and that winning a war would entail defence of mental health as well as national borders. The view was also gaining ground that this battle for mental health was inextricably linked to the defence of a democratic way of life. For both of these reasons, the psychological subjectivity of the population as a whole had the potential to become an issue of concern for politics and the state to an unparalleled degree. An examination of the psychological subject in wartime will entail uncovering the schemes that were put in place to address this concern, but also recognising limitations and emerging flaws in the attempt to equate mental health with democracy that held back these projects from full realisation.

Through the experience of shellshock, the British were aware of how potentially devastating could be the psychological impact of modern war, not just for the military effort, but also for the national economy in terms of the ongoing cost of pensions. Having received reports of the traumatic impact of aerial bombardment on civilians in the Spanish Civil War, and increasingly cognisant of mounting psychological concerns about the debilitating effect and cost of worry on the British workforce, the government also had plenty of evidence to suggest that such problems would now be translated to the civilian population as a whole. Defending the mental health of civilians would clearly be a key element in the battle to come.[95]

In 1938, the Ministry of Health received a report on reorganisation of health services in war from a group of psychiatrists. It suggested that there would be three times as many psychological as physical casualties: perhaps four million psychiatric casualties in just the first six months of war.[96] Such predictions were taken very seriously. The government expected a huge increase of psychiatric inpatients, with the view emerging that long-term patients might be placed under the supervision of non-specialists so that the limited supply of trained psychiatrists could focus on the new admissions, and plans developed for freeing beds in mental deficiency institutions by sending up to a quarter of such cases home if

[95] For reports on the Spanish Civil War: J. L. Davies, *Air Raid* (London, 1938); J. Rickman, *British Journal of Medical Psychology*, 17 (1938), 361. On industrial neurosis, see Ch. 5.
[96] R. Titmuss, *Problems of Social Policy* (London, 1950), 19–20; Shephard, *War of Nerves*, 175; T. Harrisson, *Living through the Blitz* (London, 1976), 38–9.

necessary.[97] The fear about psychological health also lay behind the radical policy of mass evacuation from cities under the threat of bombing, with some three and a half million leaving in only the first few weeks.[98]

With the outbreak of war, psychologists maintained the pressure. Having come to accept that the individual was psychologically wedded to the group, it seemed clear that civilians would not only be potential physical targets of the enemy through bombing, but would be at the cutting edge too of a 'war of nerves'—each blow to the nation likely to be suffered in the individual mind. Of course, some individuals might find it possible to separate themselves from such a strong emotional tie to the group and thereby escape such effects, but 'from the point of view of an enemy' they would have become casualties already, suggested psychoanalyst Wilfred Bion surveying the situation in the heightened nervous tension of the initial 'phoney war' of 1939–40.[99] The 'war of nerves', in its exploitation of unconscious fear and its distraction of the individual from reality, tended to be presented as the very opposite of the psychotherapeutic procedure. Ironically, in its release of psychological anxieties through aggression—something that was frustratingly absent in the 'phoney war'—warfare itself might offer something more analogous to therapy. Civilians were in great psychological danger. The factors that alleviated the problem within army life were absent on the home front: the intimate bonds, which protected against panic and fear; the opportunities to give expression to aggression; and the discipline, which curbed the instinct of self-preservation.[100] Clearly, the resources were simply not available to provide psychoanalysis as a form of treatment. Psychology instead had to find its answers in exploiting traditional institutional structures in a preventive role. The civilian population would need to be offered active, practical roles, both to release their psychological anxieties and to bring them together as a group. It might also be valuable to educate them through the social services to understand and accept their own psychological problems. But again, there was the problem of a lack of trained personnel to supervise such a process and an ongoing anxiety about democratising this knowledge as an alternative. There was also a fundamental dilemma when it came to the idea of defending morale through manipulative propaganda: psychological theory suggesting that the latter was in conflict with a national character and mental health that was so closely associated with liberal values. A British way in morale would need to be free from any taint of dictatorship if it was to be effective.[101] The irony is, therefore, that having established a strong case for the centrality of mental health in the struggle ahead, a figure such as Bion should then largely have to

[97] PRO, MH 51/664, Board of Control Circular No. 869 and ensuing debate; PRO, MH 76/101, Report of Conference between Board of Control and Ministry of Health, 10 March 1938; and Board of Control Memo, 30 March 1938.

[98] J. Welshman, 'Evacuation and Social Policy during the Second World War: Myth and Reality', *Twentieth Century British History*, 9 (1998), 28–53.

[99] W. Bion, ' "The War of Nerves": Civilian Reaction, Morale, and Prophylaxis', in E. Miller (ed.), *The Neuroses in War* (London, 1940), 180, 180–200.   [100] Ibid. 185.

[101] Ibid. 187–94.

acknowledge that psychological intervention itself could do relatively little about this, both for practical and ideological reasons. Instead, psychology would assume a role of justifying and ideologically defending the further cultivation of an existing British democratic way of life. At times, the resulting shift of strategy could seem rather comic in its retreat from ambition. Bion, for instance, ended up encouraging the active citizenship of the cookery class to bring the war effort, and thus psychological opportunities for release of energies and identification with the cause, into the private sphere of the home.[102] More significantly, we see such a retreat in the admonition to advance education and information, rather than propaganda, as a liberal British approach in this war of morale. However, rather than seeing this simply in terms of retreat, it can be argued that an important process of democratising the psychological subject was at work: both in the rejection of strategies of overt psychological control and manipulation, and in the move towards an appreciation of everyday life in understanding the psychological subject. Both processes of democratisation would be in some ways unexpected in a wartime situation that threatened to compromise democratic values.

As it turned out, the gloomy predictions about mass civilian mental breakdown had been a gross misreading of the situation. Armed conflict, when it came, appeared to ease some of the nervous tension on the home front. Bombing, particularly the concentrated Blitz on London beginning on 9 September 1940 and spreading to provincial cities before coming to a halt in May 1941, has gone down in modern British mythology as bringing people together to master nerves through a new social solidarity.[103] Contemporary propaganda supported this view. So too have participants looking back on the event from some distance. Yet actual wartime reports provide a rather less convincing picture of solidarity, highlighting both the temporary and superficial nature of bonds within the air-raid shelters and the persistence of social hostilities.[104] Looking back from the 1970s, the wartime director of Mass-Observation, Tom Harrisson, concluded that there had been 'a massive, largely unconscious cover-up of the more disagreeable facts of 1940–1'.[105] In understanding the low level of breakdown, we should perhaps pay more attention to the bonds of family. It also reflected a failure of strategy on behalf of the Germans: the experience of danger proving psychologically easier to cope with when, as so often, it was regular, as in the London Blitz, than when it came to a less well-prepared population, as in the devastation of Coventry in a single attack.[106] Here, it was also important that the Londoners who faced the nightly Blitz had avenues for escape—whether to underground shelter or countryside—and thus the type of outlet to diffuse tension and fear that had so crucially been absent in the case of the trench-bound soldier of the Great War.

Fear, bewilderment, and temporary breakdown, were nevertheless common features of the British home front, even if hysterical collapse was not.[107] Given

---

[102] Ibid. 195.   [103] A. Calder, *The Myth of the Blitz* (London, 1991).
[104] Harrisson, *Living through the Blitz*, 314.   [105] Ibid. 13.   [106] Ibid. 133–42.
[107] Ibid. 308.

this, Ben Shephard has suggested that the low level of psychiatric casualties is actually so remarkable that there is a case for suspecting that a good deal of it remained unrecognised, unreported, or unaccepted. Many of the very same doctors who had drawn the lesson from their experience with shellshock that the best thing to do was not to confirm and thereby encourage the condition, now, as the older generation, found themselves in an influential position to shape psychiatric policy on the home front. By contrast, the younger doctors who went into the army from psychodynamic backgrounds like the Tavistock Clinic were far more likely to accept psychological breakdown. Ironically, the home front had become the sterner of the two environments.[108] Given what this book has revealed about the developments within the mainstream of medicine in the interwar period, this should not come as a huge surprise.[109] Concern about the neuroses remained, but the focus of debate gradually shifted from regarding this as an issue of national security, to its implications for economic efficiency and to the problem of policing malingering.

Absence of the predicted crisis of war nerves could well have discredited psychology, even if not all psychologists were of one mind on the subject. In some circles, there are signs that it did. But it took time for this to become apparent. Meanwhile, in drawing attention to the role of morale in preventing breakdown, it offered other potential opportunities. The Ministry of Information, with responsibility for propaganda, recognised early on in the war that it needed some way of objectively assessing the morale of the population if it was to find out whether its propaganda was working or not. Employing informants to report on attitudes provoked an initial public outcry and a parliamentary debate over what the press memorably described as 'Cooper's Snoopers'.[110] Gradually a panel of about 4,000 informants was built up to work on an ongoing Social Survey, while a smaller group of Mass-Observers continued to work on the issue of morale up until April 1941. Reflecting expectations, initial reports were overly gloomy. Indeed, with the furore over exposure, there seemed a real possibility that the enterprise was doing more harm than good, simply fuelling the atmosphere of suspicion and rumour. But in highlighting the way that ignorance exacerbated public disquiet, it did encourage the move towards a policy of greater openness as a way to steady feelings, a policy that would appear to have had positive results, and which would have the support of the psychologists.

Though psychiatric social workers were among the first informants, and this may have exacerbated the initial public hostility to 'snooping', the policy as a whole was not under psychological direction.[111] Psychologists were, however, very ready to forward their advice to the Ministry. Professor of Psychology at Cambridge, Frederic Bartlett, received a serious hearing and would help steer

---

[108] Shephard, *War of Nerves*, 178–82.   [109] See Chs. 5 and 6.

[110] Named after Duff Cooper, then Minister of Information (the third in less than a year).

[111] PRO, INF/1/290, Comprehensive Report on the History, Functions and Administration of the Home Intelligence Division.

government concern towards the psychological roots of absenteeism and injury in industry. Edward Glover was recommended to the Ministry in early 1940, and would offer his own views on its work in a twenty-page memorandum. His suggestion that the amount of rumour circulating at any time was a good measure of the efficiency of the Ministry, may indeed have encouraged the move to address this problem. Unsurprisingly, he was keen to encourage the Ministry to accept a role in the maximisation of morale in war but also beyond, whether Parliament, the press, or the people liked this or not. Indeed, he suggested that the Minister of Information should be a key figure in the War Cabinet. Lying behind this support was a belief that victory depended not just on bombs and battles but also on successfully tackling the public anxieties that could erode morale. The apparatus of the Ministry offered for the first time in history the possibility of tapping the mood of the nation on a daily basis. Parliament and the press naturally resented what was in effect a fundamental challenge to their own traditional roles, and it was this resentment more than any public feeling that accounted for the outcry over 'snooping'. However, both these traditional channels had fundamental flaws as voices of the people: parliament's representative status was in effective abeyance, and anyway it was more a voice of the politicians; the press, again, was a vehicle for the political views of a few powerful owners, and was far more interested in selling copy than representing its readers' views.[112] Thus, in mid-1940, Glover had high hopes for the Social Survey, seeing it, not only as a tool for the reinvigoration of democracy, but as pointing the way towards a 'social psychiatry' in which real democratic accountability would turn the political process into something on a national level comparable to the psychotherapy of the individual.[113]

By November 1940, the Ministry had consulted, not only Glover and Bartlett, but others including the psychoanalytically-orientated Professor of Psychology at London University, J. C. Flugel, and the organically-orientated Maudsley psychiatrist Eliot Slater. But those in authority had little enthusiasm for guidance from psychological experts.[114] Lord Hankey's Scientific Advisory Committee was very unimpressed when they interviewed Bartlett, judging him impractical while at the same time complaining that much of what he said was mere common sense. As this suggests, psychologists remained easy targets for criticism whichever way they turned. 'I have the gravest suspicion of psychologists', commented the Minister concerned in a private communication in late 1940. 'I am perfectly certain they give the wrong advice. At the moment I am entangled in difficulties with Edward Glover, but I do not think he seems quite as mad as Professor Bartlett.'

---

112 PRO, INF/1/318, E. Glover, 'Memorandum on the Functions of the Ministry of Information' (1940). Mass-Observation found that the public was less hostile in practice, and Tom Harrisson's biographer suggests that 'although the British people thought they did not like to be asked questions about their private life, they actually loved it': J. Heimann, *The Most Offending Soul Alive: Tom Harrisson and his Remarkable Life* (London, 2002), 158.

113 E. Glover, 'The Birth of Social Psychiatry', *The Lancet* (24 Aug. 1940), 239.

114 PRO, INF/1/318, Memo from Henry Adams, 20 November 1940.

Glover did remain a figure for the civil servants to contend with, perhaps faring better because he was easier to deal with and a good communicator. He became Chairman of the Home Morale Advisory Committee and sat on the French Advisory Committee. In June 1941 he sent another memorandum of advice to the Ministry, complaining that only one official was familiar with psychological methods. He may have been thinking of Stephen Taylor, whose no-nonsense approach to the neuroses we have already encountered in another capacity.[115] The irony was that the appointment of this psychological expert as Director of Home Intelligence brought with it in some ways an even deeper suspicion towards the psychoanalytic approach. The latter, Taylor argued, had predicted two things about the war: first, there would be mass mental breakdown; second, only psycho-analysis would prevent it. Neither had turned out to be remotely accurate. He clearly had little sympathy for Glover: 'a slow, cautious mind, very systematic, but very dull. He is tenacious, but rather impractical. Like almost all psycho-analysts, he does not like people to hold views differing from his own.'[116] In his autobiog-raphy, Taylor recalled that defeatism was rife at the Ministry when he was appointed, and no doubt he cast some of the blame in this respect on the psycho-analysts who had encouraged the Ministry to take more seriously the culture of grumble and rumour than subsequently proved to be justified.[117] When psychol-ogists were called on in an official capacity, with the setting up of the War Time Social Survey Advisory Committee in 1944 under the direction of Taylor, it is notable that Glover was absent as were other psychoanalysts. The appointment, instead, of Frederic Bartlett, Cyril Burt, and Aubrey Lewis indicates an orienta-tion away from a concern about conflicts at the heart of human nature towards an interest in statistical analysis of the mass of material—over 280,000 interviews by this date—that had been accumulated.[118]

In his study of the wartime management of morale, Ian McLaine has argued that it was only with the appointment of Taylor that morale was at last given any kind of intelligent definition: something that was to be 'ultimately measured not by what a person thinks or says, but by what he does and how he does it.'[119] In effect, he was steering the psychology of morale from a psychoanalytic to a behaviourist orientation. The over-reaction to the atmosphere of rumour and grumble in the early stages of war seemed to support such a move, for in fact morale as measured by the population's commitment to the war effort and resilience to breakdown had remained remarkably strong. The work of psycholo-gists like Philip Vernon, interested in the practical difficulties of measuring behaviour, offered support to the reorientation, and such psychologists were now

---

[115] See Ch. 6.   [116] PRO, INF/1/318, Taylor to Mr Dodge, 1 Sept. 1941.
[117] Taylor, *Natural History of Everyday Life*, 261.
[118] PRO, INF/1/279. L. Moss, *The Government Social Survey: A History* (London, 1991), 4, 7, 11–12.
[119] I. McLaine, *Ministry of Morale: Home Front Morale and the Ministry of Information in World War II* (London, 1979), 9.

gaining favour in the advance of systems for testing aptitude when it came to officer selection.[120]

It has been rather too easy, however, for subsequent commentators to paint a picture of 'fashionable Freudians' getting things spectacularly wrong.[121] Closer analysis of the development of Glover's wartime writing offers a rather different picture, with his ideas moving on, responding to circumstances, and in continued dialogue with political circumstances. To concentrate on the prediction of mass mental breakdown is to miss the point. Figures like Glover argued that the psychopathology of war was a problem that was always present, integral to peace, and integral to making civilised democratic subjects out of potentially savage human nature. Indeed, war itself was 'part of the price of peace'.[122] One of the reasons for the absence of a psychological collapse was that war had provided an outlet for the unconscious aggression of the population.[123] It could also be argued that people were numbed to shock through its constant repetition. The aggression which lay behind war-readiness was in turn, however, provoking unconscious guilt and this was showing signs of contributing to social aggression, seen for instance in a rise of anti-Semitism and general 'scapegoating'.[124] In the context of war, questioning the peaceable instincts of the British population was difficult and might undermine morale, but as war drew to a close Glover did begin to voice such concerns more openly.[125] He and others like him had come to believe that such a perspective would be crucial to bear in mind in fashioning a post-war order.

MAKING THE PEACE

Though a certain amount of attention has been attracted by psychologists' warnings about the impact of war on civilian health, the same cannot be said of the role of psychology in the making of a peace. Unsurprisingly, war was fertile soil for a psychology that offered in its language of sickness and health a way of conceptualising and accounting for the conflict in somewhat black and white terms. This was the psychology of someone like William Brown with his wartime recasting of Germany as a sick nation. Mostly, however, the experience of war promoted a psychology that spoke more in greys, raising difficult questions about the psychological nature of the British political subject in peace as well as in war.

Evan Durbin spent his war first in the Economic Section of the Cabinet Office and then as Personal Assistant to the Deputy Prime Minister Clement Attlee.[126] In the election of May 1945 that rapidly followed the end of war in Europe and saw the surprise landslide victory of Labour, Durbin was elected as MP for

---

[120] For instance, P. Vernon, 'A Study of War Attitudes', *British Journal of Medical Psychology*, 19 (1942), 271–91.   [121] For instance, Harrisson, *Living through the Blitz*, 308.

[122] Glover, *War, Sadism and Pacifism* [1941–4], 168.   [123] Ibid. 166.   [124] Ibid. 172.

[125] Ibid. 155–6; T. Pear, 'The Social Status of the Psychologist and the Effects upon his Work', *Sociological Review*, 37 (1942), 81.   [126] Nuttall, 'Psychological Socialist', 244.

Edmonton. Stephen Taylor was also elected for Labour. The two men collaborated in setting up a weekend conference on the psychological and sociological problems of modern socialism. Invitations went out to an illustrious list of left-leaning academics and intellectuals. This included Durbin's friend psychologist John Bowlby, as well as G. D. H. Cole and his wife Margaret, sociologists Karl Mannheim and T. H. Marshall, anthropologist Audrey Richards, founder of social medicine and the subject's first professor with his appointment at Oxford, John Ryle, writer Leonard Woolf, and author of Labour's 1945 manifesto Michael Young.[127] The meeting provided a platform for advancing Bowlby and Durbin's case for rethinking socialism in light of current understanding of psychological subjectivity. There is something of a surprise here. Durbin now showed himself, not only concerned about a general problem of human nature, but to have become in some ways rather pessimistic about the innate intellectual abilities of a section of the population.[128] In a draft for a book dealing with this subject, he seemed to accept that there was little chance of action, though if there had been his sympathies might have been with quite radical solutions: 'there is really nothing much to be done except to examine the literature of the Eugenic Society and state the case'.[129] Recognising that there was simply no possibility of extending curative psychoanalysis to whole populations, he was now also less optimistic that the preventive route of education would be enough to change the character of nations like Germany or Russia: after all, 'only better parents can produce better children.'[130] Perhaps Bowlby's own emphasis on the crucial importance of the parental environment contributed to this anxiety. This post-war prognosis appears to have been significantly gloomier and less confidently democratic than that of the late 1930s. The problem of heredity, and now the quality of parenting, compounded that of a fundamental immorality. 'We are faced', Durbin concluded, 'by societies composed of persons who are much more wicked (or emotionally diseased)—than their private behaviour suggests—and judged by intellectual standards very stupid.'[131]

A draft paper from Bowlby in August 1945 contains less of this pessimism and offers more indication of ways in which a psychodynamic perspective spoke to those interested in ideological realignment. For Bowlby, psychoanalytic theory cast light on the issues of cooperation and leadership that would help to explain the phenomenon of Nazism and in turn could inform the socialism of the future. Study of play in small children revealed that the denial of individual desire in cooperative behaviour was one of man's central psychological problems. Only willing cooperation could be regarded as healthy, and this demanded regarding the common aim as of value both to the self and to loved ones. Nazism had indicated that this could take place through 'libidinisation' of the leader alone, and

---

[127] BLPES, Durbin Papers, 4/8.
[128] Ibid. Draft paper 'Character Psychology and the Problems of Democracy and Socialism', 2.
[129] 'The Sources of Social Progress', ch. 2 'Heredity and Environment', 2.   [130] Ibid.
[131] Ibid. (underlining in original).

indeed mirroring the relation to the father this was in some ways an easy transition, but it was also an unstable situation as the history of Nazism had demonstrated.[132] 'Libidinisation' of the group, the aim of democratic socialism, was a harder psychological challenge.[133] As such, Bowlby highlighted the importance from a mental health perspective of ensuring that democracy really did enable the population to identify with a common plan. Democracy, in that sense, was psychologically essential for successful socialism. Nevertheless, there was a problem, in that ideas did not usually emerge directly from the people. Leaders, then, were essential in a developed society. But what was needed was a new type of leader who was able to formulate genuinely group goals through an understanding of modern scientific method, not least psychology.[134] Julian Huxley argued that the emergence of such an intellectual-led 'group mind' would be something of a natural process, a further stage in evolution, albeit one in which culture now took over from biology, war simply providing the ideal circumstances to speed it up.[135] What had to be avoided was resort to a traditional bureaucracy, which 'uses none of the procedures for permitting the public to libidinise its ends and consequently enlists none of the psychological forces making for group co-operation.'[136]

Alongside this set of psychological challenges for democracy was another quite fundamental one for socialism itself: individual desire needed to be recognised as a psychological fact and therefore accommodated. In this respect, Labour could learn something from its political enemy:

In the present alignment of parties, the Tory party has come to represent the private goals and the Labour Party group goals. In our contempt for the Tory championship of the private concerns of a minority and our enthusiasm for achieving long sought social aims it is clearly important that we should not overlook the private concerns of the masses, their predilections in sport or entertainments, their desire to have a home and garden of their own in which they can do what they like and from which they do not frequently have to move, their preference in Seaside resorts or Sunday newspapers. The principle must clearly be maintained of permitting as great a degree of freedom in all these fields as is consistent with the achievement of the group goals chosen by the majority. Unless this principle is steadfastly applied, not only will the lives of the individuals so affected be the poorer, but the sense of frustration and hostility engendered will imperil willing co-operation.[137]

Psychology here spoke for revisionism, and Durbin would go on to make the case in relation to economics.[138] Psychological theory, then, at one and the same time pointed to the case for individualism and socialism, and in doing so it seemed that

---

[132] BLPES, Durbin papers, 4/8, Draft of untitled paper by John Bowlby, Aug. 1945.

[133] Ibid. 3.

[134] Ibid. 6. Here, James Burnham's analysis was broadly influential: *The Managerial Revolution: Or What is Happening in the World Now* (London, 1942).

[135] J. Huxley, 'The Growth of a Group Mind in Britain under the Influence of War', *Hibbert Journal*, 39 (1941), 337–50.

[136] BLPES, Durbin Papers, 4/8, Draft of paper by John Bowlby, Aug. 1945, p. 7.

[137] Ibid. 5.

[138] Though much of this remained unpublished: Durbin, *New Jerusalems*, 165–79.

it offered some solution to the conflict between individual and social needs. In truth, it may simply have highlighted the difficulty of reconciling the two: indeed, a psychological subjectivity that was individualist yet social proved in the longer term a hard balancing act and one whose appeal therefore was not that which Bowlby and Durbin appear to have hoped for in the still heady climate of 1945. As the émigré Austrian economist, F. A. Hayek highlighted in his 1944 critique of what he called *The Road to Serfdom*, war-sprung psychological theory could equally easily support the conclusion that an instinctive, impersonal, and ultimately amoral human nature was psychologically at war with what socialism was trying to do.[139]

Durbin was not alone among those in influential policy-making circles to take on board the insights of psychology. John Maynard Keynes emerged as the most influential economist of the era, and brought with him a new appreciation of economics as a psychological subject. As in the case of Durbin, this meant a reorientation towards greater appreciation of the economic subject as one driven by a desire that was neither wholly rational nor independent from social influence. This, in turn, encouraged a reorientation to an economic policy that focused on the manipulation of demand as much as supply, consumption as much as production.[140]

Another significant conduit for psychological influence was the sociologist Karl Mannheim of the London School of Economics, who invited psychologists to contribute to his influential International Library of Sociology and Social Reconstruction book series. His own influential set of essays under the title *Diagnosis of Our Time* set the tone, drawing on a psychological perspective to offer a third way between the extremes of fascism and communism: a route of 'militant democracy'.[141] In fact, Mannheim had already been interested in bringing psychology to bear on social issues in the 1930s. He was also already juxtaposing a British with a German way, suggesting that there was much to learn, though not to copy. He suggested, for instance, that the German work camp, though unpleasant, was better from a psychological point of view than the liberal strategy of the dole.[142] Britain, he thought, had something to learn from the example of its ideological counterparts. They had demonstrated the power of ideas and group life to mobilise populations. Britain had to follow suit: she faced a crisis of valuation which threatened general psychological breakdown. She had to take note of the shift in the focus of psychology from the problems of the individual to those of the group. Youth was a particular concern, with a rising problem of delinquency a clear sign of the collective psychological crisis. Mass education presented one of the most powerful potential tools for remedying this through what in effect was a

---

[139] Durbin would dismiss this as ill-informed, psychological nonsense: E. Durbin, *Problems of Economic Planning* (1949), 101–2.

[140] Skidelsky, *Keynes*, 88–9, 236–41; Winslow, 'Keynes and Freud', 549–78.

[141] K. Mannheim, *Diagnosis of our Time: Wartime Essays of a Sociologist* (London, 1943).

[142] K. Mannheim, 'Present Trends in the Building of Society', *Human Affairs*, 1 (1937), 292.

method of group analysis.[143] The individualist approach of psychoanalysis was the product of an age of liberalism, which had been shattered by the current crisis. The coming social age would need a new type of therapeutic approach, what he called 'socio-analysis'.[144] Education and the social services would be the key tools of this psychology, turning the alienated members of the crowd into groups with shared values. Though he had grossly misused these new tools of government, imposing order through submission and exploiting the psychology of repression, Hitler had shown the way with his use of group movements, notably to mobilise the energies of the young.[145] Looking forward to the challenge of both reconstructing the world on new lines and reconditioning the Nazi mind in the peace to come, democracy now had the opportunity to transform, perhaps even to rescue itself. The social thrust of psychology that had been developing since the start of the century and had been brought to the very centre of the public stage by the mid-century crisis was presented, in sum, as supporting the need for a social vision of democracy as an alternative to individualism. As Mannheim put it, with particular reference to youth, as both the key to the future and the most malleable section of the population:

the new democratic personalism will differ from the laissez-faire period in that it will restore the genuine powers of group life. It will achieve this, among other means, through the attention it will pay to the gang-age and to the potentialities which are inherent in the self-regulating forces of group existence. It must become the meaning of a nation-wide Youth movement that it breaks down the frustration which comes from isolation, exaggerated privacy and sectarianism, and mobilises instead the forces of group living in the service of the individual.[146]

Mannheim was of course a sociologist rather than a psychologist, but it has been the argument of this book that psychology often spoke through its influence on parallel disciplines, and this is a case in point. Conditions of wartime national need encouraged such dialogue.[147] However, processes of professionalisation and specialisation, accelerated in part by the expansion of the state and the economy that was a legacy of war, would make this increasingly difficult in the years to come.

Edward Glover was encouraged by the way that Mannheim and the sociologists around him were open to psychology.[148] Mirroring Mannheim's language of group analysis, Glover wrote of being happy to get rid of the term 'individual psychology' altogether; the 'group mind' part of the psychic equipment of every individual.[149] However, the socio-political diagnosis that he drew from this was somewhat different to Mannheim, with more concern about the psychological implications of an overpowering state, and with more pessimism about the implications of human nature for the peace to come. For the psychoanalyst, the family

---

[143] Mannheim, *Diagnosis of our Time*, 73–94.   [144] Ibid. 87.   [145] Ibid. 80, 99.
[146] Ibid. 52.
[147] T. Pear, 'The Relations between Psychology and Sociology', *Bulletin of the John Rylands Library*, 31 (1948), 277–94.   [148] Glover, *War, Sadism and Pacifism [1941–4]*, 153.
[149] Ibid. [1941–4], 181–3.

was a fundamental political arena, key in civilising each new generation. Both the worship of the state, heralded to some extent in Mannheim's vision, and the expansion of its power over everyday life, dramatically already taking place in wartime and with a good likelihood of continuing beyond, might be in conflict with the family.[150] Glover's concern was perhaps deeply rooted elsewhere, for post-war statism turned out to be less confident and popular than had seemed likely and tended to act to advance the centrality of the family unit.[151] He also remained concerned that new tools of democratic accountability would need to accompany state expansion if it was to work at a psychological level.[152] Indeed, it might be suggested that the lack of innovation in this area helps to explain some of the difficulties for Labour in continuing to mobilise support for the state in the post-war era.[153] It is intriguing in this respect that Stephen Taylor would lead Labour's discussion of how to use the apparatus of the survey—adapted now into testing the mood of constituents—to promote a more popular and democratic socialism.[154]

Glover believed that the international peace was being established on a set of false psychological dichotomies: pitting guilt against innocence, aggression against self-defence, and ideology against common sense. In truth, this had been a war fuelled by aggression, as well as ideology, on both sides.[155] Although its ideological nature had been complicated by the alliance with the Soviet Union, mobilisation of the British population to fight for a better post-war society had exploited an inner belief in freedom to strengthen the innate drives of aggression and self-preservation.[156] Because of this, the conflict had psychologically sown the seeds of the Cold War to come. To make the situation worse, guilt—so easy to attribute to the defeated enemy—was in fact the hidden legacy of war and its killing for the victors themselves.[157] Repressed in the unconscious, it would foster aggression toward the defeated enemy as well as the enemy to come.[158] Rather

---

[150] Glover, *War, Sadism and Pacifism* [1941–4], 221–2.

[151] Riley, *War in the Nursery*; D. Riley, 'Some Peculiarities of Social Policy Concerning Women in Wartime and Postwar Britain', in Higgonet et al. (eds.), *Behind the Lines*, 260–71.

[152] Glover, *War, Sadism and Pacifism* [1941–4], 224.

[153] N. Tiratsoo (ed.), *The Attlee Years* (London, 1991). Several essays in this volume have particular relevance for the issue of democratisation: S. Fielding ' "Don't Know and Don't Care": Political Attitudes in Labour's Britain', in Tiratsoo (ed.), *The Attlee Years*, 106–25; and T. Mason and P. Thompson, ' "Reflections on a Revolution?" The Political Mood in Wartime Britain', in Tiratsoo (ed.), *The Attlee Years*, 54–70. For criticism of this position on the popular mood: J. Hinton, 'The Apathy School', *History Workshop Journal*, 43 (1997), 266–73.

[154] S. Taylor, 'Socialism and Public Opinion', in D. Munro (ed.), *Socialism and the British Way* (London, 1948), 229–30. This is discussed in relation to what can be seen as a Labour project of improving human nature which had only limited success: S. Fielding, 'To Make Men and Women Better than they are: Labour and the Building of Socialism', in J. Fyrth (ed.), *Labour's Promised Land: Culture and Society in Labour Britain, 1945–51* (London, 1995), 16–27.

[155] Glover, *War, Sadism and Pacifism* [1945], 247–8.   [156] Ibid. [1945], 250.

[157] Ibid. [1945], 251.

[158] On the 'genocidal attitude towards Germany' in 1945: T. Kushner, *The Holocaust and the Liberal Imagination* (Oxford, 1994), 219. The pacifist Victor Gollancz described coverage of captured enemies in the press as a form of 'spiritual and sometimes physical pornography': *Our*

than peace, this was the continuation of aggression by means of diplomacy.[159] Alarmingly, the new structures of international government such as the United Nations and its Security Council were more dictatorial than democratic.[160] As such, they offered little opportunity for that marriage between authority and individual psychological need that had been heralded by the wartime emergence of new channels of accountability at the national level. The new international law was in danger of being founded on the false premise that fault lay with the 'aggressor' nations alone; that it was a matter of disciplining delinquency. Such authoritarianism was neither the right way to tackle the problem of youth rebellion in Britain itself—one of Glover's own main areas of interest as Director of the Institute for the Scientific Study of Delinquency—nor would it work transferred to the stage of international relations.[161] It was to ignore, both what had been the most fundamental insight of the crisis, and what was set to be crucial in maintaining peace in the future: that the difference between 'war-like' and 'peaceable' countries was only 'skin deep'. Indeed, in psychological terms, the 'peace-loving' nations had proved themselves the most effective fighting forces of the conflict.[162] It was these nations that now found themselves equipped with a weapon, the atom bomb, that made the civilian an even more central target, and turned war, more clearly than ever before, into an issue of extermination. The fact that fantasies of world destruction were latent in the unconscious mind was particularly alarming.[163] All this, yet there was now no more sign of government supporting research into the psychological causes of war than there had been when Glover had first begun to address the issue in 1931.

The mid-century crisis, therefore, had presented a powerful case for taking the problem of human nature and its psychological experts far more seriously than ever before, but psychology would be unable to maintain a position of influence that it had appeared on the brink of attaining in such propitious circumstances. Though the war had been good for the reputation and influence of psychodynamic psychology, bringing the analysts out of their relatively isolated pre-war world, it had also advanced a more behaviourist, empiricist, and quantitative psychology which found particularly fruitful application in selection within the military.[164] The two now stood in more obvious tension with one another. Glover pointedly remarked that those who had advanced psychology as a tool for managing subjectivity through a battery of tests in the Army might now benefit from

---

Threatened Values (London, 1946), 25. This however ran alongside a desire to forget: Kushner, *Holocaust and Liberal Imagination*, 242–3; A. Sinclair, *War like a Wasp* (London, 1989), 191.

  [159] Ibid. [1945], 263.   [160] Ibid. [1945], 263–6.

  [161] E. Glover, *The Diagnosis and Treatment of Delinquency: Being a Clinical Report of the Institute during the Five Years 1937 to 1941* (London, 1941).

  [162] Glover, *War, Sadism and Pacifism* [1945], 260.   [163] Ibid. [1945], 267–75.

  [164] In fact, the psychoanalysts were also involved in officer selection, which the British adopted reluctantly partly because of suspicion towards their ideas. Stafford Cripps proved an influential supporter, Winston Churchill a critic: Shephard, *War of Nerves*, 187–97.

'rehabilitation' to remind them of the rights of the peacetime citizen.[165] In fact, this type of psychology would find a comfortable position—managerial, apparently scientific, and morally neutral—within both the psychological discipline and the welfare state to come. By contrast, Glover's ethical, social vision, the descendant of much of what had gone before over the past half century, would never be in such a potentially influential position again. The fact that the British psychoanalytic community was so bitterly divided in these years over its own internal theoretical disputes, with Glover himself at the thick of things, cannot have helped.[166]

In two areas, in particular, the wartime encounter between psychology and ideology would have the opportunity for post-war results that reached beyond Britain: the first, de-Nazification; the second, the promotion of mental health through international organisation. The process of constructing a psychopathology of Nazism went back to the 1930s, while its roots go back even further to Trotter's study of the Great War. In the midst of the 1939–45 conflict itself, it therefore comes as no surprise to find William Brown proposing 'psycho-catharsis' to treat the German nation.[167] However, the defeat of Germany in 1945 raised the new issue of whether such a psychology might really act as a valuable practical tool in making Germany fit for democracy and peace. So intimately involved in the conflict themselves, with some of them exposed to the full horror of what Nazism had achieved in its concentration camps, when British psychiatrists were called upon now to assess the minds of Nazis and advise on post-war reconstruction, re-education, and de-Nazification, the temptation was to suggest that there was indeed some deep psychological malaise at work.[168] Henry Dicks, employed to undertake psychological analysis of high-level Germans to select for potential 'democrats', found a fundamental difference between dedicated Nazis—who had immature personalities—and those who drifted into the Party simply because of the situation and were more redeemable.[169] In that sense, psychology suggested that the situation was not hopeless; yet it still had to be recognised that there was an abnormally high percentage of authoritarians and that a full solution would only be attainable as future generations were brought up in a less authoritarian way.[170]

---

[165] Shephard, *War of Nerves*, 334–5.

[166] P. Roazen, *Oedipus in Britain: Edward Glover and the Struggle over Klein* (New York, 2000).

[167] Brown, 'The Psychology of Modern Germany', 57.

[168] On one area of this work: D. Smith, 'Juvenile Delinquency in the British Zone of Germany, 1945–51', *German History*, 12 (1994), 39–63.

[169] H. V. Dicks, 'Personality Traits and National Socialist Ideology', *Human Relations*, 3 (1950), 111–54. Dicks was used in this role well before the end of the war because of his German language skills and was involved in the psychiatric assessment of Rudolf Hess: J. R. Rees (ed.), *The Case of Rudolf Hess: A Problem in Diagnosis and Forensic Psychiatry* (London, 1947). Much later, he became involved in a multi-disciplinary project led by historian Norman Cohn investigating mass destructiveness. He described his contribution as a 'mental health man's cautionary tale', basing it on new interviews with SS killers as well as records from the time: H. V. Dicks, *Licensed Mass Murder: A Socio-Psychological Study of Some SS Killers* (London, 1972), 269.

[170] R. Money-Kyrle, *Psychoanalysis and Politics: A Contribution to the Psychology of Politics and Morals* (London, 1951), 13–15; R. Money-Kyrle, 'Social Conflict and the Challenge to Psychology', *British Journal of Medical Psychology*, 21 (1948), 215–21.

Such psychiatrists were also well aware that modern psychodynamic theory was steering them away from a sharp division between sickness and health, and thus away from a course that would have been both ideologically and emotionally attractive at a time like this. Forcing Germans to 'adjust' would also present a dilemma, in that it replaced one authoritarianism by another and ignored the fact that Germans might be normal within their own psychological context. Imposing a change of character without first changing a culture with a history that could not simply be erased overnight might indeed produce more psychological sickness than had been there in the first place. In practical terms, this was also an unrealistic challenge—after all Britain lacked the resources and personnel to address its own mental health let alone embark on full-scale therapy of the German nation—and it was soon recognised that the role would need to be left in the hands of German professionals, turning something of a blind eye to their involvement in supporting the aims of the regime.[171] The challenge of de-Nazification, in sum, presented British psychiatrists and psychologists with some difficult questions about the ideological nature of their particular conception of mental health and illness. In the circumstances of 1945, there were compelling political and emotional reasons to sidestep this problem and to uphold the pact between ideology and psychology; indeed, if anything was likely to emphasise the importance of maintaining an ethical dimension in psychology then it was seeing what this science could be made to support when such constraints were absent. However this was rooted in a contradiction, or at least a considerable tension: the social sciences, anthropology in particular, made an increasingly strong case for regarding values as a product and reflection of their own cultures; and psychology in its projection of group values into the individual psyche accepted as much.[172] By the 1960s, most notably with the emergence of the anti-psychiatry movement, such relativism would come to challenge the very idea of mental health.[173]

The post-war vision of mental health as a source of values was at its most ambitious in the World Federation for Mental Health.[174] In part, this was one strand within the post-war project of exploring the potential for world government, which has attracted relatively little attention from historians because of its perceived failures.[175] In part, it also grew out of the international mental hygiene meetings of the interwar period, which had seen the spread of mental hygiene organisations in Europe, the Americas, and even beyond. Throughout the late

---

[171] J. R. Rees, 'Work for Mental Health in Germany', *Bulletin of the World Federation for Mental Health*, 1 (1949), 15–19. On the lack of prosecution and continuity of psychiatry and psychology in Germany: M. Burleigh, *Death and Deliverance: 'Euthanasia' in Germany 1900–1945* (Cambridge, 1994), 269–90.

[172] T. Pear, 'Psychological Implications of the Culture Pattern Theory', *Bulletin of the John Rylands Library*, 29 (1945–6), 201–24. [173] Thomson, 'Before Anti-Psychiatry'; see also Ch. 8.

[174] For detail from one of those involved: P. Norman, *In the Way of Understanding* (Godalming, 1982), 151–229.

[175] The United Nations, for instance, gains just one brief and critical mention in what has emerged as the pre-eminent narrative of the century: E. Hobsbawm, *Age of Extremes: The Short Twentieth Century, 1914–1991* (London, 1994), 430.

1930s, this movement had struggled to transcend ideological differences. Now, the victors of war had a clear opportunity to revive activity and advance their own vision of mental health. In the immediate post-war period, with the Federation meeting for its first post-war congress in London in 1948, the British became highly influential.[176] J. R. Rees of the Tavistock Clinic was made President, and with other leading psychoanalytically-orientated British psychiatrists, including H. V. Dicks and J. C. Flugel, he would be in the Preparatory Commission given the role of designing a statement on world mental health aims for the new international health agencies, UNESCO and the World Health Organisation.[177] Unsurprisingly, the statement would reflect the ideologically inflected vision of mental health that had come to the fore in wartime Britain. Nevertheless, carried into the international arena, it was now suggested that in mental health the international community might find a set of common guiding values above ideology— 'a basis for common human aspiration', and through such common humanity the basis for some kind of world citizenship.[178] In turn, this world citizenship founded on mental health values would be crucial in preventing another war: 'No peace without mental health ... and at the same time no mental health without peace.'[179] Somewhat unrealistically, albeit idealistically, but again with a remarkable lack of consideration for cultural or socio-economic difference, the way forward was seen as one of promoting a single model of mental health across the globe: mental health defined in terms of a particular set of liberal values; the mapping of a western model of the necessary stages in developing mental health services (hardly a resounding success in the West's own past) onto less well-developed societies; and the projection of the West's own mental hygienist vision of how the organisation of society and lifestyle could promote psychological well-being. The World Federation hoped to act, not simply as a lobby group and steering agency on its own psychological terrain, but as a channel for promoting the central importance of mental health values to a group such as UNESCO. There were plans in 1947, for instance, for a United Nations Institute of the Human Sciences, with a remit embracing the psychological study of international relations, child development, and the idea of national character.[180] It was not long, of course, before the cultural assumptions behind the projection of a normative mental health began to attract criticism, American anthropologist Margaret Mead leading the way at the 1948 London Congress with her concern that some were trying

---

[176] Thomson, 'Mental Hygiene as an International Movement', 283–304.

[177] This story is also examined in Toms, 'Mental Hygiene to Civil Rights', 146–63.

[178] 'Statement by the International Preparatory Commission of the International Congress on Mental Health', *Human Relations*, 2 (1949), 67. On the rejection of an idea of world citizenship at the UN, though with no mention of the WFMH: D. Heater, *Citizenship: The Civic Ideal in World History, Politics and Education* (London, 1990), 139–60.

[179] 'Statement by the International Preparatory Commission of the International Congress on Mental Health', 80.

[180] 'Proposal for the Establishment of a United Nations Institute of the Human Sciences', *Human Relations*, 1 (1948), 353–72.

to turn mental health into a kind of religion.[181] The difficulty of bringing the Soviets into the fold also shattered the idea that ideological division might be a problem of the past in some brave new era in which values could be plucked from the 'neutral' territory of psychological science.[182] Those outside this community of concerned experts took little notice of the grandiose vision.[183] There was also something of a contradiction between this vision and the psychological lessons of the mid-century crisis. Recent events had surely highlighted that, however unfortunate in its potential ramifications, there was a deep psychological need for defining one's democratic subjectivity against all that lay beyond its boundaries.[184]

PSYCHOLOGY IN RETREAT

The gulf between the ambitions of psychology and its real power and influence is again apparent in attempts to extend mental health services as part of the post-war development of the British welfare state. C. P. Blacker, serving in the army as a psychiatrist but best known as Secretary of the Eugenics Society, was approached by the government in 1942 to undertake a survey of existing provision of psychiatric and psychological services. The immediate purpose was to make the most of what was currently available, promoting better coordination of military and depleted civilian resources; the ulterior motive was to develop a plan of how these services might fit in to the likely post-war reorganisation of the health services.[185] Blacker is an intriguing choice considering his high profile as a eugenicist. There was a rationale that he had links to the three main organisations concerned—the Emergency Medical Service, the Army, and the Government department dealing with mental hospitals, the Board of Control—but privately the Chairman of the Board had his doubts that such a controversial figure was appropriate. The fact that such misgivings were overridden may indicate a desire to ensure that any emerging blueprint would not be overly generous when it came to doling out public resources; here eugenicists were in their element.[186] Despite an ambitious plan of what would have been ideal—psychotherapeutic services available for all being the logical corollary arising from the psychological diagnosis of the crisis—Blacker's main finding was that there was currently a very uneven, and invariably sparse distribution of resources.[187] The conclusion that had to be drawn was that any large-scale extension of services was in fact out of the question. Unsurprisingly, Blacker found it

[181] J. Howard, *Margaret Mead: A Life* (London, 1984), 261–4.

[182] *Annual Report of the World Federation of Mental Health* (London, 1949), 29.

[183] See the review on the UNESCO conference and resulting publication *Tensions that Cause War*, concluding that 'few folk will read it and fewer study it. It will be ignored': J. L. Halliday 'Critical Notice', *British Journal of Medical Psychology*, 25 (1952), 55.

[184] Winnicott, 'Thoughts on the Meaning of the Word Democracy', 184.

[185] Blacker, *Neurosis and the Mental Health Services*, v. On reorganisation: Thomson, *The Problem of Mental Deficiency*, 270–96.   [186] On the background of the survey: PRO, MH 76/115.

[187] PRO, MH 76/115, Ministry of Health note on Blacker survey, 20 March 1944.

difficult not to fall back on the eugenic solution: try to prevent the need for such services in the first place, and develop strategies to overcome the burdensomeness of the 'social problem group'.[188] There was no sign here of the ambitious vision of psychotherapy for all; of psychology being at the heart of a project of making better men and women. Indeed, privately Blacker dismissed many of those involved in psychotherapy as unbalanced, sex-obsessed cranks.[189]

There was relief that psychiatric services found themselves in closer proximity to general health within the post-war National Health Service. However, such a victory also brought the prospect of psychiatry being the perpetual Cinderella of the new NHS. The promotion of psychotherapy in the wartime military had been spectacular, but had taken advantage of special circumstances. Returning home, progress in this direction would turn out to be much slower.[190] The post-war military reacted against those who had presided over the high wartime rates of military neurosis, and such suspicions of the 'trick-cyclists' spilled over into the domestic scene.[191] There was also the rising challenge of emerging physical treatments.[192] The most influential psychiatrist of the era, Director of the Maudsley Hospital, Aubrey Lewis, emerged from the war and the experience of surveying the problem of industrial neurosis, both aware that levels of neurosis depended on the acceptability of the condition within any given situation, and wondering whether to devolve the psychotherapeutic role to general practitioners.[193] Lewis's sympathies are evident in private correspondence to Professor F. R. Fraser, in control of surveying wartime industrial neurosis, where he advised against a strategy of simply providing more highly-trained personnel:

Diligent search for neurotics can be as bad as encouragement of neurotic symptoms, which is indeed what it may amount to.... Psychotherapy, in the usual sense of the word as continued individual treatment, need not be considered: it is too expensive a luxury and too feeble a remedy for these times.[194]

The group therapy approach pioneered within the military had been attractive, not just in the way that it supported democratic values, but also as a solution to limited resources. Yet, it would prove harder to extend on any significant scale to a peacetime Home Front where people expected individual service in tackling sensitive personal issues.[195] In reality, as already noted in relation to Stephen Taylor's

[188] PRO, MH 76/115, Blacker, 26 April 1943, p. 18; Blacker, *Neurosis and the Mental Health Services*, 103–8; C. P. Blacker, *Problem Families: Five Enquiries* (London, 1952).
[189] CMAC, EUG C21, Blacker to Dr R. H. Felix, 14 Feb. 1948.
[190] J. R. Rees, *The Shaping of Psychiatry by War* (London, 1945).
[191] Shephard, *War of Nerves*, 325.
[192] Sargant, *The Unquiet Mind*; W. Sargant and E. Slater, *An Introduction to Physical Methods of Treatment in Psychiatry* (Edinburgh, 1944).
[193] A. Lewis, 'Mental Health in War-Time', *Public Health* (Dec. 1943), 30. On Lewis: Jones, 'Aubrey Lewis, Edward Mapother and the Maudsley', in Angel, Jones, and Neve (eds.), *European Psychiatry on the Eve of War*, 3–38.
[194] PRO, MH 76/115, Lewis to Fraser, 4 March 1942, p. 4.
[195] On Bion's group therapy work at Northfield Hospital: Shephard, *War of Nerves*, 157–60. However, the idea had been pioneered by Joshua Bierer since 1938 as a way to supplement

promotion of 'good general practice', the post-war problem remained largely in the hands of the family doctors who lacked any significant expertise. Here, there was a temptation within a resource-strapped system to take a pragmatic and relatively unsympathetic approach to psychological complaints: better not to confirm illness to patients.[196]

The birth of the NHS was not then the start of a heroic new era of psychotherapy for the masses. Pioneers like the Tavistock Clinic and the Cassel Hospital may have entered the fold, signalling a new respectability for the psychotherapeutic, but they were minor partners in a now huge whole and were in some ways tamed.[197] The psychotherapists may have regarded an organicist psychiatry with suspicion, both because of what they saw as its inherent authoritarianism, and because they would dispute its scientific basis.[198] But the organicists found themselves far more at home within what was at its heart a hospital-centred, evidence-based, illness system. Moreover, a social psychological approach now met a new challenge, with the emergence of what Aubrey Lewis called 'social psychiatry' pointing away from the exploration of values towards empirical epidemiological research.[199]

The political and ideological forces that had encouraged an exploration of social values as integral to psychological subjectivity lingered in the culture of the Cold War, but were never again as pressing as they had been between the shock of the First World War and the settlement arising from the Second. To a psychoanalyst like Glover, the psychological predicament of living within the condition of the perpetual threat of extermination may have seemed more serious than ever, but circumstances of peace and prosperity helped the problem of war and therefore its psychological origins to fall away from public debate. Occasionally, a figure like Arthur Koestler would revive it, attacking the political neurosis that lay behind a 'mental iron curtain' of denial, both when it came to the left's ongoing support of the popular basis of the Soviet regime, and the refusal of the German nation to accept what had happened in the wartime extermination camps.[200] But in the post-war period, British politicians themselves appear to have remained largely unimpressed by such calls to take seriously psychological subjectivity.[201] With psychology now keen to defend its credentials as a science, the discipline too

hospital-based care: J. Beirer (ed.), *Therapeutic Social Clubs* (London, 1948). See also the experiment in group therapy by Snowden considered in Ch. 6; and the interwar Oxford Group Movement under Frank Buchman: Falby, 'Gerald Heard', 162–3.

[196] See Ch. 6.   [197] Dicks, *Fifty Years of the Tavistock*, 317.

[198] Winnicott, 'Thoughts on the Meaning of Democracy', 178–9; J. D. Sutherland, 'Psychological Medicine and the National Health Service: The Need for an Integrated Approach to Research', *British Journal of Medical Psychology*, 25 (1952), 71–85.

[199] M. Shepherd, 'From Social Medicine to Social Psychiatry: The Achievement of Sir Aubrey Lewis', in M. Shepherd, *The Psychosocial Matrix of Psychiatry* (London, 1983), 256–70.

[200] A. Koestler, 'A Guide to Political Neurosis', *Encounter*, 1 (1953), 25–32.

[201] Future research may reveal greater interest. Nuttall has recently highlighted Tony Crosland's excitement, albeit rather unsystematic, regarding Freud: 'Psychological Socialism, Tony Crosland, and the Politics of Mind', 80–2.

withdrew from the type of speculation about political values that had been common in the 1930s and 1940s.[202] The fluidity that had existed between the disciplines of anthropology, sociology, and psychology, as relatively young disciplines in the first half of the century, had in retrospect probably encouraged the social orientation of the period. Circumstances of war and its climate of democratic socialism had also been important. In the post-war period, the ideological climate changed, and academic specialisation left it harder to cross such boundaries, while appreciation of the cultural and social basis of knowledge turned psychology as an aspiring science towards the search for harder knowledge and made it more critical of the relativity of what it did say in the realm of values. As a discipline for guiding human nature, let alone statecraft, it had lost confidence. Turning inwards, it would find a new politics, a politics of the personal, but it was not for another two decades that this vision would begin to capture the public imagination.[203]

THE PSYCHOLOGY OF EVERYDAY LIFE

The role of the survey organisation Mass-Observation has already intersected with the main story of this chapter at several points and offers some striking parallels as well as significant contrasts. Founded in 1937 by the surrealist poet Charles Madge and the documentary filmmaker Humphrey Jennings, and soon joined by anthropologist Tom Harrisson, Mass-Observation was a precursor to the wartime project of surveying the mood and attitudes of the British population—a project that it would also be intimately involved in itself. Its main tools were observation, favoured by Harrisson with his anthropological orientation, and the directed diary, favoured as a route to an anthropology of the self by Madge; the two were increasingly the dominant influences.[204] Though none of the founders were psychologists, they were inspired by the new psychology and had a particular enthusiasm for exploring subconscious attitudes at both an individual and social level. As such, their enterprise was part of that spilling over of the psychological imagination from a professional to more amateur sphere that has been a feature of this book.[205] They promised to draw eclectically from different psychological schools of thought, though they appear to have been most excited by psychoanalytic ideas. And they claimed to have attracted trained psychologists to participate

[202] There has been a recent revival of interest, for instance: Andrew Samuels, *Politics on the Couch: Citizenship and the Internal Life* (London, 2001).

[203] The shift is evident in Winnicott's 'Thoughts on the Meaning of the Word Democracy'. On psychology and the politics of the personal: Ch. 8.

[204] There is no space here to go into any great depth about the history of the movement. This is well covered for this period by, for instance: A. Calder, 'Mass-Observation, 1937–1939', in M. Bulmer (ed.), *Essays in the History of Sociological Research* (Cambridge, 1985), 121–36; T. Jeffery, *Mass-Observation: A Short History* (Birmingham, 1978); and the special issue of *New Formations*, 44 (2001).

[205] Exploring this borderline position: P. Summerfield, 'Mass-Observation: Social Research or Social Movement?', *Journal of Contemporary History*, 20 (1985), 439–52.

as observers, while looking forward to psychologists being involved in training and guiding other observers.[206] Harrisson, though an anthropologist, was a rather unorthodox one, as can be seen in his *Savage Civilisation* report on the New Hebrides of 1937.[207] It should come as no surprise that the professional anthropologists and psychologists were generally dismissive of any scientific pretensions behind the project.[208] Yet it would be wrong thereby to jump to the conclusion that, particularly in the context of the time, this was insignificant work from either an anthropological or a psychological perspective. Britain's leading social anthropologist, Bronislaw Malinowski, would in fact contribute a generally very supportive essay to the report on the group's first year of work, recognising, as an anthropologist might, that the problem of reaching objective conclusions from observations that were necessarily subjective was not simply the dilemma of the untrained observer.[209] Psychologist Tom Pear, Professor at Manchester University, supported Mass-Observation as an important contribution in opening up the subject of the psychology of everyday life that the professional psychologists had thus far largely neglected.[210] He suggested that they were afraid it would undermine psychology as a serious subject.[211] Pear would share no such hesitations, bringing psychology to bear on such subjects as the art of conversation.[212] But in general, the reticence of the discipline to engage with everyday life, let alone put things forward in everyday language, set serious limits on its potential as a discipline that could ever talk to the British people. The discipline faced a dilemma that Mass-Observation did not: it was under considerable pressure to prove itself as a science; but in doing so it might find itself less well-equipped, either to address critically, or to communicate its findings, regarding the most pressing subject of its times—its own culture.[213]

Malinowski situated the Mass-Observation project within the context of anxiety about the sickness of culture and the rise of totalitarianism.[214] This sense of

[206] T. Harrisson and C. Madge, *Mass Observation* (London, 1937), 31–6.
[207] T. Harrisson, *Savage Civilisation* (London, 1937). The links with anthropology and the psychology of race are explored in Thomson, 'Savage Civilisation'.
[208] R. Firth, 'An Anthropologist's View of Mass Observation', *Sociological Review*, 31 (1939), 166–93.
[209] B. Malinowski, 'A Nation-Wide Intelligence Service', in C. Madge and T. Harrisson, *First Year's Work, 1937–8* (London, 1938), 81–121.
[210] T. Pear, 'Psychologists and Culture', *Bulletin of the John Rylands Library*, 23 (1939), 425. On Pear: A. Costall, 'Pear and his Peers', in Bunn et al. (eds.), *Psychology in Britain*, 188–204. Pear was impressed by the case put forward in American by Harvard psychologist Hadley Cantril: 'The Social Psychology of Everyday Life', *The Psychological Bulletin*, 31 (1934), 297–331. Harrisson and Madge also regarded this as an important contribution: *Mass Observation*, 50–1. They were also keen to criticise the backwardness of psychology in this respect: ibid. 12, 230.
[211] T. Pear, 'The "Trivial" and "Popular" in Psychology', *British Journal of Psychology*, 31 (1940), 115–28; T. Pear, 'The Social Status of the Psychologist and its Effects upon his Work', *Sociological Review*, 34 (1942), 73.
[212] T. Pear, *The Psychology of Conversation* (London, 1939). Also notable in this respect: J. C. Flugel, *The Psychology of Clothes* (London, 1930).
[213] T. Pear, 'Psychologists and Culture', *Bulletin of the John Rylands Library*, 23 (1939), 417–19.
[214] Malinowski, 'Intelligence Survey', 120.

crisis may well have been important in drawing people to be involved, either as informants, or simply in the more passive role as readers. By 1939, the movement was claiming to have 1,500 of these observers, while *Britain by Mass-Observation*—with a chapter on Munich, that topic of intense psychological interest—sold 100,000 copies in just the first ten days.[215] Refusing to take ideological sides in current dogmatic conflict, Mass-Observation ultimately presented another vision of knowing oneself as the route to a better society. As with Glover's wartime vision of a 'social psychiatry', the apparatus of the survey offered a way to rejuvenate democracy. Like Glover, Mass-Observation regarded the political process centring on Parliament and the press as failing in its self-proclaimed role as a valve for public feeling.[216] But whereas Glover looked to the survey to turn the political process into a kind of therapy, Mass-Observation placed far more emphasis on the importance of the observed being conscious participants in the process of observation: observation itself as a form of therapy. Ideally, it was to be 'the observation by everyone of everyone, including themselves.'[217] Of course, reality would be very different. There would be criticism, for instance, of middle-class biases. Yet this should not completely detract from the democratic ambition of this vision of psychological subjectivity. Ultimately, Mass-Observation hoped to change the way that people thought. Harrisson and Madge believed that in a mass society that had seen a technological revolution in recent years, people had become fatalistic about controlling their own destinies, increasingly reliant on expert 'technicians', finding solace only in superstition within their private lives. The current panic with regard to war and the prospect of air raids was typical of this state of mind.[218] Rather than finding a solution in the advance of the 'technicians'—the route of the psychologists, by and large—theirs would be a project of extending this role to the people, waking them from their lives of automatic habit, both making them 'more conscious of their own wishes', and cultivating a 'social consciousness' in which people would come to recognise the way that their individual behaviour was related to that of the group.[219]

At least in its embryonic form in the late 1930s, Mass-Observation presents us with a parallel social-psychological project to that of the psychologists, though one that was more democratic in its attitudes towards the public, in its approach to the accessibility of knowledge, and in its view of what constituted an appropriate psychological subject. As such, it further highlights the felt need among intellectuals for some kind of socio-psycho-anthropological alternative to either parliament or the press as channels for the integration of individual and social health. By way of contrast, it also foregrounds the democratic limitations of the mainstream psychological project. Whether a genuinely populist project of using the survey to help people to understand themselves and thereby change

---

[215] Harrisson and Madge, *Britain by Mass Observation*, 10; Heimann, *Most Offending Soul*, 149.
[216] Harrisson and Madge, *Britain by Mass Observation*, 10; *First Years Work*, 110–11.
[217] Harrisson and Madge, *Mass Observation*, 9.   [218] Ibid. 15–17.
[219] Ibid. 29–30, 37.

themselves as psychological subjects was ever a realistic possibility is another matter altogether. Collecting data so indiscriminately and in such huge volume, Mass-Observation itself never solved the problem of how to use its record of the national mood in any truly effective way.[220]

CONCLUSION

There has been considerable dispute among historians as to what the British people believed they were fighting for in the Second World War. For some, they were mobilised by a revolution in values and expectations, symbolised by the promised new world of social justice in a welfare state.[221] For Jose Harris, there was rather more 'ambiguity and contradiction' when it came to views about post-war social change, the population mobilising instead 'in defence of the untidy, atomistic, ramshackle pluralism of British social life'. There was an ideology at stake here, but rather than socialism, it was the 'strengthening and legitimation of a highly privatised and unstructured psychological individualism—an individualism that was explicitly opposed to fascism, but that also presented definite boundaries to collectivisation of all kinds.'[222] Since this chapter has made no attempt to measure popular opinion, it is in no position to arbitrate on this dimension of the debate. What it can offer, however, is insight into how contemporary psychology viewed the issue and attempted to react. What is apparent in this respect is that a 'psychological individualism' opposed to fascism was endorsed, yet also that it was invariably recast at the same time as a necessarily social and cultural phenomenon. To have embraced pure 'psychological individualism' would have meant rejecting a movement towards accepting that all psychology was social psychology that had been building in strength since the start of the century and now found vivid support in popular behaviour as Europe descended into war. In the idea of a psychological subjectivity beyond mere individualism, psychology found both a

---

[220] It struggled after the War, partly because there had been a growth in opinion polls, partly because of the advance of academic sociology: Heimann, *Most Offending Soul*, 242. On the problem of the data: Ibid. 145. This biography also provides details of Harrisson's involvement with Mass-Observation when he returned to explore the archive for his book on the Blitz in the 1970s. Housed at Sussex University, Mass-Observation would emerge as an influential source for the historian of the national mood intrigued by its rare insight into the everyday and recognising that it offered answers that were lacking in more quantitatively sound, contemporary survey material. Indicative of a growing appreciation, towards the end of the century, the directive diary project was relaunched. After the War, Madge moved into academic sociology. Here his interest in 'social eidos' has an obvious link to the Mass-Observation interest in social consciousness, though there is no mention of the earlier activity in his book on the subject: C. Madge, *Society in the Mind: Elements of Social Eidos* (London, 1964).

[221] The view was originally put forward by Richard Titmuss in his official history of the wartime social services. Significantly, this study was very aware of the role of psychologists and the nature of their message in the war. It may be the case that his view of the wartime mood was influenced by their work: Titmuss, *Problems of Social Policy*, 508.

[222] J. Harris, 'War and Social History: Britain and the Home Front during the Second World War', *Contemporary European History*, 6 (1997), 31.

way of accounting for the crisis, and its own project for overcoming it. Mere individualism set the animal within man free; culture, education, and values were the necessary psychological tools to turn this potentially dangerous instinctive creature into civilised man. So, for British psychologists this was a war that was being fought on necessarily social territory and which pointed to the need to address the social if a similar descent from civilisation was to be avoided in the future. The culture and system of values that they supported as inherently British, democratic, peaceable, and mentally healthy may indeed have been those very values of individualism and pluralism that Harris suggests were at the heart of the conflict, and hence the tension when it came to their views about expansion of state control. However, this reflected the very opposite of an individualist conception of psychological subjectivity. In psychological terms, then, Britons emerged, more than ever, in the Second World War as social subjects. This would never be as clear again.

In terms of practical achievements, this chapter suggests a contrasting picture. The foregrounding of the problem of human nature in Britain's mid-century international and ideological crisis provided a unique opportunity for the advance of psychology. In particular, it was a potential platform for a psychology with a psychoanalytic orientation, which paid particular attention to potentially destructive instincts. Here, the advance that did take place was possible because of the ongoing tendency to forge an alliance between such a psychology and existing values. In particular, we see such a psychology validating the essential mental health of British political culture and national character, and we see it also mobilised to support the defence of these virtues in post-war national and international reconstruction. However, influence depended to a considerable extent on the circumstances of the crisis itself, and thus was always liable to dissipate. Neither did longer-term academic developments help, with psychology turning to science and increasingly cautious about values, and sociology advancing as the pre-eminent discipline of the social. Moreover, such a psychology was always was far more successful in ideological rather than practical terms. When it came to the latter, as in the management of morale on the home front, and as indeed was evident in early chapters on work and health, deep suspicions remained and more pragmatic behaviourist, statistical, and physically orientated types of psychology often found favour instead.

Whether this story of the encounter between psychological and democratic subjectivity at the level of statecraft had any profound influence on the more silent currents of popular opinion is doubtful. Here, there was still a mix of practical psychology, religious and mystical strains of psychology, and an increasingly psychoanalytic strain, albeit translated into a popular idiom and in accommodation with existing values. The mix may have shifted towards the latter strain, but as the first chapters of this book showed this was already taking place. Like the First World War, then, the Second was not central when it came to popular thought and practice. Here, the idea that human nature was a problem for the nation remained of less pressing interest than the more personal problems but also the opportunities of everyday life. Here, too, gloomy prognosis of mental collapse and an inherent crisis of human nature within modern civilisation met a reality of widespread psychological resilience. However, such an experience did further embed democratic values and an increasing interest in the everyday in the psychology that came down from above, and this did accelerate a process of popular psychology increasingly being something that depended on the view of the expert.

8

Towards the Permissive Society

At the heart of this chapter is the relationship between psychology and the emergence of a more permissive postwar society. There are several reasons for believing that taking the narrative into this period offers a more satisfactory end than that other obvious juncture of 1945. First, for all the talk of war as a force for social change, recent historians have become increasingly inclined to emphasise limitations and continuities, even to regard the Britain that emerged out of war as still in many respects a very Victorian society.[1] This book provides a picture of Britain's relationship with psychology that largely supports such an interpretation. It has been a story in which the individual's relationship to the social, the spiritual, and the moral was profoundly important if not central, and in which self-overcoming, rather than an inward-looking search for authenticity, tended to be an ideal. In the Second World War, in particular, psychology had come to the fore as a profoundly ethical and social subject. The emergence of a permissive society, on the other hand, has been associated with a heightened individualism, free from social, spiritual, and moral shackles, embracing emotion and individual desire rather than suppressing it and aiming beyond. Psychology, particularly the popularisation of a psychotherapeutic psychology, has taken much of the blame. Though this critique has concentrated on the United States, Britain has not been immune and a recent book has taken to task the British 'therapeutic culture' of the last quarter of the century in much the same way.[2] This chapter will examine the extent to which one psychological culture was making way for another in the 1960s and 1970s. However, it will also highlight the presence of streams of psychological thought and practice that in their social and political orientation in some respects echoed earlier developments and reacted against some of the very things they are supposed to have fostered. Thus, from this perspective, it will recast the permissive moment as one of contradictory strains, a more complex period of transition than the cliché of social and cultural revolution that it has become. Though this period was undoubtedly an important staging post, the expansion of an individualistic therapeutic culture was something that would be more a phenomenon of the final two decades of the century. In the 1960s and 1970s, psychology was in no position

---

[1] On limits to change: R. McKibbin, *Classes and Cultures in England, 1918–1951* (Oxford, 1998), 533–6. On periodisation: Harris, *Private Lives, Public Spirit*, 252–3.
[2] F. Furedi, *Therapy Culture: Cultivating Vulnerability in an Uncertain Age* (London, 2004).

to act as midwife for such cultural change. It did align itself with premissiveness but from two radically different ideological and theoretical perspectives. This chapter explores both sides of the story.

PSYCHOLOGY AND THE POST-WAR CONSENSUS

Until relatively recently, historians have tended to accept that Britain emerged from the Second World War with a new politics of consensus, left and right meeting over the centre-ground of a welfare state and Keynesian economics.[3] That consensus fell apart with the end of the post-war economic boom in the mid-1970s and the ascendancy of a free-market right in the 1980s, and in response historians tended to become more alert to the tensions and divisions that in fact ran throughout the period.[4] Similar problems would emerge in extending the model to psychology. In some ways, consensus would be highly appropriate. In a mirror image of the acceptance of carefully limited social and economic interventionism, the Britain that emerged from war, having seen the effects of an unregulated human nature, was one that also embraced limited psychological interventionism. Psychology, as a result, came in from the margins. Less a voice for a psychological imagining of what might be, it was rather to become embroiled in the day-to-day problems of managing psychological subjectivity within complex systems like the National Health Service, the state education system, and large companies. In the taming of ambition, there is a parallel to what some would see as the story of a socialism shackled by the consensus. On the other hand, just as historians now highlight the tensions that actually existed over the new social and economic interventionism, it is possible to trace a parallel series of critiques emerging about psychology's role.[5] Not only was there division over the necessity or degree of psychological intervention, but increasingly the psychodynamic psychology of instincts and drives in need of control and cultivation encountered a challenge from biological and behaviourist models that in focusing on the individual rather than the social and ethical looked to a very different type of intervention.

Thus, although the post-war decades would see an expansion of psychology's role in the daily business of an increasingly complex welfare system, this hides some underlying weaknesses. Chapters on education, medicine, work, and war

---

[3] Here the contrast with the interwar era was crucial: P. Addison, *The Road to 1945: British Politics and the Second World War* (London, 1975).

[4] Reviewing the problem, for instance: B. Pimlott, 'The Myth of Consensus', in L. M. Smith (ed.), *The Making of Britain: Echoes of Greatness* (London, 1988); and D. Kavanagh, 'The Postwar Consensus', *Twentieth Century British History*, 3 (1992), 175–90. For signs that the further political shifts at the end of the century could encourage a revival of the interest in consensus, albeit one reframed with an institutional emphasis: B. Harrison, 'The Rise, Fall, and Rise of Political Consensus in Britain since 1940', *History*, 84 (1999), 301–24.

[5] For instance, in the case of the health service: C. Webster, 'Conflict and Consensus: Explaining the British Health Service', *Twentieth Century British History*, 1 (1990), 115–51.

have already looked forward beyond 1945 to some of these difficulties. Here, those relating to the key area of health and education will be further developed, before moving on to consider contemporary criticism of psychology's moral project and the emergence of a new sort of psychology in its place.

Within health care, psychology faced two fundamental material problems: firstly, limited funding within an overwhelmed National Health Service acted as a strong disincentive to the encouragement of any policy that might bring forth an untapped reservoir of psychological ailments; secondly, there was a severe deficit of the necessary specialists. Unless you were rich, it was still a struggle to find such a service, with an estimated 400 psychotherapists in Britain by 1960, expanding only slowly to 550 by 1976, many of these in the private sector. By far the most rapid expansion only began after this date, with 5,500 registered psychotherapists by 1999.[6]

In the post-war years, a medicine of psychological subjectivity now also met its first serious challenge from a psychiatry that reframed such subjectivity in biological terms and in the new psychotropic drugs appeared to have a powerful and readily disseminated tool to offer results. In years to come, though interest and activity in psychotherapy would grow—often outside the medical profession itself—an increasingly assertive biological approach, supported by the medical and scientific establishment, would emerge alongside it. In that sense, the central period covered in this book can be seen as something of an interlude in which science was freed from biology to think psychologically about its subject and in doing so came together with a popular audience also more inclined in this direction. Already in the decades after the Second World War, there were signs that this particular meeting of minds between science and its public was breaking down. There was no reason why another, centred on the attractions of the wonder drug might not go some way in filling its place. After all, it could be seen as absolving the individual of responsibility in a way that much psychotherapy did not. Indeed, the ongoing popularity of pills and potions for nerves throughout the period indicates a reservoir of popular demand. Now medicine, with the authority of science behind it, could capture this market. Relieved general practitioners found the drugs something of a panacea for those intractable problems that they encountered on an everyday basis and recognised as psychological but found themselves ill-equipped to solve through lengthy psychotherapy. Drugs, such as Librium, introduced in 1960, Valium from 1963, and Mogadon from 1965, offered new hope to patients and doctors alike. By the end of the 1960s, general practitioners alone were handing out 17.2 million prescriptions—some 350 million tablets—each year.[7]

[6] P. Halmos, *The Faith of the Counsellors*, 2nd edn. (London, 1981), 46; Furedi, *Therapy Culture*, 10.

[7] D. Widgery, 'Valium', *Spare Rib* (1976), 44–5. In 2002 the figure had fallen to 12.7 million GP prescriptions (from 15.8 million in 1992). However, 30% were for 56 tablets or more suggesting a high number under long-term treatment: 'Cut Down on Tranquilliser Prescriptions, GPs Warned', *Guardian*, (11 Feb. 2004).

If extending the role of managing the psychological subject to the family doctor was one way of overcoming the lack of specialist resources, another was to use social work as an auxiliary psychological service. Here, a psychological component became part of the profession's generic training and not just the preserve of the elite psychiatric social worker.[8] At the start of the 1950s, there had been little more than a handful of social workers with psychological training; by 1978, there were nearly 10,000.[9] However, in its dilution of psychological expertise, and in its emerging disquiet about the politics of psychology's focus on the personal to the detriment of the social, even this area of advance highlights some fundamental weaknesses. In the interwar period, psychology, with its demands for training, had played a key role in advancing the professional status of the social worker. However, in the process it had proved somewhat self-limiting. The psychiatric social worker emerged as the elite within the broader profession, but a small one because of the severe demands and the relatively low rewards of still being in a subservient role to the psychologist and psychiatrist. In the longer term, such tensions fostered a critique of psychological management from within. Searching for a way to make their own contribution distinctive, they returned to emphasising their superior expertise in tackling the social dimensions of a problem and their qualities compared to the other professions when it came to dealing with people on a personal level. In doing so, they forged a less authoritarian style. Psychology turned into a tool for seeing problems from the perspective of the client, and for becoming critically aware of the professionals' own reactions and prejudices.[10] More alert to the circumstances and views of their clients than the other professions, social workers could become critical of the favoured psychoanalytic approach for paying too little attention to differences of understanding when it came to their working-class clients. They also began to recognise that perhaps the most crucial role was to help such clients in the struggle for access to resources within a complex welfare system. In short, they came to view the problems of their clients as political rather than just personal.[11] The return of a concern about poverty, albeit in the relative terms set out by the influential sociological research of figures like Peter Townsend, encouraged this.[12] Indeed, the rising prominence and status of the study of sociology and social administration in training programmes now challenged the primacy of psychology. In such circumstances, the psychological approach began to be criticised for privatising social and political issues.[13]

When it came to education and child-rearing—in many ways, the most significant area of psychological influence in the first half of the century—the post-war decades again saw a further integration of such ideas into the mainstream, yet at

[8] The important training programme at the London School of Economics initiated this shift in 1954, though specialist training for psychiatric social workers persisted until 1970: M. Yelloly, *Social Work and Psychoanalysis* (New York, 1980), 86, 115.

[9] Younghusband, *Social Work in Britain*, 1, p. 34.

[10] Yelloly, *Social Work and Psychoanalysis* (New York, 1980), 97–100.

[11] J. Mayer and N. Timms, *The Client Speaks: Working Class Impressions of Casework* (London, 1970).   [12] Younghusband, *Social Work in Britain*, 1, pp. 27–35.

[13] Yelloly, *Social Work and Psychoanalysis*, 114–16.

the same time a dilution of their radical origins and a loss of confidence in the face of an emerging critique. In this area of its influence, perhaps more loudly than in any other, psychology would find itself accused of fostering the permissiveness that critics believed was now eating away at the moral fabric of British society. Such a critique is evident in the 'Black Papers' assault on progressive education at the end of the 1960s and in the early 1970s.[14] A. E. Dyson, who edited the series alongside fellow don C. B. Cox, condemned the seepage into education of a psychotherapeutic culture for encouraging a relativist mire of self-expression that pandered to irrationalism. Education, as a result, was neglecting its proper responsibilities in actively instilling values to guide future citizens, leaving children confused and increasingly disturbed. Rather than fostering mental health, the 'romantic concentration upon the self' simply exacerbated neurosis and unhappiness:

... the breakdowns which often seem to be a symptom of shapeless and irrational free-doms too completely indulged, are treated with little recourse to traditional good sense. Disturbed students are directed into still more labyrinthine ways of self-analysis, with few classical or moral yardsticks to help. The rational ideals and disciplines which education must build upon are missing and so of course is will-power: the modern 'self' is at once too sacred and too shattered to be pulled together in old-fashioned ways.[15]

The immediate context for the 'Black Papers' assault was the student unrest of 1968: diagnosed as the rotten fruit of an education system that rejected values for self-expression and whose roots went back to the entry of the 'fun morality' of the post-war childcare expert into the private space of the home. Brian Simon, the left-wing educationalist, pointed out that there was a fundamental flaw in the timing of such a theory. The students of 1968 were, in fact, largely the products of that very hierarchical, traditional system of education that the critics now looked back upon so nostalgically; the more radical changes of the last decade, such as the spread of a comprehensive system at the secondary level, would only begin to bear fruit in the decades to come.[16] Simon may have had a good case when it came to secondary education, though he was on less firm ground when it came to minimising the influence of progressivism at the primary level. A firm believer in the primacy of the socio-economic rather than the personal, he was unsympathetic to the role that psychology might play in the reform of education, and as such his outright dismissal of its influence might be regarded with a degree of caution. He did have the weight of the Government's 1967 Plowden Report on teaching within primary schools behind him on the matter: the Report concluded that radical change had taken place in only 10 per cent of state schools.[17] Yet this was still arguably a striking achievement. Moreover, the authors of the report were acutely conscious of contemporary criticism of liberal education and this may have

[14] Wooldridge, *Measuring the Mind*, 384–93.
[15] A. E. Dyson, 'The Sleep of Reason', in C. B. Cox and A. E. Dyson (eds.), *The Black Papers on Education* (London, 1971), 86.   [16] Simon, *Education and the Social Order*, 374–80.
[17] Ibid. 381.

encouraged them to downplay its real influence, preferring to emphasise better understanding of the child rather than the theory that lay behind this.[18] 'Radical change' may have been confined to just 10 per cent of schools, but reading beyond this cautious headline figure it is clear that there had been a substantial move towards placing the child's interests at the heart of the educational process, and this is particularly apparent in the description of teaching in particular subjects such as English or Mathematics.[19] One finds the same pattern in a report from advocates of progressivism published two years earlier: just 5 per cent of primary schools were 'truly' permissive, but a further 45 per cent had moved visibly in a progressive direction, while at least 80 per cent showed the influence in particular areas of the curriculum like art.[20]

Bearing in mind the influence that psychology was already having on pedagogy in the interwar period, this presence should come as no surprise.[21] After the Second World War, with the extension of secondary education for all, and the number of trained teachers rising from 30,000 in 1958, to 107,000 in 1970, psychology had the opportunity to spread its influence considerably further.[22] From the perspective of the 1960s advocacy of progressivism, this advance may have seemed disappointing, but this was partly because expectations in such a situation had been so great. In fact, this would be a key period for the flow of progressive ideas into the secondary system, with the new Secondary Modern Schools still relatively free to experiment, not yet shackled by pressure for results in external examinations, and invigorated by an influx of newly trained teachers under the influence of progressive textbooks. The designation of these schools as sites for 'concrete' learning, as opposed to the more academic learning of the grammar schools, tends to be criticised for its dismissal of the potential of a huge segment of the population. In fact, it also echoed the sentiments of the psychological progressivism of learning by doing and suggested that this would be an ideal home for such an approach. However, the idealism of progressive pedagogy would struggle to survive when faced by the practical problems of teaching in these schools. It soon became clear that cultural deprivation was invariably a more important impediment to progress than mere educational technique. And as the Secondary Moderns struggled for status in what soon came to be recognised as a hierarchical, rather than tripartite system, they responded to pressure, not only from parents more interested in results than creativity, but from children increasingly driven by the demand for educational qualifications as a passport in the world of work, and from teachers keen to advance themselves professionally by escaping the ghetto of low scholastic expectations. Inevitably, they became more traditionally academic and examination-orientated.[23]

---

[18] Department of Education and Science, *Children and the Primary Schools. A Report of the Central Advisory Council of Education (England)*, 1 (London, 1967), 266–7.   [19] Ibid. 218–35.
[20] Boyd and Rawson, *The Story of the New Education*, 185–6.   [21] See Ch. 4.
[22] Simon, *Education and the Social Order*, 374.
[23] W. Taylor, *The Secondary Modern School* (London, 1963), 90–4, 140–2, 161.

For those who had looked to change the world through progressive pedagogy, the post-war situation was a huge disappointment. Dora Russell lamented the way that progressivism had been swamped by the demands of modern technological and industrial society to turn out results rather than human beings.[24] Nevertheless, she now found herself in the position of having to dismiss the idea that psychology was to blame for a generation of delinquents who even had the audacity to exploit the language of psychology to excuse their own behaviour.[25] A. S. Neill, still headmaster at Summerhill, was equally pessimistic about the future for the progressive approach, seeing 'signs of stagnation, even of retrogression'. He now questioned whether the intense hopes surrounding psychology had been justified.[26] Greater freedom, rather than any psychological therapy, had always been the real key to unlocking the potential of the child. 'We were so naïve', he reflected. 'Make the unconscious conscious and the world will be a Utopia without greed and hate and crime and war. So we kept being dug into and digging into others. We never paused to think that many important people had never had analysis.'[27] Expansion of progressivism within the independent sector, in stark contrast to growth after the First World War, had also come to a halt. Some of the schools closed; others became more orthodox. In the immediate aftermath of war, there was a brief flurry of anxiety about the need to foster freedom of the individual as a counter to authoritarianism, but within an increasingly meritocratic society the priorities of progressive middle-class parents were firmly fixed on schooling that offered the best academic results.[28]

In sum, much of what happened in the advance of psychology's influence within post-war education was a continuation, albeit taking advantage of new opportunities such as the expansion of the secondary system, of something that had already been set in place. However, earlier pioneering enthusiasm and utopianism had faded. Struggling to maintain its influence both in the face of escalating pressures for academic results and the challenge of sociology to its primacy as an inspiration, psychology and its progressive pedagogy was certainly far from the triumphant position of the Black Papers mythology. At the primary level, and within the progressive independent sector, development had been more remarkable in the first four decades of the century. If progressive education really did lead to permissiveness, one might ask why this had not happened much earlier. Of course, 'Spockism in child-rearing' shared the blame as far as the critics were concerned.[29] Again, however, this assumes too sharp a contrast between psychology fostering a disciplinary approach before the war and a permissive one after it.[30] In fact, the 'fun-morality' reflected, far more than it shaped, the culture of its time, and there was in practice often a huge gulf between the strictures of advice and reality within the home.[31]

---

[24] D. Russell, *The Tamarisk Tree*, 2 (London, 1980), 202–5.   [25] Ibid. 201.
[26] A. S. Neill, *Summerhill* (London, 1971), 10.
[27] A. S. Neill, *'Neill!, Neill! Orange Peel': A Personal View of Ninety Years* (London, 1972), 210.
[28] Boyd and Rawson, *The Story of the New Education*, 113–38.   [29] *Black Papers*, 14, 94.
[30] See pp. 136–8.
[31] J. and E. Newson, 'Cultural Aspects of Childrearing in the English Speaking World', in M. Richards (ed.), *The Integration of a Child into a Social World* (Cambridge, 1974), 53–82.

THE POPULAR PSYCHOLOGY OF
PERMISSIVENESS REFRAMED

At the heart of criticism about psychology's role in the rearing and education of children was the idea that it undermined values. What such criticism often failed to recognise was that psychological permissiveness invariably rested on its own very clear sense of liberal-democratic values. Barbara Wootton would recognise this in her critique of the way that the mental health professions were extending their own values and mental diagnoses into what had previously been, and should rightly remain in her view, the territory of legal judgement.[32] From a different ideological stance, anti-psychiatry and its followers would echo this critique of the value-laden nature of a concept such as mental health.[33] Yet in 1964, one of the first serious British accounts of 'permissiveness' would suggest that 'the psychiatrists' were playing an important role in fostering open-mindedness, undermining moral traditions, and turning people inwards. In particular, these experts offered scientific support for the new diffidence in disciplining children, criminals, and sexual behaviour, shifts that were coming to symbolise and indeed were fostering a more general transformation of human morality.[34] Likewise in its 1969 enquiry into the permissive society, the *Guardian* included Freud and Spock in a list of seventeen 'Priests and Prophets of Permissiveness', described R. D. Laing as the 'Psychiatrist of Liberation', and agreed that a progressive pedagogy was at the very root of the new permissiveness.[35]

Such contemporary commentary on the relationship between permissiveness and psychology in fact brought together some very different types of thought and practice. The obvious temptation is to assume that a rejection of values was lead by the counter-cultural vanguard. The second half of the chapter will raise some problems with this assumption. Here it turns to four examples from the other side of the cultural barricades of the era. This is important for two reasons. First, it was on this side that a more silent majority, and thus perhaps the more popular psychology of the era, still lay, and we need reminding of this. Secondly, we cannot fully appreciate any relationship between psychology and permissiveness without looking across what was by this time a broad and contested terrain of psychological thinking. Ironically, it is on this other side of the barricades that we find a retreat from values at its clearest.

---

[32] B. Wootton, *Social Science and Social Pathology* (London, 1959).

[33] For introductions to anti-psychiatry in Britain: A. Clare, *Psychiatry in Dissent* (London, 1976); P. Sedgwick, *Psycho-Politics: Laing, Foucault, Goffman, Szasz and the Future of Mass Psychiatry* (London, 1982). For later reflections and the impact on historiography: M. Gijswijt-Hofstra and R. Porter (eds.), *Cultures of Psychiatry and Mental Health Care in Post-war Britain and the Netherlands* (Amsterdam, 1998).

[34] C. H. and W. Whiteley, *The Permissive Morality* (London, 1964), 11–13, 48–68. This supports the theory of sociologist Christie Davies that permissiveness in Britain centred on a shift from 'moralism' to 'causalism': *Permissive Britain: Social Change in the Sixties and Seventies* (London, 1975). Davies, though, did not discuss the role of psychology.

[35] The *Guardian* Enquiry, *The Permissive Society* (London, 1969), 9, 3–6, 47–50, 58.

An unshackling of psychology from values is evident when we turn to the man who emerged as Britain's best-known psychologist of the era: Hans Eysenck. Though his populism and controversial style would irritate others within the profession, it represented an attempt to assert the appeal of a psychology of science over that of meaning and mysticism that had so engaged the public in the past. Psychoanalysis and its offspring would fall in the latter camp, with Eysenck doing his utmost to undermine its reputation.[36] He would be an almost constant presence through appearances in the press, radio, and television.[37] He also reached out to a huge audience in a trilogy of essay collections, published by Penguin. The titles cut to the heart of his mission to clean up popular understanding: *Uses and Abuses of Psychology* (1953); *Sense and Nonsense in Psychology* (1957); and *Fact and Fiction in Psychology* (1964). Each went into multiple editions, and Eysenck claimed that total sales were in the millions.[38] In the 1960s, another popular Penguin series would provide scientific guidance for an audience apparently eager to test its own intelligence, drawing on a television series on the same theme for which he had designed the IQ tests.[39] Further popular publications would follow in the 1970s and the early 1980s.[40] One of the things that distinguished this so clearly from the popular psychology of the interwar era was that it drew such a fundamental line between 'sense and nonsense'. Eysenck was scathing about popular understanding and on a mission to reform it rather than reach out and engage with it. Though he continued to lament the public ambivalence about what psychologists did, suggesting that they still preferred to turn for their psychological advice to a motley assembly of populist philosophers and 'unspecified dons of ancient vintage', the very popularity of his own work in fact suggests that a shift in relationship between the popular and the professional was under way.[41] If so, it also heralded a shift in taste with strikingly permissive implications.

Eysenck's was a psychology that rejected any spiritual or ethical pretensions. In his view, it could offer no guidance to the good life. It was a science. It offered facts about behaviour, not values. In the mid-century crisis, psychology had overreached itself becoming embroiled in a pseudo-scientific attempt to offer itself as a secular guide to salvation. The danger of crossing such a boundary was now evident in criticism of science for its association with the atom bomb. The scientist, he believed, should not have to worry about the potential political or ethical implications of what was a truth, and he seems to have borne a desperate compulsion to prove this in relation to psychology in his own career.

[36] For instance, H. Eysenck, *The Effects of Psychotherapy* (New York, 1966); H. Eysenck and G. Wilson, *The Experimental Study of Freudian Theories* (London, 1973).
[37] H. Eysenck, *Rebel with a Cause*, 165–6.   [38] Ibid. 163–5.
[39] *Know your Own IQ* (London, 1962); *Test your own IQ* (London, 1964); *Check your own IQ* (London, 1966). On the background: Eysenck, *Rebel with a Cause*, 166–7.
[40] For instance, *Psychology is about People* (London, 1972); (with G. D. Wilson), *Know your own Personality* (London, 1975); *You and Neurosis* (London, 1977); (with M. Eysenck), *Mindwatching* (London, 1981); *Decline and Fall of the Freudian Empire* (London, 1985). For a full bibliography: Eysenck, *Rebel with a Cause*, 292–8.   [41] Eysenck, *Sense and Nonsense in Psychology*, 11–13.

The permissive character of Eysenckian psychology also has something to do with the style in which it was delivered. In a deeply personal sense—both as a believer in the theory of personality types, and as an émigré from authoritarianism—Eysenck saw himself as being the one on the permissive side of any cultural barricade. Coming into a stuffy British profession dominated by an older generation of men like Cyril Burt who maintained strict formality in personal relations, this handsome son of a film-star mother and stage-actor father, who presented himself as an anti-authoritarian exile from Nazi Germany, on first-name terms with his students and often far more intimate with a coterie of attractive young women which included his second wife-to-be, the 'Monroe-like' Sybil, and with a compulsion to rebel against out-dated convention, whether in social life, or in a psychology still infatuated with a psychoanalysis that had never been supported by proper scientific evidence, Eysenck styled himself as a 'rebel with a cause'. Before his departure from Germany in 1934, he claimed to have been something of a wild youth, defending Jewish schoolmates against the Hitler Youth and coming into conflict with the Nazis; though his critics always found it easier to imagine his Aryan looks and politics in the other camp. In his academic career, he would appear almost pathological in the way that he looked for fights with authority figures and with whatever was the orthodoxy of the day; typically, he refused to discount the possibility that there was a scientific basis for extrasensory perception or even astrology. In his private life, he embraced the modern. He loved what he would recall as the Cinerama-like abundance of America, in contrast to the black and white of Britain's post-war austerity.[42] He became a keen jitterbugger and jiver. He maintained a youthful enthusiasm for playing sport, especially tennis, at which he excelled, and in football would follow Chelsea, West Ham, Crystal Palace, and eventually Manchester United, revealing a characteristic taste for the flamboyant and fashionable, rather than any tribal loyalty. And he was open and enthusiastic in his attitude regarding sex.[43] The popularity of his writing would be greatly assisted by the fact that he was so at ease with the popular culture of his time and so ready to engage with it. It would be impossible to name a comparable figure for the interwar era. Eysenckian psychology, then, was not only to be scientific and value free, but it was also willing to be fun; the latter quality, just as much as the former, marked it out from the ethical earnestness of the past.

Politically, despite becoming something of a bête noire to the left, Eysenck had arrived in Britain with leftist sympathies. Indeed, his main early reading would come from the *New Statesman* and the Left Book Club. This soon dimmed. This was partly a case of a falling out with the left over his psychological ideas. They were offended, initially by his claim that ideological affiliation was a matter of personality more than values, with much therefore in common between far left and far right, and then by his emergence as a figurehead for the increasingly controversial hereditarianism of IQ theory. The political shift also however reflected Eysenck's

42 Eysenck, *Rebel with a Cause*, 120–1.
43 Ibid. H. B. Gibson, *Hans Eysenck: The Man and his Work* (London, 1981), 105–6.

own disenchantment, for instance through his experience of comprehensive schools and union power in the 1970s. His sympathies turned towards what he described as 'civilised anarchy'; he might have used the word permissiveness.[44]

As if in some psychological equation, the personality of the psychologist and his belief in a psychology of facts, not values, added up to research whose implications invariably pointed in a permissive direction; a result which suggests how spurious the idea of value-free psychology really was. It was not only the findings that had a permissive character, but also the subject matter that he chose to investigate: for instance, the causes and effects of smoking, the relationship between crime and personality, and the effects on behaviour of violence and sex on television and film. As often as not, what he had to say would set the authority of science against attempts to hold back a loosening of moralism.

Typical of this was his position on smoking. Backed, notoriously, by the funds of the tobacco industry, he would spend considerable energy arguing that a causal relation between smoking and cancer had not yet been proven. In the absence of definitive clinical proof, it rested on epidemiology alone. In Eysenck's opinion, the statistical reasoning of such epidemiology was seriously flawed. But there is a clear sense that what he objected to most of all was the pathologisation of what was an act of individual choice. He attacked, for instance, the way that smoking was coming to be seen as a psychological 'addiction'. The term—now so widely and variously used that it was becoming meaningless—completely overlooked the importance of individual psychology. Eysenck himself had been a keen smoker since boyhood but had given up with little problem when he realised that it reduced his stamina playing tennis: he preferred tennis to smoking, so that was that. The question, like so many others of its nature needed to be turned around: why did people like smoking? The reorientation towards a psychological calculus of pleasure, rather than approaching individual behaviour in terms of problems of adjustment to a normality based on assumed moral standards, is typical of the essentially permissive nature of the Eysenckian outlook.

The same was true when it came to issues like crime or sexual orientation. Such behaviour was not going to be erased by the threat or actuality of punishment; it was not simply the fault of individual 'maladjustment'. But neither did he accept the determinism that rooted something such as sexual behaviour in innate instinct. Environment did shape behaviour. The permissive society, like an extraverted personality, had chosen to encourage certain forms of behaviour. For instance, within 'biological limit', it had 'chosen to maximise sexual arousal'. So although he accepted that media depictions of sex, like those of violence, did influence the behaviour of viewers, he avoided moralising about it. Pornography did change people: that was a psychological fact. Whether this was a good or a bad thing was a matter of opinion, not psychology.[45] This was a psychology, in sum, that

---

[44] Eysenck, *Rebel with a Cause*, 23, 46, 191–2, 270–1; Gibson, *Hans Eysenck*, 239. The remark comes from 1979.

[45] Eysenck, 'The Uses and Abuses of Pornography', in *Psychology is about People*, 236–86.

highlighted the dilemma of balancing individual freedom and social good that lay at the heart of the permissive debate; but apart from an insistence, largely in vain, that the psychologist should be to the fore in offering advice on such matters, it did not proffer ideal solutions, and it moved away from that mapping of mental health onto a language of right and wrong that had been such a tendency with the psychological culture of the first half of the century.

To highlight the permissive qualities of an Eysenckian psychology is also to highlight something of an irony. For Eysenck would come to be a prime object of attack by the 1970s from groups who saw themselves as supporters of permissivism, but who objected, both to the facts about behaviour so provocatively aired by Eysenck, and to his assault on a more humanist, ethical psychology as unscientific, and his support for behaviourism in its place. He would find himself subjected to public pillory, even blamed for the war in Vietnam, by what he regarded as a 'drug-induced' audience when invited to debate the merits of behaviour therapy with anti-psychiatry guru David Cooper.[46] And in 1972 and 1973, he encountered student and left-wing protests when he spoke at the universities of Birmingham, Leicester, and the London School of Economics, the last event in particular attracting national attention, and he found himself banned from speaking at events organised by the National Union of Students.[47] Indeed, to a certain extent, the existence of an Eysenckian psychology would be an important spur—as something to identify against—in bringing to the fore the type of counter-cultural, radical psychology of the 1970s that one might more obviously associate with the permissive society, and this point will be amplified in due course. Eysenck, however, would claim that the majority of students were in fact 'utterly indifferent' to his ideas.[48] He revelled in the irony of the protest painted across the front walls of Birmingham University: 'Fascist Eysenck has no Right to Speak! Uphold Genuine Academic Freedom'.[49] Who, here, was the real permissive, who following in fascist footsteps? As this suggests, and the same would be true when it comes to our broader understanding of the permissive moment, we need to be wary about assuming that the counter-cultural minority either stood for the whole or represented what was the most significant permissive shift of the era: in both instances, the changing tastes and individualist, de-moralised appetites of a more silent majority may in the long term have been even more significant.

In the 1950s, the independent and unorthodox style of the early-twentieth-century practical psychology culture appears to have fallen into abeyance. A popular psychology remained, but it was far more likely to relay the findings of professional psychology than offer up its own version, and it tended to dwell on

---

[46] Eysenck, *Rebel with a Cause*, 189–90.

[47] See coverage of the LSE protest in *The Times*: 9–11, 14, 16, 17, 18, 28 May 1973.

[48] Gibson, *Hans Eysenck*, 238.

[49] In Gibson's highly sympathetic biography the syntax is different with the effect of emphasising illogicality; 'Uphold Genuine Academic Freedom: Fascist Eysenck has no Right to Speak': *Hans Eysenck*, 217–18. The syntax in the text follows the photographs reproduced in Eysenck's autobiography: *Rebel with a Cause*, 152–3.

the lifestyle of the individual, rather than look towards the individual's relationship to a greater social or spiritual whole: it had been tamed. The trend was already becoming apparent towards the end of the interwar era, for instance in the popular magazine *Psychology* published in Britain from 1937 following a glossy, individualist model already successful in the United States, which was soon claiming a readership of 100,000.[50] Such a publication would find itself well placed to make the transition to post-war affluence, whereas much of the more spiritually orientated and actively practical literature fell away. In the mid-1960s it was renamed *Psychology and Successful Living*, the shift indicative of its main orientation. There would be occasional sorties to address wider concerns. For instance, in 1965, the editor would tie the paradox of absence of peace of mind in an 'age of plenty' to the ever-present threat of the atomic bomb and the pace of the 'machine age'. However, this would be framed in narrowly individualist terms: there was no paean to the role of psychology in fostering a more peaceful humanity; instead, the focus was the resulting anxieties of the age and how best to cope—the problem of lack of sleep and the mounting reliance on sleeping pills was a regular theme.[51] A year later, he was lamely addressing the broader world through the epithet of the 'age of security' and worrying that in such circumstances true individualism was in danger of dying out.[52] This was ironic: with its endless advice about avoiding the traps and pitfalls of emotional life, a magazine like this can only have further fostered such a claustrophobic security. Its offer of true individualism—of standing out from the crowd through the cultivation of personality—was essentially inward-looking and narcissistic in its appeal. The increasing attention given to the beautiful and the sexual body was the physical counterpart of this, and again contrasts with the far more politicised appeal of vegetarianism, yoga, clothing reform, and breathing exercises that filled popular psychological journals in the first decades of the century.

Psychology Today, which began publication in Britain in 1975, represents a rather different but equally significant shift. Though it appropriated the well-established populist strategy of applying psychological knowledge to the problems of everyday life, the aim of 'creating a better you' was largely set aside and in its place there emerged a reasonably serious attempt to inform the public about recent developments within psychological science.[53] C. P. Snow, the voice of the establishment's anxiety about a distancing of science from the public, welcomed it as a 'shake up' in this respect.[54] Part of its appeal still rested on its provision of

---

[50] *Psychology* (June, 1937), 5. Henry Knight Miller brought this influence from the United States: 'The Man of the Moment', *Psychology* (Feb., 1939), 4–5; J. Crowell, 'Henry Knight Miller: Apostle of the School of Courage', *Psychology*, (Feb., 1939), 19–21.

[51] Editorial, *Psychology* (April, 1965), 5. The problem of sleep was a regular issue.

[52] 'This Age of Security', *Psychology and Successful Living* (April, 1966), 5.

[53] The full title indicates the desire to embrace the reader's everyday world but also broader educational horizons: *Psychology Today: About Human Experience, Society and You*. It followed its namesake established by psychologists in the United States.

[54] Letter, *Psychology Today*, 1 (May, 1975), 6.

insights for self-development. To some extent the journal deliberately exploited this, with a scattering of articles and advertisements that appealed to this market, and an opening editorial that promised that it would guide readers on a path to better understanding of self and others; though such a project was now recast in a scientific idiom, with life turning into 'a lived-in psychological experiment'.[55] However, it also had to satisfy the academics who used it as a forum for disseminating their ideas to an educated audience and were inherently suspicious of 'D.I.Y.' populism. Indeed, the journal promoted its ability to offer a direct line of communication, 'without middle men to blur the facts'; in doing so, publicly identifying itself against the amateurism of popular psychology in the past. There would be 'no articles on how to become happy in fourteen days'.[56] The new relationship with the professionals was not the only factor behind this reorientation; it was also the type of psychology now promoted. The psychodynamic and psychotherapeutic was not wholly absent, but it took a back seat. In the foreground, instead, was the psychology of brain and behaviour, biofeedback and IQ. It should come as no surprise to see Eysenck as a contributor. The style and content mirrored his own: science for the masses, which aimed to be serious yet fun and slightly racy, and which did not preach from any pulpit. The independence and the ethical and spiritual ambition of an earlier popular and practical psychology had disappeared. An article on the 'Sixth Form Psychologist'—Advanced Level study in the subject now on general offer in schools after a period of experiment since 1972—emphasises how far things had changed: the extent to which psychology had become a different sort of knowledge.[57]

The evolution of Mensa, the group for people of high intelligence set up in Britain in the aftermath of the War, provides a final fresh perspective to consider the relationship between psychology, the popular, and the permissive. The idea went back to a broadcast talk by Cyril Burt in 1945. Speaking in a series on industrial psychology, he had provided an account of utopian visions and had ended with this one of his own, a kind of cross between the BBC's *Brain's Trust* and the Gallup Poll. As explored earlier, there had been considerable wartime interest in using the tool of the opinion survey as a way to improve democracy, with psychologists presenting their qualities as experts to interpret this material.[58] Burt's was a vision which cut out the ignorant or irrational mass and looked to use the expertise of psychology instead in selecting out those equipped with superior intelligence as a panel—the Latin term *Mensa* suggested a roundtable—to guide national policy. The proposal was attacked, not only as outlandish, but as anti-democratic. Burt's defence was that there was nothing inherently undemocratic about a scheme that though based on intelligence was also in his view one founded on equality of opportunity.[59]

[55] 'The Puzzle and the Pleasure', *Psychology Today*, 1 (April, 1975), 4.
[56] For instance, letter from Ian Vine, Lecturer in Social Psychology, University of Bradford, *Psychology Today*, 1 (July, 1975), 6.
[57] 'Enter the Sixth Form Psychologist', *Psychology Today*, 1 (June, 1975), 10.
[58] See pp. 226–31.
[59] V. Serebriakoff, *IQ: A Mensa Analysis and History* (London, 1966), 11–21.

The real constituency for the idea was one, both frustrated by the apparently levelling tendencies of the day, and looking for a new way to advance eugenic concerns in an ideological climate that had sidelined the prevalent interwar strategies of segregating or sexually sterilising the less able. For a man such as Roland Berrill, a barrister whose attention was drawn to Burt's idea in discussion at Oxford about the merits of the opinion poll, there was a real danger that democracy might come to be dominated by a majority who were ill-informed (a very high proportion of such survey results were in the 'don't know' category) and easily swayed by emotion from rational conclusion. There was also the feeling that such an organisation might offer a way to promote the corporate and eugenic interests of people with high intelligence.[60]

Initially, Mensa had a limit on membership set at six hundred. The idea of using the organisation to provide government with a new type of public opinion was central but much of the energy was devoted to the creation of a community of intelligence. A monthly magazine was published from 1947 and there was a regularly updated register of members' interests and skills to foster networks of mutual support. The exclusive Masonic tone was capped by Berrill's idea that each member would be given an ornamental tile, decorated with the Mensa symbol of three masked figures in Ku-Klux-Klan style clothing seated at a round table, which was to be incorporated in the hearths of their homes as a secret symbol of membership.[61]

The eccentric Berrill resigned in 1952, and in the mid-1950s the society was in a state of poor health and lacked clear direction. Membership had struggled to reach 280 by 1952, and now fell to just 100 by 1956. The elitism of the initial vision had clearly been extraordinarily out of place in the post-war social climate. But a psychological movement based around intelligence did have potential now, in the way that perhaps it did not in the interwar era, if it could find a more democratic style. There had certainly been no comparable movement before the war. Concern about intelligence had found a home in the eugenics movement; a home that, as the failure of Berrill's vision indicated, was no longer viable. However, the popular psychological movements of the pre-war era had been relatively uninterested in intelligence, or had regarded it as a rather dehumanising approach to the wonders and untapped potential of the mind. Victor Serebriakoff, appointed Secretary of the society in 1956, believed that the climate was now more favourable, a focus on intelligence resonating with the upwardly mobile ambitions of the affluent society. Mensa was to create a new excitement that intelligence was 'the most human thing about a human'.[62] A working-class Russian émigré, Serebriakoff's life had been transformed when he had been tested for intelligence by British army psychologists. Astonished by his score, they had placed him in charge of a Military Education Centre. After the war, he had brought this interest into industrial management. His mission was one of

[60] V. Serebriakoff, *IQ: A Mensa Analysis and History* (London, 1966), 89.
[61] Ibid. 98.   [62] Ibid. 132.

releasing the potential of others like himself. Under Serebriakoff, Mensa was to abandon its role as an elite sect and turn evangelical. Advertisements were placed in the press to publicise the society, the limit on membership was cast aside, and the entrance qualification was lowered. By 1960, Mensa was attracting some 10,000 applications every year. By 1966, with a growth in the international following, membership had risen to 110,000.[63]

Experience had dimmed the earlier grandiose expectation that government might turn to Mensa as a kind of think tank.[64] However, the regular practice of surveying members on their views continued, with the panel idea now re-energised as it met the hunger of members for a channel of public expression that transcended normal politics and its sectarian divisions. Indeed, the pages of the society's journals were bursting with debate over the topics of the day. The mission shifted to one rescuing society from the 'abdication of the intellectual'. Rational thinking was being swamped by the nihilistic and anarchistic tendencies of the emerging beat generation on the one hand, and the dominion of market values on the other. The most intelligent members of society were either caving in to these forces and selling their ability for the purpose of mass manipulation of public opinion—the 'hidden persuaders'—or they were retreating into their shells within an increasingly anti-intellectual climate.[65] The solution to the problem of an affluent society, that had gained material comfort but in the process lost its sense of deeper ethical purpose, lay in re-engaging these lonely, neglected figures. Within a democracy, the hope was that if the intelligent were given a voice they would be able to influence the others; the worry was that mass communications gave more power to special interest groups than isolated intellectuals. Mensa now advanced itself on the basis that the future of world peace depended on creating a dialogue of the intelligent—a 'self-conscious world-wide cadre of the able'—who alone might overcome the irrationality at the heart of the Cold War.[66]

There was a part of this that echoed mid-century liberal anxieties about democracy and world peace, with psychology offering solutions, again albeit in a rather different guise. It remained difficult, however, to hide the inherent elitism. Membership may have multiplied, but this was still a sect that was predicated on exclusivity and which struggled therefore to overcome a reputation for snobbery, or at best a certain boffinish eccentricity, which left it open to ridicule in the press.[67] Worse still, there was a mounting critique of the reliability and ideological desirability of intelligence testing. Serebriakoff was humiliated before a nation of viewers, when Alan Whicker grilled him on IQ testing on the BBC's 'Tonight' programme.[68] Even Mensa members appear to have become less confident about either the accuracy of testing or the idea that the views of the intelligent minority were of that much greater value than those of the majority, or even necessarily that

---

[63] Ibid. 105–9.   [64] Ibid. 105.
[65] The term comes from Vance Packard's analysis, *The Hidden Persuaders* (London, 1957).
[66] Serebriakoff, *IQ*, 121–32.   [67] 'Vox Populi', *Mensa Correspondence*, 4 (May, 1959), 1.
[68] *Mensa Correspondence* (April, 1960), 1.

distinctive.[69] Indeed, the surveys of Mensa opinion reveal an irony: rather than evincing an 'abdication of the intellectual', retreating in horror from the levelling tendencies of mass culture, we find a community of the intelligent that was generally happy with the cultural shifts of the era, and indeed was more often at the permissive end of opinion than not. Intelligence, in fact, turned out to be largely beside the point. Saving democracy and the world through the values of the intelligent had descended into little more than a trivial pursuit: psychology had become a source of fun, perhaps a way of defining oneself, not a route to salvation.

BACK TO VALUES?

Part of the story when it comes to the post-war decades, then, is of the emergence of a popular psychology that was becoming more individualist in character, was less concerned about values, was under closer guidance from the profession, and was generally less swept up as a result in some mystical worship of the unconscious and more inclined to be open to the authority and more limited psychological horizons of intelligence testing, behavioural therapy, and drug therapy. Psychology, presented as fun and largely devoid of its earlier danger, was perhaps more available than ever before but was also less radical in its potential. With its limited ethical ambitions, it happily fitted into the increasingly permissive post-war climate.

Such development, however, does not necessarily point towards the therapeutic culture of the last decades of the century. The latter would centre on the liberation of emotion, whereas in these post-war decades, there was either continuing reticence about this or the focus turned elsewhere altogether, in particular towards interest in the machinery of mind. What follows in the second half of this chapter will be a contribution towards explaining this shift. The late 1960s and 1970s would see a reaction in radical circles against the consensual nature of the psychological culture that was emerging, a revival of the tension between the professional and the popular, and attempts to reinvigorate psychology as something with a moral or spiritual purpose. This purpose would centre on a discovery of emotional authenticity. For the radicals who were often at the forefront of such a shift, there would ultimately be a fundamental tension in reconciling the politics of the personal and the social, particularly since some of the psychological models that had served this purpose earlier in the century had lost credibility. In the long term, as these radical projects stumbled on their own contradictions, the emphasis on emotional authenticity would reveal itself a much more broadly based phenomenon, taken up within popular psychological culture, embedded in the culture of the new 'New Age', and an increasingly integral part of a confessional popular

---

[69] For instance, M. Spence, 'Can Intelligence be Measured?', *Mensa Correspondence*, 4 (May, 1959), 6–7; *Mensa Correspondence* (April, 1960), 7; *Mensa Correspondence*, 22 (Dec., 1960), 2–3.

culture.[70] This owed something to the way that psychology had made such a culture available, but more to the deeply-rooted social and economic changes that lay behind acceptance and demand.

By the 1960s, there was growing unease in Britain towards the purchase of social contentment, through affluence and a welfare state, at the expense of impoverishment when it came to ethical life. For some, a growing fascination with psychotherapy was a symptom of this problem; for others, it offered a line of critique and a way beyond. This section of the chapter will deal briefly with the first category, what we might call the diagnosticians, before moving on to those more actively involved in the response.

In his book, *The Secular Priests* of 1972, the British writer Maurice North argued that industrialisation had led to a new dichotomy between the public and private spheres and that this set up a parallel dichotomy within the individual psyche, resulting in confusion and alienation. In the post-war era, the situation had been exacerbated as the nature of employment, marketing, and the mass media led to individual isolation. In the earlier period, religion had played an ameliorating integrative role—a source of meaning and guidance for locating the private self within a larger moral community—but its influence had rapidly eroded in an era of secularisation.[71] The 'psychotherapeutic ideology' had stepped into this breach. Sceptical about its scientific basis, North readily highlighted the parallels with religious faith: it was 'actually a form of inverted transcendence, a neo-mysticism in which the "real self" is discoverable not by an ascent to heaven but by a descent into the depths with a guide'.[72] What was taking place was a 'strange reversal of the disenchantment of the world', as science turned into religion.[73] In North's view, Britain was peculiarly ripe for the spread of such a culture, since the 'therapeutic society is more of a paradigm of social thought in Britain than anywhere else in the world.'[74] Welfare-state Britain offered particularly fertile soil for a regime of counselling that shifted responsibility for fault from individuals to their upbringing, and that offered solutions through expert intervention, rather than individual action; by contrast, it had provided poor soil for the behaviourist psychology, with its emphasis on individual responsibility, which thrived in the United States.[75] The spread of such a therapeutic culture had also been fostered by the conditions of affluence and increasing consumerism which, alongside the rather desperate search for new values and moral guidance, lay behind what sociologist Peter Berger had described as a burgeoning 'private identity market'.[76] North, too, would emphasise this consumerist drive in his follow-up book, *The Mind Market*. Recognising that other post-war psychological culture explored in

[70] P. Heelas, *The New Age Movement: The Celebration of Self and the Sacralization of Modernity* (Oxford, 1996); F. Nudelman, 'Beyond the Talking Cure: Listening to Female Testimony on *The Oprah Winfrey Show*', in Pfister and Schnog (eds.), *Inventing the Psychological*, 297–315.

[71] M. North, *The Secular Priests* (London, 1972), 19.   [72] Ibid. 25.   [73] Ibid. 25–6.

[74] Ibid. 38–9.   [75] Ibid. 38–42.

[76] P. Berger, 'Towards a Sociological Understanding of Psychoanalysis', *Social Research* (1965), 26–41.

this chapter, he divided the market into two parts: those like the behaviourists who approved of the technological society; and those like the psychotherapists who favoured 'rehumanisation' (even if they were actually 'technicists' in practice).[77] The development of this market, in its heightening of social comparison, in turn did little to alleviate, much in fact to fuel, the underlying problem of individual insecurity.[78] This was an essentially pessimistic diagnosis. Psychotherapy might be a solution to personal unhappiness, but it came at the cost of individual liberty on the one hand, and a radical political consciousness on the other. Power, as in so many other areas of modern life, went to the technician: the psychotherapist was little more than 'a policeman in a white coat'.[79]

North's analysis brings together many of the better-known lines of critique that had already been established or that were to emerge over the decades to come, mainly in relation to the United States. Therapy was a replacement for religion.[80] The obsession with the psychological was both response to and further cause of a privatisation of life.[81] The therapeutic was essentially narcissistic, epitomising a dominant trait of modern life.[82] And despite outward appearances it was a new form of governance with real power going not to the patient but to the professionals.[83] Despite his prescience in the latter three instances, and the fact that he was applying these ideas to Britain, there is no indication that he was regarded as a seminal thinker at the time. Indeed, the impression, instead, is of a writer who was articulating a broader emerging consciousness about the psychotherapeutic as an increasingly central, but also problematic, aspect of modern life in the early 1970s. Bearing in mind what has already been said about the real limitations of such a culture in the post-war decades, he was almost certainly overstating his case. But the consciousness is important in its own right. It suggests two things. First, that critiques such as this may have acted as a further brake on the development of such a culture in the British context: the existence of the critique as much a sign of weakness as strength. Secondly, that in that flurry of cultural excitement that has come to be known as 'the sixties' and that was the immediate context for North's account, there may have been developments that encouraged such a diagnosis.[84] An exploration of the developments within the counterculture of the period, overlooked thus far, will follow shortly.

If North now offered a critical diagnosis of the problem of a crisis of values and its resolution in psychotherapy, a decade earlier, in his Reith Lectures broadcast on the BBC, G. M. Carstairs, Professor of Medical Sociology at Edinburgh University had done much to stir up a debate about declining values in Britain.

---

[77] M. North, *The Mind Market* (London, 1975).   [78] North, *The Secular Priests*, 52–3.

[79] Ibid. 288–92; North, *The Mind Market*, 176.

[80] P. Rieff, *The Triumph of the Therapeutic: Uses of Faith after Freud* (London, 1966).

[81] R. Sennett, *The Fall of Public Man* (London, 1977).

[82] C. Lasch, *The Culture of Narcissism* (London, 1980).

[83] Rose, *Governing the Soul* (London, 1989).

[84] On the 'sixties': A. Marwick, *The Sixties: Cultural Revolution in Britain, France, Italy and the United States, c.1958–1974* (London, 1998).

Carstairs, however, had been highly optimistic that the spread of more sophisticated psychological understanding would do much to fill the void. In understanding ourselves, we would become more tolerant and more perceptive of the need of others. A popularisation of psychology, in short, was the key in adjusting to a world of unstoppable social change and in forging a new morality for a permissive age.[85]

In 1965, sociologist Paul Halmos would take up this baton. Again, he would recognise the crisis of values, but rather like Carstairs he would see psychology as the way to reintroduce a life centred on values rather than as a symptom and further cause of retreat.[86] For Halmos, such values would spread from above in the counselling role of doctors, psychologists, and social workers. However, he resisted the idea that they would function as mere human engineers, managing the happy but ultimately passive population of an apolitical, technocratic society. Instead, he emphasised the qualities of inspiration, conviction, and love, the reverence for the individual psychological subject, and the powerful moral stance that accompanied such work. Halmos was inclined to regard it as akin to a new direction for religion: 'the faith of the counsellors', as he called it.[87] Indeed, he would portray it as ultimately strengthening traditional ethical regimes, such as Christianity, founded on love and sympathy.[88] In what many were coming to regard as a post-political age, the 'faith of the counsellors' provided a new humanistic vision of progress. Social workers, with their potential for greatly extending the reach of counselling through numerical superiority to the other professions and an ability to reach into the home, and now with the powers of communication and influence that came with psychological insight, would be the shock troops of the movement. Armed with psychotherapy, an intervention to address suffering and unhappiness, which previously had been opposed as meddling and prying, would be given new scientific legitimacy.[89] The result would be a demoralisation and politicisation of the personal. Although Halmos recognised that the new 'faith' contributed to, as well as benefited from the more general decline in political ambition, he was convinced that it would ultimately prove a positive, reinvigorating force. Here, he aligned himself with E. P. Thompson's prediction of a new kind of politics, in response to the dwindling faith in the old, in *Out of Apathy*: 'a new rebellious humanism'.[90] What was taking place through the

---

85 G. M. Carstairs, *This Island Now: The BBC Reith Lectures of 1962* (London, 1963).

86 P. Halmos, *The Faith of the Counsellors* (London, 1965). This grew out of his earlier interest in the problem of a sense of individual isolation in modern society: *Solitude and Privacy: A Study of Social Isolation, its Causes and Therapy* (London, 1952). As such, it had roots in the concerns considered in Ch. 7. The emphasis here on Halmos's optimism is a rather different one to that recently put forward by Furedi, who sets Halmos alongside critics of the therapeutic like Lasch: *Therapy Culture*, 84, 92.

87 Halmos, *Faith of the Counsellors*, 7.   88 Ibid. 191–5.   89 Ibid. 44–7, 176–7.

90 Ibid. 30; E. P. Thompson, 'Outside the Whale', in E. P. Thompson et al., *Out of Apathy* (London, 1960), 188. Though in the one essay in this volume to directly address psychology, it was argued that Freud had been domesticated from being an apostle of freedom to a tool for conformist adjustment, a line of analysis much closer to the critics like North: MacIntyre, 'Breaking the Chains of Freedom', 231–2. Referring to the crisis in values when it came to the working class, it is intriguing

emerging faith of the counsellors, suggested Halmos, was not the 'end of ideology', but a 'transvaluation in our social concerns'.[91]

PSYCHOLOGY AND THE COUNTERCULTURE

Between the optimism of Halmos and the later pessimism of North there arose a moment of psychological experimentation and excitement that has parallels with the situation explored at the start of this book. Here, the anti-psychiatric theatrics of R. D. Laing, David Cooper and Kingsley Hall have come to dominate our picture. With books like *The Divided Self*, Laing emerged as a key figure in the British counter culture, reopening the self as the kind of exciting territory for existential exploration that it had been at the start of the century, providing the bored young of an increasingly secure society with opportunities for intellectual adventure.[92] Already the subject of extensive biographical and historical study, there is little point in dwelling in too much detail on his contribution here. That said, a few points are particularly pertinent.[93] The first is to highlight the way that the anti-psychiatric critique of normative mental health values—a world of definite boundaries between madness and sanity—was something of a ticking time bomb waiting to explode. As already noted, the mid-century crisis had provided the ideological conditions to cement a relationship between mental health and values, but it had done so at a time when there was also a clear awareness that culture shaped values and that all psychology was social psychology. Relativism about mental health was therefore intellectually pressing, but ideologically suppressed. Laing and the anti-psychiatrists could expose this and gain a following, not because their insight was so radically new, but because ideological conditions had changed.[94] The second point is that in questioning the authority of psychiatric values, such figures were adding to the series of other factors set out earlier in this chapter that retarded the development of the mid-century psychological vision. Anti-psychiatry was acting therefore as less of a lone rogue than was sometimes assumed, and looked at in this way had some surprising allies.[95] Similarly, for all anti-psychiatry's association with an assault on authority, the guru-like status of a Laing hardly represented any such retreat, and in truth it reconfigured and radicalised the role of psychotherapy rather than rejected it altogether. In the favour

that in the same volume, Stuart Hall (ibid. 93) would talk in the language of psychology: 'a loss of any social psychology . . . a crisis in the psychology of the working class'.

[91] Halmos, *Faith of the Counsellors*, 48.

[92] For a vivid fictionalised account of the atmosphere from one of those involved: C. Sigal, *Zone of the Interior* (New York, 1976).

[93] A. Laing, *R. D. Laing: A Biography* (London, 1994); D. Burston, *The Wing of Madness: The Life and Work of R. D. Laing* (Cambridge, Mass. and London, 1996); J. Clay, *R. D. Laing: A Divided Self: A Biography* (London, 1996).   [94] Thomson, 'Before Anti-Psychiatry'.

[95] Hence, the criticism from a left more concerned with the defence of services: Sedgwick, *Psycho-Politics*.

shown for tools like group therapy it actually followed a democratisation whose roots went back to the Second World War, as well as several earlier experiments in the interwar period, and had evolved in a less dramatic process of psychiatric reform in the post-war era.[96]

To gain a fuller flavour of this anti-psychiatric mood, it would be helpful for our understanding if we moved beyond Laing and his small band of followers to a series of lesser known but more broadly based movements for psychiatric reform.[97] One such group was People not Psychiatry, founded by Michael Barnett in 1969, which claimed to have drawn 10,000 people into its networks by 1973. Identifying himself as a schizophrenic—reconfigured, in a topsy-turvy Laingian climate, from cause for commitment, to a kind of passport to a world of insight— Barnett returned in the late-1960s from the hippy trail in the East to a London blossoming with a counterculture. Through a mix of meditation and the ideas of Zen, Krishnamurti, and Don Juan, the Yacqui Indian Shaman, he participated in the activities of the 'Psychenautics Institute for Journeys into Inner Space', sitting for hours, together with a few others in a white-walled room stripped of furniture and comforts, gazing into the depths of his mind. The aim was one of breaking down, unburdening the self, rather than building it up: 'emotions, pains—these were not to be expressed but probed, peeled, broken up, unravelled, dissolved, and thereby true detachment from them reached.' He also became involved in the activities of the Campaign against Psychiatric Activities, which was organising demonstrations against the use of electric shock treatment and neurosurgery in the biological psychiatry that had made such gains since the War. He left when he learnt of the group's links to Scientologist opposition to psychiatry.[98] Instead, he proposed a new organisation—'People for a New Psychiatry'—setting out his aims in the underground magazine, *International Times* in 1969, alongside inter-views with R. D. Laing and Mick Jagger. As the new name indicated, he was not convinced by the kind of whole-scale attack on psychiatry mounted by the Campaign against Psychiatric Activities; nor was he a supporter of Laing's denial

[96] J. Andrews, 'R. D. Laing in Scotland: Facts and Fictions of the "Rumpus Room" and Interpersonal Psychiatry', in Gijswijt-Hofstra and Porter (eds.), *Cultures of Psychiatry*, 121–50.

[97] The existence of such a network of social movements has recently begun to be charted by soci-ologist Nick Crossley in a series of essays: 'R. D. Laing and British Anti-Psychiatry: A Socio-Historical Analysis', *Social Science and Medicine*, 47 (1998), 877–98; 'Fish, Field, Habitus and Madness: On the First Wave Mental Health Users Movement in Britain', *British Journal of Sociology*, 50 (1999), 647–70; 'Working Utopias and Social Movements: An Investigation using Case Study Materials from Radical Mental Health Movements in Britain', *Sociology*, 33 (1999), 809–30.

[98] The movement had been brought to Britain from the United States by psychologist L. Ron Hubbard in the early 1950s. By the end of the decade, the world centre of the movement's publica-tion efforts had been set up in East Grinstead. Scientologist opposition was partly a consequence of their support for dianetics, a form of psychotherapy. As well as the CAPA campaign, it had been involved in a thwarted attempt to take over the National Association for Mental Health in 1969. Growth of the movement and reports of its manipulation of followers led to the introduction of restrictions on immigration of those involved and then a public inquiry which took a less alarmist view and rescinded the measures: J. Tarbit, 'The Road to Total Furore: Dianetics, Scientology, and their Detractors in Fifties and Sixties Britain', MA thesis (University of Warwick, 2003).

of the reality of mental illness and its suffering. There was a massive response to his article and to further pieces, not only in the *International Times*, but also in the more mainstream progressive forum *New Society*. Before long, networks were forming across the country. Barnett recognised that the movement had drawn in many people under the impression that they might cure themselves without recourse to psychiatry. If it managed to do so, this was because the very structure of the movement functioned as an adjunct to cure. It offered both the support of being able to talk to others who had similar experiences and a public identity to people who suffered in silent isolation; and it helped people come to terms with themselves, rather than trying to change them. As such, it would provide a bridge to the emerging growth movement, and Barnett himself would move in this direction as his organisational role ended.

In this example, we see anti-psychiatry as being located in something of a melting pot of movements and ideas. A concern with humanising psychiatry sat alongside an interest in mind expansion. Interest in the psychology of the growth movement came in part organically from below through experience of the therapeutic value of group activity within a social movement. Eastern thought, even the new religion of the West in the form of Scientology, intermingled with the psychology of the West. In the closely interconnected world of the counterculture, all this could sit alongside the Rolling Stones, offering it no doubt an added allure. The picture is of an exploration of mind and self that went well beyond narrow psychiatric boundaries. It would not be wholly inappropriate to draw a parallel with some of the more bohemian enthusiasm for new psychological ideas and practices at the start of the century.

Analysis of the underground press, unleashed by the coincidence of an explosion of social movements and technological advances in lithography, would seem to confirm this.[99] Coverage in the important forum *International Times* has already been noted, but there were a host of other magazines that either aligned themselves with an attack on the dominant psychiatry and psychology of the day—particularly biological psychiatry, behaviourism, and intelligence testing— or supported a reorientation to put people in charge of their own therapy. *Humpty Dumpty* presented itself as the voice of 'dissenting psychologists in public' and ran critical articles covering special education for handicapped children, conditions within mental hospitals, IQ, and behavioural modification. *Red Rat* likewise attracted disaffected psychological professionals and academics: 'We being psychology students in academia or psychology workers in the business world', it announced in its first edition of May 1970, 'do hereby give notice to the interested of our intention to reject the established roles our professional forebears created.'[100] This meant setting themselves up against not only behaviourism but

[99] For general accounts, though with no indication of coverage of the psychological: N. Fountain, *The London Alternative Press, 1966–1974* (London, 1988); E. Nelson, *The British Counter-Culture, 1966–73: A Study of the Underground Press* (Basingstoke, 1989).

[100] *Red Rat*, 1 (May, 1970), 3.

also Freud, and moving instead towards the humanistic psychology that will be considered shortly.[101] A *Red Rat* conference at Keele University attracted two hundred participants, and the group would go on to forge links with academics at the London School of Economics, People not Psychiatry, and even the Gay Liberation Front.[102] Psychology was less central elsewhere but still an important issue. *Science for the People* ran articles on 'Psychiatric Treatment or Social Degradation' and 'The Politics of Psychological Testing'. The libertarian *Off our Backs* supported a self-help approach towards therapy. There was also interest from a psychedelic perspective in publications like *Heavy Daze*. Even *Peace News* offered regular coverage of the emerging patients' movement, pointing to a congruence of interest that was alluded to in discussion of the Second World War.[103] When it came to the New Left, there was always more ambivalence. A psychological vision of becoming whole seemed a suspiciously religious idiom, and one that ignored both the centrality of conflict and the inevitability of incompleteness. However, engagement with the ideas of Sartre, Laing, Cooper, and Lacan via Althusser in the pages of an influential forum like the *New Left Review* did herald some reorientation. The challenge of taking the psychological turn but still catering to more traditional leftist concern about social and economic inequality will be considered further in the final sections of this chapter.[104]

SELF AND SOCIETY

The dialogue between the counterculture, the left, and psychology can be explored in more detail through a case study of the forum provided by *Self and Society: The Journal of Humanistic Psychology*. Founded in 1973, it drew inspiration from the development in the 1960s of a humanistic psychology movement in the United States. Again, it distanced itself from the determinism of Freud on the one hand and behaviourism on the other. In Britain, it had roots both within the discontents of a younger generation of academic psychologists and within the heady atmosphere of countercultural rebellion and experimentation.

Self and Society announced itself with an editorial that highlighted the wholly inadequate reach and social exclusivity of existing psychotherapeutic provision. Medicine was unable to cope with the mental problems experienced by two out of every five persons within a population struggling to adjust to changing values. The unhappy had little alternative but to turn to their general practitioners, whose 'reach

---

101 Ibid. 13–14.   102 Ibid. 5.

103 For a listing of articles: J. Noyce (ed.), *The Directory of the British Alternative Periodicals* (Brighton, 1975); and J. Spiers (ed.), *The Underground and Alternative Press in Britain (Bibliographical Guide to the Harvester Social Sources Press Collection)* (Brighton, 1975); M. Smith, *The Underground and Education: A Guide to the Alternative Press* (London, 1977). Further coverage came in: *Hard Cheese; Rat, Myth and Magic; Red Rat;* and in pamphlets like Keith Paton's *The Great Brain Robbery*.

104 A. McRobbie, 'An Interview with Juliet Mitchell', *New Left Review*, 176 (1988), 81–7.

me down' solution of drug therapy was causing as many problems as it solved. Humanistic psychology, echoing currents at the start of the century, proposed the alternative solution of a new way of life and a reclaiming of people's at-oneness with their humanity that seemed to have been a victim of the modern age. Understanding what it was to be human emerged as a source of values in an age where religion and political ideology seemed to have lost much of their appeal. Humanistic psychology would therefore go far beyond mere treatment. It would address the central psycho-logical malaise of the age: the sense that life was dull and unsatisfactory. With per-haps a subconscious recognition of how the urge to escape from a life which had shackled the full expression of the emotions mirrored a détente-era hope for release from the suffocation of living within a Cold War culture, it was about 'coming in from the cold'.[105] It would release modern man and woman to 'live more fully. Enjoy more. Suffer more. Feel more.... Be more human.'[106]

An Association for Humanistic Psychology had been founded in the United States in the early 1960s. Britain followed later, and thus with somewhat different emphases, in 1969.[107] The writing of the American humanist psychologists Abram Maslow and Carl Rogers was an important influence, but the movement also eclectically drew on Adler, Rank, Jung, Marcuse, Reich, Szasz, and Norman Brown. The 'bad animal' model shared by behaviourism and Freud, was rejected for one that emphasised the potentiality of human nature.[108] Initially the move-ment emerged out of social psychology and social psychiatry and operated on the fringes of the British Psychological Society, but the decision to establish a journal of its own reflected disenchantment with the ethical position of the discipline and a move in reaction towards a psychology from below.[109] It was 'a whole different way of looking at psychological science'. This was to be a psychology which included 'love, involvement and spontaneity, instead of systematically excluding them'. Its object was not 'the prediction and control of people's behaviour, but the liberation of people from the bonds of neurotic control'.[110] This was a rebellion from within. It signalled growing unease about a psychology that had lost its ethical vision in the search for scientific credibility and now looked like little more than an instrument of control.

Psychoanalysis and treatment made way for growth as the key paradigm. Following the prototype of the Esalen Institute at Big Sur in California, growth centres began to appear in Britain, offering a range of therapeutic techniques, including encounter groups, Gestalt therapy, bio-energetics, psychodrama, mas-sage, and Yoga.[111] The leading centres—Quaesitor, founded in 1969, and Kaleidescope—were both in London.[112] John Rowan, Chairman of the

---

[105] C. Lutz, 'Epistemology of the Bunker: The Brainwashed and Other New Subjects of Permanent War', in Pfister and Schnog (eds.), *Inventing the Psychological*, 245–67.
[106] Editorial, *Self and Society*, 1/1 (1973), 2–3.
[107] J. Rowan, *Ordinary Ecstasy: Humanistic Psychology in Action* (London, 1976), 7, 137.
[108] Ibid. 8.   [109] Ibid. 138–41; J. Rowan, *The Science of You* (London, 1973).
[110] Rowan, *Ordinary Ecstasy*, 3.   [111] *Self and Society*, 1/1 (1973), 26–7.
[112] Rowan, *Ordinary Ecstasy*, 137.

Association, described the atmosphere as one of open-minded, transgressive experimentation, which went well beyond the intentions of the founders of the humanistic psychology.[113] The silence and cold, impersonal judgement of the psychoanalytic relationship had been thrown out; but so too had what Barnett described as the intellectualising 'mind-fuck' of attempting to step outside of one-self to enable objective analysis.[114] Instead, psychology was a tool to enhance being through activity. The centrality of talking about oneself, about emotion, and about relationships within the encounter group was radically different from the generally non-introspective approach of practical psychology. But this talk was seen as a bar-rier of consciousness which had to be stripped away before the real work could begin on a self that lay beyond, and in this sense there was a parallel between the two. With further echoes of their early-twentieth-century antecedents, the focus on avoiding the analytical and striving to get in touch with one's full self meant that experience of the physical—though now increasingly focusing on sexuality—moved to the centre of psychological concern.[115] Another parallel was their open-mindedness towards Eastern religion as a counterpart to Western psychology, though the counterculture's experimentation with drugs such as LSD was now added to this armoury.[116] The new movement, like its forebears, emphasised the importance of transcending a conscious state and was just as imaginative in map-ping out a landscape of consciousness. Rowan, for instance, pointed to a realm beyond the waking state of the preconscious, the psychodynamic unconscious, the ontogenetic unconscious, the trans-individual unconscious, the phylogenetic unconscious, the extra-terrestrial unconscious, the superconscious, and the void. Travel to these states was pictured as a journey of ecstasy.[117] Once again, growth was about overcoming the limitations of individualism: 'one becomes far more oneself at the very same time as one flows with the whole universe.'[118] Existential consciousness of being totally alone and totally responsible was cultivated, but would be made bearable through the cultivation alongside this of intense group experience and consciousness of the pattern and unity of the universe.[119]

With its leaderless dynamics and its aim of intensifying the quality of human relationships, the encounter group epitomised the orientation of the movement. Listings of the activities of growth centres indicate that they were extending from London to cities across the country, and that such methods were being spread into schools and colleges by enthusiastic teachers.[120] By the start of the 1980s, twenty-eight courses and seventy-three centres had been established.[121] However, the

---

[113] J. Rowan, 'Humanistic Psychology and the Revolution', *Self and Society*, 1/6 (1973), 1.
[114] M. Barnett, *People not Psychiatry* (London, 1973), 29.
[115] Hence the appeal of the writing of Marcuse, Reich, Brown, and of practices such as bio-energetics, yoga, and massage.   [116] Rowan, *Ordinary Ecstasy*, 11, 15–25.
[117] J. Rowan, 'Ecstasy', *Self and Society*, 3/4 (1975), 18–20.
[118] Barnett, *People not Psychiatry*, 31.   [119] Rowan, *Ordinary Ecstasy*, 13.
[120] *Self and Society*, 1/1 (1973), 28. See also the focus on education in the September 1973 edition.
[121] J. Rowan, *The Reality Game: A Guide to Humanistic Counselling and Therapy* (London, 1983), 173–80.

limited and largely middle-class audience was a persistent problem for a movement which had partly justified itself in terms of providing an answer to the elitism of psychoanalysis. One female correspondent supported the journal's basic ideas but questioned whether it would ever reach the people who really needed to read it. In catering to their own circle in trendy metropolitan London, they were 'patting one another on their backs with satisfaction' and simply 'encouraging the neurotic to be more neurotic'. The real problem was a hidden mass of 'emotionally subdued people' in the suburbs.[122] The Association responded, acknowledging the seriousness of this issue of dissemination. It had previously considered the idea of promoting the movement's activities through a publicity campaign and large experiential events but claimed to have been deterred by a sense that fear and prejudice were the prevailing public attitudes. Instead, it fell back on the more cautious and slow strategy of building up a committed following through the activities of small local groups and links to other groups. The co-counselling movement within feminism was an example of the potential for such cross-fertilisation.[123] By the mid-1970s links were also being forged with the men's and homosexual movements.[124] There was even a report of such activities within the labour movement, though it was acknowledged that there were real practical problems in combining long working hours with a commitment to 'growth'.[125] How to be both radical and popular remained a persistent dilemma.[126] It was also a concern that in practical terms, an anti-authoritarian style made effective organisation and united action difficult.[127]

From the perspective of those on the left within the movement, the criticism of exclusivity was particularly serious. Many remained uncomfortable over whether the movement's activities were essentially frivolous and self-indulgent. One leftist critic suggested that AHP might stand for the 'Association of Hedonistic Pursuits'. It was hard to believe that the movement could fully overcome the contradiction at the heart of all previous psychotherapy: a desire to be free was gained only through a loss of autonomy to the therapist.[128] It was also worrying that America—the country at the very centre of developments in humanistic psychology—had seen such psychology acting as a training ground for industrial and other psychologists who appeared to be committed to furthering the interests of the ruling class.[129]

[122] Letter from S. Hyams, *Self and Society*, 1/10 (1973), 15.
[123] Ibid. and response: 'Spreading the Good Stuff Around', *Self and Society*, 1/10 (1973), 16–17.
[124] J. Rowan, 'The Four-Way Workshop', *Self and Society*, 3/5 (1975), 16–19.
[125] J. Southgate, 'The Dialectics of the Growth Movement', *Self and Society*, 1/10 (1973), 22.
[126] A strategy of promotion through the media and through links to the British Psychological Society was also considered: *Self and Society*, 2/4 (1974), 18–19. For further criticism of the lack of politics within the growth movement: B. Richards, 'Against Humanistic Psychology', *Self and Society*, 2/8 (1974), 2–6. See also the Editor's defence: *Self and Society*, 2/8, (1974), 1.
[127] J. Liss, 'What is the Movement's Future?', *Self and Society*, 2/12 (1974), 15.
[128] J. Southgate, 'The Dialectics of the Growth Movement', *Self and Society*, 1/10 (1973), 21–2.
[129] J. Rowan, 'Humanistic Psychology and the Revolution', *Self and Society*, 1/6 (1973), 2–3.

Editor of *Self and Society*, Vivian Milroy, argued that there was little point in channelling energies into the political process or even into an internal struggle within psychology itself: 'I want all the energy, time, love to be directed to shewing [sic] what positive life alternatives we can offer, and not wasted on criticizing each other, knocking the conventional life, proving how wrong Freud, the behaviourists, traditional psychology are (even if they are).'[130] For others, 'self-actualization' was both the path to individual happiness, identity and meaning in life, and the key thereby to transforming the world.[131] As Rowan put it, describing his own ideological odyssey:

I don't believe any more in revolution which is only about structural changes in social institutions and says nothing about how we live our lives. I see the revolution as basically about better social relationships, and as being achieved through better social relationships, which in themselves force structural change.[132]

As he pointed out, politics had been one of the major themes in the journal during its first three years.[133] In May 1974, a meeting of some three hundred to listen to speakers including Jerry Rubin, the American Yippie who had taken a path from political activism to the growth movement, helped to increase self-consciousness about this being a turning point from one sort of politics to another.[134] The psychological route was not to be seen as a retreat from the political, but as a rein-vention of it. Neither was it simply other-worldly talk or self-obsession: its thera-peutics was about activity, and it could offer practical solutions to real problems. Nor was therapy a tool for adjustment and passification within existing social structures. Although it would be able to help people cope with the alienation caused by redundancy, or adjust to the three-day week and increased leisure heralded by the economic crisis of 1974, it would also arm them to engage in strategies of social change.[135]

From 1972, Rowan, Chairman of the AHP, had come into increasing contact with feminism. He had been particularly impressed by an article by Angela Hamblin in the first issue of the *Women's Liberation Review*, and this would later be republished in the pages of *Self and Society*. Hamblin's argument was that both sexes had lost touch with their inner selves and needed to be freed from the alienating roles which had been imposed on them by society. This appeared to mirror the problem at the heart of humanistic psychology. Rowan soon came into contact with the emerging men's movement in London, with its journal *Brothers*, and also the homosexual movement. By the mid-1970s, he was coming to accept the political nature of a heterosexual male identity and was contributing to *Men*

[130] V. Milroy, 'Feedback', *Self and Society*, 3/6 (1975), 14–15.

[131] J. Southgate, 'The Dialectics of the Growth Movement', *Self and Society*, 1/10 (1973), 23.

[132] J. Rowan, 'Humanistic Psychology and the Revolution', *Self and Society*, 1/6 (1973), 1. Rowan had lectured for many years on Social Psychology for the Extramural Department of the University of London. [133] J. Rowan, 'AHP Activities', *Self and Society*, 3/12 (1975), 16.

[134] From *Psychology Today* (Sept. 1973), quoted in the report on the meeting, *Self and Society*, 2/6 (1974), 17. [135] 'What about the Crisis?', *Self and Society*, 2/1 (1974), 12.

against Sexism.[136] In the men's movement, Rowan came together with Keith Paton, both earlier involved in *Red Rat* and now active within the AHP. In a highly personal and self-critical examination in *Self and Society* of the relationship with his wife, Paton also argued that an engagement with feminism was key to the future direction of the movement.[137] Essentially, what the encounter with the women's movement highlighted was the political nature at the heart of personal relationships and identity; as such, it pointed towards the new sort of politics that humanistic psychologists like Rowan were searching for.[138]

It would be wrong to assume that all who were drawn to the personal growth movement were looking for some kind of replacement for political ideology. Others became involved hoping to meet new people or simply because it was a fashionable thing to do. Neither did all feel comfortable about the results. As one woman recalled, encounter sessions could be dominated by a self-conscious anxiety that one looked right—stretch denim jeans or tricel jersey trousers, hip-length tunic of cotton jersey or towelling with a zip front, 'no gaping necklines to show unintentional bras'—and the group experience could be more embarrass-ing and awkward than liberating. It simply made her guilty about her femininity and more anxious about her body shape. Indeed, she emerged thinking that the manipulation of behaviourism might do more to help her: 'somewhere, some-how, we shall find some conundrum, even some Eysenckian conditioning machine, to enable us to cope once and for all with the self-destroying curse of bread, cakes, biscuits, bananas, chocolates, wine, whisky or almond fudge.'[139] Such women would increasingly turn not to Eysenck, but to the emerging women's movement.

WOMEN'S CONSCIOUSNESS RAISED

Historian and feminist, Sheila Rowbotham, who lived through the excitement of the emergence of second-wave feminism in the Britain of the late 1960s, recalls ideas 'rushing through the air to be grabbed'.[140] As such, it is unsurprising that the movement was open to the influence of the psychological theories and practices that were surfacing at just the same time. Looking back on the origins of the British women's movement, participants have often recalled the excitement gener-ated by the anti-psychiatry movement and the writing of Laing in particular, even if they sometimes struggled to understand it, while others soon came to criticise its

---

[136] J. Rowan, 'The Four-Way Workshop', *Self and Society*, 3/5 (1975), 16–19; A. Hamblin, 'Ultimate Goals', *Self and Society*, 3/12 (1975), 1–6.

[137] K. Paton, 'Crisis and Renewal', *Self and Society*, 2/2 (Feb., 1974), 9–14. *Red Rat*, 1 (May, 1970), 5.   [138] 'AHP Activities', *Self and Society*, 2/2 (1974), 15.

[139] M. Kuttna, 'In and out of Encounter', *Self and Society*, (1974), 16, 14–19.

[140] S. Rowbotham, *A Century of Women* (London, 1997), 348.

limitations.[141] The attention to psychoanalysis within the American feminist movement was also influential.[142]

By the early 1970s, the British women's movement was actively fashioning its own psychological positions and its own therapeutics. Analysis of the journal *Spare Rib*, founded in 1972 and a key forum for the movement in Britain, reaching an estimated audience of 20,000, provides a flavour of this.[143] As early as 1972, we find reports of a Women's Self-Help Therapy Scheme. 'Therapy', on its own, would have suggested a need for remoulding of the sick individual which had unpleasant connotations for many women; 'self help', echoing the culture of practical psychology half a century earlier, was attractively more self-affirming.[144] A 'Red Therapy' group followed in 1973, emphasising again an identity distinct from anything within the established mental health arena. Over the next three years, dozens of these groups would emerge around the country.[145] Regular coverage in a forum like this helped to spread the new consciousness of consciousness to a broader audience still.

One of the reasons for the prominence of this issue within the early days of the women's movement was that by the end of the 1960s psychology had come to be considered a powerful force in the oppression of women. The writing of Laing had shown schizophrenic women seemingly made mad by the conditions of family life. And psychological theory, notably in the form of Bowlbyism and its claim that separation of mothers from young children resulted in psychological deprivation, was increasingly open to criticism for the way it confused a social with a biological role to keep mothers in the home.[146] Frequent use of terms such as 'psychological conditioning' and 'brainwashing' within the counter-culture had associated psychology with the defence of the existing moral order, albeit often indirectly, and this language was now co-opted in a critique of women's resignation to a subordinate role in society.[147]

Criticism was most intense when it came to psychiatry. Feminists attacked diagnoses of mental illness for ignoring the fundamental social causes of widespread female unhappiness. Labelling women as mentally ill let society off the hook and perpetuated a myth of innate female weakness. 'Confinement', electric shock treatment, and the burgeoning tranquilliser culture were all condemned as 'inhuman'

[141] Historian Sally Alexander recollects a frustration at being unable to read Laing's *Divided Self* and giving up after a chapter. Juliet Mitchell was among those who engaged with anti-psychiatry: M. Wandor, *Once a Feminist* (London, 1990), 86, 109; A. McRobbie, 'An Interview with Juliet Mitchell', *New Left Review*, 176 (1988), 81.
[142] Mitchell's own interest in the psychological went back to an exposure to the ideas of Wilhelm Reich via her anarchist upbringing in the 1940s. It also reflected her early academic work on the theme of child development in literature: McRobbie, 'Interview with Juliet Mitchell', 81.
[143] For background material on *Spare Rib* and a survey of its coverage: M. Rowe (ed.), *Spare Rib Reader* (London, 1982). See also, N. Fountain, *Underground: The London Alternative Press, 1966–74* (London, 1988), 171–80.
[144] C. Morrell, 'Why is Liberation an Emotional Struggle?', *Spare Rib* 14 (1973), 37.
[145] S. Ernst and L. Goodison, 'Unconsciousness Raising', *Spare Rib*, 113 (1981), 19.
[146] S. Lipshitz, 'Are children loved enough, too much or too little', *Spare Rib*, 14 (1973), 15–16.
[147] For psychological conditioning: J. Miles, 'Jealousy', *Spare Rib*, 15 (1973), 9.

and as leaving women defenceless within a psychiatric machine which had little interest in listening to them.[148] There was of course a long history of women being represented as victims of wrongful incarceration; however, the intensity of the critique came to a head on the back of the anti-psychiatry of the late 1960s.[149] Echoing Laing and Cooper's influential assault on the family, psychiatric therapy was also attacked as failing to grapple with what was the fundamental problem: the oppressed position of women within a patriarchal society.[150] In returning 'disturbed' women to a state of dependency, psychiatry simply reconfirmed and reinforced that femininity which had been at the heart of the unhappiness in the first place. There were similar concerns, however, about a psychotherapeutic relationship which placed women in subordination and prone to the manipulation of male doctors. The shocking inadequacy of support in the move towards 'community care' was also highlighted, and there was early concern that this would simply place a further burden on women as carers within the home.[151]

A 'Women and Psychiatry' workshop was organised at the 1972 Women's Liberation Conference in Bristol, with a follow-up conference the next year and the formation of several local groups dedicated to addressing the issue. The movement also allied itself with an emerging self-help culture among mental patients and their families, directing readers not just towards the 'Women and Psychiatry Group', but also the 'Mental Patients Union', 'Mind', 'Cope', and 'Gingerbread'.[152] There remained a tension within the movement between those who looked to a reformed psychiatry and those who persisted with the kind of anti-psychiatric position which had been forged by Laing at the end of the 1960s. When schizophrenia was discussed in *Spare Rib* as a real disease, some readers expressed outrage. As one of them put it, the coverage would have looked more at home in the pages of *Woman's Own*:

As most liberals or radicals should, by now, be aware, the acceptance of the proposition that 'schizophrenia is most probably a genetically inherited, biochemically mediated disease' is a sign of gross reaction . . . Many a housewife, having been convinced by G.P. or Psychiatrist that she is 'suffering from the mental "illness" of depression or anxiety' has had her last feeble, disguised protest swamped by largactyl or electric shocks. Women suffer doubly from the incredibly powerful chauvinism of the medical profession. Please don't let Spare Rib increase the mysticism.[153]

Interestingly, this particular Laingian enthusiast was a male psychology lecturer, rather than someone writing from personal experience. Nonetheless, the anti-psychiatric position was clearly significant as a polemical vehicle for rallying women and persisted as a strain within the feminism of the early 1970s. Phyllis

[148] For instance, the case of 'Ann': C. Morrell, 'Why is Liberation an Emotional Struggle?', *Spare Rib*, 14 (1973), 36–7.

[149] E. Showalter, *The Female Malady: Women, Madness and English Culture, 1830–1980* (London, 1987).

[150] D. Cooper, *The Death of the Family* (London, 1972).

[151] Corrine, 'Bringing it all Back Home', *Spare Rib*, 46 (1976), 32–4.   [152] Ibid. 34.

[153] Letter from Hugh Coolican, *Spare Rib*, 30 (1974), 3. Response to article by C. Morrell, 'Schizophrenia', *Spare Rib*, 27 (1974), 34–5.

Chesler's *Women and Madness*, in which mental illness was recast as a female refusal to conform to society's expectations and the road to sanity set out as 'mother-sisterhood', was thus recommended to *Spare Rib*'s readers as 'impassioned' and 'inspiring'.[154] In contrast, Juliet Mitchell's theoretical defence of psychoanalysis was described as sending 'us off to the library, not into our own psyches'.[155]

In sum, established theories and practices of psychology and psychiatry provided the women's movement with a powerful enemy to identify themselves against. Cast in the well-established melodramatic trope of the woman wronged by psychiatry, this was an easily understood message and one which could act as a significant rallying call to the movement. What made it more powerful still, however, was the attack on psychological values: the assertion that the labelling of women as mentally ill was an act of political subjugation. As one reader put it, 'I have been led into believing I am crazy because I find it so difficult in a male orientated world. Then I read your magazine and I find I am right—life is hard, bloody hard.'[156] The critique of psychology, as such, acted as a vehicle for a much broader mobilisation against the prevailing values of society, its exposure of injustice appealing to both the growing number of women with personal experience of the mental health services and others who could empathise with the narrative of the 'bloody hard' life.

However, feminists did not reject the psychological route altogether. They also reshaped it in a 'consciousness-raising' project, which became central to liberation: psychological practice in particular emerged as a route towards a new politics and new values. Feminist writers invariably distanced themselves from Laing and the anti-psychiatric position. The inequalities of the doctor–patient relationship were still at the very heart of Laingian therapy: for all of its radical theatrics, anti-psychiatry was still psychiatry. And despite its valuable analysis of madness as a female strategy within the family, it did little to address women's problems in their own right.[157] Instead, in small leaderless groups or in 'co-counselling' pairs—the tools of a democratic psychotherapy—women were to be encouraged to become conscious of their oppressed condition and formulate strategies of resistance by talking about it. The personal and psychological would lead to the social and political.[158] In the narration of individual female journeys from mental subordination to self-assertion, the movement would find a powerful personal medium for projecting the potential of consciousness-raising. The personal stories of suffering, depression, and the struggle for recovery also did much to shatter the romanticising of madness in the fashion of anti-psychiatry.

However, there was clearly a concern that it would be too easy for critics to dismiss the political nature of consciousness-raising if they could pass it off as

---

[154] Chesler was reviewed by C. Morrell, *Spare Rib*, 26 (1974), 39–40.

[155] Mitchell was reviewed by M. Walters, *Spare Rib*, 23 (1974), 42. For an overview of the relationship between feminism and psychoanalysis in this period: L. Appignanesi and J. Forrester (eds.), *Freud's Women* (London, 1993), 455–74.

[156] Letter from Clair, 'Crazy is as Crazy is Done to', *Spare Rib*, 24 (1974), 3.

[157] Showalter, *Female Malady*, 220–47.

[158] J. Mitchell, *Woman's Estate* (London, 1971), 61.

mere therapy and self-exploration. There was also the danger that an attraction to the therapeutic might be seen as confirming the emotional, irrational nature of women, their interest in the personal and private, rather than the political and public. So, consciousness-raising and self-help had to be presented as fundamentally different to therapy. It needed to be clear that this was an approach in which the social causes of unhappiness were central, and which was about people helping one another rather than being treated. The language of 'consciousness-raising', with its echoes of a Marxist struggle against false consciousness, emphasised a political rather than merely therapeutic lineage.

Yet tensions clearly remained, echoing the problems of reconciling psychology and social radicalism in the humanistic movement. This can be highlighted by looking at the experiences of an individual like Amaya, attracted by the potential of therapy but subsequently becoming disenchanted and rejecting it for a more politicised approach to consciousness-raising. Initially, she had turned to psychoanalysis as a way to address problems in the relationship with her male partner. She had already read some Freud, and she and her friends frequently spoke about his ideas: 'It was our cultural background, a whole way of looking at things in terms of motives people wouldn't really admit to.'[159] In its favour was the disapproval of her parents, who saw it as risqué and unscientific. So too was the fact that university psychology had dismissed it, focusing instead on rats in mazes and people as information-processing machines. However, psychoanalysis soon shifted, from being a source of rebellion, to becoming the new authority against which to rebel. Amaya came to question the supposed neutrality of the analyst and experienced a growing clash of values as she became more deeply involved in a collective form of living: the analyst 'kept saying I seemed to have a whole lot of friends who were highly disturbed, all sick people.'[160] She began to find the act of being in analysis politically disturbing: 'It was completely split off from the rest of my life. You go off to see him, you have this completely unequal relationship when you get there, everything that you experience as a problem is explained by things in you.'[161] She was now coming to believe that the process of living side-by-side within a community could foster relationships that were far more valuable in terms of her psychological development. She constantly confronted interpersonal situations, for in joining such a community you had accepted a responsibility largely absent in the outside world of monogamous relationships. Recognising the similarities between such communal living and the ethic of the women's movement, she soon moved to an all-women collective, distancing herself from the inequalities and values that she had come to find in psychotherapy.

Others within the movement remained more positive in their attitude towards psychotherapy. Marsha Rowe, one of the founders of *Spare Rib* and herself involved in Jungian therapy in the 1970s, recognised the value and political nature of both psychotherapy and consciousness-raising. She distinguished the

---

[159] M. Rowe, 'False Consciousness', *Spare Rib*, 30 (1974), 67.   [160] Ibid. 69.   [161] Ibid.

two, but saw each as having a political role: 'Psychoanalysis locates the self in family history. Consciousness-raising locates the self in social history. Both ways of understanding have political consequences.'[162] Juliet Mitchell, an influential theorist and the most significant defender of psychoanalysis within the British movement, criticised the idea that therapy was necessarily non-political. Consciousness-raising, was 'speaking the unspoken': the opposite of the 'nattering together' which critics accused it of being; but so too was serious psychoanalysis. The social relations of a patriarchal society had become internalised in the structures of mind. One had to use the best available tools—and this meant psychoanalysis—to understand and change this.[163]

Recounting her own experiences of therapy in *Spare Rib*, Frances Seton lent support to Mitchell's view.[164] Although she had come to therapy with the recommendation and support of a few close friends who were in therapy themselves, she also had to cope with others who were 'horrified or embarrassed by what seemed an admission on my part of a terrible disease, or deforming blemish'.[165] For a feminist, there was the additional awkwardness that psychiatry was now supposed to be something of an enemy. Her defence of therapy was addressed to these anti-psychiatric critics, as much as traditional stigma. Reading and talking about herself, she had taken the feminist journey towards awareness that her suffering had a social origin, but found that this did little to relieve the actual distress that she was experiencing. She had taken psychology into her hands, but initially found that it simply provided her with a series of labels to hide behind. Turning to a female therapist, however, she was encouraged to recognise her feelings about events in the past—particularly, her attitudes towards her dead mother—not to change them, but to change how she now felt and acted. Transference of feelings for her mother onto the matriarchal figure of the psychotherapist played a vital role in this. Also important was the acceptance of the unconscious side of her personality: she had known about this, but not really believed in it until demonstration through therapy. Her natural inclination had always been to resist losing self-control. Therapy had broken down this resistance. Consciousness-raising, with its focus on just one side of this equation, did not provide the same opportunity. The therapeutic relationship could provide two things which the camaraderie of the group could not: it reproduced the authoritarian relationship which had to be re-explored in order to liberate the individual from the psychological straightjacket of family history; and the face-to-face encounter was so intense that it shook up the unconscious. Liberating the individual from past experiences, 'unconscious-ness-raising' was thus an even more important political tool than its conscious partner. Although a lengthy period of therapy was the necessary first stage, a process of 'permanent revolution' could continue as individuals took up the tools of therapy and applied them to an understanding of social constraints.

---

[162] Ibid. 66. Brief biographical details for Rowe are provided in Rowbotham, *A Century of Women*, 631. [163] Mitchell, *Woman's Estate*, 61–3.
[164] F. Seton, 'Opening Myself to Change', *Spare Rib*, 44 (1976), 30–2. [165] Ibid. 30.

'Unconsciousness-raising' would make women self-determined, rather than 'patterned', autonomous rather than dependent. However, it was not a route to individualism. On the contrary, Seton claimed to have become 'more profoundly and constructively political' through psychotherapy. Group therapy, by contrast, could be 'interesting, informative and in some ways helpful', but the format did not 'generate enough pressure to enable individuals to change or equip them to fight'.[166]

Other personal accounts of experience in self-help therapy lend some support to this. Amaya, whose rejection of psychoanalysis has already been discussed, saw consciousness-raising as playing a valuable role in the development of personal relations but did not believe that it had helped people work out their political views.[167] *Spare Rib* also published an account based on five women's experience of setting up a self-help group which highlighted the limitations of taking therapy into one's own hands. The idea of the group had been raised at a local women's centre meeting in 1975. Even among active feminists, there was clearly still something of an aura of embarrassment about being involved in an activity which so publicly exposed one's private life and personal fallibilities and feelings. A number of the participants were looking for therapeutic solutions to personal problems: one had 'cracked up' a year before; another was having difficulty coping with day-to-day life. Others were simply looking for a 'more structured setting than friendship' where they could express fears without guilt. They shared a suspicion about the psychiatric establishment, regarding it as the 'way in which women were adjusted to their limited roles and oppressed position'. Instead, the group created a warm, 'indulgent and supportive atmosphere', so that the women would feel comfortable about being openly emotional. The emphasis was on easing conflict and emotional trauma, rather than fostering it for catharsis, as was more likely within the growth movement. The experience of being able to talk about oneself with the full attention of a sympathetic audience could leave one feeling 'purged', even 'really high'. However, it was difficult for all of them to have the same opportunity to hold centre stage. More seriously, they found it difficult to move beyond the initially liberating feeling of being heard. As feminists, they schooled themselves in a rational way of thinking about women's conditioning within society, and they found it difficult to break away from this. When problems arose, they would be calmly analysed; but there was little space for the venting of violent emotions. The gentle environment fostered timidity about expression of anger or criticism of others within the group. The predisposition against authority also emerged as a handicap. Eventually, the group adopted a system of rotating leadership to provide direction and energy. Insecurity about lacking expert psychological understanding was harder to overcome. Ultimately, in response to the question of whether self-help provided a genuine alternative to therapy, the group responded that it was hardly a question of alternatives: the NHS provided only 50 psychotherapists for some 50 million

166 F. Seton, 'Opening Myself to Change', *Spare Rib*, 44 (1976), 32.
167 Rowe, 'False Consciousness', *Spare Rib*, 69.

people. It was this 'appalling lack of public, free, progressive provision' which made the work of groups such as theirs necessary.[168]

By the beginning of the 1980s, the psychological had become a much more marginal subject within the pages of *Spare Rib*. An article on consciousness-raising noted that the topic had attracted little attention since the early 1970s and set this down to an increasing emphasis on campaigning as an alternative focus of feminist activity. A group was set up to re-evaluate the practice.[169] Although its members reported back with some enthusiasm, what they represented as consciousness-raising had shifted some way since its origins a decade earlier. There was now no sign of any engagement with psychological theory. Indeed, there was an anxiety to point out that consciousness-raising should not be construed as having anything at all to do with therapy: 'let us hear no more about consciousness raising being self-indulgent middle-class therapeutic support groups for women who lack confidence to join "real" political groups and who just want to sit around cosily counting orgasms.' On the contrary, it 'transforms us into highly sensitised and politicised, highly dangerous women. Consciousness raising will never make us happy.'[170] When on a rare occasion the issue of therapy was broached, the tone of justification was distinctly defensive. It was now framed in utilitarian terms of providing necessary assistance to the one in nine desperate British women who suffered from mental problems, and as a preferable solution to the common alternative of pacifying pills. The claim that therapy might be the way forward to a new politics—politicising personal unhappiness—was far less prominent. The acceptance that these women really did have mental problems—that this was not simply an issue of male doctors placing a medical label on female dissent—highlights the distance from the anti-psychiatric atmosphere of the early 1970s. Women's support groups were now more likely to form around the recognition of particular problems, such as eating disorders, rather than act as a broad forum for exploring what it meant to be a psychological subject as a woman.[171]

Elaine Showalter's influential history of women as victims of psychiatry ends on a positive note with the emergence of a feminist therapy movement in the early 1970s.[172] Other commentators have been less sanguine, portraying the move to therapy as part of a broader, inward-looking, and ultimately individualist cultural turn, paying less credence to a trajectory in which psychology may have fostered a new social consciousness and politics. In Rose's view, the narrative of emotions and relationships, which lay at the heart of this feminist therapeutics, was still essentially a technique for a new individualism: 'we should not be misled by the rhetoric of sharing and communality which we find in these tales'.[173] Likewise, it has been argued that despite its sometimes anti-psychiatric rhetoric, feminist therapy 'can only be viewed as in some ways extending the existing field of the

---

168 F. McKay, 'Self-Help Therapy', *Spare Rib*, 48 (1976), 14–16.
169 G. Philpott, 'Consciousness-Raising: Back to Basics', *Spare Rib*, 92 (1980), 49.
170 Ibid. 54.   171 Ernst and Goodison, 'Consciousness Raising', 18–24.
172 Showalter, *Female Malady*, 250.   173 Rose, *Governing the Soul*, 253.

psychiatric system, and not as subverting or supplanting it'.[174] There has been a sense that the women's-movement project of politicizing the personal through consciousness-raising and self-help therapy floundered on its own contradictions or became debased as it evolved into the kind of testimonies of suffering which have come to be such a popular public spectacle of late-twentieth-century therapeutic culture, most notably in the baring of personal problems by audiences and celebrities alike on television chat shows.[175]

This brief survey of one aspect of this culture lends some support to such criticisms. There were unresolved tensions about being anti-psychiatric yet turning to the psychological as a key to personal transformation; and there were further tensions between this focus on the self, on the one hand, and social consciousness and political action, on the other. Such contradictory aspirations would prove increasingly hard to hold together as the decade progressed. For those feminists who prioritised political and social campaigning, a consciousness-raising therapeutics could easily appear something of a middle-class indulgence. For others, who continued to explore the internalisation of the social order within the individual psyche, it was increasingly unclear whether changes in the law and social conditions would be sufficient to transform what was such a deep-rooted psychological issue.[176] Yet such debate would increasingly colonise the realm of theory more than practice, emerging as extremely influential within a post-structuralist academic and intellectual world heavily influenced by feminism. It would be largely inaccessible when it came to guiding the majority of British women.

However, this survey has also highlighted an importance of the psychological within the women's movement of the late 1960s and 1970s which has not always been given due emphasis in histories of either subject.[177] For all its flaws, consciousness-raising was more than a mere prelude or epiphenomenon of an increasingly self-centred therapeutic society. The attempt to draw together an exploration of self with a political critique of society was historically important. It is significant that it came to be seen as the way forward by many within the broader growth movement: men as well as women. In bringing the psychological into the centre of its politics, the feminism of this era achieved what the male politics of the social had invariably failed to do, despite the increased importance of psychology as a key to understanding human action, since the start of the century. Most importantly, the feminist recognition of the importance of the social order in constructing femininity as a psychological category is in marked contrast to the lesser attention paid to gender differences earlier in the century,

---

[174] H. Allen, 'Psychiatry and the Feminine', in P. Miller and N. Rose (eds.), *The Power of Psychiatry* (Cambridge, 1986), 104.

[175] This view is discussed and criticised in Nudelman, 'Beyond the Talking Cure'.

[176] For some of these tensions: B. Caine, *English Feminism, 1780–1980* (Oxford, 1997), 266–71.

[177] On the socialist wing of the movement, Sheila Rowbotham, for instance, perhaps unsurprisingly pays little attention to the engagement with the psychological in her various studies of the British women's movement. Sally Alexander, however, has highlighted the lack of attention given to the important relationship and pointed to some intriguing parallels between the histories of psychoanalysis and feminism over the century as a whole: *Becoming a Woman and Other Essays in Nineteenth and Twentieth Century Feminist History* (London, 1994), 225–30, 244–5.

and to the focus on the biological rather than social as the main cause of those differences which were noted.

CONCLUSION

This chapter has been keen to contribute to an emerging interest in the cultural and social history of this post-war period. Thus far, the dominant framework in such work has been that of the emergence of a permissive society, hence the focus here. This framework has proved illuminating for considering the subject of psychology. However, the chapter has also attempted to question conventional assumptions about both who and what was permissive. By way of a series of case studies, it has charted the development of psychological thought and practice in the period from the late 1950s to the mid-1970s. It has considered the extent to which this period saw significant shifts at both the popular and professional levels, and the extent to which any such shift reflected or contributed to permissiveness, real and imagined. In certain respects, the contrasts with the first half of the century have been striking. Equally, significant, however, have been certain parallels.

The chapter has suggested that two streams of psychological thinking emerged in relation to permissiveness. Both had some permissive qualities, though often different ones, and to some extent they were in tension or even open conflict. The more obvious is that of representatives of the counter culture, here epitomised by the case studies of the humanistic psychology and feminist movements. Such a psychology was permissive, not just in the sense that it lined up with the forces of change, but also because it looked to openness in emotions and relationships and attacked psychology as a potential tool of control. Less obvious is the stream represented by a figure like the hugely popular Eysenck, but also the popular psychological books and magazines, even a group like Mensa or more generally the interest in intelligence, and the growing influence of behaviourism and a biological psychiatry, particularly evident in the expanding use of the drug as a therapeutic tool. This was important in providing something for a countercultural anti-psychiatry and anti-psychology to mobilise against; but in its move away from values, it too had a key permissive characteristic.

The comparison of these streams with the currents of psychological thought and practice in the first half of the century is also intriguing. Consciousness-raising and self-help therapy centred on the value of talk and depended on rationalisation; practical psychology had tended to avoid introspection, concentrating on doing rather than discussing. However, the stream epitomised by a figure like Eysenck presents us with some equally significant differences the past, particularly in its distancing of psychology from values, and its turn to behaviourism and biology. In fact, the countercultural stream had certain features in common with its forebears. It still looked to psychology in a rather utopian way as a source of values and meaning for life. It remained fascinated by the path to higher levels of consciousness. In the use of the social movement, it maintained an interest in both practice and the power of thinking in groups. Even the anti-psychiatric and anti-psychological strain echoed an earlier misgiving and ongoing tension about the democratisation of psychological knowledge.

Here, the chapter also adds a further twist to the story of popular–professional relations. In their populism, Eysenck and a journal like *Psychology Today* suggest a new confidence from the profession in this respect and a more relaxed attitude to mass culture, no longer feeling that they needed to protect themselves in a cocoon of science, and now increasingly assertive about an evangelising mission to break down abuse and nonsense. Their success also suggests a public open to this message. Yet the picture was more confused than this. Another section of the profession, as evident in anti-psychiatry and humanistic psychology, was in active dispute with professional power and looked to a popular audience for allies. For several rather different reasons, then, the dialogue across the popular–professional divide once again became particularly intense in this period.

Finally, a major theme in this book has been the relationship between psychological thinking and values. The book has argued that psychology, rather than necessarily undermining values, for much of the century acted to reconfigure and reinvigorate them. This is one of the reasons for continuing the analysis to a period seen as so fundamental in the breakdown in values. The case studies of this chapter offer several insights in this respect. As already noted, one of the streams of psychological thought did tend to divorce itself from values, regarding the dialogue in the past as something that compromised psychology's scientific reputation. Critics, meanwhile, blamed psychology for permissiveness, most notably through its role in child rearing and education, but also in turning issues of right and wrong into issues instead of mental health. However, this chapter has suggested that this exaggerates the real influence of psychology. If values changed or collapsed, the more fundamental reasons lay elsewhere in broader social processes. It also overlooks the fact that this period saw a flourishing of idealism about psychology potentially providing the values for a society that was fast losing them. This has been a major theme in the chapter, whether in the vision of a 'faith of the counsellors' or in a new type of politics within the humanistic psychology and feminist movements. On the other hand, the tensions in such visions also rapidly became apparent. First, there was ambivalence from the anti-psychiatric perspective. Secondly, there was growing pessimism by the mid-1970s that such utopianism about self-realisation and therapy would struggle to either transcend its middle-class base or overcome the more fundamental social and economic inequalities. Psychological practice would expand rapidly after this period, but in terms of idealism, and utopian expectations about psychology—a phenomenon that had been so acute since the start of the century—this period may well have been one in which the vision finally reached a breaking point in face of its mounting contradictions.

Conclusion

This has been a study of the shifting character of psychological thought and practice in twentieth-century Britain. It has also involved testing the extent to which one can usefully push such exploration well beyond the normal territories of either the academy and profession or a Freudian intellectual elite; though it has suggested that we might look afresh at these areas too when set within the context of a broader cultural whole. It has been particularly interested in a type of popular thought beyond the well-trodden territory of the reception of Freud among the educated public. Here, it has unearthed systems of thought and practice whose character and considerable appeal call for us to reconsider some of our assumptions about what sort of psychology mattered in this period. Thus, alongside the existing story of the popularisation of Freud, which is certainly not discounted here, even if it does need careful contextualisation as part of a broader phenomenon, with due emphasis too on adaptation and accommodation, we find an often striking array of options. This is particularly evident in the early decades of the century, before it gradually changed because of mounting professional authority on the one hand, and a greater willingness of these professionals to engage with a popular audience on the other. In these years, one finds a rich and diverse culture of practical psychology, called such because of its emphasis on the centrality of independent and active practice. This culture ranged from the sheer pragmatism of self-improvement practices like Pelmanism, to embracing the potential of 90 per cent of the mind hidden in the unconscious through the key of Couéist autosuggestion, to the mystical visions of transcending self in some sort of cosmic consciousness, and to the burgeoning market for practical psychological advice on managing personal life. The book has also highlighted the impact of psychological thinking on groups, subjects, and debates not normally part of any history of psychology. We have seen, for instance, the interest in psychology within workers' education organisations, and later within the feminist movement, but also in relation to thinking about human nature (not just trauma) in relation to war, to the problem of adjusting to a machine age, and last of all to the very idea of a permissive society. We have also seen the interest among teachers, social workers, doctors, preachers, employers, advertisers, and even politicians, highlighting the importance of intermediate levels of popularisation and translation. Although practice was fundamentally important at the popular level of the self-help cultures, elsewhere it was invariably held back by economic problems, lack of adequately trained personnel, and concern about psychological theory such as psychoanalysis being too dangerous to pass into untrained hands. Therefore, often more important was the way psychology emerged as a powerful source of ideas for envisaging not just the good person but also the good society. Backwardness in terms of academic and professional development provided space for a flourishing and diverse popular culture. It also meant that even at the academic and professional level, such a psychology tended to accommodate itself to existing values in order to gain validation and often found its most significant manifestation not in policy but in values, acting as a bridge to ease cultural transitions. The book has highlighted, in particular, a role of offering values to ameliorate the difficulty of adjusting to and embracing secularisation, democratisation, expanding state welfare (here focusing on health care and education), mechanisation, consumerism (giving an ethical gloss to salesmanship and advertising but also, via self-realisation and personality, to the commodification of everyday problems and identity), total war, and permissiveness.

In uncovering this richer terrain of psychological influence, the book indicates that we may need to modify and temper the two main narratives of the impact of psychology within twentieth-century society. The first, particularly influential now in the British context, centres on the advance of applied psychology and its tools and regimes of normalisation, regulation, and control in governing, and in its extreme form, making subjectivity. The second narrative has been most associated with developments in the United States, though it remains a powerful framework for charting psychological modernity and often for considering Britain as relatively backward. This centres on the advance of a psychology inspired by Freud that promoted a new openness to emotions and relationships, and ultimately according to critics resulted in a narcissistic obsession with therapy. In terms of the first narrative, a theme throughout this book has been limitations of extent, resistance, and modification in practice. It has also highlighted the existence among the experts, who have been situated at the heart of this narrative, of more romantic strains of thought about the implications of psychology for their subjects and, most important, a desire and need in terms of approval from a position of insecurity to accommodate psychology to existing values. In terms of the second narrative, the book has explored some of the cultural barriers that either channelled psychology in a more pragmatic, self-improving, and less introspective direction, or modified and directed towards ethical, social, and spiritual ends a psychology centred on exploring individual emotion and relationships. If the first stands for the narrative of discipline within modernity, and the second for liberty, what has emerged as a dominant theme of this book is a strain of psychological thinking that looked to reconcile the two. For much of the century, popular audiences, public intellectuals, and professionals alike were not wholly comfortable with either of the first two options. Instead, they used the space opened up by psychological thinking to imagine and design practices for cultivating a subjectivity that was free but not self-centred, and that transcended mere individualism in its ethical, social, and even spiritual ambitions.

In order to establish this case, to chart and contextualise shifts over time, and to further open up the subject of psychology's potentially broad implications for the general rather than the specialist historian, *Psychological Subjects* has focused on the relationship of this strain of thinking to the four dominant narrative frames for writing the British history of the period. In each case, contemporary concern and excitement about human—by this time, increasingly psychological—nature was an integral element. This is an important but hitherto largely neglected subject, and one of the main aims of the book has been to help open up a history that looks outwards from psychology, exploring in particular its relation to the constitution of social democratic subjectivity in twentieth-century Britain.

Suggesting a relationship between the psychological and the first of the frames—the turn-of-the-century 'new age'—has been less original than in the other cases. However, in stretching our understanding of what we might mean by popular psychology in this period, and in highlighting the differences and tensions between the culture of practical psychology and the more culturally-elite interest in Freud that still dominates our perspective of the early twentieth-century 'change in human character', our picture of this episode is nevertheless modified. At the start of the century, the appeal of psychological thinking was partly that it provided a bridge between new pressures and opportunities and an existing ethics and associated practices of the self. In this sense, despite the importance of the feeling that human character was coming to be understood in a new way, the story is also one that supports the view of a certain cultural continuity stretching from the late-Victorian era to a more fundamental challenge to the centrality of values in the final decades of the twentieth century. The culture of practical psychology was one in which character—that fixation of Victorian culture and ethics—still mattered very much, even if it now found itself translated into a more psychological idiom. For this reason, practice and often service were also central. Continuities with a religious ethics of the self are equally apparent. Together, this added up to a psychological culture in which self-realisation was about transcending the mere boundaries of individual selfishness to a consciousness of one's relationship, not only to a hidden psychic world within, but also to one without. Thus, self-realisation was invariably a social and often a spiritual project. What it did not rest upon was a pole of abnormality. For that reason, the tensions between popular and professional psychology, including often psychoanalysis, for all their commonalities, were at times intense; and this marks out the earlier period. All this emphasis on continuity, however, is not to say that a sense of change could not also be important. Indeed, one of the most striking findings has been the intense excitement, often verging on the utopian, which crossed the boundaries between popular and professional psychological communities, about new psychological understanding and practice and its implications, not just for the individual, but also for society, in the early decades of the century.

The second context of the problems of industrial civilisation has been a less obvious one to develop. This has been part of the attraction in exploring it: it has provided the opportunity to begin considering the extent to which the ramifications of psychological thinking extended beyond the merely personal to matters social, economic, and even political. Here, the book has downplayed the significance of perhaps the most well appreciated development—that of industrial psychology. Instead, it has pointed to a wider dialogue. Even the discipline, in the formative years at the start of the century, was not immune from such questions and grand ambitions. It was also an area of interest among some critics of industrial society, not just within the workers' movements of the era, but also within some of the intellectual circles explored. In terms of policy, it was an underlying inspiration behind the project of rescuing the consciousness of the working-class child through a new pedagogy. Ultimately, however, such a frame also highlights the limitations of psychology's influence. It attracted attention on the political and economic margins, but with some significant exceptions aside would struggle to make a transition to the mainstream in relation to questions more readily addressed as political or economic. Class relations and inequalities would also inhibit the expansion of a psychological approach not only within industry, but also in medicine, which would struggle to overcome suspicions about malingering on the one hand, and lack of resources on the other.

By the 1930s, a powerful second set of anxieties, exposed by the irrationality and aggression of man in war and now peace, joined those relating to economic man to push psychological subjectivity from the status of a private to a public issue. Again, however, the story in relation to the mid-century international crisis is as much one of ultimately unfulfilled visions, as of concrete or lasting achievements. Though the gendering of the issue was rarely explicit, the fact that the central psychological subject of war, like that of the problem of industrial civilisation, was a male one was significant in bringing it to the fore of public concern. Also important were the circumstances for relating mental health to both democracy and national identity, with psychology emerging as a tool for reinvigorating the former through its naturalisation and valorisation of the latter. However, such propitious circumstances would be temporary, even if given a further spur by the prospects of reconstruction at home and abroad. In this area, like so many others, a wartime impetus would be hard to maintain far beyond it.

Bringing psychology and particularly a more Freudian psychology to the fore and providing it with a new degree of public authority, war also accelerated a process of professional specialisation that had the effect of closing down the space for psychologies from below. An ongoing feminisation of popular psychology also increasingly directed it towards psychoanalytic experts and their advice on gender, childrearing, relationships, and sexuality. At the same time, the bonds of associational culture, that had been such an important factor behind the practical psychology culture of the first decades of the century, were weaker now. For a complex of reasons, then, the popular psychology of the post-war era moved away from its earlier independent and unorthodox character. Because of this, the emphasis on the importance of practice waned, as did resistance to policies of control, regulation, and measurement based on psychology. There would also be a new opportunity for psychologies that cast their subjects in biological or behavioural terms. The critiques of the 1960s and 1970s would reflect disquiet about this new balance of power. At times, they would also echo the earlier movements, with their language of self-transcendence, the search for a new system of values in a deeper understanding of being human, and an emphasis on practice rather than passivity. A new radicalism would also emerge which recognised the potential in psychological thinking for subverting, rather than supporting, existing gender roles, as had tended to be the case for most of the century. Particularly through the influence of feminism, there was again excitement about the use of psychology in forging, not just people, but also a new type of politics. What such use of psychological thinking shared with a strong strain that had preceded it was a commitment to values. In that sense at least, we should be cautious about seeing the counterculture as the home for a newly permissive type of psychological thinking. If permissiveness centres on greater openness about relationships and emotion, then this culture was indeed an important site, both for expressing this and using psychological thought and practice to turn it into a lifestyle project. If it centres, instead, on a rejection of the place of values as a guide to individual and social life, the psychological roots lay in two rather different lines of development. Firstly, a loss of confidence in the coupling of psychology and ideology that culminated in the Second World War, and in the rise of a psychology that, as part of its struggle to defend itself as a science, objected to being embroiled in the search for values, and was more reticent about interdisciplinary exchange. Secondly, the advance of a type of individualism that found its roots in much broader structural processes, rather than in psychology itself: the psychology had been there since the start of the century to foster narcissism; cultural circumstances, as this book has argued, had meant that this had been far from the only, let alone the dominant story.

It is because of the importance of such cultural circumstances that this story may be, at least in some respects, a peculiarly British one. Ultimately, this is for others with a stronger understanding of different national contexts to judge, though it may be helpful here to highlight some potential lines of inquiry. The obvious focus for comparison is the United States, a country that was particularly fertile ground for the emergence of the dominant form of psychological modernity, for a combination of cultural, institutional, economic, and even psychological reasons. Rather than comparing Britain against such a model, this book has preferred to consider development here in its own right to suggest the possibility of reframing it from one of backwardness (hence the lack of attention from historians) to one of difference instead, emphasising the tendency for accommodation with existing values which tended to accentuate national difference. However, America clearly did sometimes act as a springboard for ideas: a subject that deserves more consideration. Equally interesting is the way that emerging consciousness of an American model could provide something to identify against and thereby legitimate an alternative path in difficult circumstances. In this regard, Germany, or at least an idea about the relation between mental health and German culture, played a crucial role too in the first half of the century. In terms of lines of influence from America, the book has touched on several significant examples. At the start of the period, we see the passage across the Atlantic of new thought movements and of a commodification of psychology through magazines, the funding and attempted steering of professional development from American philanthropy, and Clifford Beers' inspiration for the idea of mental hygiene. By the end, we again see American roots, for instance in the humanistic growth movement and the use of psychology within feminism. However, in many such instances, one also finds rhetoric that differentiated, by way of justification, a British way in psychology. British industrial psychologists presented themselves as humanising work, in contrast to American efficiency engineering. We see the cultivation of personality and truth to offer a British way in business, advertising, and salesmanship, an ethical dimension supposedly missing in the United States. For much of the century, the British also tended to present themselves as unreceptive to the determinism of a behaviourism that flourished in the United States. Later, the British humanistic psychologists were also keen to distance their radicalism from American developments.

When it came to actual practice, actual policies, actual institutional developments, sheer economics were ultimately even more crucial than culture in differentiating British development from that in the United States. Throughout the period, there was a gross disparity in the level of academic and professional development. This meant British psychology had to work hard at cultural accommodation in order to be accepted, and this probably encouraged a divergence in style in line with broader cultural tendencies. Economics were also important at the popular level where class was a powerful factor in the British story. This may have given a particularly self-improving but also social orientation to British practical psychology. This was even evident in an explicitly working-class psychology within the workers' education movement. The private market for expensive therapy, by contrast, was much smaller, and the economic limitations of the state system fostered suspicion of opening any psychological floodgates in terms of therapy. We also see the way that a psychology centred on the power of personality could actually sharpen divides between elites and the masses, epitomised by the orientation of figures as diverse as McDougall, Mitrinovic, and Casson, or even the scepticism about the mental ability of the masses in the labour movement, or the concerns about popularisation among psychoanalysts. However, the problem of bridging this divide tended to turn British engagement with the psychological in a social democratic orientation, most notably in the context of the mid-century crisis. In the longer term, the normative values at the heart of an ideology of mental health, the undemocratic nature of power within the therapeutic relationship, and the ongoing failure to tackle what remained more vital underlying social inequalities were always liable to critique from a radical perspective, as was indeed the case in the 1960s and 1970s. In short, this problem of class and the struggle to overcome it through a social democratic form of psychological subjectivity, like the associated strong ethical orientation and accommodation with existing values more generally, and the relatively weak institutional development that accompanied a more statist orientation, all help to mark out a distinctively British story.

Bibliography

1. ARCHIVES

Rockefeller Archive Centre, Tarrytown, New York
  Papers of the Commonwealth Foundation
  Papers of the Rockefeller Foundation
Modern Records Centre, University of Warwick
  Trades Union Congress Papers
British Library of Political and Economic Science, London School of Economics
  Evan Durbin Papers
  National Institute of Industrial Psychology Papers
Contemporary Medical Archives Centre, Wellcome Trust Library, London
  John Bowlby Papers
  British Medical Association Papers
  Eugenics Society Papers
  Ranyard West Papers
National Archives, London
  Ministry of Health
  Ministry of Information

2. GOVERNMENT PUBLICATIONS

Board of Education, *Report of the Consultative Committee on Infant and Nursery Schools* (London, 1933).

Board of Education, *Report of the Consultative Committee on the Primary School* (London, 1931).

Department of Education and Science, *Children and the Primary Schools: A Report of the Central Advisory Council of Education (England)*, 1 (London, 1967).

Ministry of Education, *Report of the Committee on Maladjusted Children (Underwood Report)* (London, 1955).

Report as to the Practice of Medicine and Surgery by Unqualified Persons in the United Kingdom (London, 1910).

Report of the Royal Commission on Medical Education, 1965–1968 (London, 1968).

Report of the War Office Committee of Enquiry into 'Shell-Shock' (London, 1922).

3. OTHER REPORTS

Annual Reports of the World Federation of Mental Health.

Report of the Feversham Committee: The Voluntary Mental Health Services (London, 1939).

4. PERIODICALS AND NEWSPAPERS

Adelphi
Applied Psychology
British Journal of Educational Psychology
British Journal of Guidance and Counselling
British Journal of Medical Psychology
British Journal of Psychology
British Medical Journal
Bulletin of the John Rylands Library
Burial Reformer
Daily Herald
Daily Mirror
Efficiency Magazine
Encounter
Evening News
Health Record
Hibbert Journal
Highway
Human Affairs
Human Factor
Human Relations
International New Thought Alliance Record
International Times
Journal of Mental Science
Journal of the National Institute of Industrial Psychology
Journal of the Royal College of General Practitioners
Manchester Daily Dispatch
Manchester Guardian
Mensa Correspondence
Mental Hygiene
Nature
New Adelphi
New Age
New Albion
New Britain
New Era
New Ideals Quarterly
New Left Review
New Society
New Statesman
New Thought
New Thought Journal
Occupational Psychology
Peace News
Picture Post
Practical Psychologist

Practical Psychology
Psychology
Psychology Today
Psycho-Therapeutic Journal
Public Health
Purpose
Red Rat
Scrutiny
Self and Society
Sheffield Telegraph
Sociological Review
Spare Rib
The Emblem
The Freewoman
The Lancet
The Plebs
The Realist
The Times
You

5. BOOKS AND ARTICLES

Adams, J., *The Herbartian Psychology Applied to Education* (London, 1897).

Addison, P., *The Road to 1945: British Politics and the Second World War* (London, 1975).

Alexander, S., *Becoming a Woman and Other Essays in Nineteenth and Twentieth Century Feminist History* (London, 1994).

—— 'Men's Fears and Women's Work: Responses to Unemployment in London between the Wars', *Gender and History*, 12 (2000), 401–25.

Allderidge, P., 'The Foundation of the Maudsley Hospital', in Berrios and Freeman (eds.), *150 Years of British Psychiatry*, 1, pp. 79–88.

Allen, H., 'Psychiatry and the Feminine', in P. Miller and N. Rose (eds.), *The Power of Psychiatry* (Cambridge, 1986).

Andrews, J., 'R. D. Laing in Scotland: Facts and Fictions of the "Rumpus Room" and Interpersonal Psychiatry', in Gijswijt-Hofstra and Porter (eds.), *Cultures of Psychiatry*, 121–50.

Angel, K., 'Defining Psychiatry: Aubrey Lewis's 1938 Report and the Rockefeller Foundation', in K. Angel, E. Jones, and M. Neve (eds.), *European Psychiatry on the Eve of War: Aubrey Lewis, the Maudsley Hospital and the Rockefeller Foundation in the 1930s* (London, 2003) 57–63.

Anon., *Test your Intelligence: Questions and Replies from General Knowledge* (London, 1940).

Anon., *Test Yourself: Intelligence Quizzes based on Official Tests and Arranged as Party Games* (London, 1951).

Anton, E., 'The Biography of an Idea—Pelmanism', *The Times* (28 Jan. 1918).

Appignanesi, L. and Forrester, J. (eds.), *Freud's Women* (London, 1993).

Argyle, M., 'The Development of Social Psychology in Oxford', in Bunn et al. (eds.), *Psychology in Britain*, 333–43.

Armstrong-Jones, Sir R., 'Mind and Body', in Sir W. Arbuthnot Lane (ed.), *Safer Motherhood and the Hygiene of Life* (London, 1934).

Armytage, W. H. G., *Heavens Below: Utopian Experiments in England, 1560–1960* (London, 1961).

Ash, E. L. H., *Nerves and the Nervous* (London, 1911, 1921).

—— *Faith and Suggestion* (London, 1912).

—— *Mental Self-Help: A Practical Handbook* (London, 1912, 1920).

—— *'Can't Waiters' Or How You Waste Your Energy* (London, 1913).

—— *The Nursing of Nervous Patients* (London, 1913).

—— *Nerves in War-Time* (London, 1914).

—— *Stammering and Successful Control in Speech and Action* (London, 1916).

—— *How to Treat by Suggestion, with and without Hypnosis: A Notebook for Practitioners* (London, 1914).

—— *Middle Age Health and Fitness* (London, 1922).

—— *I Am and I Will: Twelve Practical Lessons in Mental Science* (London, 1924).

—— *Facts about Stammering* (London, 1925).

—— *On Keeping Our Nerves in Order* (London, 1928).

—— *An ABC of Treatment by Personal Influence, Suggestion, Medical Hypnosis, and Psychomagnetic Methods* (London, 1929).

—— *Therapy of Personal Influence* (London, 1929).

—— *Melancholia in Everyday Practice* (London, 1934).

—— *Manipulative Methods in the Treatment of Functional Disease* (London, 1935).

—— *Diagnosis of Some Delusional Types in General Practice* (London, 1936).

—— *The Mental Nurses Dictionary* (London, 1942, 1952).

Ashman, J., *Psychopathology or the True Healing Art* (London, 1874).

Auden, W. H., 'Psychology and Art', in G. Grigson (ed.), *The Arts To-day* (London, 1935), 1–24.

Aveling, F., *Personality and Will* (London, 1931).

Babini, V., 'Science, Feminism and Education: The Early Work of Maria Montessori', *History Workshop Journal*, 49 (2000), 44–67.

Badouin, C., *Suggestion and Autosuggestion: A Psychological and Pedagogical Study Based Upon the Investigations made by the Nancy School* (London, 1920).

Baily, C. W., *The Brain and Golf: Some Hints for Golfers from Modern Mental Science* (London, 1923).

Balfour, M., *Propaganda in War, 1939–45: Organisation, Policies and Publics in Britain and Germany* (London, 1979).

Balint, M., *The Doctor, the Patient and the Illness*, 2nd edn. (London, 1964).

Ballard, P. G., *Thomas George Tibby: A Lecture in his Memory* (London, 1936).

Barham, P., *Forgotten Lunatics of the Great War* (New Haven and London, 2004).

Barke, M., Fribush, R., and Stearns, P., 'Nervous Breakdown in Twentieth-Century American Culture', *Social History*, 33 (2000), 565–84.

Barker, B. (ed.), *Ramsay MacDonald's Political Writing* (London, 1972).

Barnett, M., *People not Psychiatry* (London, 1973).

Barrow, L., *Independent Spirits: Spiritualism and English Plebians, 1850–1910* (London, 1986).

Bartlett, P. and Wright, D. (eds.), *Outside the Walls of the Asylum: The History of Care in the Community, 1750–2000* (London, 1999).

Bartlett, Sir F., Ginsberg, M., Lindgren, E. J., and Thouless, R. H. (eds.), *The Study of Society: Methods and Problems* (London, 1939).

Bartrip, P., *Workmen's Compensation in Twentieth-Century Britain* (Aldershot, 1987).

Bates, W. H., *The Cure of Imperfect Sight by Treatment without Glasses* (New York, 1920).

Beale, M., *The Modernist Experience: French Elites and the Threat of Modernity, 1900–1940* (Stanford, Calif., 1999).

Beales, H. L. and Lambert, R. S. (eds.), *Memoirs of the Unemployed* (London, 1934).

Beirer, J. (ed.), *Therapeutic Social Clubs* (London, 1948).

Bennett, J. G., *Witness: The Autobiography of John G. Bennett* (London, 1974).

Benson, J., *The Rise of Consumer Culture in Britain, 1880–1980* (London, 1994).

Berger, P., 'Towards a Sociological Understanding of Psychoanalysis', *Social Research* 32 (1965), 26–41.

Berrios, G. and Freeman, H. (eds.), *150 Years of British Psychiatry, 1841–1991*, 2 vols. (London, 1991 and 1996).

Berry, M., *Teacher Training Institutions in England and Wales: A Bibliographical Guide to their History* (London, 1973).

Berry, P. and Bostridge, M., *Vera Brittain: A Life* (London, 2001).

Bingham, A., *Gender, Modernity, and the Popular Press in Inter-War Britain* (Oxford, 2004).

Bion, W., ' "The War of Nerves": Civilian Reaction, Morale, and Prophylaxis', in E. Miller (ed.), *The Neuroses in War* (London, 1940), 180–200.

Birchenough, C., *History of Elementary Education in England and Wales from 1800 to the Present Day* (London, 1925).

Bishop, A., 'The Battle of the Somme and Vera Brittain', in M. Roucoux (ed.), *English Literature of the Great War Revisited* (Amiens, 1987), 125–42.

Blacker, C. P., *Neurosis and the Mental Health Services* (London, 1946).

—— *Problem Families: Five Enquiries* (London, 1952).

Bland, L., *Banishing the Beast: English Feminism and Sexual Morality, 1885–1914* (London, 1995).

Boden, M., 'Purpose, Personality, Creativity: A Computational Adventure', in Bunn et al. (eds.), *Psychology in Britain*, 353–62.

Bogacz, T., 'War Neurosis and Cultural Change in England 1914–1922: The Work of the War Office Committee of Enquiry into "Shell-Shock" ', *Journal of Contemporary History*, 24 (1989), 227–56.

Bottome, P., *Alfred Adler: Apostle of Freedom* (London, 1939).

Bourke, J., *Dismembering the Male: Men's Bodies, Britain and the Great War* (London, 1996).

Bowlby, J., *Maternal Care and Mental Health* (Geneva, 1952).

—— *Child Care and the Growth of Love* (London, 1953).

—— and Durbin, E., *Personal Aggressiveness and War* (London, 1939).

—— and Durbin, E., 'Personal Aggressiveness and War', in E. Durbin, J. Bowlby, I. Thomas, D. Jay, R. Fraser, R. Crossman, and G. Catlinz (eds.), *War and Democracy: Essays on the Causes and Prevention of War* (London, 1938), 3–150.

Bowler, P., *The Eclipse of Darwinism: Anti-Darwinian Evolution in the Decades around 1900* (London, 1992).

—— *Reconciling Science and Religion: The Debate in Early Twentieth-Century Britain* (Chicago, 2001).

Boyd, W. (ed.), *Towards a New Education: Based on the Fifth World Conference of the New Education Fellowship at Elsinore, Denmark* (London, 1930).
—— and Dawson, W., *The Story of the New Education* (London, 1965).
Brackenbury, H., *Patient and Doctor* (London, 1935).
Braddock, A. P., *Applied Psychology for Advertisers* (London, 1933).
Brehony, K. J., 'Montessori, Individual Work and Individuality in the Elementary School Classroom', *History of Education*, 29 (2000), 115–28.
British Institute of Practical Psychology, *Complete Course on Psychology* (London, 1933).
British Institute of Practical Psychology, *Personal Adjustment and Vocational Guidance through Personalysis* (London, 1934).
British Phrenological Society, *In Commemoration of Bernard Hollander* (London, 1965).
Brittain, I., *Fabianism and Culture: A Study in British Socialism and the Arts, c.1884–1918* (Cambridge, 1982).
Brittain, V., *Testament of Youth: An Autobiographical Study of the Years 1900–1925* (London, 1933).
Brome, V., *Ernest Jones: Freud's Alter Ego* (London, 1982).
Brooke, S., 'Evan Durbin: Reassessing a Labour "Revisionist"', *Twentieth Century British History*, 7 (1996), 27–52.
Brooker, P., *Bohemia in London: The Social Scene of Early Modernism* (Basingstoke, 2004).
Brooks, C. H., *The Practice of Autosuggestion by the Method of Emile Coué* (London, 1922).
Brown, A. Barratt, *The Machine and the Worker* (London, 1934).
Brown, H., *Advanced Suggestion (Neuroinduction)* (London, 1918).
—— *Modern Medical Methods* (London and New York, 1925).
Brown, J. A. C., *Freud and the Post-Freudians* (London, 1961).
Brown, W. (ed.), *Psychology and the Sciences* (London, 1924).
Brown, W., *Mind and Personality: An Essay in Psychology and Philosophy* (London, 1926).
—— *Science and Personality* (London, 1929).
—— *War and Peace: Essays in Psychological Analysis* (London, 1939).
—— 'The Psychology of Modern Germany', *British Journal of Psychology*, 34 (1944), 43–59.
Buchan, J., *The Gap in the Curtain* (London, 1932).
Bulmer, M., 'The Development of Sociology and Empirical Social Research in Britain', in M. Bulmer (ed.), *Essays on the History of British Sociological Research* (Cambridge, 1985), 3–36.
Bunn, G., Richards, G., and Lovie, S. (eds.), *Psychology in Britain: Historical Essays and Personal Reflections* (Leicester, 2001).
Burleigh, M., *Death and Deliverance: 'Euthanasia' in Germany 1900–1945* (Cambridge, 1994).
Burnett, J. (ed.), *Destiny Obscure: Autobiographies of Childhood, Education and Family from 1820 to the 1920s* (London, 1982).
Burnham, J., *The Managerial Revolution: Or What is Happening in the World Now* (London, 1942).
Burnham, J.C., *Paths into American Culture* (Philadelphia, 1988).
Burns, C. Delisle, *Industry and Civilisation* (London, 1925).
Burston, D., *The Wing of Madness: The Life and Work of R. D. Laing* (Cambridge, Mass. and London, 1996).
Burt, C., *Young Delinquent* (London, 1925).

—— 'An Inquiry into Public Opinion Regarding Educational Reforms', Part I, *Occupational Psychology*, 17 (1943), 157–67.

—— 'An Inquiry into Public Opinion Regarding Educational Reforms Part II', *Occupational Psychology*, 18 (1944), 13–23.

—— (ed.), *How the Mind Works* (1932).

Buzzard, E. F., 'The Dumping Ground of Neurasthenia', *The Lancet*, (4 Jan. 1930), 1–4.

Caesar, A., *Taking it Like a Man: Suffering, Sexuality and the War Poets* (London, 1993).

Caine, B., 'The Stracheys and Psychoanalysis', *History Workshop Journal*, 45 (1998), 144–69.

Calder, A., 'Mass-Observation, 1937–1939', in M. Bulmer (ed.), *Essays in the History of Sociological Research* (Cambridge, 1985), 121–36.

—— *The Myth of the Blitz* (London, 1991).

Cameron, D. E., *Auto-Psychology* (London, 1934).

Cameron, L., 'Histories of Disturbance', *Radical History*, 74 (1999), 5–13.

Cantril, H., 'The Social Psychology of Everyday Life', *The Psychological Bulletin*, 31 (1934), 297–331.

Cardwell, M., *How to Keep Well: A Simple Outline of the Proved Laws of Health* (London, 1938).

Carlson, M., *'No Religion Higher than Truth': A History of the Theosophical Movement in Russia, 1875–1922* (Princeton, 1993).

Carpenter, E., *The Art of Creation: Essays on the Self and its Powers* (London, 1904).

—— *The Drama of Love and Death* (London, 1912).

Carstairs, G. M., *This Island Now: The BBC Reith Lectures of 1962* (London, 1963).

Carswell, J., *Lives and Letters: A. R. Orage, Beatrice Hastings, Katherine Mansfield, John Middleton Murry, S. S. Koteliansky, 1906–1957* (London, 1978).

Casey, F., *Method in Thinking* (Manchester, 1933).

Casson, E. E., *Postscript: The Life and Thoughts of Herbert N. Casson* (London, 1952).

Casson, H. N., *Ads and Sales: A Study of Advertising and Selling from the Standpoint of Scientific Management* (London, 1911).

—— *The Story of My Life* (London, 1931).

—— *Efficiency Mentality* (London, 1933).

—— *Twelve Tips of Brain-Making* (London, 1935).

—— *Twenty Tips in Psychology* (London, 1936).

Catts, M., *A Weaver's Life: Ethel Mairet, 1872–1952* (Bath, 1983).

Chadwick, M., *Chapters about Childhood: The Psychology of Children from 5–10 Years* (London, 1939).

Chapman, R. W., 'Wilfred Trotter's "Instincts of the Herd in Peace and War"', *Sociological Review*, 35 (1943), 44–7.

Charles, E., *The Twilight of Parenthood* (London, 1934).

Chesterton, G. K., 'The Game of Psychoanalysis', *Century Magazine*, 106 (1923), 34–43.

Child, J., *British Management Thought: A Critical Analysis* (London, 1969).

Church, R., 'Advertising Consumer Goods in Nineteenth-Century Britain: Reinterpretations', *Economic History Review*, 53 (2000), 621–45.

Clare, A., *Psychiatry in Dissent* (London, 1976).

Claremont, C. A., 'Montessori and the New Era', *New Era*, 1/1 (1920), 11–16.

Clark, M., 'The Rejection of Psychological Approaches to Mental Disorder in Late Nineteenth-Century British Psychiatry', in A. Scull (ed.), *Madhouses, Mad-Doctors, and Madmen: The Social History of Psychiatry in the Victorian Era* (London, 1981), 271–312.

Clay, J., *R. D. Laing: A Divided Self. A Biography* (London, 1996).

Cohen, M., *What Nobody Told the Foreman* (London, 1953).

—— *I was one of the Unemployed* (Wakefield, 1978).

Collini, S., *Public Moralists: Political Thought and Intellectual Life in Britain, 1850–1930* (Oxford, 1991).

Collins, M., *Modern Love: An Intimate History of Men and Women in Twentieth-Century Britain* (London, 2003).

Colls, R., *Identity of England* (Oxford, 2002).

—— and Dodd, P. (eds.), *Englishness: Politics and Culture, 1880–1920* (London, 1986).

Conn, Revd J. C. M., *The Menace of the New Psychology* (London, 1939).

Cook, H., 'Sex and the Doctors: the Medicalization of Sexuality as a Two-Way Process in Early to Mid-Twentieth-Century Britain', in W. de Blécourt and C. Usborne (eds.), *Cultural Approaches to the History of Medicine: Mediating Medicine in Early Modern and Modern Europe* (Basingstoke, 2004), 192–211.

—— *The Long Sexual Revolution: English Women, Sex and Contraception 1800–1975* (Oxford, 2004).

Cooper, D., *The Death of the Family* (London, 1972).

Cooter, R., *The Cultural Meaning of Popular Science: Phrenology and the Organization of Consent in Nineteenth-Century Britain* (Cambridge, 1984).

—— (ed.), *In the Name of the Child: Health and Welfare, 1880–1940* (London, 1992).

—— 'Malingering and Modernity', in R. Cooter, M. Harrison and S. Sturdy (eds.), *War, Medicine and Society* (Sutton, 1999), 125–48.

Costall, A., 'Pear and his Peers', in Bunn et al. (eds.), *Psychology in Britain*, 188–204.

Coster, G., *Psycho-Analysis for Normal People*, 3rd edn. (London, 1932).

—— *Yoga and Western Psychology: A Comparison* (London, 1934).

Coué, E., *Self Mastery through Conscious Autosuggestion* (London, 1922).

—— and Brooks, C. H., *Better and Better Every Day: Two Classsic Texts in the Healing Power of Mind* (London, 1960).

—— and Orton, J. L., *Conscious Auto-Suggestion* (London, 1924).

Cox, C. B. and Dyson, A. E. (eds.), *The Black Papers on Education* (London, 1971).

Crammer, J., 'Training and Education in British Psychiatry 1770–1970', in Berrios and Freeman (eds.), *150 Years of British Psychiatry*, 2 (1996), 209–36.

Cronin, J., *Labour and Society in Britain, 1918–1979* (London, 1984).

Crook, P., *Darwinism, War and History: The Debate over the Biology of War from the 'Origin of Species' to the First World War* (Cambridge, 1994).

Crookshank, F. G., *The Mongol in Our Midst: A Study of Man and his Three Faces* (London, 1924).

—— 'The Importance of a Theory of Signs and a Critique of Language in the Study of Medicine', in C. K. Ogden and I. A Richards, *The Meaning of Meaning*, 2nd edn. (London, 1927), 337–55.

—— 'Types of Personality with Special Reference to Individual Psychology', *The Lancet* (8 Mar. 1930), 546.

—— *Individual Psychology, Medicine, and the Bases of Science*, Individual Psychology Pamphlet 3a (London, 1932).

—— *The New Psychology and the Health of the People*, Individual Psychology Pamphlet (London, July–Sept 1932).

—— *Individual Psychology and Nietzsche*, Individual Psychology Pamphlet 10 (London, 1933).

—— (ed.), *Anorexia Nervosa*, Individual Psychology Pamphlet 2 (London, 1931).

Cross, G., *Time and Money: The Making of a Consumer Culture* (London, 1993).

Crossley, N., 'R. D. Laing and British Anti-Psychiatry: A Socio-Historical Analysis', *Social Science and Medicine*, 47 (1998), 877–98.

—— 'Fish, Field, Habitus and Madness: On the First Wave Mental Health Users Movement in Britain', *British Journal of Sociology*, 50 (1999), 647–70.

—— 'Working Utopias and Social Movements: An Investigation using Case Study Materials from Radical Mental Health Movements in Britain', *Sociology*, 33 (1999), 809–30.

Crozier, I., 'Taking Prisoners: Havelock Ellis, Sigmund Freud and the Construction of Homosexuality, 1897–1951', *Social History of Medicine*, 13 (2000), 447–66.

Culpin, M., 'A Study of the Incidence of the Minor Psychoses: Their Clinical and Industrial Importance', *The Lancet* (4 Feb. 1928), 220–4.

—— 'The Need for Psychopathology', *The Lancet* (4 Oct. 1928), 725–6.

—— 'Some Cases of "Traumatic Neurasthenia"', *The Lancet* (1 Aug. 1931), 233–7.

Dainlow, M., *Personal Psychology: A Practical Guide to Self-Knowledge, Self-Development, and Self-Expression*, 2nd edn. (London, 1936).

Dale, P., 'Implementing the 1913 Mental Deficiency Act: Competing Priorities and Resource Constraint Evident in the South West of England before 1948', *Social History of Medicine*, 16 (2003), 403–18.

Davies, C, *Permissive Britain: Social Change in the Sixties and Seventies* (London, 1975).

Davies, T. G., *Ernest Jones, 1879–1958* (Cardiff, 1979).

Davies, W. T. and Shepherd, T. B., *Teacher Training: Begin Here* (London, 1949).

Dawson, G., *Soldier Heroes: British Adventure, Empire and the Imagining of Masculinities* (London, 1994).

de Chardin, P. T., *The Phenomenon of Man* (London, 1959).

De Groot, G., *Blighty: British Society in the Era of the Great War* (London, 1996).

de Man, Paul, *The Psychology of Socialism* (London, 1928).

—— *Joy in Work* (London, 1929).

Delap, L., 'The Superwoman: Theories of Gender and Genius in Edwardian Britain', *Historical Journal*, 47 (2004), 101–26.

Devaleny, E., *D. H. Lawrence and Edward Carpenter: A Study in Edwardian Transition* (London, 1971).

Dicks, H. V., 'Neurasthenia: Toxic and Traumatic', *The Lancet* (23 Sept. 1933), 683–6.

—— 'Personality Traits and National Socialist Ideology', *Human Relations*, 3 (1950), 111–54.

—— *Mental Health in the Light of Ancient Wisdom* (London, 1959).

—— *Fifty Years of the Tavistock Clinic* (London, 1970).

—— *Licensed Mass Murder: A Socio-Psychological Study of Some SS Killers* (London, 1972).

Digby, A., *The Evolution of British General Practice, 1850–1948* (Oxford, 1997).

Dixon, J., *Divine Feminine: Theosophy and Feminism in England* (Baltimore, 2001).

Dumville, B., *Child Mind: An Introduction to Psychology for Teachers*, 2nd edn. (London, 1931).

Dunlop, C. A., *Practical Psychology: Embodying the New Principle for the New Age in the Art of the Science of Living* (London, 1930).

Durbin, E., *New Jerusalems: The Labour Party and the Economics of Democratic Socialism* (London, 1985).

Durbin, E., *The Politics of Democratic Socialism: An Essay in Social Policy* (London, 1940).

—— *Problems of Economic Planning* (London, 1949), 101–2.

Davies, J. L., *Air Raid* (London, 1938).

Eder, M. D., 'Psycho-Analysis and Politics', in E. Jones (ed.), *Social Aspects of Psycho-Analysis: Lectures Delivered under the Auspices of the Sociological Society* (London, 1924).

—— 'On the Economics and the Future of the Super-Ego', *International Journal of Psycho-Analysis*, 10 (1929), 249–55.

—— 'Psychology and Value', *British Journal of Medical Psychology*, 10 (1930), 175–85.

—— 'The Myth of Progress', *British Journal of Medical Psychology*, 12 (1932), 1–14.

Ellenberger, H., *The Discovery of the Unconscious: The History and Evolution of Dynamic Psychiatry* (New York, 1970).

Elsdon, R., *Notes on Class Lectures on Practical Psychology* (Colne, 1925).

Ennever, W. J., *Brain Building for Success* (London, 1938).

—— *Your Mind and How to Use it* (London, 1942).

Evans, B. and Waites, B., *IQ and Mental Testing: An Unnatural Science and its Social History* (London, 1981).

Eysenck, H., *Sense and Nonsense in Psychology* (London, 1957).

—— *Know your Own IQ* (London, 1962).

—— *Test your own IQ* (London, 1964).

—— *Check your own IQ* (London, 1966).

—— *The Effects of Psychotherapy* (New York, 1966).

—— *Psychology is about People* (London, 1972).

—— *Rebel with a Cause: The Autobiography of H. J. Eysenck*, (London, 1990).

—— and Wilson, G., *The Experimental Study of Freudian Theories* (London, 1973).

Fennelly, P., *Practical Psychology* (Hull, 1929).

—— *Charts for Reading Physiological and Psychological Data* (Sheffield, 1935).

—— *Practical Analysis* (Southport, 1935).

Fielding, S., ' "Don't Know and Don't Care": Political Attitudes in Labour's Britain', in Tiratsoo (ed.), *The Attlee Years*, 106–125.

—— 'To Make Men and Women Better than they Are: Labour and the Building of Socialism', in J. Fyrth (ed.), *Labour's Promised Land: Culture and Society in Labour Britain, 1945–51* (London, 1995), 16–27.

Firth, R., 'An Anthropologist's View of Mass Observation', *Sociological Review*, 31 (1939), 166–93.

Fleming, C. M., 'The Place of Psychology in the Training of Teachers', *British Journal of Educational Studies*, 3 (1954), 17–23.

Fletcher, P., *How to Practice Auto-Suggestion* (London, 1939).

Flood, W. E. and Crossland, R. W., 'The Origin of Interest and Motives for Study of Natural Sciences and Psychology among Adult Students in Voluntary Courses', *British Journal of Educational Psychology*, 18 (1948), 105–17.

Flugel, J. C., *The Psychology of Clothes* (London, 1930).

—— *A Hundred Years of Psychology, 1833–1933* (London, 1933).

—— *Man, Morals and Society: A Psycho-Analytic Study* (London, 1945).

Forrester, J., ' "A Whole Climate of Opinion": Rewriting the History of Psychoanalysis', in M. Micale and R. Porter (eds.), *Discovering the History of Psychiatry* (New York and Oxford, 1994), 174–90.

—— and Cameron, L., ' "A Nice Type of the English Scientist": Tansley and Freud', *History Workshop Journal*, 48 (1999), 64–100.

Fountain, N., *Underground: The London Alternative Press, 1966–74* (London, 1988).

Fox, H., *Dreamland Speeches on Homeland Problems: The Practical Psychology of Life* (London, 1914).

Francis, M., 'Tears, Tantrums, and Bared Teeth: The Emotional Economy of Three Conservative Prime Ministers, 1951–1963', *Journal of British Studies*, 41 (2002), 354–87.

Freeden, M., *Liberalism Divided: A Study in British Political Thought, 1914–1939* (Oxford, 1986).

Furedi, F., *Therapy Culture: Cultivating Vulnerability in an Uncertain Age* (London, 2004).

Fussell, P., *The Great War and Modern Memory* (Oxford, 1975).

Gardner, D. E. M., *Susan Isaacs* (London, 1969).

Garland, D., *Punishment and Welfare* (Aldershot, 1985).

Gauld, A., *The Founders of Psychical Research* (London, 1968)

Gay, P., *Freud for Historians* (Oxford and New York, 1985).

—— *The Bourgeois Experience: Victoria to Freud: The Tender Passion* (Oxford, 1986).

Geppert, A. C. T., 'Divine Sex, Happy Marriage, Regenerated Nation: Marie Stopes's Marital Manual *Married Love* and the Making of a Best-Seller, 1918–1955', *Journal of the History of Sexuality*, 8 (1988), 389–433.

Gibson, H. B., *Hans Eysenck: The Man and his Work* (London, 1981).

Gibson, Sir R., *The Family Doctor: His Life and History* (London, 1981).

Gijswijt-Hofstra, M. and Porter, R. (eds.), *Cultures of Psychiatry and Mental Health Care in Post-war Britain and the Netherlands* (Amsterdam, 1998).

—— and Marland, H. (eds.), *Cultures of Child Health in Britain and the Netherlands in the Twentieth Century* (Amsterdam, 2003).

Giles, J., *Women, Identity, and Private Life in Britain, 1900–1950* (London, 1995).

Gillespie, R. D., 'Mental Hygiene as a National Problem', *Mental Hygiene*, 4 (Dec. 1931), 1–9.

Ginsberg, M., *The Psychology of Society* (London, 1921).

—— 'National Character and National Sentiment', in J. A. Hadfield (ed.), *Psychology and Modern Problems* (London, 1935), 29–50.

Glover, E., *The Diagnosis and Treatment of Delinquency: Being a Clinical Report of the Institute during the Five Years 1937 to 1941* (London, 1941).

—— *War, Sadism and Pacifism* (London, 1946).

Goldman, L., *Dons and Workers: Oxford and Adult Education since 1850* (Oxford, 1995).

Gollancz, V., *Our Threatened Values* (London, 1946).

Graham, J.M., *Neurasthenia: Its Nature, Origin and Cure* (London, 1936).

—— *Personality: How it Can be Developed* (London, 1938).

Graves, R., and Hodge, A., *The Long Weekend: A Social History of Great Britain, 1918–1939* (London, 1971).

Greenleaf, W., *The British Political Tradition. Volume I: The Rise of Collectivism* (London, 1983).

Griffiths, R., *A Study in Imagination in Early Childhood* (London, 1935).

Guardian Enquiry, *The Permissive Society* (London, 1969).

Haddock, F. C., *Practical Psychology: An Advance Manual in the Science of Mental Development in Eleven Lessons* (London, 1915).

Hadfield, J. A., *Psychology and Morals: An Analysis of Character* (London, 1923).

—— (ed.), *Psychology and Modern Problems* (London, 1935).

Haggard, H. W., *T'isn't What you Know But are You Intelligent?* (London, 1927).

Hale Jr., N., *Freud and the Americans: The Beginnings of Psychoanalysis in the United States, 1876–1917* (New York, 1971).

—— *The Rise and Crisis of Psychoanalysis in the United States: Freud and the Americans, 1917–1985* (Oxford, 1985).

Hall, L. and Porter, R., (eds.), *The Facts of Life: The Creation of Sexual Knowledge in Britain, 1650–1950* (New Haven and London, 1995).

Hallam, A., *The Key to Perfect Health* (London, 1912).

—— *Practical Psychology* (London and Philadelphia, 1922).

Halliday, J. L., *Psychosocial Medicine: A Study of the Sick Society* (London, 1948).

Halmos, P., *Solitude and Privacy: A Study of Social Isolation, its Causes and Therapy* (London, 1952).

—— *The Faith of the Counsellors* (London, 1965; 2nd edn. 1981).

Halpern, D. B., 'A Table Showing the Balance of Subjects in WEA Classes, 1913–58', *Rewley House Papers*, 3 (1959–60), 23–5.

Hamley, H. R., 'The Place of Psychology in the Training of Teachers', *BJEP*, 6 (1936), 1–7.

Hardyment, C., *Dream Babies: Child Care from Locke to Spock* (London, 1983).

Harrington, R., 'On the Tracks of Trauma: Railway Spine Reconsidered', *Social History of Medicine*, 16 (2003), 209–24.

Harris, J., 'Political Thought and the Welfare State, 1870–1940: An Intellectual Framework for British Social Policy', *Past and Present*, 135 (1992), 116–41.

—— *Private Lives. Public Spirit: A Social History of Britain, 1870–1914* (Oxford, 1993).

—— 'War and Social History: Britain and the Home Front during the Second World War', *Contemporary European History*, 6 (1997), 17–35.

Harrison, B., 'The Rise, Fall, and Rise of Political Consensus in Britain since 1940', *History*, 84 (1999), 301–24.

Harrison, C., *English Art and Modernism, 1900–1939* (London, 1981).

Harrisson, T., *Savage Civilisation* (London, 1937).

—— and Madge, C., *Mass Observation* (London, 1937).

—— (ed.), *War Factory: A Survey by Mass-Observation* (London, 1943).

—— *Living through the Blitz* (London, 1976).

Harte, R., *The New Psychology, or the Secret of Happiness, Being Practical Instructions as to How to Develop and Employ Thought Power*, 3rd edn. (London, 1903).

Hayes, N. and Hill, J. (eds.), *'Millions Like Us'? British Culture in the Second World War* (Liverpool, 1999).

Hayward, R., ' "Our Friends Electric": Mechanical Models of Mind in Postwar Britain', in Bunn et al. (eds.), *Psychology in Britain*, 290–308.

—— 'The Tortoise and the Love-Machine: Grey Walter and the Politics of Electro-Encephalography', *Science in Context*, 14 (2001), 615–41.

—— 'Demonology, Neurology, and Medicine in Edwardian Britain', *Bulletin of the History of Medicine*, 78 (2004), 49–50.

Heard, G., *The Third Morality* (London, 1937).

—— *The Five Ages of Man: The Psychology of Human History* (New York, 1963).

Hearnshaw, L., 'What is Industrial Psychology', *Occupational Psychology*, 23 (1949), 3–8.

—— *A Short History of British Psychology, 1840–1940* (London, 1964).

—— *Cyril Burt, Psychologist* (London, 1971).

Heater, D., *Citizenship: The Civic Ideal in World History, Politics and Education* (London, 1990).

Heelas, P., *The New Age Movement: The Celebration of Self and the Sacralization of Modernity* (Oxford, 1996).

Heimann, J., *The Most Offending Soul Alive: Tom Harrisson and his Remarkable Life* (London, 2002).

Hendrick, H., *Images of Youth: Age, Class and the Male Youth Problem, 1880–1920* (Oxford, 1990).

Herle, A. and Rouse, S. (eds.), *Cambridge and the Torres Strait: Centenary Essays on the 1898 Anthropological Expedition* (Cambridge, 1998).

Heyck, T., 'Myths and Meanings of Intellectuals in Twentieth-Century British National Identity', *Journal of British Studies*, 37 (1998), 192–221.

Higham, Sir C., *Advertising: Its Use and Abuse* (London, 1925).

Hinshelwood, R. D., 'Psychodynamic Psychiatry before World War I', in Berrios and Freeman (eds.) *150 Years of British Psychiatry*, 1 (1991), 197–205.

Hinton, J., 'The Apathy School', *History Workshop Journal*, 43 (1997), 266–73.

Hobman, J. B., (ed.), *David Eder: Memoirs of a Modern Pioneer* (London, 1945).

Hobsbawm, E., *Age of Extremes: The Short Twentieth Century, 1914–1991* (London, 1994).

Hobson, J. A., *Confessions of an Economic Heretic* (1st edn. 1938; London, 1976).

Hogan, S., *Healing Arts: The History of Art Therapy* (London, 2001).

Holden, A., *Teachers as Counsellors* (London, 1969).

Hollander, B., *Scientific Phrenology: Being a Practical Mental Science and Guide to Human Character* (London, 1902).

Holmes, E., *What is and What Might Be* (London, 1911).

—— *In Quest of an Ideal: An Autobiography* (London, 1920).

—— 'The Meaning of Self-Realization', *New Ideals Quarterly*, 1, 3 (Sept. 1925), 6–9.

Holmes, J., *John Bowlby and Attachment Theory* (London, 1993), 22–5.

Homans, P., *The Ability to Mourn: Disillusionment and the Social Origins of Psychoanalysis* (Chicago, 1989).

Hose, C. and McDougall, W., *The Pagan Tribes of Borneo*, 2 (London, 1912).

Howard, J., *Margaret Mead: A Life* (London, 1984).

Howe, E. G., *A Psychologist at Work* (London, 1952).

Howland, A., 'Anna Maud Hallam and Her Followers at Toronto', *Psychology*, 1/4 (Aug. 1923), 24–5.

Hughes, J. W., *Major Douglas: The Policy of a Philosophy* (Glasgow, 2002).

Hughes, R. E., *The Making of Citizens* (London, 1902).

Humphries, S., *Hooligans or Rebels: An Oral History of Working-Class Childhood and Youth, 1889–1939* (Oxford, 1981).

Hurry, J. B., *The Vicious Circles of Neurasthenia and their Treatments* (London, 1915).

—— *The Vicious Circles of Sociology and their Treatment* (London, 1915).

—— *The Vicious Circles of Disease*, (3rd edn.: London, 1919).

—— *Poverty and its Vicious Circles* (London, 1917, 1921).

Huxley, A., *After Many a Summer* (London, 1939).
—— *The Art of Seeing* (London, 1943).
Huxley, J., 'The growth of a Group Mind in Britain under the influence of War', *Hibbert Journal*, 39 (1941), 337–50.
Huxley, J., *The Humanist Frame* (London, 1961).
—— (ed.), *Essays of a Humanist* (London, 1964).
Hyndman, H. M., *The Future of Democracy* (London, 1915).
Hynes, S., A *War Imagined: The First World War and English Culture* (London, 1990).
Inch, T., *Self Analysis: A Book of Practical Psychology* (London, 1947).
Inge, Revd Dean of St Paul's, 'Psychology and the Future of Religion', in Hadfield (ed.), *Psychology and Modern Problems*, 215–37.
Irvine, E. F., *A Pioneer of the New Psychology, Hugh Crichton Miller, 1877–1959* (Chatham, 1963).
Isaacs, S., *The Nursery Years: The Mind of the Child from Birth to Six Years* (London, 1929).
—— *Social Development in Young Children: A Study of Beginnings* (London, 1933).
—— *Children and Parents: Their Problems and Difficulties* (London, 1948).
Jackson, B., and Marsden, D., *Education and the Working Class* (London, 1966).
James, W., *Varieties of Religious Experience* (London, 1902).
Jeffery, T., *Mass-Observation: A Short History* (Birmingham, 1978).
Jones, Edgar., 'Aubrey Lewis, Edward Mapother and the Maudsley', in Angel, Jones, and Neve (eds.), *European Psychiatry on the Eve of War*, 3–38.
Jones, Ernest., *Free Associations: Memories of a Psycho-Analyst* (London, 1959).
Jones, G., 'Women and Eugenics in Britain: The Case of Mary Scharlieb, Elizabeth Sloan Chesser, and Stella Browne', *Annals of Science*, 52 (1985), 481–502.
Jones, L. G. E., *The Training of Teachers in England and Wales* (London, 1924).
Joyce, P., *Democratic Subjects: The Self and the Social in Nineteenth-Century England* (Cambridge, 1994).
Jung, C. G., *Studies in Word Association*, tr. M. D. Eder (London, 1918).
Kavanagh, D., 'The Postwar Consensus', *Twentieth Century British History*, 3 (1992), 175–90.
Keith-Lucas, A., 'Enlightened Education: A Discussion of the Young Child and Cultural Problems', *Scrutiny*, 1 (1932), 96–101.
Kennedy, J. M., 'The Psychology of Sex', *The Freewoman* (23 Nov. 1911), 14–15.
Kennedy, J., *Worry: Its Cause and Cure* (London, 1937).
—— *Will Power: Ways to Develop it* (London, 1938).
Kenney, R., *Westering: An Autobiography* (London, 1939).
Kent, S. K., *Making Peace: The Reconstruction of Gender in Interwar Britain* (Princeton, 1993).
Kerr, R. B., *Our Prophets* (Croydon, 1932).
Kidd, B., *The Science of Power* (London, 1918).
Kimmins, C. W. and Rennie, B., *The Triumph of the Dalton Plan* (London, 1932).
Kirkham, P., 'Beauty and Duty: Keeping up the Home Front', in P. Kirkham and D. Thoms (eds.), *War Culture: Social Change and Changing Experience in World War Two Britain* (London, 1995), 13–28.
Kirkham, S. D., *The Philosophy of Self-Help: An Application of Practical Psychology to Daily Life* (London, 1909).
Knights, L. C., 'Will Training Colleges Bear Scrutiny?', *Scrutiny*, 1 (1932), 247–63.

Koestler, A., 'A Guide to Political Neurosis', *Encounter*, 1 (1953), 25–32.

Kohon, G. (ed.), *The British School of Psychoanalysis: The Independent Tradition* (London, 1986).

Kornhauser, A., *How to Study*, (2nd edn.: London, 1941).

Kuklick, H., *The Savage Within: The Social History of British Anthropology, 1885–1945* (Cambridge, 1991).

Kushner, T., *The Holocaust and the Liberal Imagination* (Oxford, 1994).

Kyle, W. H. (ed.), *The History of the Guild of Personal Psychology, 1936–1970* (London, 1970).

Ladell, R., *The First Five Years from Birth to School: How to Help your Child Develop its Personality* (London, 1939).

—— *The Parents' Problem: Or How to Tell Children about Sex* (London, 1941).

—— *Blushing: Its Analysis, Causes and Cures* (London, 1949).

—— *A Dictionary of Psychological Terms with Definitions and Explanations* (London, 1951).

Lafourcade, G., *Arnold Bennett: A Study* (London, 1939).

Laing, A., *R. D. Laing: A Biography* (London, 1994).

Lambert, M., 'Radical Schoolteachers and the Origins of the Progressive Movement in Germany, 1900–1914', *History of Education Quarterly*, 40 (2000), 22–48.

Landau, R., *God is my Adventure: A Book on Modern Mystics, Masters and Teachers* (London, 1935).

Lane, H., *Talks to Parents and Teachers* (London, 1928).

Langdon Brown, W., 'The Return to Aesculapius', *The Lancet* (7 Oct. 1933), 821–2.

—— et al., *Individual Psychology and Psychosomatic Disorders (I)*, Individual Psychology Pamphlet 4 (London, 1932).

—— *The History of the Medical Society of Individual Psychology of London*, Individual Psychology Pamphlet 23 (London, 1943).

Langham, I., *The Building of British Social Anthropology: W. H. R. Rivers and his Cambridge Disciples in the Development of Kinship Studies, 1898–1931* (London, 1981).

Lasch, C., *The Culture of Narcissism* (London, 1980).

Lawrence, C., 'Still Incommunicable: Clinical Holists and Medical Knowledge in Interwar Britain', in C. Lawrence and G. Weisz (eds.), *Greater than their Parts: Holism in Biomedicine, 1920–1950* (Oxford, 1998), 94–111.

Lawson, M. D., 'The New Education Fellowship: The Formative Years', *Journal of Educational Administration and History*, 13 (1981), 24–8.

Layton, L., 'Vera Brittain's Testaments(s)', in M. Higgonet et al. (eds.), *Behind the Lines: Gender and the Two World Wars* (New Haven and London, 1987), 70–83.

Lears, T. J. Jackson, 'From Salvation to Self-Realization', in R. W. Fox and T. J. Jackson Lears (eds.), *The Culture of Consumption: Critical Essays in American History, 1880–1980* (New York, 1983).

—— *Fables of Abundance: A Cultural History of Advertising in America* (New York, 1994).

Lee, H., *Virginia Woolf* (London, 1996).

Lee, J., *Management: A Study of Industrial Organisation* (London, 1921).

—— (ed.), *Pitman's Dictionary of Industrial Administration*, 2 vols. (London, 1928).

Lee, L. F., 'The Dalton Plan and the Loyal, Capable Intelligent Citizen', *History of Education*, 29 (2000), 129–38.

Leese, P., *Shell Shock: Traumatic Neurosis and the British Soldiers of the First World War* (Basingstoke, 2002).

Lerner, J. C. and Newcombe, N., 'Britain between the Wars: The Historical Context of Bowlby's Theory of Attachment', *Psychiatry*, 45 (1982), 1–12.

Lewin, S., 'Economics and Psychology: Lessons for Our Own Day from the Early Twentieth Century', *Journal of Economic Literature*, 34 (1996), 1293–1323.

Lewis, A., 'Mental Health in War-Time', *Public Health* (Dec. 1943), 30.

Light, A., *Forever England: Femininity, Literature, and Conservatism between the Wars* (London, 1991).

Lloyd-Evans, A., 'The Place of Psychology in the Training of Teachers', *BJEP*, 5 (1935), 257–64.

Loewenberg, P., *Decoding the Past: The Psychoanalytic Approach* (New York, 1983).

Lord, J. R., *Mental Hospitals and the Public* (London, 1927).

Lovie, S., 'Three Steps to Heaven: How the British Psychological Society Attained its Place in the Sun', in Bunn et al. (eds.), *Psychology in Britain*, 95–114.

Low, B., *Psychoanalysis: A Brief Account of the Freudian Theory* (London, 1920).

Lowe, R. A., 'Eugenicists, Doctors and the Quest for National Efficiency: An Educational Crusade, 1900–1939', *History of Education*, 8 (1979), 293–306.

Lowndes, G. A. N., *The Silent Social Revolution: An Account of the Expansion of Public Education in England and Wales, 1895–1935* (Oxford, 1937).

Lutz, C., 'Epistemology of the Bunker: The Brainwashed and Other New Subjects of Permanent War', in Pfister and Schnog (eds.), *Inventing the Psychological*, 245–67.

Lynch, A. J., *Individual Work and the Dalton Plan* (London, 1924).

Macbride, W.J., *The Conquest of Fear through Psychology* (London, 1936).

—— *The Inferiority Complex: Its Meaning and Treatment* (London, 1936).

MacDonald, J. R., *Socialism and Society* (London, 1905).

McDougall, W., *Anthropology and History* (Oxford, 1920).

—— *The Group Mind* (Cambridge, 1920).

—— *Is America Safe for Democracy?* (New York, 1921).

—— *National Welfare and National Decay* (London, 1921);

—— 'Our Neglect of Psychology', *Edinburgh Review*, 245 (1927), 299–312.

—— *Love and Hate: A Study of the Energies of Men and Nations* (London, 1931).

—— *Religion and the Sciences of Life* (London, 1934).

—— *The Frontiers of Psychology* (London, 1934).

—— in C. Murchison (ed.), *A History of Psychology in Autobiography*, 1 (New York, 1961; 1st edn., 1930), 191–223.

—— *Introduction to Social Psychology* (London, 1967; 1st edn. 1908).

McIlroy, J., 'Independent Working Class Education and Trade Union Education and Training', in R. Fieldhouse (ed.), *A History of Modern British Adult Education* (Leicester, 1996), 271–3.

MacIntyre, S., 'British Labour, Marxism and Working Class Apathy in the Nineteen-Twenties', *Historical Journal*, 20 (1977), 479–96.

—— *A Proletarian Science: Marxism in Great Britain, 1917–1933* (London, 1980).

McIvor, A., *A History of Work in Britain, 1880–1950* (Basingstoke, 2001).

Mackenzie, C., 'Women and Psychiatric Professionalization, 1780–1914', in London Feminist History Collective (eds.), *The Sexual Dynamics of History* (London, 1983), 107–19.

MacKenzie, N. and J., *The First Fabians* (London, 1977).

McKibbin, R., *The Evolution of the Labour Party, 1910–1924* (Oxford, 1975).

—— 'Why was there no Marxism in Great Britain?', *English Historical Review*, 99 (1984), 297–331.

—— 'The "Social Psychology" of Unemployment in Interwar Britain', in R. McKibbin, *The Ideologies of Class: Social Relations in Britain, 1880–1950* (Oxford, 1991), 228–58.

—— *Classes and Cultures in England, 1918–1951* (Oxford, 1998).

McLaine, I., *Ministry of Morale: Home Front Morale and the Ministry of Information in World War II* (London, 1979).

McMillan, M., *Education through the Imagination* (London, 1904).

Macnaghten, H., *Emile Coué: The Man and his Work* (London, 1922).

McRobbie, A., 'An Interview with Juliet Mitchell', *New Left Review*, 176 (1988), 81–7.

Maddox, B., *The Married Man: A History of D. H. Lawrence* (London, 1994).

Madge, C., *Society in the Mind: Elements of Social Eidos* (London, 1964).

Maguire, U., 'The School Counsellor as Therapist', *British Journal of Guidance and Counselling*, 3 (1975), 160–71.

Mairet, P., *Autobiographical and Other Papers* (Manchester, 1981).

Malinowski, B., 'A Nation-Wide Intelligence Service', in C. Madge and T. Harrisson, *First Year's Work, 1937–8* (London, 1938), 81–121.

Mallon, T., 'The Great War and Sassoon's Memory', in J. Hildebidle and R. Kiely (eds.), *Modernism Reconsidered* (Cambridge, Mass. and London, 1983), 81–99.

Mannheim, K., 'Present Trends in the Building of Society', *Human Affairs*, 1 (1937), 278–300.

—— *Diagnosis of our Time: Wartime Essays of a Sociologist* (London, 1943).

Mannin, E., *Confessions and Impressions* (London, 1930).

Marett, R., 'A Sociological View of Comparative Religion', *Sociological Review*, 1 (1908), 48–60.

—— *Psychology and Folk-Lore* (London, 1920).

Margrie, W., *Brainy Britons and Brainless Britons* (Peckham, 1947).

Marinker, M., 'Medical Education and Human Values', *Journal of the Royal College of General Practitioners*, 24 (1974), 445–62.

Martin, D. and Rubinstein, W. (eds.), *Ideology and the Labour Movement* (London, 1979).

Marwick, A., *The Sixties: Cultural Revolution in Britain, France, Italy and the United States, c.1958–1974* (London, 1998).

Mason, M., *The Making of Victorian Sexuality* (Oxford, 1994).

Mason, T. and Thompson, P., ' "Reflections on a Revolution?" The Political Mood in Wartime Britain', in Tiratsoo (ed.), *The Attlee Years*, 54–70.

Mass-Observation, *Puzzled People: A Study in Popular Attitudes to Religion, Ethics, Progress and Politics in a London Borough* (London, 1947).

Maxim, H., *Practical Psychology of Cooperative Conduct* (London, 1920).

Mayer, J. and Timms, N., *The Client Speaks: Working Class Impressions of Casework* (London, 1970).

Medhurst, A., 'Myths of Consensus and Fables of Escape: British Cinema, 1945–51', in J. Fryth (ed.), *Labour's Promised Land: Culture and Society in Labour Britain* (London, 1995), 289–301.

Mews, S., 'The Revival of Spiritual Healing in the Church of England, 1920–26', in W. J. Shiels (ed.), *The Church and Healing* (Oxford, 1982), 299–331.

Michael, P., *Care and Treatment of the Mentally Ill in North Wales, 1800–2000* (Cardiff, 2000).

Middlemas, K., *Politics in Industrial Society* (London, 1979).

Miles, A., 'Workers' Education: The Communist Party and the Plebs League in the 1920s', *History Workshop Journal*, 18 (1984), 102–14.

Miller, E., 'The Artist in Modern Civilisation', in Hadfield, *Psychology and Modern Problems*, 159–86.

Miller, H. Crichton, *Hypnotism and Disease: A Plea for Rational Psychotherapy* (London, 1912).

—— *The New Psychology and the Preacher* (London, 1924).

—— 'Mental Hygiene and Preventive Medicine', *Mental Hygiene*, 2 (1936), 160.

—— 'The Priest and the Doctor in the Treatment of Nervous and Mental Disorder', *Mental Hygiene*, 2 (1936), 23–9.

Mini, P., *Keynes, Bloomsbury and the 'General Theory'* (London, 1991).

Mitchell, A., *Harley Street Psychiatrist* (London, 1960).

Mitchell, J., *Woman's Estate* (London, 1971).

Money-Kyrle, R., 'Social Conflict and the Challenge to Psychology', *British Journal of Medical Psychology*, 21 (1948), 215–21.

—— *Psychoanalysis and Politics: A Contribution to the Psychology of Politics and Morals* (London, 1951).

Moore, J., *Gurdjieff: A Biography* (Shaftesbury, 1991).

Morgan, L., *Psychology for Teachers* (London, 1894).

Moskowitz, E., 'The Therapeutic Gospel: Religious Medicine and the Birth of Pop Psychology, 1850–1910', *Prospects: An Annual of American Cultural Studies*, 20 (Cambridge, 1995), 57–86.

Moss, L., *The Government Social Survey: A History* (HMSO, 1991).

Myers, C. S., 'The Human Side of Industry', *Journal of the National Institute for Industrial Psychology*, 1/8 (1923), 309–12.

—— 'The Efficiency Engineer and the Industrial Psychologist', *Journal of the National Institute for Industrial Psychology*, 3 (1927), 168–72.

—— *Industrial Psychology in Great Britain* (2nd edn.: London, 1933).

—— *In the Realm of the Mind* (Cambridge, 1937).

National Institute for Industrial Psychology, *The Worker's Point of View: A Symposium* (London, 1933).

Neary, F., 'A Question of "Peculiar Importance": George Croom Robertson, *Mind* and the Changing Relationship between British Psychology and Philosophy', in Bunn et al. (eds.), *Psychology in Britain*, 54–71.

Neill, A. S., *Summerhill* (London, 1971).

—— *'Neill! Neill! Orange Peel': A Personal View of Ninety Years* (London, 1972).

Nelson, E., *The British Counter-Culture, 1966–73: A Study of the Underground Press* (Basingstoke, 1989).

Newson, J. and E., *Patterns of Infant Care in an Urban Community* (London, 1963).

—— 'Cultural Aspects of Childrearing in the English Speaking World', in M. Richards (ed.), *The Integration of a Child into a Social World* (Cambridge, 1974), 53–82.

Nichols, B., *Cry Havoc!* (London, 1933).

Norman, P., *In the Way of Understanding* (Godalming, 1982).

North, M., *The Secular Priests* (London, 1972).

—— *The Mind Market* (London, 1975).

Northfield, W., *Curing Nervous Tension* (London, 1936).

—— *Sound Sleep: Proved Methods of Attaining It* (London, 1937).

—— *Frayed Nerves: Simple Ways of Restoring their Tone* (London, 1940).

Nottingham, C., *The Pursuit of Serenity: Havelock Ellis and the New Politics* (Amsterdam, 1999).

Noyce, J. (ed.), *The Directory of the British Alternative Periodicals* (Brighton, 1975).

Nudelman, F., 'Beyond the Talking Cure: Listening to Female Testimony on *The Oprah Winfrey Show*', in Pfister and Schnog (eds.), *Inventing the Psychological*, 297–315.

Nuttall, J., 'Psychological Socialist; Militant Moderate: Evan Durbin and the Politics of Synthesis', *Labour History Review*, 68 (2003), 235–52.

—— 'The Labour Party and the Improvement of Minds: The Case of Tony Crosland', *The Historical Journal*, 46 (2003), 133–53.

Oppenheim, J., *The Other World: Spiritualism and Psychic Research in England, 1850–1914* (Cambridge, 1985).

—— *Shattered Nerves: Doctors, Patients and Depression in Victorian England* (New York, 1991).

Orage, A. R., *The Active Mind* (London, 1954).

Orwell, G., *Collected Essays, Journalism and Letters*, 3 (London, 1968).

Otis, L., *Organic Memory: History and the Body in the Late Nineteenth and Early Twentieth Centuries* (London, 1994).

Owen, A., 'Occultism and the "Modern" Self in *Fin-de-sièck* Britain', in B. Reiger and M. Daunton (eds.), *Meanings of Modernity: Britain from the Late-Victorian Era to World War II* (Oxford, 2001), 71–96.

—— *The Darkened Room: Women, Power and Spiritualism in Late Victorian England* (London, 1989).

—— 'The Sorceror and his Apprentice: Aleister Crowley and the Magical Exploration of Victorian Subjectivity', *Journal of British Studies*, 36 (1997), 99–133.

—— *The Place of Enchantment: British Occultism and the Culture of the Modern* (Chicago and London, 2004).

Packard, V., *The Hidden Persuaders* (London, 1957).

Park, J., *Bertrand Russell on Education* (London, 1964).

Passerini, L., *Europe in Love, Love in Europe: Imagination and Politics in Britain between the Wars* (London, 1999).

Paul, E. and C., *Creative Revolution: A Study of Communist Ergatocracy* (London, 1920).

—— —— *Proletcult* (London, 1921).

Pear, T., 'Psychologists and Culture', *Bulletin of the John Rylands Library*, 23 (1939), 417–35.

—— *The Psychology of Conversation* (London, 1939).

—— 'The "Trivial" and "Popular" in Psychology', *British Journal of Psychology*, 31 (1940), 115–28.

—— 'The Social Status of the Psychologist and its Effects upon his Work', *Sociological Review*, 34 (1942), 68–81.

—— 'Psychological Implications of the Culture Pattern Theory', *Bulletin of the John Rylands Library*, 29 (1945–6), 201–24.

—— 'The Relations between Psychology and Sociology', *Bulletin of the John Rylands Library*, 31 (1948), 277–94.

Pekin, L. B., *Progressive Schools: Their Principles and Practice* (London, 1934).

Pfister, J., and Schnog, N., (eds.), *Inventing the Psychological: Toward a Cultural History of Emotional Life in America* (New Haven and London, 1997).

Phillips, M., 'Professional Courses in the Training of Teachers: A Report on an Enquiry into Values', *British Journal of Educational Psychology*, 1 (1931), 225–44.

Philp, H. L., *Memory: How to Make the Most of It* (London, 1936).

Pick, D., *War Machine: The Rationalisation of Slaughter in the Modern Age* (London, 1993).

—— *Svengali's Web: The Alien Enchanter in Modern Culture* (New Haven and London, 2000).

Pick, D., 'The Id Comes to Bloomsbury', *Guardian* (16 Aug. 2003).

Pierson, S., 'Edward Carpenter, Prophet of a Socialist Millennium', *Victorian Studies*, 13 (1970), 301–18.

Pimlott, B., 'The Myth of Consensus', in L. M. Smith (ed.), *The Making of Britain: Echoes of Greatness* (London, 1988).

Pines, M., 'The Development of the Psychodynamic Movement', in Berrios and Freeman (eds.), *150 Years of British Psychiatry*, 1 (London, 1991), 206–31.

Placzek, B. R., *Record of a Friendship: The Correspondence between Wilhelm Reich and A. S. Neill, 1936–1957* (London, 1982).

Plebs League, *An Outline of Psychology*, 2nd edn. (London, 1921).

Pogson, B., *Maurice Nicoll: A Portrait* (London, 1961).

Porter, D., 'Changing Disciplines: John Ryle and the Making of Social Medicine in Britain in the 1940s', *History of Science*, 30 (1992), 137–64.

—— 'John Ryle: Doctor of Revolution', in D. and R. Porter (eds.), *Doctors, Patients and Society: Historical Essays* (Amsterdam, 1993), 247–74.

—— (ed.), *Social Medicine and Medical Sociology in the Twentieth Century* (Amsterdam, 1997).

Porter, R., *Mind Forg'd Manacles: A History of Madness in England from the Restoration to the Regency* (London, 1987).

—— 'Two Cheers for Psychiatry! The Social History of Mental Disorder in Twentieth Century Britain', in Berrios and Freeman (eds.), *150 Years of British Psychiatry: The Aftermath*, 2 (1996), 383–406.

Psychologist, *Nervousness: Its Cause, Prevention and Cure* (London, 1936).

Pursell, C., 'Domesticating Modernity: The Electrical Association for Women, 1924–1986', *British Journal for the History of Science*, 32 (1999), 47–67.

Rabinbach, A., *The Human Motor: Energy, Fatigue and the Origins of Modernity* (New York, 1990).

Rait, S., 'Early British Psychoanalysis and the Medico-Psychological Clinic', *History Workshop Journal*, 58 (2004), 63–85.

Rapp, D., 'The Reception of Freud by the British Press: General Interest and Literary Magazines, 1920–1925', *Journal of the History of the Behavioural Sciences*, 24 (1988), 191–201.

—— 'The Early Discovery of Freud by the British General Educated Reading Public, 1912–1919', *Social History of Medicine*, 3 (1990), 217–45.

Rawlinson, Rev. A. E. J., 'Psychology and Theology', in W. Brown (ed.), *Psychology and the Sciences*.

Raymond, E. (ed.), *The Autobiography of David* (London, 1946).

Reddy, W., *The Navigation of Feeling: A Framework for the History of Emotions* (Cambridge, 2001).

Rée, J., *Proletarian Philosophers: Problems in Socialist Culture in Britain, 1900–1940* (Oxford, 1984).

Reed, D., *Insanity Fair* (London, 1938).

Rees, J. R., *The Shaping of Psychiatry by War* (London, 1945).

—— 'Work for Mental Health in Germany', *Bulletin of the World Federation for Mental Health*, 1 (1949), 15–19.

—— (ed.), *The Case of Rudolf Hess: A Problem in Diagnosis and Forensic Psychiatry* (London, 1947).

Richards, G., 'Of What is History of Psychology a History?', *British Journal for the History of Science*, 20 (1987), 201–11.

—— ' "To Know our Fellow Men to do them Good": American Psychology's Continuing Moral Project', *History of the Human Sciences*, 8 (1995), 1–24.

—— 'Britain on the Couch: The Popularization of Psychoanalysis in Britain, 1918–1940', *Science in Context*, 13 (2000), 183–230.

—— 'Psychology and the Churches in Britain, 1919–1939: Symptoms of Conversion', *History of the Human Sciences*, 13 (2000), 57–84.

—— 'Edward Cox, the Psychological Society of Great Britain (1875–1879) and the Meanings of Institutional Failure', in Bunn et al. (eds.), *Psychology in Britain*, 54–71.

Richards, T., *The Commodity Culture of Victorian England: Advertising and Spectacle, 1851–1914* (London, 1991).

Rieff, P., *The Triumph of the Therapeutic: Uses of Faith after Freud* (London, 1966).

Rigby, A., *Initiation and Initiative: An Exploration of the Life and Ideas of Dimitrije Mitrinovic* (Boulder Colo./New York, 1984).

Riley, D., *War in the Nursery: Theories of the Child and Mother* (London, 1983).

—— 'Some Peculiarities of Social Policy Concerning Women in Wartime and Postwar Britain', in M. Higgonet et al. (eds.), *Behind the Lines: Gender in the Two World Wars* (London and New Haven, 1987), 260–71.

Rivers, W. H. R., *The History of Melanesian Society*, 2 (Cambridge, 1914).

—— 'Sociology and Psychology', *Sociological Review*, 9 (1916), 1–13.

—— 'Dreams and Primitive Culture', *Bulletin of the John Rylands Library*, 4 (1917–18), 387–410.

—— *Psychology and Ethnology* (London, 1926).

Roazen, P., *Oedipus in Britain: Edward Glover and the Struggle over Klein* (New York, 2000).

Robb, M., 'The Psychology of the Unemployed from the Medical Point of View', in Beales and Lambert (eds.), *Memoirs of the Unemployed*, 271–85.

Robinson, A. L., *William McDougall: A Bibliography* (Durham, NC, 1943).

Rodaway, A., *A London Childhood* (Bath, 1985).

Roiser, M., 'Social Psychology and Social Concern in 1930s Britain', in Bunn et al. (eds.), *Psychology in Britain*, 169–87.

Roper, M., 'Between Manliness and Masculinity: The "War Generation" and the Psychology of Fear in Britain, 1914–1950', *Journal of British Studies*, 44 (2005), 343–62.

Rose, J., *The Edwardian Temperament, 1895–1919* (London, 1986).

—— *The Intellectual Life of the British Working Classes* (New Haven and London, 2001).

Rose, M., *Industrial Behaviour: Theoretical Development since Taylor* (London, 1975).

Rose, N., *The Psychological Complex: Psychology, Politics, and Society in England, 1869–1939* (London, 1985).

—— *Governing the Soul: The Shaping of the Private Self* (London, 1989).

—— *Inventing Ourselves: Psychology, Power and Personhood* (Cambridge, 1996).

—— 'Assembling the Modern Self', in R. Porter (ed.), *Rewriting the Self: Histories from the Renaissance to the Present* (London, 1997), 224–48.

Rosenberg, C., 'Body and Mind in Nineteenth-Century Medicine: Some Clinical Origins of the Neurosis Construct', *Bulletin of the History of Medicine*, 63 (1989), 187–8.

Rosenfield, M., 'Industrial Psychotherapy', *Human Factor*, 10 (1936), 360–5.

Ross, T. A., *The Common Neuroses: Their Functional Treatment by Psychotherapy* (London, 1923).

Ross, T. A., *An Enquiry into Prognosis in the Neuroses* (Cambridge, 1936).

—— 'Some Evils of Compensation', *Mental Hygiene*, 3, 4 (1937), 141–5.

Rouse, R., and Miller, H. Crichton, *Christian Experiences and Psychological Processes* (London, 1917).

Rowan, J., *The Science of You* (London, 1973).

—— *Ordinary Ecstasy: Humanistic Psychology in Action* (London, 1976).

—— *The Reality Game: A Guide to Humanistic Counselling and Therapy* (London, 1983).

Rowbotham, S., *A Century of Women* (London, 1997).

—— and Weeks, J., *Socialism and the New Life: The Personal and Sexual Politics of Edward Carpenter and Havelock Ellis* (London, 1977).

Rowe, M. (ed.), *Spare Rib Reader* (London, 1982).

Royal College of General Practitioners, *The Future General Practitioner—Learning and Teaching* (London, 1972).

Russell, B. and D., *The Prospects of Industrial Civilisation* (London, 1923).

—— —— *The Right to be Happy* (London, 1927).

Russell, D., *The Tamarisk Tree*, 2 (London, 1980).

Sadler, Sir M., *John Adams: A Lecture in his Memory. The Second John Adams Lecture* (London, 1935).

Sampson, O., *Child Guidance: Its History, Provenance and Future* (London, 1980).

Samuels, A., *Politics on the Couch: Citizenship and the Internal Life* (London, 2001).

Sargant, W., *The Unquiet Mind: The Autobiography of a Physician in Psychological Medicine* (London, 1967).

—— and Slater, E., *An Introduction to Physical Methods of Treatment in Psychiatry* (Edinburgh, 1944).

Satter, B., *Each Mind a Kingdom: American Women, Sexual Purity, and the New Thought Movement, 1875–1920* (Berkeley and Los Angeles, 1999).

Saville, J. and Bellamy, J. (eds.), *Dictionary of Labour Biography*, 9 (London, 1993).

Sayers, D. L., *Murder Must Advertise* (London, 1933).

Schivelbusch, W., *The Railway Journey: The Industrialization of Time and Space in the Nineteenth Century* (Berkeley, Calif., 1986).

Schofield, A. T., *The Management of a Nerve Patient* (London, 1906).

—— *The Mind of a Woman* (London, 1919).

—— *A Harley Street Doctor's Story* (London, 1930).

Schon, L., *The Psychology of Golf* (London: Methuen, 1922).

Scott, C., *My Years of Indiscretion* (London, 1924).

Scull, A., *Museums of Madness: The Social Organisation of Insanity in Nineteenth-Century England* (London, 1970).

—— *The Most Solitary of Afflictions: Madness and Society in Britain, 1700–1900* (New Haven, 1993).

Seabrook, J., *Working-Class Childhood* (London, 1982).

Sedgwick, P., *Psycho-Politics: Laing, Foucault, Goffman, Szasz and the Future of Mass Psychiatry* (London, 1982).

Selleck, R. J. W., *The New Education, 1870–1914* (London, 1965).

—— *English Primary Education and the Progressives 1914–1939* (London, 1972).

Sennett, R., *The Fall of Public Man* (London, 1977).

Serebriakoff, V., *IQ: A Mensa Analysis and History* (London, 1966).

Shamdasani, S., 'Claire, Lise, Jean, Nadia, and Gisèle: Preliminary Notes towards a Characterisation of Pierre Janet's Psychasthenia', in M. Gijswijt-Hofstra and R. Porter (eds.), *Cultures of Neurasthenia: From Beard to the First World War* (Amsterdam, 2001), 363–85.

Shephard, B., 'Digging up the Past', *Times Literary Supplement* (22 March 1996).

—— *A War of Nerves: Soldiers and Psychiatrists, 1914–1994* (London, 2000).

Shepherd, M., 'From Social Medicine to Social Psychiatry: The Achievement of Sir Aubrey Lewis', in M. Shepherd (ed.) *The Psychosocial Matrix of Psychiatry* (London, 1983), 256–70.

Shorter, E., *From Paralysis to Fatigue: A History of Psychosomatic Illness in the Modern Era* (New York, 1992).

Showalter, E., *The Female Malady: Women, Madness and English Culture, 1830–1980* (London, 1987).

Sicherman, B., 'The Uses of Diagnosis: Doctors, Patients and Neurasthenia', *Journal of the History of Medicine*, 32 (1977), 33–54.

Sigal, C., *Zone of the Interior* (New York, 1976).

Simmons, D., *Private Lessons in Practical Psychology (The Realization System)* (Manchester, 1936).

Simon, B., *Educational Psychology in the USSR* (London, 1952).

—— *Psychology in the Soviet Union* (London, 1957).

—— *A Life in Education* (London, 1998).

Sinclair, A., *War like a Wasp* (London, 1989).

Skidelsky, R., *English Progressive Schools* (London, 1969).

—— *John Maynard Keynes: The Economist as Saviour*, 2 (London, 1991).

Slobodin, R., *W. H. R. Rivers* (New York, 1978).

Smiles, S., *Character* (London, 1908).

Smith, D., 'Juvenile Delinquency in the British Zone of Germany, 1945–51', *German History*, 12 (1994), 39–63.

Smith, M., and Maule, H. G., *Industrial Psychology and the Laundry Trade* (London, 1947).

—— Culpin, M., and Farmer, E., 'A Study of Telegraphists' Cramp', *Industrial Health Research Board Report No. 43* (HMSO, 1927).

Smith, M., *The Underground and Education: A Guide to the Alternative Press* (London, 1977).

Smith, R., 'Biology and Human Values: C. S. Sherrington, Julian Huxley and the Vision of Progress', *Past and Present*, 178 (2003), 210–42.

—— 'Brain and Mind in the Age of C. S. Sherrington', in Bunn et al. (eds.), *Psychology in Britain*, 223–42.

—— 'Does the History of Psychology have a Subject?', *History of the Human Sciences*, 1 (1988), 147–77.

Smith, S., 'Personalities in the Crowd: The Idea of the "Masses" in American Popular Culture', *Prospects*, 19 (Cambridge, 1994), 273–83.

Snowden, E. N., 'Mass Psychotherapy', *Lancet* (21 Dec. 1940), 769–70.

Soffer, R., *Ethics and Society in England: The Revolution in the Social Sciences 1870–1914* (Berkeley, Calif., 1978).

—— 'The New Elitism: Social Psychology in Prewar England', *Journal of British Studies*, 8 (1989), 111–40.

Spice, N., 'I Must be Mad', *London Review of Books* (8 Jan. 2004), 11–15.

Spiers, J. (ed.), *The Underground and Alternative Press in Britain (Bibliographical Guide to the Harvester Social Sources Press Collection)* (Brighton, 1975).

Stansky, P., *On or About December 1910: Early Bloomsbury and its Intimate World* (Cambridge, Mass., 1996).

Stearns, C. and P., (eds.), *Emotion and Social Change: Toward a New Psychohistory* (New York and London, 1988).

Steedman, C., ' "The Mother Made Conscious": The Historical Development of a Primary School Pedagogy', *History Workshop Journal*, 20 (1985), 149–63.

—— *Childhood, Culture and Class: Margaret McMillan, 1860–1931* (London, 1990).

—— *Strange Dislocations: Childhood and the Idea of Human Interiority, 1780–1930* (London, 1995).

Steinberg, H. (ed.), *The British Psychological Society 1901–1941: Supplement to the Bulletin of the British Psychological Society* (London, 1961).

Stone, D., *Breeding Superman: Nietzsche, Race and Eugenics in Edwardian and Interwar Britain* (Liverpool, 2002).

Stone, M., 'Shellshock and the Psychologists', in W. Bynum, R. Porter and M. Shepherd (eds.), *The Anatomy of Madness*, 2 (London, 1985), 242–71.

Stopes, M., *Married Love* (London, 1918).

Summerfield, P., 'Mass-Observation: Social Research or Social Movement?', *Journal of Contemporary History*, 20 (1985), 439–52.

Susman, W., 'Personality and the Making of Twentieth-Century Culture', in J. Higham and P. Conkin (eds.), *New Directions in American Intellectual History* (Baltimore, 1979), 212–26.

Sutherland, G., *Ability, Merit and Measurement: Mental Testing and English Education, 1880–1940* (Oxford, 1994).

Sutherland, J. D., 'Psychological Medicine and the National Health Service: The Need for an Integrated Approach to Research', *British Journal of Medical Psychology*, 25 (1952), 71–85.

Suttie, I., *The Origins of Love and Hate* (London, 1935).

Tait, I., 'Person-Centred Perspectives in Medicine', *Journal of the Royal College of General Practitioners*, 24 (1974), 151–60.

Tanner, D., 'Ideological Debate in Edwardian Labour Politics' in E. Biagini and A. Reid (eds.), *Currents of Radicalism: Popular Radicalism, Organised Labour, and Party Politics in Britain, 1850–1914* (Cambridge, 1991).

Tansley, A. G., *The New Psychology and its Relation to Life* (London, 1922).

Taylor, G., *Orage and the New Age* (Sheffield, 2000).

Taylor, S., 'The Suburban Neurosis', *The Lancet* (26 Mar. 1938), 759–61.

—— 'Socialism and Public Opinion', in D. Munro (ed.), *Socialism and the British Way* (London, 1948).

—— *Good General Practice* (London, 1954).

—— *A Natural History of Everyday Life: A Biographical Guide for Would-be Doctors of Society* (Cambridge, 1988).

Taylor, W., *The Secondary Modern School* (London, 1963).

Teear, C. H., *The Art of Making Friends* (London, 1939).

—— *Mastering Shyness* (London, 1941).

Temple, A., *Good or Bad—It's Life* (London, 1944).

Thom, D., 'The 1944 Education Act: The Art of the Possible?', in H. Smith (ed.), *War and Social Change* (Manchester, 1986), 101–28.

—— 'Wishes, Anxieties, Play and Gestures', in R. Cooter (ed.), *In the Name of the Child: Health and Welfare, 1880–1940* (London, 1992), 200–19.

—— 'The Healthy Citizen of Empire or Juvenile Delinquent? Beating and Mental Health in the UK', in Gijswijt-Hofstra and Marland (eds.), *Cultures of Child Health*, 189–212.

Thomas, J. B., 'Mistresses of Method: Women Academics in the Day Training Colleges 1890–1914', *Journal of Education and Administrative History*, 29 (1997), 93–107.

Thomas, R., 'The New Psychology at Work in the School', *The New Era in Home and School*, 17/1 (1936), 185–8.

Thompson, E. P. et al., *Out of Apathy* (London, 1960).

Thomson, M., 'Mental Hygiene as an International Movement', in P. Weindling (ed.), *International Health Organisations and Movements, 1919–1939* (Cambridge, 1995), 283–304.

—— 'Before Anti-Psychiatry: "Mental Health" in Wartime Britain', in Gijswijt-Hofstra and Porter (eds.), *Cultures of Psychiatry*, 43–60.

—— 'Status, Manpower and Mental Fitness: Mental Deficiency in the First World War', in R. Cooter, M. Harrison and S. Sturdy (eds.), *War, Medicine and Society* (Stroud, 1998), 149–66.

—— *The Problem of Mental Deficiency: Eugenics, Democracy, and Social Policy in Britain, 1870–1959* (Oxford, 1998).

—— ' "Savage Civilisation": Race, Culture, Mind in Britain, 1898–1939', in W. Ernst and B. Harris (eds.), *Race, Science and Medicine, 1700–1960* (London, 1999), 235–58.

—— 'Constituting Citizenship: Mental Deficiency, Mental Health and Human Rights in Inter-War Britain', in C. Lawrence and A. Mayer (eds.), *Regenerating England: Medicine and Culture in Inter-War Britain* (Amsterdam, 2000), 231–50.

—— 'Neurasthenia in Britain', in M. Gijswijt-Hofstra and R. Porter (eds.), *Cultures of Neurasthenia: From Beard to the First World War* (Amsterdam, 2001), 77–96.

—— 'Psychology and the Consciousness of Modernity', in B. Rieger and M. Daunton (eds.), *Meanings of Modernity: Britain from the Late-Victorian Era to World War II* (Oxford, 2001), 97–115.

—— 'The Popular, the Practical and the Professional: Psychological Identities in Britain, 1901–1950', in Bunn et al. (eds.), *Psychology in Britain*, 115–32.

Thouless, R. H., *Introduction to the Psychology of Religion* (Cambridge, 1923).

Tiratsoo, N. (ed.), *The Attlee Years* (London, 1991).

Titmuss, R., *Problems of Social Policy* (London, 1950).

Todd, S., ' "Boisterous Workers": Young Women, Industrial Rationalization and Workplace Militancy in Interwar England', *Labour History Review*, 68 (2003), 293–310.

Tomlinson, J., 'Mr Attlee's Supply-Side Socialism', *Economic History Review*, 46 (1993), 1–22.

Trombley, S., *'All that Summer She was Mad': Virginia Woolf and her Doctors* (London, 1981).

Trotter, W., *Instincts of the Herd in Peace and War* (London, 1919).

Tsuzuki, C., *Edward Carpenter, 1844–1929: Prophet of Human Fellowship* (Cambridge, 1980).

Turner, E. S., *A Shocking History of Advertising* (London, 1952).

Turner, T., 'James Crichton Browne and the Anti-Psycho-Analysts', in Berrios and Freeman (eds.), *150 Years of British Psychiatry: The Aftermath*, 2 (1996), 144–55.

Urwick, L. and Brech, E. F. L., *The Making of Scientific Management*, 2 vols. (London, 1957).

Vernon, P., 'A Study of War Attitudes', *British Journal of Medical Psychology*, 19 (1942), 271–91.

Vincent, J., *Inside the Asylum* (London, 1948).

Walden, G., *We Should Know Better: Solving the Educational Crisis* (London, 1996).

Walker, K., *Venture with Ideas* (London, 1951).

Wallas, G., *Human Nature in Politics* (1908).

—— *The Great Society: A Psychological Analysis* (London, 1914).

Wandor, M., *Once a Feminist* (London, 1990).

Washington, P., *Madame Blavatsky's Baboon: Theosophy and the Emergence of the Western Guru* (London, 1993).

Waterhouse, E. S., *Psychology and Religion: A Series of Broadcast Talks* (London, 1930).

—— *An ABC of Psychology: For Sunday School Teachers and Bible Students*, 4th edn. (London, 1933).

Waters, C., ' "Dark Strangers" in Our Midst: Discourses of Race and Nation in Britain, 1947–1963', *Journal of British Studies*, 36 (1997), 207–38.

—— 'Havelock Ellis, Sigmund Freud and the State: Discourses of Homosexual Desire in Interwar Britain', in L. Doan and L. Bland (eds.), *Cultural Sexology: Labelling Bodies and Desires, 1890–1940* (London, 1998), 165–79.

Watson, J. B. and McDougall, W., *The Battle of Behaviourism, An Exposition and an Exposure* (London, 1928).

Watson, W. F., *Machines and Man: An Autobiography of an Itinerant Mechanic* (London, 1935).

Watts, A., *The Legacy of Asian and Western Man* (London, 1937).

—— *Psychotherapy East and West* (London, 1961).

—— *In My Own Way: An Autobiography, 1915–1965* (London, 1973).

Weatherhead, L., *Psychology and Life* (London, 1934).

Webb, J., *The Harmonious Circle: The Lives and Works of I. D. Gurdjieff and P. D. Ouspensky and their Followers* (London, 1980).

Webster, C., 'Conflict and Consensus: Explaining the British Health Service', *Twentieth Century British History*, 1 (1990), 115–51.

Weeks, J., *Sex, Politics and Society: The Regulation of Sexuality since 1800* (London, 1981).

Welch, L., *Orage with Gurdjieff in America* (London, 1982).

Welshman, J., 'Evacuation and Social Policy during the Second World War: Myth and Reality', *Twentieth Century British History*, 9 (1998), 28–53.

West, R., *Psychology and World Order* (London, 1945).

Westwood, L., 'A Quiet Revolution in Brighton: Dr Helen Boyle's Pioneering Approach to Mental Health Care, 1899–1939', *Social History of Medicine*, 14 (2001), 439–57.

Whitbread, N., *The Evolution of the Nursery-Infant School* (London, 1972).

Whiteley, C. H. and W., *The Permissive Morality* (London, 1964).

Whitson, K., 'Scientific Management and Production Management Practice in Britain between the Wars', *Historical Studies in Industrial Relations*, 1 (1996), 47–76.

Wiener, M., *Between Two Worlds: The Political Thought of Graham Wallas* (Oxford, 1971).

—— *English Culture and the Decline of the Industrial Spirit, 1850–1950* (Cambridge, 1981).

Wilde, R. W., *Psychology: How it Can Help You* (London, 1942).

Williams, W. E. and Heath, A. E., *Learn and Live: The Consumer's View of Adult Education* (London, 1936).

Wills, W. D., *Homer Lane: A Biography* (London, 1964).

Wilson, E. C., *Catherine Isabella Dodd, 1860–1932: A Memorial Sketch by her Friend and Colleague* (London, 1936).

Winnicott, D. W., *Getting to Know your Baby: Six Broadcast Talks* (London, 1944).

—— 'Some Thoughts on the Meaning of the Word Democracy', *Human Relations*, 3 (1950), 175–86.

Winslow, T., 'Keynes and Freud: Psychoanalysis and Keynes's Account of the "Animal Spirits of Capitalism" ', *Social Research*, 53 (1986), 549–78.

Winter, A., *Mesmerized: Powers of Mind in Victorian Britain* (Chicago, 1998).

Winter, J., *Sites of Memory, Sites of Mourning: The Great War in European Cultural History* (Cambridge, 1995).

—— 'Shell-Shock and the Cultural History of the Great War', *Journal of Contemporary History*, 35 (2000), 7–12.

Wolfenstein, M., 'Fun Morality: An Analysis of Recent American Child-Training Literature', in M. Mead and M. Wolfenstein (eds.), *Childhood in Contemporary Cultures* (Chicago, 1955).

Wolters, A. W., 'Psychology in the Training of Teachers', *British Journal of Educational Psychology*, 5 (1935), 250–6.

Wooldridge, A., *Measuring the Mind: Education and Psychology in England, c. 1860–1990* (Cambridge, 1994).

Wootton, B., *Social Science and Social Pathology* (London, 1959).

Yelloly, M., *Social Work and Psychoanalysis* (New York, 1980).

Yellowlees, H., *Out of Working Hours: Medical Psychology on Special Occasions* (London, 1943).

Yeo, S., 'Notes on Three Socialisms—Collectivism, Statism and Associationism—Mainly in Late-Nineteenth- and Early-Twentieth-Century Britain', in C. Levy (ed.), *Socialism and the Intelligentsia, 1880–1914* (London, 1974), 219–70.

—— 'The Religion of Socialism in Britain, 1883–1896', *History Workshop Journal*, 4 (1977), 5–56.

Young, J. C., 'An Experiment at Fontainebleau—A Personal Reminiscence', *The New Adelphi*, 1 (1927), 26–42.

—— 'Implications of Adlerism', *Adelphi*, 4 (1932), 517–24, 581–9.

Younghusband, E., *Social Work in Britain, 1950–1975*, 2 vols. (London, 1978).

Zangwill, O. L., 'Doubts and Queries about Psychology', *Rewley House Papers*, 3 (1953), 38–43.

Zelizer, V., *Pricing the Priceless Child: The Changing Social Value of Children* (New York, 1985).

6. UNPUBLISHED THESES AND PAPERS

Coupland, P., 'Voices from Nowhere: Utopianism in British Political Culture 1929–1945', Ph.D. thesis (University of Warwick, 2000).

Ellesley, S., 'Psychoanalysis in Early Twentieth Century England: A Study in the Popularisation of Ideas', Ph.D. thesis (University of Essex, 1995).

Falby, A., 'Gerald Heard (1884–1971) and British Intellectual Culture between the Wars', D.Phil. thesis (University of Oxford, 2000).

Gartrell-Mills, C. F., 'Christian Science: An American Religion in Britain, 1895–1940', D.Phil. thesis (University of Oxford, 1991).

Hayward, R., 'Popular Mysticism and the Origins of the New Psychology, 1880–1910', Ph.D. thesis (University of Lancaster, 1995).

Long, V., 'Changing Public Representations of Mental Illness in Britain 1870–1970', Ph.D. thesis (University of Warwick, 2004).

Nuttall, J., 'Psychological Socialism, Tony Crosland, and the Politics of Mind', D.Phil. thesis (University of Oxford, 2001).

Pols, J., 'Managing the Mind: The Culture of American Mental Hygiene, 1910–1950', Ph.D. thesis (University of Pennsylvania, 1997).

Root, S., 'Healing, Touch and Medicine, *c*.1890–1950', Ph.D. thesis (University of Warwick, 2006).

Tarbit, J., 'The Road to Total Furore: Dianetics, Scientology, and their Detractors in Fifties and Sixties Britain', MA thesis (University of Warwick, 2003).

Thomson, M., 'Mind in Socialism: Montague David Eder, Socialist, Psycho-Analyst, and Zionist' (unpublished paper).

Toms, J., 'Mental Hygiene to Civil Rights: MIND and the Problematic of Personhood, *c*.1900 to *c*.1980', Ph.D. thesis (University of London, 2005).

Travell, J. C., 'Psychology and Ministry with Special Reference to the Life, Work and Influence of Leslie Dixon Weatherhead', Ph.D. thesis (University of Sheffield, 1990).

Westwood, L., 'Avoiding the Asylum: Pioneering Work in Mental Health Care, 1890–1939', Ph.D. thesis (University of Sussex, 1999).

Whitelaw, B., 'Industry and the Interior Life: Industrial 'Experts' and the Mental World of Workers in Twentieth Century Britain', Ph.D. in progress (University of Warwick).

7. WEBSITES

Museum at Ditchling, displaying work by early members of the community discussed in Chapter 3: http://www.ditchling-museum.com/arts_crafts-intro.html

Diaries of General Lionel Dunsterville: http://www.gwpda.org/Dunsterville/Dunsterville_1921.html

B. Hunter, 'Combining Good and Truth, Now: An Homage to Dr Maurice Nicoll', *Gurdjieff International Review*: http://www.gurdjieff.org/hunter1.htm

Mitrinovic's New Atlantis Foundation: http://www.hlss.mmu.ac.uk/pap/politics/naf1.htm

Index